SAP Performance Optimization

SAP Technical Support Guides
Editor: Bernhard Hochlehnert, SAP AG

SAP PRESS is a joint initiative of SAP and Galileo Press. The know-how offered by SAP specialists combined with the expertise of the publishing house Galileo Press offers the reader expert publications in the field. SAP PRESS features first hand information, expert advice and provides useful skills for professional decision making.

SAP PRESS offers a variety of books on technical and business related topics for the SAP-user. For further information, please also visit our website: www.sap-press.de

Paul Read
SAP Database Administration
with Microsoft SQL Server 2000
2002, 384pp., ISBN 1-59229-005-1

Sue McFarland Metzger, Susanne Röhrs
SAP R/3 Change and Transport Management
2002, 600pp., ISBN 3-89842-282-8

Liane Will
SAP APO-Systemadministration (German Edition)
2002, 280pp., 3-89842-248-8

A. Rickayzen, J.Dart, C. Brennecke, M. Schneider
Practical Workflow for SAP
2002, 504pp., ISBN 1-59229-006-X

Thomas Schneider

SAP Performance Optimization

Analyzing and Tuning SAP Systems

Galileo Press

German Edition first published in 2002 as
SAP-Performanceoptimierung. Analyse und Tuning von SAP-Systemen
ISBN 3-89842-192-2

Translation: Lemoine International, Inc., Salt Lake City, UT
Editing: Florian Zimniak
Proofreading: Bruce Mayo, Konstanz, Germany
Cover design: department, Cologne, Germany
Production: Sandra Gottmann
Typesetting: Lemoine International, Inc., Salt Lake City, UT
Printed and bound by Bercker Graphischer Betrieb, Kevelaer, Germany

Contents

Foreword to the Series of Books

At SAP AG our first priority is to ensure that the SAP software solutions in your enterprise run effectively and at a minimal cost. This *Lowest Cost of Ownership* is achieved with fast and efficient implementation, together with optimal and dependable operation. SAP Active Global Support is actively and consistently at hand to help you achieve this. *Safeguarding* is the new strategy. This new service program helps customers to plan their implementation in such a way as to avoid technical problems at a later stage. With this support team, SAP assumes the role of the central contact party and shares all of its knowledge with partners and customers; something that should help to increase customer satisfaction considerably.

With the "SAP Technical Support Guides" series of books, SAP Active Global Support has set itself the goal of providing you with the most up-to-date knowledge possible. This series gives you a detailed overview of technical concepts for managing SAP software solutions. The themes of the books range from the planning phase of an implementation through to running a system and the corresponding database systems.

Whether you are new to SAP system management or wish to gain further qualifications, you will find it helpful to consult the books for their wealth of practical experience and first-hand information. With this range of books SAP also endeavors to help prepare you for qualification as a "Certified Technical Consultant". Please note, however, that these books cannot replace, nor do they attempt to replace, personal experience gained from working with the various different SAP solutions! Rather, the authors give recommendations for daily work with the software that will expand the scope of your competence.

SAP solutions are constantly subject to change and new innovations are continuously being integrated; this means that new demands are frequently made on system management, too. The demands made on the customer's own or external support organizations also increase. The competences and knowledge of these organizations can be of great assistance in avoiding problems with SAP software. One of the core tasks of this series of books is to teach skills for problem solving. Even in this Internet age, books prove to be an ideal medium for imparting knowledge in a compact form. Furthermore, their content complements new service and support portals such as SAP Solution Manager and other new services offered by SAP. The series provides background knowledge for the operation and functioning of these new SAP solutions and in this way, contributes to customer satisfaction.

Gerhard Oswald
Member of the Executive Board of SAP AG

Dr. Uwe Hommel
Senior Vice President of SAP AG
SAP Active Global Support

Walldorf, November 2001

Acknowledgments

As a result of the huge success of the first edition of this book—one can say without a doubt that not only has it become a cornerstone in performance training among customers but also for many SAP employees—the need has arisen to publish an updated and extended edition. It is with great pleasure that I set out to satisfy this need. For the most part, the selection and presentation of themes is conceived on the basis of the experience gained by my colleagues and I in concrete environments, working with many SAP systems in production operation—whether in SAP's Early Watch and GoingLive Check services, in training courses for performance analysis or, not least of all, during on-site analysis of systems with critical performance problems. Based on this experience we are confident that in this book we cover a broad range of important performance-related themes.

This book would not have been possible without the collaboration of many competent discourse partners. First of all I would very much like to mention our colleague and mentor Augustinus Wohlfahrt, whose sudden and untimely death left us all deeply shaken. As one of the initiators of this series of books, he played a central part in putting together this publication. I would like to dedicate this book to him.

I would also like to thank the following colleagues by name: Hartwig Brand, Bernhard Braun, Matthias Blümler (SAP Development Client Server Technology), Ralf Hackmann, Brigitte Huy, John Landis, Vivian Luechau-de la Roche, Ulrich Marquard (SAP Development Performance & Benchmarks), Dirk Müller, Jens Otto, Marc Thier, Fabian Tröndle, Gerold Völker and Liane Will. Unless otherwise stated, they work at SAP AG in SAP Global Support.

I would like to thank the team from Galileo Press for their outstanding collaboration.

Dr. Thomas Schneider
SAP Active Global Support

Introduction

Performance

Why is the performance of your e-business application important? Users will only be motivated and work efficiently with an application if response times are good. A slow system leads to downtime and frustration. Should the situation deteriorate further, in the worst case, you no longer have the throughput necessary for running business processes. The results are overtime, delays in production and financial loss. In contrast, the systematic, proactive optimization of performance considerably increases the value of your e-business application.

The performance of a data processing system is defined as the system's ability to fulfill given requirements as regards response time and data throughput. The system may, for example, be required to achieve a throughput of 10,000 printed invoices in one hour or a response time of under one second for the creation of a sales order. Good performance is, however, not an absolute characteristic of an e-business application. Rather, it should always be viewed as relative to the demands made on the application.

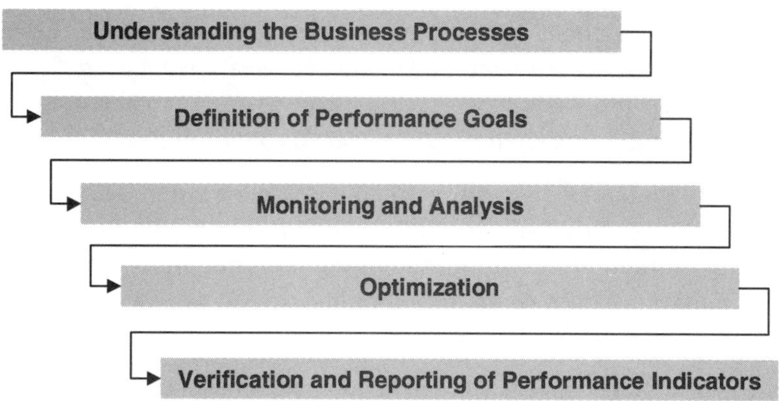

Figure 0.1 Performance optimization in five phases

Performance Optimization

By *Performance optimization* in this book we refer to a process that *always includes five phases*: The first two phases are *understanding the business processes* and *setting and quantifying performance goals*. These steps involve all participating parties, that is to say, technicians and application experts. Optimization can only be successful on the basis of these prerequisites. Phases three to five involve the *systematic monitoring, identifying and analysis* of problems, the *implementation of optimization measures* and further analysis to *verify the success of the* measures introduced (Figure 1). We warn against randomly tinkering with configuration parameters and similar impulsive tuning measures! Rather, the objective of this book is to enable you to identify and analyze performance problems in order to deal with them purposefully.

Technical Optimization

From a technical point of view, an e-business application is made up of many different components. On the one hand there are the logical components: processes and services, threads or work processes and memory areas such as buffers and user contexts. On the other there are the physical components such as processors (CPU), main memory (RAM), hard disks and network segments. Each of these components allows for a maximum throughput and optimal response time. If the interplay between the components is not appropriately balanced or if an individual component has reached its performance limit, wait situations can occur which have a negative effect on throughput and response time. In this book, *Technical Optimization* refers to the identification, analysis and solution of such problems by tuning the components and distributing the workload that occurs within the system.

Application Optimization

The second important task of performance optimization is to avoid unnecessary workload. Performance can be weakened by inefficient programs or the inefficient use of programs. The optimization of individual programs is referred to as *application optimization*.

The goal of optimization is, first of all, to improve the system settings and the applications to achieve the desired performance on the basis of the existing hardware resources. If the existing resources are not sufficient, they must be extended according to the knowledge gained in the analysis.

How much tuning is necessary?

How much effort is involved in the performance analysis and tuning of a mySAP.com solution? The answer to this question depends largely on the size of the system. For a small or medium sized installation without modifications to the SAP standard and without customer developments, it is normally sufficient to do performance optimization just before and shortly after the start of production and after large-scale changes, for example, after upgrades, large data transfers or client transports, or when new mySAP.com solutions or additional users are introduced in the system. Of course, it is also necessary to intervene when there are acute performance problems. The tuning potential and, with it, the effort involved in analysis and optimization increase in proportion to the size of the system. Experience shows that many performance bottlenecks are caused by customer developments and modifications to the standard SAP software. The most common reason for this is insufficient testing, but problems may also arise as a result of time constraints or a lack of experience on the part of the developer. The extreme case would be a large, constantly developing installation with several hundred users, complicated process chains, a dozen or more developers (often from different consulting firms, working on the system at different times and in different places) and outsourced system management. In such a system environment it is absolutely necessary that a small group of administrators and developers has an overview of the entire system and keeps an eye on performance.

SAP's remote services offer help with performance analysis and tuning. These are, namely, the GoingLive™ Check, which enables your system to make a smooth transition to production operation and the EarlyWatch® Service, which monitors your system and suggests additional optimizations.

Proactive performance-management

How does *proactive performance management* help you attain your objective of successfully running of an e-business application? Two influencing factors should be borne in mind if this objective is to be achieved: the satisfaction of users and the costs of running the e-business application. Operating costs come, on one hand, from the cost of hardware (infrastructure, CPU, main memory, hard disks and networks) and personnel (administration, maintenance, fault analysis). However, the costs that arise if an application is not available or does not achieve the required performance should not be overlooked. In these cases losses incurred in a few hours or days can exceed the average amount invested in proactive performance optimization in one year. The cost of these risks must be compared to the cost of proactive performance management. The following table demonstrates the value of proactive performance management using two concrete examples.

Proactive measure	Effect on the system	Immediate value thanks to increased user satisfaction	Immediate value thanks to lower operating costs	Diminished risk of deterioration
SQL statement optimization	Reduction of the database load	Faster response times for certain transactions	Hardware investments (database server, memory system) can be stretched	Overloading of the database system can be avoided
Proactive data management (Data avoidance, archiving, reorganization)	Database growth reduced Shorter times for maintenance work on the database (backup/ recovery, upgrade, migration, system copy)	Faster response times for certain transactions Shorter downtime during maintenance work	Hardware investments can be stretched Lower personnel requirements for maintenance work	Database size remains "manageable"

Table 0.1 Examples of the value of proactive performance management

From SAP R/3 to mySAP.com

With the development of the Internet there has been a shift of paradigm in the world of business software: software is no longer aimed at highly specialized employees; rather, it is aimed at Internet or intranet users.

With SAP R/3, the classical strategy of process automatation was based on highly-specialized users accessing their ERP (Enterprise Resource Planning) system from fixed work centers via installed SAP GUIs. The role of these specialized agents, who had to be trained to use the software, is becoming unnecessary in many cases. Instead, the end user can get direct access to the enterprise's ERP systems via Internet or an Intranet. Today, for example, in many enterprises the employees can enter their work and absence times, travel expenses etc. into the system themselves via the Internet, where previously this would have been done by central users. Increasingly, customers are ordering their products directly on the

Internet and no longer by means of a letter, fax or telephone call to a sales center. Experts also speak of the "popularization" or even "democratization" of ERP software. The following statement from an analyst sums up the issue in a nutshell: "ERP software is made for clerks, but we aren't talking about clerks anymore." With the changeover from R/3 to the e-business platform mySAP.com, SAP has completed the change of paradigm in the development of their software, with the consistent expansion of their Web technology on the one hand and more emphasis on solutions, on the other.

SAP describes the significance of the mySAP.com e-business platform for their customers as follows: "In order to be able to survive profitably and competitively in the Internet influenced business world of today, successful companies must be put in a position that enables them to collaborate beyond traditional corporate boundaries and cooperate within virtual global networks. In mySAP.com, SAP combines sound business and industry-specific know-how with a comprehensive e-business platform for solutions, services and technologies. By linking their business strategies with mySAP.com, enterprises achieve a long-term competitive advantage, assessable added value and the best possible return on investment."

In an advertising slogan SAP makes the claim that their software does not merely execute "add to shopping basket", but also deals with "load to truck"—in allusion to the unsuccessful Internet connection attempts of many enterprises with "isolated applications", not linked with their business processes. The e-business platform mySAP.com on the other hand, offers integrated solutions—from Customer Relationship Management to Enterprise Resource Planning through to Supply Chain Management.

What are the consequences of the changeover from SAP R/3 to mySAP.com for system management and for performance management in particular? There are two specific consequences that we would like to deal with here in the first instance: firstly, the increasing user demands and secondly, the growing complexity of the system landscape linked with the growing need to recognize IT as a service.

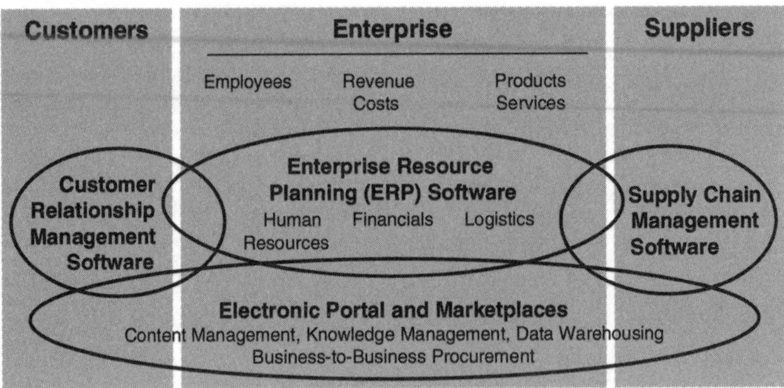

Figure 0.2 From SAP R/3 to mySAP.com: SAP R/3 is typical ERP software covering the areas of human resources, financials and logistics. mySAP.com includes solutions for the enhanced linking of the enterprise with customers and partners, for example, via the Internet.

User expectations

The expectations of a user as regards the usability and performance of an e-business solution are disproportionately higher than the classical employee's expectations as regards their ERP system. The employee relies on his or her own ERP system, and if it normally helps to make his day-to-day work easier, he accepts it and even puts up with minor errors or weak points in performance. The Internet user is quite different: If the applications offered on the Internet do not work easily and effectively, users can immediately change over to the competition and, for example, make their purchases there ("the competition is only a mouse-click away"). In addition, the Internet does not finish work at 5 p.m.—an e-business solution on the Internet will be required to be available and working well 365 days a year, 24 hours a day.

IT services

The demands for an open, flexible software architecture require specialized, independently running software components, which are linked via interfaces. That means that a business process involves several software components. The constantly growing number of solutions and components presents an administrative challenge for computer centers—the number has gone from the "manageable" SAP R/3 (with SAP instances, database, hardware/operating system) to a constantly growing range of technologies—including products that SAP does not produce itself, but that it offers as a reseller.

Consistent with this, the business process operator counters this trend by integrating more and more service partners into the running of the business process. This outsourcing may involve only the hardware (computer performance, hard disk memory, network resources etc.) or also the application itself (application service providing, ASP). For example the services of an Internet product catalog can be completely given over to a service provider instead of operating the catalog software in the enterprise itself. This means that it is not only necessary to monitor hardware and software components, but monitoring must also go beyond company and component boundaries.

Overall, completely new requirements arise for the administration and monitoring of mySAP.com solutions which cannot be dealt with using past concepts.

About This Book

The new edition of this book takes advantage of the opportunity to deal appropriately with current trends in SAP product development and also with the aforementioned trends in the world of IT. As a result, new sections are dedicated to the following key areas.

Key area: Service Level Management

Behind a service offered to the user there is often a network of partners, each of which contributes a part of the solution. Many parts are supplied by different service providers, sometimes external. To deal with the complexity of this, many service providers and customers introduce a *Service Level Management (SLM)* solution. SLM refers to a structured, proactive method that aims to guarantee an adequate level of service to the users of an IT application, in accordance with the business objectives of the ordering party and at an optimal cost. In this book we will show the tools and methods needed to introduce SLM for a mySAP.com solution.

Key area: Internet connection

Since 1997 (SAP R/3 3.1) SAP R/3 can be directly accessed from a Web browser via the SAP Internet Transaction Server (SAP ITS) and a working Web server. With the release of SAP R/3 4.6 all functions were made available on the Web. Other important SAP e-business solutions, such as mySAP Workplace, mySAP Customer Relationship Management (Internet Sales), mySAP Marketplace, mySAP Enterprise Buyer Professional and mySAP Business Intelligence also use SAP ITS. For many customers it will thus be a strategically important component of their mySAP.com solution landscape for years to come.

Key area: Interfaces

Even in the past e-business solutions made up of a single monolithic R/3 were a rarity—as a rule they are open solutions made up of several components, and linked via interfaces.

Key area: SAP Basis 4.6

As part of the EnjoySAP initiative started in 1997, SAP has put increasing emphasis on user-friendly and intuitive software and has developed personalized user interfaces for SAP software. With *SAP R/3 4.6* and other software components, SAP presents a redesign of their software to this end. Technically, the new design is based on a completely new interaction model for communication between the presentation and application levels, the controls.

Key area: Server consolidation

Server consolidation—the concentration of all services on a few, very powerful computers—has been, without a doubt, an important trend in the IT market in recent years. This is normally accompanied by the introduction of 64-bit main-memory addressing technology. We explain everything that you should take into account if you want to use these technologies efficiently.

Apart from these main points, we have taken advantage of the opportunity presented by a new edition to expand on some smaller themes as well.

Structure of the book

The methods for performance analysis and optimization presented in this book reflect the methods used by experts in the *EarlyWatch® service* and the *GoingLive™ Check* and they are included in the SAP Basis training courses *BC315 Workload Analysis* and *BC490 Optimization of ABAP programs*.

Chapter 1, "Performance Management of a mySAP.com Solution", is directed at SAP administrators, SAP consultants, application developers and SAP project leaders. It deals with the following fundamental questions about performance analysis on a non-technical level:

- Which preventative measures must be taken to guarantee the optimal performance of a mySAP.com solution?
- What performance tuning measures should be taken into consideration?
- Who is involved in the tuning process?

Performance analysis is presented in **Chapters 2 to 4**. After having read these chapters you should be in a position to carry out a systematic performance analysis.

In this book, we initially follow the bottom-up analysis strategy, starting in **Chapter 2,** "Monitoring Hardware, Database and SAP Basis", with an examination of the operating system, database, SAP memory management and SAP work processes. At the same time, solution

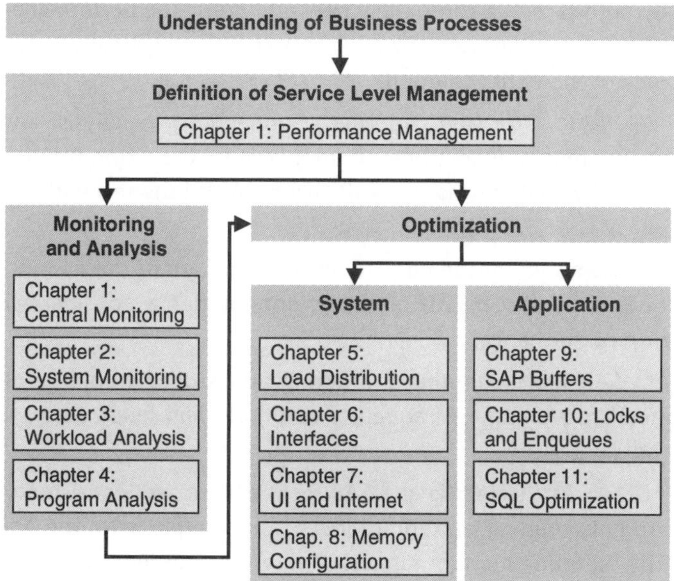

Figure 0.3 The chapters in this book and how they correspond to the phases of performance optimization

proposals are provided which should enable the administrator or consultant to solve the most important performance problems. For small and medium sized installations this level of tuning is often sufficient.

Then in **Chapter 3,** "Workload Analysis", the more complex workload analysis is discussed as an example of top-down analysis. In **Chapter 4,** "Performance Analysis for ABAP-Programs", you will find methods for analyzing individual programs, using the tools SQL trace and ABAP debugger, among others.

The remaining **Chapters 5 to 11** present knowledge necessary for a more indepth performance analysis. They are intended for SAP consultants responsible for the efficient functioning of large systems who seek and need to reach the full tuning potential of their system. Chapters 5 to 11 are independent units to a large extent, and they can be read in any order once you are familiar with the content of the first four chapters.

The topics are:

- Chapter 5, "Workload Distribution": Optimal workload distribution of dialog, update and background requests helps to ensure optimal use of hardware and avoids bottlenecks brought about by nonoptimal configuration.

- Chapter 6, "Interfaces" (a completely new addition): The performance of interfaces between software components contributes greatly to the performance of the entire solution.
- Chapter 7, "SAP GUI and Internet Connection": Analysis and configuration recommendations demonstrate the optimization potential of linking GUIs (classical SAP GUI or Web browser) with the application.
- Chapter 8, "Memory Management": The configuration of the memory areas allocated by the mySAP.com component has a considerable influence on performance.
- Chapter 9, "SAP Table Buffering": Buffering tables on the application servers speeds up access to frequently read data and helps ease the load on the database.
- Chapter 10, "Locks": Database and SAP locks ensure data consistency. With an optimized administration of locks (for example, with the ATP server or by buffering number ranges) throughput bottlenecks can be avoided.
- Chapter 11, "Optimizing SQL Statements": Ineffective SQL statements make heavy demands on the database and thus become a problem for the performance of the entire application. An entire chapter is therefore devoted to optimizing SQL statements.

Target groups We have already differentiated between technical optimization and application optimization. Chapters 2, 5, 6. 7 and 8 deal with technical optimization and are mainly aimed at SAP system administrators and technical consultants. Chapters 4, 9, 10 and 11 deal with the analysis and tuning of individual programs (or applications) and as such form part of application optimization. This part of the analysis is also of interest to those responsible for SAP applications (employees in the department, application consultants and developers). Chapters 1 and 3 are relevant to both areas.

Prerequisites This book assumes both theoretical and practical knowledge of the administration of mySAP.com components. You should be familiar with the use of *Computer Center Management Systems (CCMS)* in particular. "R/3 System Administration" (see appendix G, "Information Sources") should serve as good preparation. Parts of this book, e.g. Chapters 4, 9, 10 and 11 assume familiarity with the programming language ABAP, with the functioning of relational databases and with SQL.

The book does not cover the following topics:

Limitations of this book

- **Hardware and network tuning**
  Although this book helps you to identify a bottleneck in the CPU, main memory, I/O or network, a detailed analysis requires the tools of the hardware or network provider. In view of the enormous number of products offered, this area (especially tuning the hard disk) cannot be included.
- **Databases**
  In the Computer Center Management System (CCMS), SAP offers tools that standardize most administrative and analysis tasks for different database systems. However, for those who wish to do more in-depth database tuning, you need to know the different database system architectures. It is impossible to go into the fine points of all seven database systems that can be used in conjunction with mySAP.com in sufficient detail in this book. In any case, this is not necessary because reference material on tuning is available for all database systems. This book cannot replace such material, nor does it endeavor to do so. Rather, the emphasis in this book is on the SAP-specific context of database tuning and on explaining concepts common to all database systems. The concrete examples used always refer to individual database systems. In the appendix you will find an overview of the most important monitors for analyzing all database systems.
- **Application tuning**
  Many problems with performance can only be solved with detailed knowledge of the application and of the individual mySAP.com modules. A change to the customizing settings often solves the problem. This book does not provide know-how for tuning individual mySAP.com modules. However, this book does provide you with analysis strategies so that you can limit performance problems to certain applications and then consult the appropriate developer or consultant.

Release dependency

One question that was heatedly discussed before this book was published concerns the extent to which release-dependent and time-dependent information should be included; this would affect, for example, menu paths, recommendations for configuration parameters and guide values for performance counters. A new version, a patch (for the mySAP.com component, the database or the operating system), a new generation of computers—these and other factors could render previous information useless overnight. In the worst case, obsolete recommendations could even have negative effects on performance. We are aware of this risk.

Nevertheless we have decided to include time-dependent information and rules in the book. Only in this way can the books of this series be used as works of reference for daily work in SAP administration. On the other hand, it is clear that this is not a book of fixed rules and regulations, and anyone who considers performance optimization to mean mechanically following rules is mistaken. This book cannot replace direct analysis of the solution, SAP online help or up-to-date SAP Notes on SAP's Service Marketplace—it only hopes to support them.

SAP Basis 4.6

All details on menu paths, references to performance monitor screens and guideline values for performance counters refer to SAP Basis 4.6.

You will find important Notes and Tips in sections marked with this symbol.

This symbol indicates an Example.

Caution, sections marked with this symbol warn of potential errors and pitfalls!

UNIX
Windows

Sections referring to specific features of the UNIX and Windows operating systems will be marked as such.

www.sap-press.de

As was the case for the first edition, we will provide up-to-date information, and further texts on the subjects dealt with in this book will appear on the publisher's Web site *www.sap-press.de*. This service is available to you as a registered reader. Information on online registration can be found on the last page of this book.

1 Performance Management of a mySAP.com Solution

Customers who implement SAP solutions do so with the expectation that the solutions will be reliable and easy to maintain. They assume that the standard-setting levels of excellence achieved with SAP R/3 can be upheld in mySAP.com solutions (such as CRM, SCM, BI). In addition SAP not only offers its tried and tested platform for ERP and e-business solutions with the most high-performance architecture on the market, but also—according to analysts—an innovative service concept.

In this chapter we will present the architecture and the service concept. In the first section we will deal with the architecture in which mySAP.com solutions are constructed and outline the potential for optimizing the system. At this stage we deliberately dispense with technical details. In the second section we deal with organizational questions regarding the running of a mySAP.com solution, such as the creation of a monitoring and optimizing plan with SAP Solution Manager. Two elements play a key role here: on the one hand, there is a plan for the continuous monitoring of availability and performance of the business process, and on the other there is the Service Level Management method.

When should you read this chapter?

You should read this chapter if you want to develop a monitoring and optimization plan for a mySAP.com solution. We recommend that you read this chapter first, to get an overview of the contents of this book before getting into more detail in subsequent chapters.

mySAP.com Architecture

The architecture of mySAP.com is described below. First of all we will look at the different mySAP.com solutions and components. Then follows a section on client/server architecture.

mySAP.com Solutions and mySAP.com Components

The make up of a mySAP.com solution landscape

In the past SAP software was built on a single technological component, *SAP Basis*, which served as the base for SAP R/3. With *mySAP.com* the business processes of an enterprise are no longer reproduced in a single R/3 system; rather, this is done with several software components.

Figure 1.1 shows an example of the components that make up a mySAP.com solution.

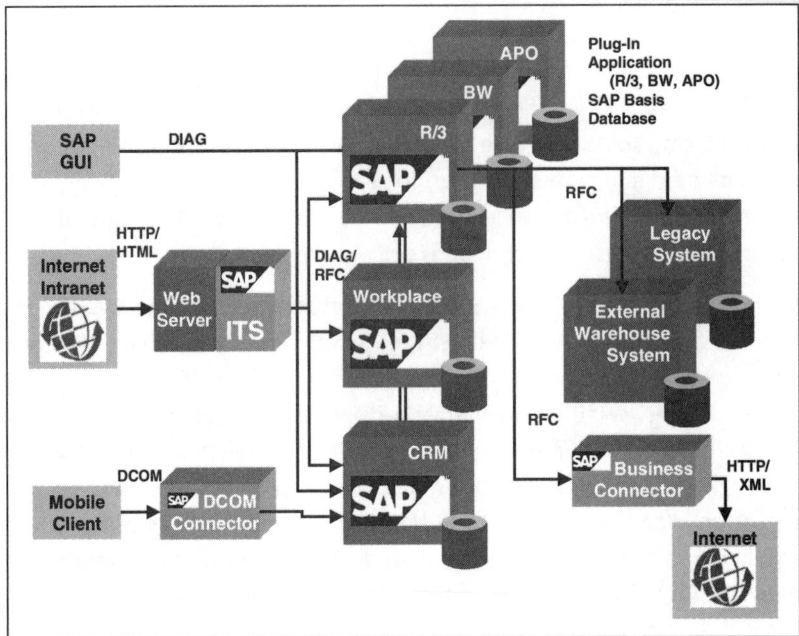

Figure 1.1 The technical make up of a mySAP.com solution with multiple software components (example)

As with SAP R/3, many of the new mySAP.com software components have SAP Basis with *Development Workbench* and Basis tools such as the *Computer Center Management System (CCMS)*. They also have their own database (with a three figure database ID, which must be unique in a mySAP.com solution landscape). Application-specific software components complete the SAP Basis system and form an SAP R/3, an SAP BW or an SAP APO. Namely:

- SAP R/3 Enterprise
- SAP Advanced Planner and Optimizer (SAP APO)
- SAP Business Information Warehouse (SAP BW) and SAP Strategic Enterprise Management (SAP SEM)
- SAP Customer Relationship Management (SAP CRM) and SAP Enterprise Buyer Professional (SAP EBP)
- SAP Workplace (up to 2.11)

In this book we will refer to this collection of software components with SAP Basis as *SAP systems*.

mySAP.com solutions are complemented by other independent software components without the conventional SAP Basis, for example:

- SAP Internet Transaction Server (SAP ITS)
- SAP liveCache
- SAP Business Connector (SAP BC)

The great variety of smoothly meshed components forms the strong point of mySAP.com technology. Figure 1.1 shows an example of how the technical foundations of a mySAP.com solution can appear.

Linking systems with RFC

Every mySAP.com component can run independently (that means, for example, can be started, stopped and maintained independently of others). Data is exchanged between components using *Remote Function Calls (RFCs)*. SAP has created its own standard for the electronic exchange of business documents: Data are converted into what are known as *IDocs* and sent via RFC. With RFC, components of different versions can communicate with each other.

So that SAP R/3 and, for example, SAP APO or SAP BW can work together, software transports, known as plug-ins, have to be implemented in SAP R/3.

User connection

On the left hand side of Figure 1.1 you can see the interfaces via which the user can logon to the system (GUI interfaces). These are the *SAP GUI for Windows Environment*, the *SAP GUI for Java Environment* and the *SAP GUI for HTML*. Specialized users use the SAP GUI for Windows or Java environments. The disadvantage of the SAP GUI for Windows environment is that it must be installed on the desktop computer. (The Java GUI must also be installed on the desktop computer, but installing it is much easier than installing the SAP GUI for Windows.) Typical users of the Windows or Java GUIs are controllers, planners and employees in sales centers (such as telesales).

Occasional users (Internet or intranet users) log on using a Web browser. The advantage of this form of logon is that no special GUI program needs to be installed on the desktop computer. All input and output screens are presented in a Web browser in HTML format. Communication between the Web browser and the SAP application level is effected on the Internet level (see below).

A third possible means of access is with what are known as *Mobile Clients*, laptop computers or handheld devices, that are not continuously linked to the central system but only exchange data with the system periodically.

This method of access is useful, for example, for field sales or service employees. Access can take place via a CRM server and a DCOM connector.

mySAP Workplace *mySAP Workplace* standardizes access to all systems in a system landscape. A user only logs on to the Workplace once and the Workplace server creates what is known as a "portal page" for that user, on which all access information needed by this user for day-to-day work is recorded: this includes reference to transactions on the mySAP.com components and non-mySAP.com components, Internet and intranet links and to additional information (called *MiniApps* or *iViews*). From this portal page the user can execute all day-to-day tasks, without having to worry about logging on to different systems. In addition to employees, portal pages can also be created with mySAP Workplace for customers and business partners.

Client/Server Architecture

The technology of a mySAP.com component is based on a multi-layer client/server architecture, as presented in Figure 1.2. The presentation level consists of the frontends and is where the users perform data input and output. The actual processing is carried out on the application level, which represents the business process. The database level is for the permanent storage and preparation of data.

Presentation level Presentation servers are normally set up as PCs. The GUI program is the traditional SAP GUI (SAP GUI for Windows or Java environments), which must be installed on the desktop computer or as a Web browser (provided by Microsoft of Netscape, for example).

Application level Once a user has ended a data entry, the presentation server sends this data to the *application level*. The application level contains the application logic and the presentation logic. The application level also forms the integrated Internet connection of the SAP Web Application Server (SAP Web AS, from SAP Basis 6.10).

Application logic is encapsulated in transactions, screens, reports or function modules.

There are three possibilities for connecting Internet users to the SAP application level. The first possible solution is to use the SAP Internet Transaction Server (SAP ITS) and a Web server provided by a third party (for example Microsoft or Netscape). Typical SAP ITS applications are self-service applications in the area of human resources (ESS applications such

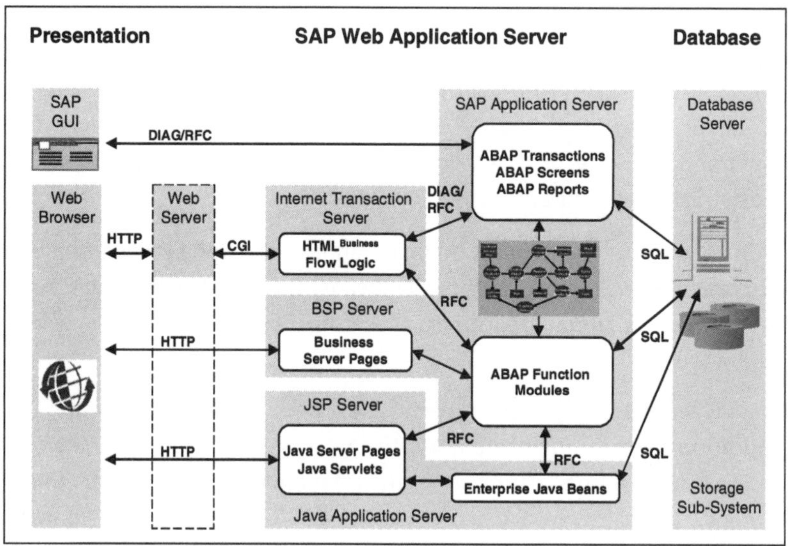

Figure 1.2 Client/Server architecture (SAP Web Application Server)

as time recording and travel accounting), Business-to-Business Procurement applications (Enterprise Buyer Professional) and Internet sales (product catalog, online store in SAP R/3). Since SAP R/3 3.1, SAP Internet Transaction Server and Internet applications, such as product catalog, online store and Employee Self Service, have been delivered with R/3. With the release of SAP R/3 4.6 all functions were made available on the Web. Easy Web Transactions (EWTs, with the SAP Script languages HTML^{Business} and Flow Logic), Internet Application Components (IACs), SAP GUI for HTML, and Web-RFC are available as technologies for generating HTML pages.

Business Server Pages (BSP) is the second programming model. With it, HTML pages can be dynamically generated using ABAP or JavaScript as the scripting language. The technical advantage of this programming model is that no other software components need to be installed; Business Server Pages are generated directly in the normal SAP application instances. A special Web server is not absolutely necessary. However, from the point of view of security, it is recommended that you install a separate Web server as a security buffer. Business Server Pages form a part of SAP Basis 6.10.

The third possibility for connecting Internet users to the SAP application level is to use a JSP server or a Java Application Server. The languages used are HTML and Java, the programming models are Java Server Pages

(JSP) or Java Servlets. On the basis of the compatibility of Java developments, you can replace SAP's own Java Application Server with a Java Application Server from a third party (such as BEA or IBM), once this has been authorized by SAP. Examples of solutions that use this programming model for realizing presentation logic are mySAP CRM Internet Sales 3.0 and Enterprise Portal 5.0.

In future, parts of the application logic can even be done in Java in a Java Application Server (as Enterprise JavaBeans, EJB). At the time this book goes to press, large applications have not been created using this technology.

Database level

If data is required to process a user request and this data is not yet in the application server's main memory, the data is read from the database server. The relational database is the medium used for permanently storing data. Apart from SAP's own database (SAP DB), SAP also supports the use of databases from other large producers (IBM, Oracle, Microsoft).

Aspects of performance and tuning potential

Because presentation servers are normally set up as PCs, no further tuning is required on this level, once the hardware conforms to the recommendations current for the respective SAP release.

The situation is different for the other levels in the client/server architecture, where requests share processes and memory areas.

Process configuration

We shall explain this using the example of the application server: Requests from users or from other systems are processed in the application server by *SAP work processes*. SAP systems are typically configured in such a way that an average of 5—10 active users share one SAP dialog work process. This assumes that users need around 10 times as long to enter data in the screen and interpret the results, as the SAP system needs to process the user requests. Therefore, there should always be enough free work processes available to be able to process user requests without delay. If individual users start reports with very long response times (perhaps even several at the same time), they occupy work processes for several minutes. There are then not enough remaining work processes to process other users' requests quickly, and wait times occur. The SAP system does not prioritize users. If a bottleneck occurs, all users, regardless of their corporate role or the urgency of their request, must get in the queue and wait their turn. However, methods of load distribution offer the possibility of reserving application servers for certain user groups. Apart from requests for dialog or online transactions, a mySAP.com component also processes background, update and print tasks. There is a different type of

SAP work process for each of these request types. Appropriate tuning in this area enables the workload to be distributed optimally in line with system requirements. For Internet and database level servers, the processes must also be suitably configured for the parallel processing of requests.

Buffers (Caches)

On all levels, *buffers* (also called *caches*) ensure that once data has been loaded in a server it is then held in the main memory of that server and is available for subsequent requests. In the case of application servers, for example, programs, table and field definitions and data about customizing tables are held in the buffers. When optimally configured, these buffers ensure that a minimum amount of data needs to be read directly from the database server. Reading data from an SAP buffer is around 10 to 100 times faster than reading from the database server.

Database tuning

Database tuning is divided into three areas. The first of these is the optimal setting of database buffers and other database parameters. The second area is optimizing the layout of the hard disks of the database to distribute the workload as evenly as possible across the hard disks so as to avoid wait situations when writing to or reading from the hard disk. The third aspect of database tuning is the optimization of expensive, i.e. long-running SQL statements.

Network

Network transfer speed and data throughput between the different levels of the client/server architecture is of considerable importance. These can affect the performance of the entire mySAP.com solution.

mySAP.com architecture is conceived in such a way that most data communication occurs between the application and database levels. This can be reduced by optimizing expensive SQL statements; however, in practice, the application and database levels will be linked by a *Local Area Network (LAN)*. Data transfer between presentation and application, on the other hand, is as low as possible because the network connection can be achieved either with a LAN or a *Wide Area Network (WAN)*.

Internet

When using a the Web browser as a GUI, care should be taken with programming to ensure that as little data as possible is transferred between the presentation and Internet levels. If elaborate HTML pages are generated, there is clearly a greater risk that the user will be limited by network runtimes, than if the classical SAP GUI is used (as it uses SAP's own DIAG protocol). Tuning potential depends greatly on the programming model used. Given that the Internet level is used purely as a transfer level between presentation and application levels (such as SAP GUI for HTML), optimizing potential is limited to configuration. The more logic that is stored on Internet level (for example, field checking), the greater the need for analyzing programs on this level.

Hardware It should be checked on both the database server and on the application servers if there is sufficient *hardware* (CPU and main memory) available to manage the existing load. You should also ensure that the operating system parameters and network parameters are optimally set to achieve good hardware performance. You should also refer to the tools and literature provided by the manufacturer on this matter.

Scalability mySAP.com components are scalable as client/server systems. By vertical *scalability* we refer to the fact that the software components on all levels can be installed either centrally on one computer (server) or distributed over several computers. (However, because not all software components are authorized for all operating systems, the centralized installation of all components is only possible on certain platforms.)

Within the client/server level the load that occurs can be distributed over several logical instances, which can run on different computers. This is known as horizontal scalability. Presentation levels are thus generally distributed on PCs or terminal servers. The application level is realized by SAP instances and the Internet level by ITS instances and Web server instances. In principle, for some database systems (Oracle and DB2/390) it is possible to arrange several database instances in parallel to form the database level. However, in practice this possibility is rarely used.

Client/server architecture means that it is possible to increase the number of application, Internet and presentation servers to almost as many as you wish, to cope with the increased demand produced by growing numbers of users. The database level is formed by a database server (the exceptions of Oracle Parallel Server and DB2/390 are not discussed here). In principle, certain processes on the database server cannot be distributed (for example, lock management). Experience shows that performance problems in large SAP installations with more than ten application servers are most often caused by bottlenecks in the database server. As a result, tuning the database becomes increasingly important as a system grows. When a system has been running in production operation for some time, most tuning settings, such as buffer settings, load distribution, and so on, will have been satisfactorily optimized and will require no further change.

By contrast, the tuning of expensive SQL statements becomes increasingly important as the database data volume grows, and is an ongoing tuning process.

The Monitoring and Optimization Plan for a mySAP.com Solution

The following sections deal with the monitoring and optimization plan for a mySAP.com solution. First of all we should discuss the requirements of such a plan.

Requirements of a Monitoring and Optimization Plan

To meet the expectations of a mySAP.com user, it is necessary to have a monitoring and optimization plan. Just as SAP has come to present itself to customers as a solution provider, rather than as a software provider, the task of monitoring has also changed. Instead of the traditional system monitoring, today we speak of solution monitoring, which no longer merely monitors the individual system components, but monitors the business process as a whole.

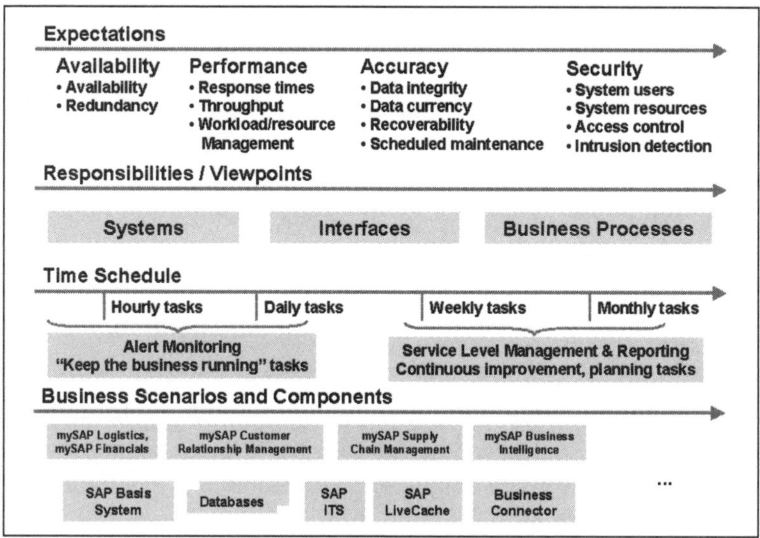

Figure 1.3 Requirements for monitoring a mySAP.com solution (Solution Monitoring)

User expectations

The users of a mySAP.com application are either the employees, customers or partners (for example, suppliers) of the enterprise that owns the application. As a result, user satisfaction is one of the first objectives to be achieved in the operation of the application. We therefore require that our monitoring plan meets user expectations.

You should ask yourself: What exactly are your expectations as regards an Internet application that you use to order goods or conduct a bank transaction, for example? You will come up with four requirements: First, the application should be available when you need it; second, the performance should be reasonable; third, it should run correctly (in other words: you wish the product presented on the Internet to be delivered and the price invoiced should be the same as that offered on the Internet); and fourth, you want to be sure that the application is secure, i.e. that nobody can manipulate your data.

Availability

To guarantee *availability*—the first expectation a user makes of an application—most system management platforms on the market offer hardware and software component monitoring. However, this is not enough to guarantee that the business process is available. For a user, an application is also unavailable if an interruption in communication between components or a serious application error means that it is not possible to enter or request data. An availability monitor must therefore guarantee that the entire business process is available, not just the individual components.

Performance

Poor *performance* in an e-business application is an easy way to annoy customers. In this respect, performance concerns the dialog part of the application, that is to say, the part in which data is entered and saved, as well as the automatic background processing which processes data even if the customer is not online. Poor performance in the dialog application affects the customer as soon as they enter data, while poor performance in the associated background applications affects the customer indirectly when, for example, it prevents the products ordered from being delivered by the agreed date.

As a rule, the performance of the dialog applications and the background applications should be evaluated separately. The distribution of resources according to needs forms part of performance monitoring if both types of application run on a technical IT system (this is normally the case). Normally, dialog applications are given higher priority than background applications. However, there are exceptions to prove this rule: Background applications with a strict deadline should be given the highest priority. As an example, consider the printing of shipping documents (delivery note, address labels, invoices etc). If these are not completed by a particular time, there may in some circumstances be a delay of up to 24 hours (mail collection!).

To guarantee the *integrity* (or correctness) of an application, the following areas should be taken into consideration in the monitoring plan:

Integrity

- **Integrity of data**
  Violations of data integrity may include: corrupt data on the database, network errors, errors in interfaces.
- **Software components and data are up-to-date and consistent**
  If software components or master and customizing data are not correctly updated, there may be inconsistency in documents, for example an Internet catalog may display a price that is not the same as that recorded in the billing system and as a result, the bill the customer receives is not correct.
- **Backup of databases and file systems and their recoverability**
  If the content of a production database is irretrievably damaged due to a hardware or software defect, you must be able to reproduce it using a backup.

Monitoring *backup* is generally as time consuming as the backup plan itself. This area will not be treated in detail in this book.

Backup

At best, traditional system monitoring checks each software component individually. Given the number of components that are involved in a solution, however, it may happen that although each component functions correctly by itself, the overall business process does not work well, optimally and securely for the end user. This can be due to poor communication between components. As a result, solution monitoring must have a specific section to monitor the overall business process, beyond the boundaries of individual components (see second area in Figure 1.3).

In the third area of Figure 1.3 we can see that a monitoring plan must refer to different time horizons. In other words: Alert information is dealt with on different time scales. We will explain this with the aid of an example: When a production component goes down, alert information is relevant on the minutes time scale. On the other hand, an alert to inform you that a backup that has gone wrong during the previous night, must be dealt with in a matter of hours. Another type of alarm may inform the administrator that the extrapolated database growth will exhaust the hard disk space in four weeks. While this is also useful information that should persuade the administrator to deal with the problem (perhaps the administrator can start archiving, rather than ordering extra hard disk capacity), nobody would want a red light to be displayed in the alert monitor for four weeks. Therefore, a monitoring plan must provide for both short-term monitoring—checking on exceptional situations—and also for medium and long-term reporting and optimizing.

Central monitoring and extensibility

Finally—this aspect of the monitoring plan leads to the fourth area of Figure 1.3—the constantly growing number of solutions and components presents an administrative challenge for computing centers—the number has gone from the "manageable" SAP R/3 (with SAP instances, database, hardware/operating system) to a constantly growing range of technologies—including products that SAP does not produce itself, but offers as a reseller. As a result of this development, each computing center manager demands a monitoring method that is both centralized (all information in one tool) and can also be expanded to included new components.

Summary

Up to now, we have presented the following requirements for a monitoring and optimizing plan (Figure 1.3):

- A monitoring and optimizing plan has to cover the areas of availability, performance, correct functioning and backup.
- A monitoring and optimization plan should not only take individual hardware and software components into account. Rather, it must monitor and optimize the information flow of business processes between components.
- Different time scales should be taken into account in the monitoring: From error situations which must be dealt with as soon as possible, to long-term planning and the analysis of trends.
- If possible, the plan should cover all business processes and components in one central tool.

To deal with these requirements for monitoring mySAP.com solutions, SAP has created the Solution Management program, of which SAP Solution Manager is the central tool. We shall present it in the following sections.

Tools and Methods for the Monitoring and Optimization Plan

The SAP Basis system includes a range of powerful programs for monitoring and performance analysis, which are constantly added to with the experience of SAP performance experts. Firstly, there is the central monitoring architecture, which continuously measures the performance of all hardware and software components. There is also a central workload monitor and further expert tools for more detailed analysis.

Central control monitor

Continuous system monitoring checks that all components are available and work well. If this is not the case, an alarm is triggered. Continuous monitoring can be automated using the central monitoring architecture. You can use the central CCMS (Computing Center Management System) alert monitor to continuously monitor the system (transaction code RZ20). Define one SAP system as the central monitoring system, and all reports of errors from all mySAP.com components will be sent to this system. Up to now, data on the SAP instances, databases, operating systems and other mySAP.com components, such as SAP IT, have been linked in the *central alert monitor*. Other data suppliers, also for non-SAP components such as catalog software, Clarify and Commerce One, are also available.

Central workload monitor

The Central *Workload Monitor* gives you an overview of the workload distribution in your mySAP.com solution throughout all software components. With a technical analysis, for example, problems on the database, in the SAP Basis system or the Internet Transaction Server can be identified and analyzed. In an application analysis, transactions, programs and users that generate high system load can be identified and analyzed.

Expert monitors for performance analysis

Other *expert monitors* for performance analysis of SAP systems are listed in the performance menu (transaction code STUN):

Tools · Administration · Monitor · Performance or
Tools · CCMS · Control/Monitoring · Performance menu

The performance monitors available for analyzing Basis and applications are listed in Table 1.1

Monitors for technical analysis	
Operating System Monitor (ST06)	Monitors the load on the CPU and the physical main memory
Database Monitor (ST04)	To check load on the database buffers, database locks and other wait situations; read and write accesses to hard disks; monitor SQL statements
SAP Memory Configuration Monitor ("Setup/Buffers", ST02)	To monitor load on the SAP buffer and other memory areas, SAP work processes

Table 1.1 SAP performance monitors

Monitors for technical analysis	
Work Process Overview (SM50)	To monitor load on SAP work processes
Workload Monitor (ST03)	Overview of load distribution in the SAP system. In a technical analysis, for example, problems on the database, in SAP memory management or SAP buffers can be identified and analyzed.
Monitors for application analysis	
Workload Monitor (ST03, ST03N, ST03G)	Overview of load distribution in the SAP system. In an application analysis, transactions, programs and users that place a heavy load on the system can be identified and analyzed.
Application monitors (ST07, ST14)	To monitor the use of resources according to SAP modules
SQL Trace (ST05); ABAP Trace (SE30)	Trace functions for a detailed analysis of ABAP programs

Table 1.1 SAP performance monitors (contd.)

SAP software components that are not based on SAP Basis are delivered with their own expert tools for administration, monitoring and analysis.

Interfaces All SAP performance monitors have open *interfaces* which enable SAP partners to call up performance data related to SAP systems. This means that if you use external system management software for monitoring your system, you can access SAP performance data and in this way monitor your mySAP.com solution system-wide. Examples of monitoring tools which can access SAP performance data include OpenView (HP), Tivoli (IBM) or Patrol (BMC Software). It should be pointed out that only system monitoring is possible with these products (we call this the outside-in approach). With these products it is not possible to monitor applications. We will deal with this in greater detail in the next section.

Monitoring services With the help of these powerful tools you can now put together a monitoring and optimizing plan with three fundamental elements: first, Service Level Management, in which the performance objectives of your application will be defined and controlled; second the plan for continuous monitoring, which can identify deviations from normal operation (preventatively if possible) and reinstate normal operation in so far as possible; and third the optimization plan, which covers the continuous optimization of the application by building on the results of Service Level Management and continuous monitoring. Below you will find concrete instructions on how to plan these three elements.

Service Level Management

Apart from the short-term Alert Monitoring, what is referred to as *Service Level Management* (SLM) is of central importance for long-term monitoring and optimization. This has already been implemented by many IT organizations to manage the relationship between individual service providers and the owner of the business process. Service Level Management refers to a structured, proactive method that aims to guarantee an adequate level of service to the users of an IT application—in accordance with the business objectives of the ordering party and at an optimal cost. This method includes clearly defined, verifiable goals and clear communication between the business process holder and the operators of a solution (for servers, databases, networks and so on, there may be several internal or external operators). Service Level Management is made up of, first of all, a Service Level Agreement in which the goals to be achieved as regards availability, performance, correctness and security are defined. How the achievement of these objectives is to be measured and communicated is also laid down. Service Level Reporting describes how objectives are attained in a certain period of time. The first aim of Service Level Reporting is thus to determine whether or not the operating goals have been achieved and to indicate potential for optimization.

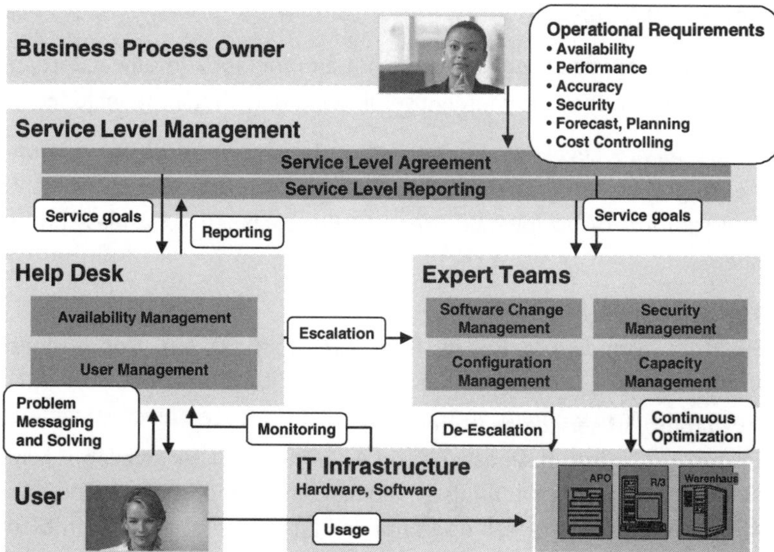

Figure 1.4 The interconnection between the fields of Service Level Management, Alert Monitoring and continuous system monitoring

In addition, the business process holder would like to achieve the satisfaction of the end user at optimal cost of ownership. Apart from monitoring availability, performance, correctness and security, Service Level Management should thus also make costs transparent (hardware and personnel costs, for example). Looking after communication between business process holders and service providers—which in practice can often be difficult—is another requirement of Service Level Management.

Arranging service level management

To achieve successful Service Level Management in your SAP project, first of all you should come to a Service Level Agreement in which you record which objectives are to be attained by the individual service partners, you set measures that should be put in place if objectives are not met, and you agree how the achievement of objectives is to be measured and presented. A Service Level Agreement should cover the following agreements:

- Definition of business hours
- Database backup and restoration
- Performance
- Content of reports

Please note that our observations are not a model for a legally watertight contract. Rather, they are merely useful items that should be included.

Definition of business hours

Start the Service Level Agreement with a description of business hours. For example, you may wish to define three different types of hours of business: Hours of business A, B and C. For each set of business hours, define:

- **Period of application**
  Example: Monday to Friday, 8:00 a.m. to 5:00 p.m. for business hours A.
- **Availability of service personnel**
  Example: During business hours A, a helpdesk is available with sufficient capacity to administer requests from end users. In addition, all experts necessary for operation and for any necessary problem solving are also available. During B and C business hours only emergency service is available. During business hours B, experts are on-call.

- **Availability, planned and unplanned downtimes**
  Example: In business hours A, planned downtimes are not possible; unplanned downtimes can be a maximum of 2 hours in one day, with a maximum of 4 hours per month. During business hours B, planned downtimes are only possible after consultation with business process holders; unplanned downtimes can be a maximum of 4 hours per day, maximum of 12 hours per month. During business hours C, downtimes are possible at any time. (An exception to this are special situations, such as software upgrades, which may lead to extended downtimes).

All planned and unplanned downtimes must be included in the Service Level Report, with details on the reason for the downtime.

Backup and recovery

The Service Level Agreement should set down responsibilities for backup and recovery of databases and, if necessary, file systems (Backup and Recovery). You should set out the scope of the backup to be carried out. Define a procedure for the recovery of databases and file systems in the event of error, in accordance with regulations. The maximum time necessary for this is calculated from the maximum time allowed for unplanned downtime.

Performance

Service providers often give guarantees for average dialog response times. A generally accepted rule of thumb is that good performance is indicated by an average response time of 1 second or less. However, a broad generalization of this nature is not always valid for all the different requirements of mySAP.com components.

Rather, agreements should be reached on the monitoring of SAP dialog transactions. SAP dialog transaction response times can be analyzed with both the central Alert Monitor and with the Workload Monitor. To reach a useful Service Level Agreement, proceed as follows:

1. Choose around 10 to 20 critical transactions, the performance of which should be monitored. You can decide whether or not a transaction is "critical" using the following criteria:
   - If a transaction performs poorly do you suffer immediate economic damage (contract penalties, lost orders and so on)?
   - Does the poor performance of a transaction mean that the image of your company is seriously damaged? Is the transaction directly accessible by your customers or partners (via the Internet, for example) or is the transaction used in direct dealings with customers or partners (for example, in telesales)?

- Is it one of the most frequently executed transactions (you can check this in the transaction profile of the Workload Monitor)?

Please note that it will not be possible to agree on a complete performance monitoring of business processes in a Service Level Agreement. Nevertheless the selected transactions should form the most representative sample possible of your most important applications.

2. Measure the average response time of the transaction in production operation over a given period of time (in the transaction profile of the Workload Monitor). At the same time, find out if the user is satisfied with the response time experienced. If so, set the measured response time plus a margin of around 50% as threshold value for good performance.
3. Agree that weekly details on the response times for the selected transactions will be given in Service Level Reporting.
4. Link the selected transactions to the CCMS monitor (see the section "Continuous Monitoring" on page 47).
5. Agree that in the event that the set threshold value is exceeded, an analysis will be carried out on all persons participating in the transaction. A general action plan should be drawn up and the people named in it should execute assigned measures to restore stable performance.

Problem solving

Errors in the regular operation come to the attention of the system or application manager in two ways: either a user reports the errors, or they become evident through active monitoring.

In the Service Level Agreement you should set out priorities for errors and reaction times for problem solving.

In communication between SAP and customers, four priorities are used (SAP Note 67739):

- Very high (negative impact, which causes the entire system or a critical process to stop responding)
- High (considerable impact on a critical process)
- Medium (impact on a process)
- Low (small problem, additional questions)

You should also fix the initial reaction time, that is to say, when is error analysis started, and the entire processing time, that is to say the time from which an error must be dealt with.

You should also describe which error situations are to be monitored by the monitoring team. These include:

- Interrupted updates
- Interrupted background processes
- Interrupted interface processes (transactional RFC, queued RFC, Ioc, ALE)

Define how problem solving should look. In the following example, we indicate how the problem solving process for interrupted updating should look: (Interrupted or un-executed updates lead to a situation where documents entered or changed by users are not finally saved in the corresponding application table and are thus non-existent for the user. The daily checking of updating tasks is therefore an important task of the SAP system administrator. If interrupted updates are not investigated immediately, once a few days have passed there is little chance of finding the cause of the error.) The monitoring team monitors interrupted updates in all production systems. For business hours A, one hour is set as initial reaction time (in this case, this refers to the time between the occurrence of the error and the monitoring team noticing the error). The monitoring team passes the error information on to the relevant expert. To do this, the monitoring team has a list of transaction codes and of the corresponding consultants. The specialist contacts the user for whom the error has occurred, resolves the interrupted updating in the system and clears up any other necessary steps in the department so that similar error situations do not occur again. A maximum processing time can be set for this, which once again depends on the importance of the transaction for the operation of business. As a guideline value we suggest 8 hours of working time (during business hours A) for transactions critical to business.

Finally, you should arrange that the number of interrupted updates over a given period of time is recorded in the Service Level Report.

Escalation procedure

If at a particular time it can be foreseen that a problem cannot be resolved within the agreed service target, the problem must be "escalated", which means that a person in a position of higher responsibility must decide how to proceed with this problem.

In the Service Level Agreement you should give details of who is to be notified in the event of escalation and when. If necessary, you should define several escalation levels. The *escalation procedure* should cover all hierarchy levels of the customer enterprise and the service provider. Establish that details of an escalation must be included in the Service Level Report.

Service level reporting

In the *Service Level Report*—apart from the key figures already mentioned—you should include other statistics characteristic of the SAP system. Examples are:

- Number of users logged on and number of transaction steps
- Average response time for dialog and update tasks
- Average response time during the hour with the greatest system load
- CPU and main memory load during the hour with the greatest system load
- Size of database and its rate of growth

Medium and long-term trends can often be traced from this information, which in turn allows for a timely intervention (for example, archiving measures in the event of high database growth).

Record how often a Service Level Report should be written (we recommend weekly) and to whom it should be distributed.

SAP Solution Manager

Service Level Management in *SAP Solution Manager*, which we shall describe in the last section of this chapter, covers the aspects described above. It is made up of a Setup, in which you enter the different parameters of your Service Level Agreement (e.g. hours of business or critical transactions that should be monitored carefully). Based on this data, SAP Solution Manager draws up a Service Level Report each week. Service Level Reporting in SAP Solution Manager includes the following functions:

- Automated setup, for example, for starting critical transactions
- Presentation of selected performance indicators, error messages and optimization advice for all components of a mySAP.com solution, based on the results of SAP EarlyWatch Alert services.
- Presentation of performance indicators, error messages and optimization recommendations, grouped according to system and according to business area.
- Graphic presentation of the time spans of selected performance indicators (trend analysis), for example hardware load
- Automatic generation of instructions and reference to other SAP services

Continuous Monitoring

CCMS (*Computing Center Management System*) contains a monitor with which you can monitor all aspects of your mySAP.com solution. Together with SAP Solution Manager, this forms a complete solution for the continuous monitoring of your system. The monitor offers:

- Complete, detailed monitoring (performance indicators) of mySAP.com software components, servers, databases and third-party (non-SAP) components
- Status indicators (Alerts: green, yellow, red) for performance indicators if threshold values are exceeded or not met
- Alert tracking and administration
- Expansion possibilities, thanks to the open structure (also for non-SAP software components)
- A graphical interface for monitoring and following up errors in conjunction with SAP Solution Manager

The central Alert Monitor is available with SAP Basis 4.0. The system to be monitored should be at least SAP Basis 3.0.

After introducing the Alert Monitor, this section presents concrete recommendations such as how to adapt the "tree" in the monitor to suit your mySAP.com solution, how to organize an escalation procedure, for example messaging by e-mail or pager, and how to link the Alert Monitor to the graphical interface of the Solution Manager. Taken together, these measures define a complete monitoring solution.

Performance indicators

The status of an IT solution is illustrated by what are known as *performance indicators*. Performance indicators can be:

- Counters, for example, average response times, throughput statistics, degree of process workload or the fill level of memory areas
- Text information, for example, error messages (an error message "processing of document X has been terminated" is also an indicator of poor performance in a system). In this sense, performance refers not merely to runtime performance, but it also evaluates availability and error situations.

The task of the solution monitoring is to generate, record, aggregate and evaluate performance indicators. SAP central Alert Monitor integrates performance indicators from dozens of "expert monitors" and brings them together in monitoring trees. These expert monitors act as suppliers of data to the Alert Monitor. The advantage of the central Alert Monitor is that you need to use the expert monitors only in particular exceptional situations, but not for the normal monitoring of components. The expert monitors linked to the indicators are deposited in the central Alert Monitor under the name of analysis methods. From the Alert Monitor you can go directly to the corresponding expert monitor (also if you are logged on to a remote system).

The Alert Monitor automatically generates alerts if an indicator threshold value is exceeded or not reached. Standards are supplied for threshold values, which can be individually adapted to suit your needs.

Not all performance indicators are of equal importance as regards evaluating whether or not your mySAP.com solution is running optimally. As you gain experience, some indicators will emerge as being of particular importance. We refer to these as *Key Performance Indicators* (KPIs). One objective of putting together a monitoring plan is thus to filter out the KPIs relevant to you from the wealth of information available. We would like to give some instructions to help you do this.

Working with the Alert Monitor

You can call the Alert Monitor as follows:

1. **CCMS · Tools · Control/Monitoring · Alert Monitor,** or use transaction code RZ20. The system displays the CCMS monitor collections.
2. You can expand one of the monitor collections by placing the cursor over "CCMS monitor sets" and then selecting **Process · Expand tree**.
3. Display the **"Entire System"** monitor in the "SAP CCMS Monitor Templates" collection by placing the cursor over it and selecting **Load monitor**. The monitor displays the tree in the presentation last used. The Monitoring tree is a hierarchical display of the monitor objects (system components) and monitor attributes (information on types of object) in the system. The **"Entire System"** Monitoring tree displays all objects and attributes presented in the expert view and objects from other views for which there are alerts. Expand the tree if the entire hierarchy is not displayed. Place the cursor in the "Entire System" row and select **Edit · Tree · Expand tree · Expand sub-tree**.

Apart from the "Entire System" monitor, there are other pre-defined monitors for special purposes. For example, if you are a database administrator you can open the "Database" monitor instead of the "Entire System" monitor. "CCMS self monitoring" is one of the special monitors in the "SAP CCMS Technical Expert Monitors" collection. This monitor displays possible problems in the Alert Monitor and in the monitoring architecture. In this monitor you can check if all data collection methods started by the Alert Monitorare running properly. If no data is given for a monitoring element, the monitoring tree is displayed in gray (see Figure 1.5).

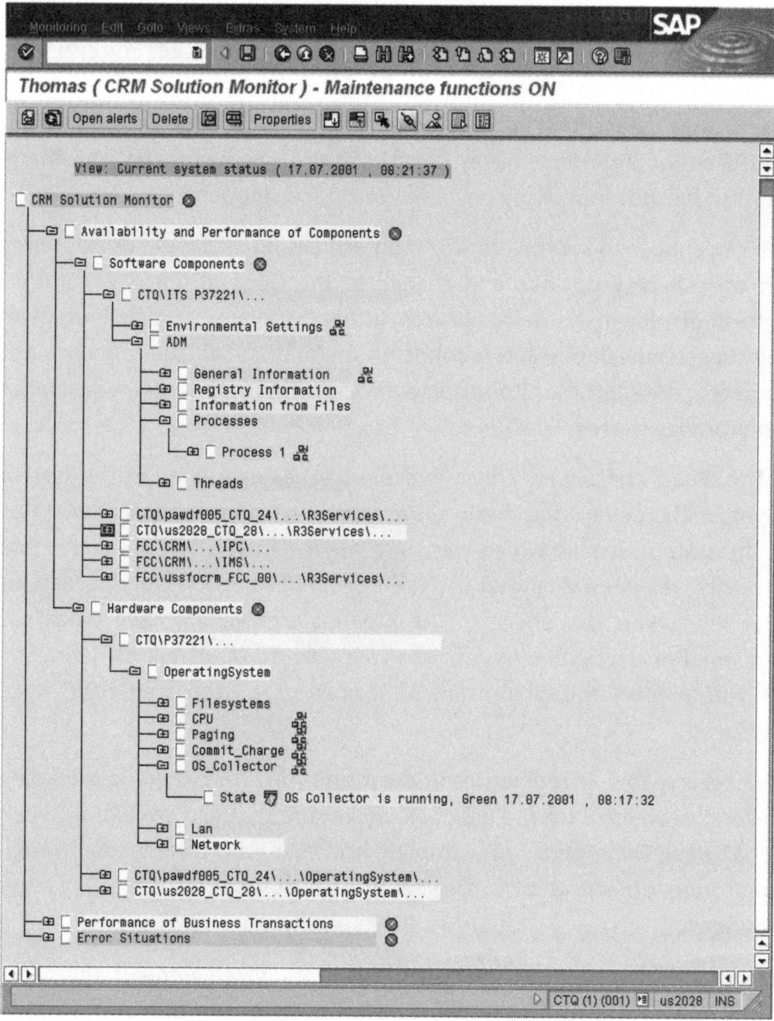

Figure 1.5 Central CCMS Alert Monitor for a mySAP CRM solution: Alerts on the availability and performance of software and hardware components

Alert propagation Check the current status of your mySAP.com components by displaying the current system status in your monitor. In the list of buttons, select **Current status** (if the button does not appear in the list, then this view is already displayed). In the "Current status" view you can see the latest performance values and status information reported to the control monitor. Older alerts that are still open (meaning that they have not been dealt with) are not displayed in color. To view a legend of the colors and symbols used in the control monitor, select **Extras · Legend**. The Alert Monitor gives the highest alert level in the monitoring tree. For example, if the monitoring object with the name of your mySAP.com component is green, this means that all components in the monitoring tree of the mySAP.com component have "green" status. This means that the Alert-monitor has not found any problems in this component.

Refresh display You can choose to set the display to refresh automatically. To do so, select **Extras · Display options** and change to the **General** tab page. Within **Refresh display** mark the option **Yes, interval** and enter a refresh interval. The suggested value is 300 seconds or longer. If automatic refresh is not activated, the Alert Monitor displays the data that was available when the monitor was started.

Current status and open alerts In the **Open alerts** view check to see what has happened in the system recently. The color code in this view does not tell you the current status of the system; it tells which alerts are open. Open alerts are alerts that have not yet been analyzed. At the beginning of your working day, or after lunch you can check in the **Open alerts** view to see what has happened in the system in your absence. The monitor records the alerts for you, even if the circumstances that triggered the alert have since improved.

Reacting to an alert If you see yellow or red entries in the monitoring tree, there is a warning (yellow) or an error (red). First of all, make sure that you are in the "Open alerts" view. The monitor now displays how many alerts there are for each monitoring object. It also displays the most important waiting alert messages.

Place the cursor over a yellow or red monitoring tree element and select **display alerts**. The system opens the alert browser and displays the open alerts for the corresponding monitoring object. The alert browser shows all alerts in the branch of the tree that you have marked. Move the cursor further up the monitoring tree to display a larger range of alerts. If you position the cursor on a monitoring object on the lowest level, you display only alerts on this monitoring object.

Each row in the alert browser gives overview information on an alert, including the alert message. The browser offers two further sources of information. First of all, mark an alert.

Methods of analysis

- Double-click on a monitoring object to start the corresponding analysis method. The analysis methods are expert tools for performance analysis, which are also discussed in other chapters of this book.
- Select **Display details**, to view details on the monitoring tree element. These include the most recent values or status reports, the alert threshold values and the performance data for the last control period (only for performance monitoring tree elements). You can represent performance data graphically, by marking the corresponding row and selecting **Display performance values graphically**.

Dealing with alerts

When you have analyzed the problem and resolved it or made sure that it can safely be ignored, set the alert to "resolved". Mark the alert and select **Complete alert**. The Alert Monitor deletes the alert from the list of open alerts.

Arranging monitoring trees

In principle, the CCMS Alert Monitor is ready to use immediately after installation. However, an optimized control should be adapted to suit your solution. You can also define and change monitoring objects and monitoring trees. Any changes made can also be transferred between systems.

The most important performance indicators that you should take into account for your daily monitoring and for which you should adjust the CCMS Alert Monitor are described in this section.

As can be seen in Figure 1.5, we divide performance indicators into three groups:

- **Availability and Performance of Components**
  The objective of monitoring in this branch is to ensure the availability and system performance of the hardware and software components participating in the mySAP.com solution. In other words: An alert in this area indicates that a component is not working at all or is working very slowly. All components are included in the monitoring, regardless of whether or not they come from SAP.

- **Performance of Business Transactions**
  The performance of SAP online transactions is monitored. The transaction-based monitoring of response times has the advantage that it is possible to react to performance problems flexibly and individually. This means, for example, that you can react to a transaction in the sales area with higher priority than to a transaction in the area of accounts. In particular, you should monitor the transactions for which a Service Level Agreement has been reached.
- **Error Situations**
  Errors in the regular operation are monitored here.

Availability and performance of SAP systems

By default, the Alert Monitor examines the mySAP.com component in which it is started. However, you can also examine several mySAP.com components with a single control monitor.

To do this, identify a mySAP.com component to your central system for monitoring. The central system should have the most up-to-date version of SAP Basis possible, so that you always have access to the latest monitoring possibilities. Depending on the size of your installation, you may need to use a dedicated SAP system for this. If you use SAP Solution Manager, assign it and the central CCMS monitoring to one system.

Make the other mySAP.com components known to the Alert Monitor. You will find a more detailed description of how to link an SAP system to the Alert Monitor in SAP online help.

Monitoring of remote components occurs via an RFC connection. From a single system you can monitor as many mySAP.com components as you want. Technical factors such as the speed of your network and the traffic in your network limit the number systems that can be monitored. This becomes particularly noticeable if a component in your system landscape is already down or the performance is already particularly bad. In this case it is neither useful nor desired to generate all performance indicators. In order to be able to react in such a case, the central Alert Monitor offers a special form of the availability control function, with which you can monitor the availability of remote mySAP.com components and their application servers. Monitoring availability means that you can determine whether or not a component and its server are running and are available for work.

The availability control uses the alert and display functions included in the monitoring architecture. It uses an "agent" for data entry (to determine whether a remote system is active and available). An agent is an independent program that runs externally of the mySAP.com component. By using an agent the availability of several remote systems can be checked from one central system, without the risk that a non-active system will cause the Alert Monitor to display "system crash". The availability of a large number of components can be monitored efficiently. An RFC connection to the remote systems is not necessary. The Alert Monitor does not have to log on to a remote component to check its availability. As a result, the data entry procedure with which the availability of even hundreds of systems can be checked from a central CCMS Alert Monitor is extremely fast. The availability monitor also has a short wait time, in case a component is not available.

Computers without SAP software

With the CCMS Alert Monitor you can check the availability and performance of any computers in your system landscape—not only those running SAP systems. To do this you need to install what is known as a "monitoring agent" on the computers that you wish to monitor.

Software components without SAP Basis

You can also monitor mySAP.com components without SAP Basis using SAP monitoring agents and include them in the central monitor. The procedures are described in detail in SAP Notes (for example, SAP Note 418285 for SAP ITS).

External software components

The open structure of CCMS monitoring architecture means that you can stipulate your own data supplier for the Alert Monitor so that you can also monitor software components that do not come from SAP.

For further information on SAP monitoring agents and their enhancements, see SAP Service Marketplace under *http://service.sap.com/systemmanagement*.

Summary of component monitoring

Figures 1.5 and 1.6 show *component monitoring* in the central monitor as it would be arranged for mySAP Customer Relationship Management (mySAP CRM). In the **Availability and Performance of Components, Software Components** branch, the monitoring of three SAP instances of the CTQ system (R/3 backend) and FCC (CRM Server) hangs, as do other components of the Internet Transaction Server (ITS) solution, Internet Pricer & Configurator (IPC) and the Index Management Server (IMS) (Figure 1.5). In the **Hardware Components** branch we find the performance indicators of the computers on which the SAP systems CTQ and FCC run, as well as a computer (P37221), on which SAP ITS runs (this is monitored by agents, as described above).

Performance specific transactions

With the Alert Monitor you can track the response times of certain clients or SAP transactions. This is of particular importance for transactions you have included in the service level agreement. In SAP Basis 4.6C the Alert Monitor contains the "Transaction specific dialog monitor" in the "SAP CCMS Monitors for optional components" collection. Further information is available in SAP online help. In our example (in Figure 1.6) the transaction "Create Sales Order" is included in the check.

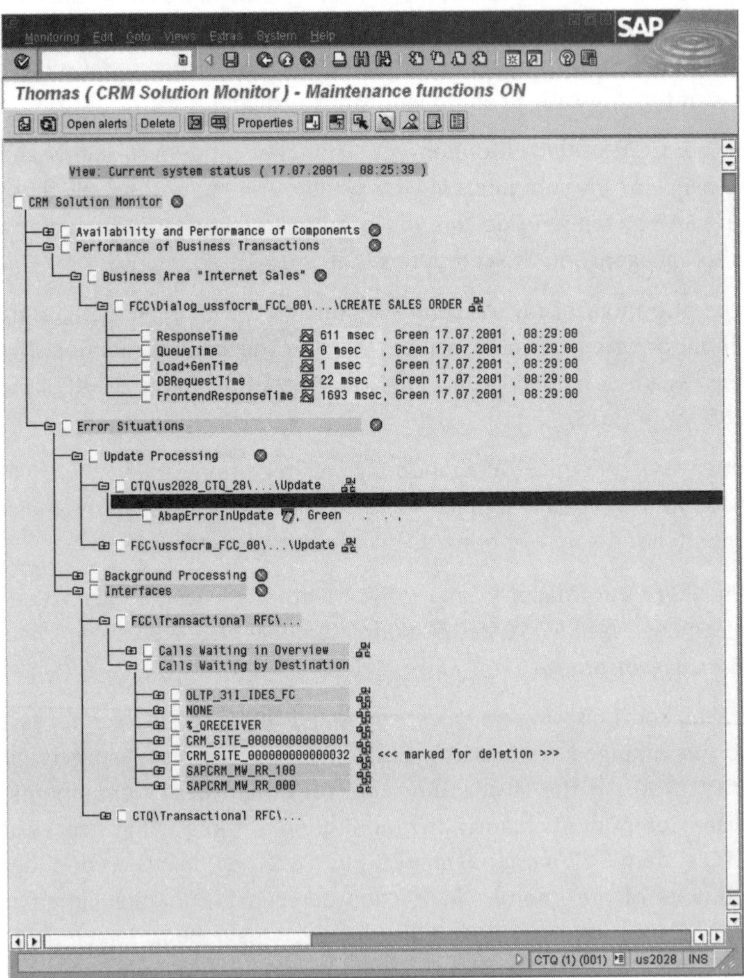

Figure 1.6 Central CCMS Alert Monitor for a mySAP CRM solution: Alerts on the performance of business process steps and error situations within update, background and interface processing

The most important error situations, which you should constantly monitor for all mySAP.com components, are: **Error situations**

- Interrupted updates
- Interrupted background processes
- Interrupted interface processes (transactional RFC, queued RFC, Idoc) Important alerts for interrupted interface processes can be found in the monitoring branch **Transactional RFC**.

The **Error Situations** branch in Figure 1.6 shows what error situations should be monitored in our mySAP CRM example.

Arranging automatic alert messaging

Starting with SAP Basis 4.6 you can allocate "auto-reaction methods" to critical performance indicators so that you will be informed of an alert by e-mail, fax or pager even if you are not currently working with the Alert Monitor. The Alert Monitor can automatically dial a pager or send an e-mail or fax to the following addressees:

- A Business Workplace user in client 000. The e-mail is sent 0 to 5 minutes after the occurrence of the alert and is delivered immediately.
- A distribution list or an external e-mail address. The e-mail is sent 0 to 5 minutes after the occurrence of the alert. Depending on the settings in SAPconnect there can be a delay before mail is sent to external e-mail addresses (that is to say, addresses of users that are not defined in client 000 or in the SAP system). You should set the time delay for the SAPconnect send process to less than one hour.

The message text of the e-mail contains the same information that is displayed in the Alert Monitor, which includes what the problem is, where and when it occurred and the degree of urgency of the alert (a red alert indicates a problem or an error, an amber alert is a warning). Further information is available on SAP online help and in SAP Note 176492.

Using the graphical interfaces of Solution Manager

Particularly for complex component landscapes, the structure of the alert trees quickly becomes too big to get an overview. If you include the SAP Solution Manager, which we will describe in the last section of this chapter, you can arrange the alerts in your business process and summarize them in the form of graphics. The business process graphics make it easier to find your way around, and you can see at a glance whether or not a particular business process is affected or not. Figure 1.7 shows an example of an alert graphic for a business process.

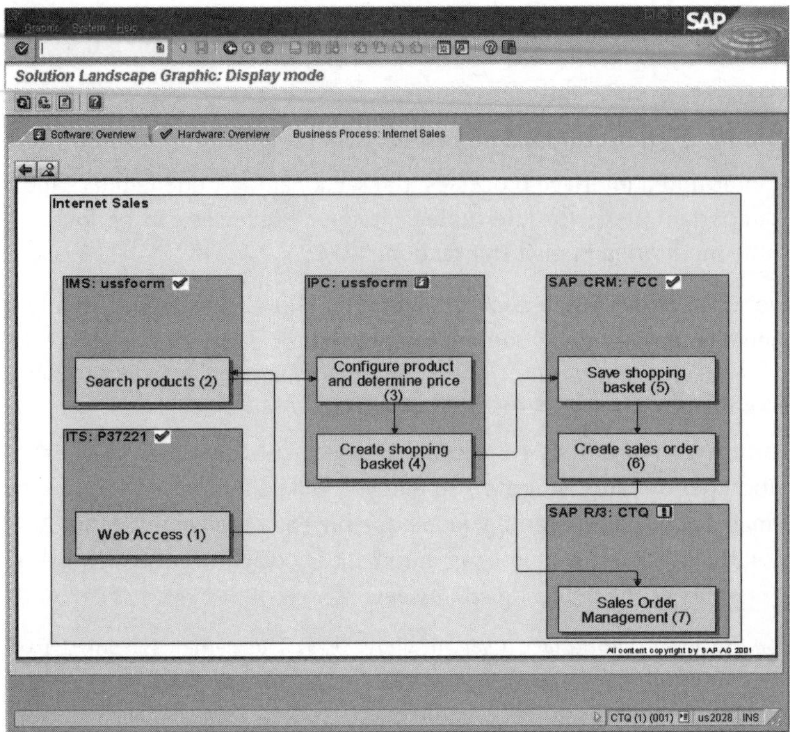

Figure 1.7 Business process graphic in the SAP Solution Manager with error messages. The business process graphics make it easier to find your way around a monitor, and you can see at first glance whether or not a particular business process is affected by an error or not.

For the component "IPC: ussfocrm" (Internet Pricing and Configurator) a (red) lightening symbol is displayed which indicates that a serious error has occurred in this component. You can see at first glance which process steps are affected by this error. You can then navigate to the corresponding expert monitor via the graphic.

Summary In principle, the CCMS Alert Monitor is ready to use immediately after the installation of your SAP system. In practice, however, you should adapt it to suit your own specific mySAP.com solution. Monitoring includes:

- Central monitoring of availability and performance of all hardware and software components participating in the mySAP.com solution via the SAP Monitoring Agent (the agent can easily be extended to cover non-SAP software)
- Monitoring the performance of the most important SAP online transactions

- Monitoring error situations in online transactions, updates, background processing and interfaces

For alerts that you identify as particularly critical, you can define automatic reaction procedures, for example that e-mails or SMS messages are sent so that constant monitoring is guaranteed even if you do not constantly have an eye on the Alert Monitor.

SAP Solution Manager offers you a graphical interface for presenting your business processes and the corresponding alert situations. This makes monitoring considerably simpler, particularly for complex processes and software landscapes, and it visualizes the connection between business process and software.

Plan for Continuous Performance Optimization

Optimization potential can be gathered from Service Level Management and feedback from continuous monitoring. Performance optimization measures can be divided into two categories:

- **Technical tuning actions**
  With technical tuning all components belonging to the system are set in such a way that load created by the users can be optimally processed by the system and no performance bottlenecks occur. Operating system, database, SAP application server and networks are all subject to technical tuning.
- **Application tuning measures**
  Application tuning works at program level. The main emphasis is on checking application-specific procedures as regards requirements and effectiveness. The aim of this is to minimize use of main memory and CPU resources, network transfers and hard disk accesses. Typical application tuning actions include the effective use of SAP transactions or performance tuning of customer-developed ABAP programs.

Technical tuning is necessary for each IT application. The need for application tuning grows proportionally to the size of the installation, and in particular with regard to the volume of data, the number of users and the number of customer-developed programs and modifications.

Whereas technical tuning optimally distributes the load generated by applications on the system, application tuning aims to keep system resources, such as CPU consumption, main memory consumption and I/O activity on the database server and application servers low. This is usually a matter of setting applications as efficiently as possible so as to avoid unnecessary load on the system in the first place.

Therefore, within the context of workload analysis, first of all a list is drawn up showing transactions and programs that place a heavy load on the system and could be optimized. These programs are then examined according to the following criteria:

- Which programs or transactions consume most resources?
- Which SQL statements are putting a high load on the database? From which programs do these statements come?

Optimization of SAP standard functions

The first tuning measure in application tuning is the efficient use of *SAP standard functions*. As a rule there are many equivalent business possibilities for portraying business processes in mySAP.com components. Among these possibilities, which only differ as regards technical implementation, there are more powerful or less powerful solutions, the effects of which for the user will result in higher or lower response times. Any customizing done to the mySAP.com component will also influence subsequent performance.

Program optimization

Another tuning measure is *program optimization*. This measure is mainly used for customer-developed programs, modifications of SAP standards and user exits. Unfortunately, quality control of the performance of customer-developed programs is hardly ever done in SAP projects. Rather, more often than not, programs are written during the implementation phase—often by inexperienced developers or under a lot of time pressure—and tested with a completely unrepresentative dataset. As the dataset grows in production, the performance of these programs continuously deteriorates and can finally lead to problems for the entire system. At this point in time, the original developer is often not available and any subsequent performance optimization involves a lot of work.

Future performance must be borne in mind, for both customizing and customer-developed programs and modifications, right from the implementation of the SAP system. If the development work is carried out by a consultant partner, this partner must be responsible not only for the functionality of developments, but also their performance.

There are also notes for SAP standard programs on adjusting coding in order to improve performance. You should consult the SAP Service Marketplace regularly to see if there are up-to-date error corrections or recommended modifications for your most important transactions.

Search the Service Marketplace for notes on your performance-critical transactions using the key word **Performance** and the corresponding transaction code program or table name.

Table buffering and indexing

Other possibilities for reducing database load is the correct use of the SAP buffer and the definition of suitable database indexes (secondary indexes) which can greatly reduce the database load for read operations. Table buffering and indexes are already set when mySAP.com components are installed. For optimizing the runtime of individual programs, however, it may be necessary to change these pre-settings. For customer-developed tables these settings must be carried out by the developer.

Summary: "Better to avoid workload rather than distribute it"

Table 1.2 shows an overview of the most important tuning measures. In the "Person" column the person responsible for each activity is listed: M: IT management; S: those responsible for the system (administrators, basis expert); A: Application consultant (employee of the department, application administrator, developer); U: User.

In general, several solutions can be performed to resolve a performance problem. In deciding which measures should be carried out in what order, one rule of thumb is: *It is better to avoid workload than distribute it*. There are, of course, exceptions. In certain cases, or as a temporary solution, it may be better to compensate for inefficient customizing and inefficiently written customer programs with technical measures such as creating indexes, increasing the size of the buffer or installing better and faster hardware. The actual list of measures for performance tuning must therefore be adapted according to the results of a performance analysis and by taking local circumstances into account.

Technical tuning	Person
Setting system parameters for operating system, database and SAP Basis system (database buffer, SAP buffer, number of work processes and so on)	S
Optimization of the database layout (I/O balancing)	S
Definition of daily, weekly and monthly workload distribution (for example, background processing, logon groups)	A, S, U, M
Installation of additional and more powerful hardware	S, M

Table 1.2 Tuning measures

Application tuning	
Looking for and applying SAP Notes from the SAP Service Marketplace (patches, error correction or recommended modifications)	A, S
Optimizing the Customizing of standard SAP transactions to improve performance.	A
Optimizing coding for customer-developed programs and modifications	A
Defining table buffering	A, S
Creating, changing or deleting secondary indexes	A, S

Table 1.2 Tuning measures (contd.)

Example: Technical tuning and application tuning

The interplay between technical optimization and application optimization is explained in the following example. It shows a performance analysis and a range of possible measures for performance optimization. The technical details of the analysis are purposely omitted.

Let us imagine a situation where SAP R/3 users are complaining of massive performance problems in Production Planning (SAP module PP), for example, in the creation of requirement lists and stock lists.

A performance analysis has come up with the following results:

- The SAP Work Process Overview shows that several programs repeatedly spend a long time reading from table RESB.
- An analysis of the database shows that all tables with transaction data reside on one hard disk. All transaction data together amounts to 8 GB, of which table RESB accounts for 2 GB.
- The operating system monitor shows that the hard disk on which, among other things, the RESB table resides, is fully loaded (80-100% load, response times of over 100 ms per access).

System administrators and application consultants sit down together to solve the problem. From the system administrator's point of view, the following technical solution strategies need to be discussed:

- The data buffer on the database server could be made bigger, so that it will be able to hold a large part of the RESB table on the main memory of the database server.
- The RESB table could be placed on a separate hard disk. The database hard disk layout could also be changed so that the RESB table could be distributed over several hard disks.

- The use of the ATP server would make it possible to buffer partial RESB table results on the application server main memory and thus reduce database accesses to this table.
- As a last resort, the installation of faster hard disks could be considered.

From the application administrator's point of view, the following measures are possible:

- The RESB table contains the reservation and dependent requirements of materials, components and assemblies used in production planning. It is read during availability checks, in particular. It may be that skillful customizing of the availability check would reduce the size and read frequency of table RESB. The following issues must be examined:
  - Could the availability check be simplified for some materials? Examples of this are screws, cable ties and other small parts that are used in all products. Is it really necessary to check the availability of these materials for each production order or can an individual check for this type of material be deactivated? This measure would reduce the expansion of table RESB and the frequency of accesses to it and as a result raise the performance of the availability check.
  - How often is the content of the RESB table archived and deleted? Is there still very old planning data in the table?
  - Table RESB also contains future planning data. Has the table grown so much because planning goes too far into the future?

It is evident that given the many possible measures, system administrators and application consultants have to work out a solution together. The most effective method for optimizing performance is often to deactivate unnecessary application functions. The application administrator needs the system administrator's analyses to know what should be deactivated or simplified in customizing. Therefore, a joint effort is necessary in order to find the best solution.

The SAP Solution Management Program

The SAP Solution Management program provides customers and partners with tools and procedures to support all SAP solutions over their entire lifecycle. In this way customers can use mySAP.com to its full potential.

SAP Solution Manager for monitoring

From day-to-day life you know that even the best tool kit is of no use if the person planning to use it does not have the necessary knowledge of how to use the tools. Apart from the well known media with which customers and partners have accumulated this knowledge up to now (including SAP online help, training courses, SAP Service Marketplace with SAP Notes and other documentation and of course this book), since 2001 SAP has also provided partners and customers with service procedures. These let you implement your mySAP.com solutions in an efficient way and put them into productive use.

SAP Solution Manager is the portal for accessing these services and it gives you centralized access to tools and service procedures for performance monitoring and optimization. Technically, the Solution Manager is an add-on to SAP Basis 4.6 (minimum version 4.6C). With the Solution Manager, SAP systems starting with SAP Basis 3.1, can be monitored and optimized.

A core element of SAP Solution Manager is Solution Monitoring, which makes it possible to monitor mySAP.com solutions. Unlike classical system monitoring, which is limited to hardware elements and software components, Solution Monitoring checks the functionality of the entire business process. The Solution Management method comprises three steps: the first step covers the most important business processes and the implementation of these as a mySAP.com solution, in order to identify which hardware and software components participate in the solution. In a second step it is determined which indicators (for example, response times, error messages) should be monitored in order to ensure problem free operation. To this end SAP delivers templates for each business process with a standardized monitoring plan. These templates can be downloaded from the SAP Service Marketplace to SAP Solution Manager, and they can be adapted to the needs of the customer, so that an individual monitoring plan can be created with a minimum of effort. In the third step, a monitoring plan suited to the customer's business processes emerges. Figure 1.7 displays the graphical representation of a business process and its status in the form of alarm symbols (in this case, for example: green ticks and red lightening symbols). The SAP EarlyWatch Alert Service, already used by most customers, is also an element of Solution Monitoring, as is Service Level Management based on monitoring data.

One important feature that differentiates between Solution Monitoring in SAP Solution Manager and monitoring with previous system management programs is that the Solution Manager focuses on the business process. It bears in mind the network of relationships that exists between software components when a business processes runs over several components. Up to now, system management only monitored each component individually, without recognizing the relationship between them. Therefore, we could say that the SAP Solution Manager monitors a business process practically "from the inside" whereas previous system monitoring only provided monitoring "from the outside".

SAP Solution Manager for optimizing

SAP Solution Manager not only helps you with performance monitoring, but also with performance optimization. Let us assume, as an example, that monitoring has found numerous expensive SQL statements which are placing a high load on your database, frequently leading to bottlenecks. The EarlyWatch Alert Service identifies the statements in question and also recommends a service that should be carried out to optimize SQL statements. This service can also be downloaded from SAP Service Marketplace to the SAP Solution Manager and executed there. The SAP Solution Manager interacts with your system landscape on the one hand, to load the necessary statistics and other data, and on the other hand it interacts with the agent that carries out the service. Using a repetitive procedure, it finds ways to improve performance. It is clear that a service program of this type can be much more detailed than, for example, this book or a training course. The service mentioned here for optimizing SQL statements covers over 500 individual optimization possibilities—beginning with common pitfalls and misused features in database software, with recommendations for optimizing indexes through to recommendations for re-formulating SQL statements. From these 500 cases the agent will certainly be able to find those that apply to the problem in hand.

Apart from service procedures which help you optimize during production, there are other service procedures which help achieve an optimal setting for your system landscape right from implementation. In this case, SAP Solution Manager also works with both the system and the agent, which can achieve optimal configuration with the help of the service.

After you have downloaded the service procedures from SAP Service Marketplace onto the SAP Solution Manager once, you can, in principle, carry out these services yourself. Alternatively, you can decide to have these services provided by SAP or your service partner as a remote or on-site service. You can thus decide, according to your needs, if you wish to build up specific know-how in your organization or prefer to acquire it externally. This choice exists, for example, for the EarlyWatch service. The EarlyWatch Service has been available as a remote service since 1984. It is provided by SAP in collaboration with numerous service partners (including SAP's main hardware partners). Since 2001 employees of SAP customers can also take part in a training course and qualify for certification in the EarlyWatch Service, to be able to perform the service in their own enterprise. As a result, customers can choose to build up this know-how in-house or, as in the past, to use external know-how. Your service and support center can give you details of service provision.

Summary SAP Solution Manager

Table 1.3 explains the most important services in the SAP Solution Manager as regards performance monitoring and optimization.

Service	Objective	Prerequisites	See also chapter(s)
Solution monitoring	Monitoring a mySAP.com solution	Certified Technical Consultant (recommended)	1, 2
Service Level Management	Reporting on whether or not objectives regarding availability, performance and error situations are achieved.	Certified Technical Consultant (recommended)	1, 3
SAP EarlyWatch Alert service	Identifying medium and long-term optimization potential	Certified Technical Consultant (recommended)	1, 2, 3
SAP EarlyWatch service	Detailed system analysis and optimization	Service-specific certification (EarlyWatch)	all

Table 1.3 SAP Solution Manager services in the area of performance monitoring and optimization. Your service and support center can give you further details, or you can find more information on the Internet page http://service.sap.com/solutionmanager.

Service	Objective	Prerequisites	See also chapter(s)
Customer Program Optimization	Optimization of customer-developed programs	Service-specific certification	4, 9, 10, 11
SQL statement optimization	SQL statement optimization	Service-specific certification	2, 9, 11
System administration	Optimization of system administration, including Service Level Management and Monitoring	Service-specific certification	1, 2, 3
Storage subsystem optimization	Optimization of the storage system with regard to configuration and data distribution		
Interface management	Optimization of interfaces	Service-specific certification	6, 7
Data management and archiving	Reduction of occurring data by avoiding data (optimized customizing) and archiving	Service-specific certification	
Business process performance optimization	Optimizing performance of processes	Service-specific certification	
Business process management	Optimization of business processes	Service-specific certification	
SAP GoingLive Check	Checking transition to production operation	Service-specific certification	all
SAP GoingLive Functional Upgrade check	Verify production operation after a software upgrade	Service-specific certification	all

Table 1.3 SAP Solution Manager services in the area of performance monitoring and optimization. (contd.)

Summary

There are two important prerequisites for good system performance:

- The cooperation of all those involved in setting up a mySAP.com solution and in the execution and administration of customizing or developments.

- Long-term planning of performance monitoring and optimization. For this you can use Service Level Management methods and the central monitoring architecture of CCMS in the SAP Solution Management program.

What are the concrete advantages of a structured monitoring and optimization plan? First of all, clearly defined and measurable goals and communication structures improve the IT organization's understanding of the requirements of end users and business process owners. The quality of the IT organization's service improves because it can work in a more purposeful way and as a result, customer satisfaction also increases. Indirectly, Service Level Reporting makes the current cost structure (for example, use of hardware and IT) transparent and allows for forecasting. Finally, well executed Service Level Management should have a positive effect on the motivation of employees of the IT organization because, given clear objectives, they can also see that they are doing all they can to achieve a high level of customer satisfaction. (Anyone who has experienced the often indiscriminate finger pointing in IT organizations and knows the frustration employees feel when they have subjectively done their best can well understand this point!)

The tasks of performance monitoring and optimization are carried out by very different people. Employees who carry out error monitoring and generate Service Level Reporting generally have a good basic knowledge of the technology and the applications, but don't normally have specialist knowledge. This is due to the fact that system monitoring must be maintained 24 hours a day, 7 days a week, and specialists from all areas cannot be available for these tasks at all times. During monitoring or Service Level reporting, a helpdesk employee or manager must be in a position to decide whether or not a specialist should be consulted. In other words: you should not need a database expert to decide whether or not a database expert is needed!

The planning or arrangement of monitoring and the continuous optimization of the application, on the other hand, generally require greater specialist knowledge. Technical tuning requires knowledge of the operating system, the database and the SAP Basis system. Consequently, it is usually carried out by an SAP Basis administrator or by an SAP Basis consultant. If necessary the database and network administrators are available to help.

Application tuning requires a broader knowledge of the mySAP.com solution and mySAP.com technology:

- Knowledge of the database will help decide when to create additional database indexes or how to formulate SQL statements effectively
- Knowledge of SAP Basis will help you to buffer tables optimally
- Knowledge of the ABAP programming language will help you to use ABAP commands effectively
- Knowledge of the mySAP.com solutions will help ensure that SAP programs and transactions are used effectively
- Knowledge of business processes within the enterprise will help you recognize time-critical processes and adapt important transactions to suit users.

It is generally impossible for one person to have such a broad overview of the SAP system. As a result, it is important to form teams. For a large SAP project it would be necessary to set up a *performance forum* to ensure regular meetings between people who represent the various aspects of performance optimization.

Important terms in this chapter

After studying this chapter you should be familiar with the following terms:

- mySAP.com solution and mySAP.com software component
- Client/Server technology, SAP Web Application Server
- SAP Solution Manager
- Central CCMS Alert Monitor
- Service Level Management

2 Monitoring Hardware, Database and SAP Basis

This chapter explains how to monitor and analyze the performance of your hardware, database, SAP memory configuration and SAP work processes. Procedure roadmaps at the end of each section summarize the most important analysis paths and clarify when to use the various monitors.

Simple recommendations are provided to help you optimize each component, except where in-depth explanations are required (these are given in subsequent chapters). Unnecessary background information is intentionally kept to a minimum so that even application consultants or system administrators with limited experience in performance analysis can use this chapter to improve the performance of their system. For example, monitoring and customizing SAP extended memory is described without explaining SAP extended memory in detail. More detailed information can be found in Chapters 5 to 9. Our experience suggests that you can solve many performance problems in the operating system, database and SAP Basis using simple instructions, without delving into technical details.

When should you read this chapter?

You should read this chapter if you want to use the SAP system to technically monitor and optimize the performance of your SAP system, database or operating system.

Basic Terms

This section explains how the terms *computer, server, application server, SAP instance, database, database server* and *database instance* are used throughout this book:

A *computer* will always mean a physical machine with a CPU, a main memory, an IP address and so on.

An *SAP application instance*, also referred to as *SAP instance*, is a logical unit. It consists of a set of SAP work processes that are administered by a dispatcher process. It also includes a set of SAP buffers located in the host computer's shared memory and accessed by the work processes. There can be multiple SAP instances on one computer. As a result there will be multiple dispatchers and sets of buffers. An *application server* is a computer with one or more SAP instances.

Every SAP system has only one *database*. The term *database* refers to the set of data that is organized in files, for example. The database may be thought of as the passive part of the database system.

The active part of the database system is the *database instance*, a logical unit that allows access to the database. A database instance consists of database processes with a common set of database buffers in the shared memory of a computer. A *database server* is a computer with one or more database instances. A computer can be both a database server and an application server if a database instance and an SAP instance run on it.

In the SAP environment there is normally only one database instance for each database. Examples of database systems where multiple database instances can access a database are DB2/390 and ORACLE Parallel Server. The special features of these *parallel database systems* are not covered in this book.

We refer to SAP software components as *SAP systems*, which are based on SAP Basis. These are, namely, SAP R/3, SAP BW, SAP APO, SAP CRM/EBP and SAP Workplace 2.

Throughout documentation and literature the term *server* is used in both a hardware sense and a software sense. Thus the term can be used to refer to a computer, for example in the term *database server*, and also to a logical service, such as in the terms *message server* and *ATP server*.

Monitoring Hardware

The SAP performance monitors are tools for analyzing performance. They are listed together in the performance menu (transaction code STUN). To call this menu, select:

> **Tools · Administration · Monitor · Performance** or
> **Tools · CCMS · Control/Monitoring · Performance menu**

The Operating System Monitor is the tool for analyzing hardware bottlenecks and operating system problems.

To start the Operating System Monitor for the application server you are currently logged on to, select

Tools · Administration · Monitor · Performance · Operating system · Local · Activity

or enter the transaction code ST06. The main screen of the operating system monitor "Local OS Monitor" appears.

To start the Operating System Monitor for a database server or an application server other than the one you are logged on to, use transaction code OS07, or select:

Tools · Administration · Monitor · Performance · Operating system · Remote · Activity (transaction code OS07)

After selecting the desired server, the screen "Local OS Monitor" for that server will appear.

Alternatively the Operating System Monitor can be called from the server overview using Transaction SM51 or by selecting:

Tools · Administration · Monitor · System Monitoring · Server

Mark the desired application server and choose **OS Collector**.

Analyzing a Hardware Bottleneck (CPU and Main Memory)

The main screen of the Operating System Monitor lists the most important performance data for the operating system and the hardware. All data is renewed every 10 seconds by the auxiliary program `saposcol`. To update the data on the screen (after 10 seconds or longer), choose **Refresh display**.

CPU Workload

Under the header CPU in the Operating System Monitor initial screen are the fields **Utilization user**, **system** and **idle**. These values indicate the percentage of the total CPU capacity that is currently being used by user processes (by the SAP system, the database and other processes), the percentage being used by the operating system itself and what percentage is not being consumed. The **count** field indicates the number of processors. **Load average** is the average number of work processes waiting for a free processor and is indicated for the previous minute, 5 minutes and 15 minutes. The other values listed under CPU are less significant for analyzing system performance.

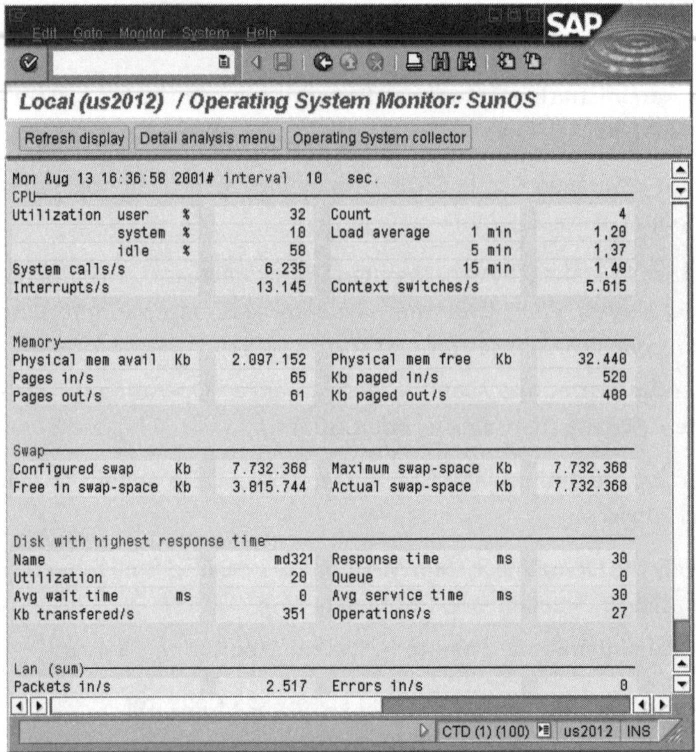

Figure 2.1 Main screen of the Operating System Monitor

Field	Explanation
Utilization user	CPU workload caused by user processes (SAP system, database etc.)
Utilization system	CPU workload caused by the operating system
Utilization idle	Free CPU capacity. This value should be at least 20%, optimally 35%.
Count	Number of processors (CPUs)
Load average	Number of processes waiting for CPUs, averaged over 1, 5 or 15 minutes
Physical mem avail Kb	Available physical main memory (RAM) in KB

Table 2.1 Fields in the Operating System Monitor

Main memory workload

Under the header Memory in the Operating System Monitor initial screen, you will find the amount of available physical main memory

(**Physical mem avail Kb** field) and the operating system paging rates and paged data quantities.

Swap space

Under the header **Swap** you will find the amount of currently allocated *swap space*. The swap space should be about three times as large as the physical main memory and at least 3.5 GB.

If the sum of the physical memory and swap space is smaller than the total amount of memory required by the SAP system, the database and other programs, this may cause program terminations or even operating system failure. You should therefore ensure that there is sufficient swap space.

History: CPU and main memory

To display the CPU workload over the previous 24 hours, select the following buttons in the initial screen of the Operating System Monitor:

Detail analysis menu · Previous hours: CPU

The screen **Local CPU last 24 hours** appears. The column headers are the same as in the fields under CPU in the Operating System Monitor initial screen, except that the values given are for one hour. There is a similar overview for main memory usage:

Detail analysis menu · Previous hours: Memory

and similarly for the swap space and so on.

When is there a CPU or main memory bottleneck?

The unused CPU capacity (indicated as "CPU utilization idle") should normally be at least 20% on average per hour. This enables the system to accommodate temporary workload peaks. A reading of 35% idle CPU capacity is even better. The paging rate should not become too large. As a rule of thumb, paging is not critical if, every hour, less than 20% of the physical main memory is paged. For operating systems that page asynchronously (for example, Windows NT), the value indicated in the Operating System Monitor as Paged-in Rate is the key statistic on paging performance. For other operating systems that page only when necessary (such as most UNIX derivatives), the key statistic is the Paged-out Rate.

If the Operating System Monitor sometimes shows values that exceed these guideline values, this does not automatically mean that there is a hardware bottleneck. Rather, the Workload Monitor should be used to check whether the high CPU workload or the paging rate is associated with poor response times. Corresponding analyses can be found in Chapter 3 in the section "Analyzing General Performance Problems" on page 132.

Main memory bottleneck

If you observe high paging rates on several computers, calculate the virtual main memory allocated to the SAP instances and the database. (To calculate the virtual memory, see the sections "Displaying the Allocated Memory" on page 103 and "Analyzing the Database Buffer" on page 80 in this chapter.) Compare this with the available physical main memory. Experience shows that, as a rule of thumb, there should be around 50% more virtual memory than physical memory.

Causes of hardware bottlenecks

If you do detect a hardware bottleneck on one or more computers in the SAP system, it may be due to one or more of the following causes:

Nonoptimal workload distribution

In a distributed system with multiple computers, if you discover a hardware bottleneck on at least one computer, while other computers have unused resources, the workload is probably not optimally distributed. To improve performance, redistribute the SAP work processes and the user logons.

It is extremely important that the database server has enough resources. A CPU or main memory bottleneck on the database server means that the required data cannot be retrieved quickly from the database, which causes poor response times in the entire system.

Individual processes that consume too much CPU

In the Operating System Monitor (transaction code ST06) select:

Detail analysis menu · Top CPU processes

The overview of the operating system processes is displayed. Here you can see all processes currently active and the demand they are making on resources. Identify the processes causing high CPU load: SAP work processes are indicated with the process name "disp+work" (Windows NT) or "dw_<instance>" (UNIX). Database processes are normally indicated by brand names such as Oracle or Informix that appear in the columns Process name or User name.

To check whether individual processes are placing a heavy load on the CPU for long periods of time, refresh the monitor periodically and observe any changes in the value CPU Util [%]. If SAP work processes are causing high CPU load, open a new user session and call the Local Work Process Overview (see "Analyzing SAP Work Processes" on page 107 in the present chapter). You can use the process ID to identify this SAP work process. From the Work Process Overview, note the name of the ABAP program and the user corresponding to the PID. It may be necessary to consider an in-depth performance analysis for this program. If a database process is causing high

CPU utilization over a long time period, call the Database Process Monitor (see "Identifying Expensive SQL Statements" on page 85). With this monitor, you can find out which SQL statements are currently running.

Thus, using the Operating System Monitor in conjunction with the Work Process Overview and the Database Process Monitor, you can fairly easily identify programs, transactions, and SQL statements that cause high CPU load.

External processes

External processes can also cause a CPU bottleneck. In the Operating System Monitor, if you find external processes (that is, processes that are neither SAP work processes nor database processes) with a high CPU consumption that cause a CPU bottleneck, you should find out whether these processes are really necessary for your system, or whether they can be switched off or moved to another computer. Examples of external processes are: administrative software, backups, external systems, screen savers, and so on.

Suppose you notice a CPU bottleneck during times of peak user activity. The process overview in the Operating System Monitor reveals a single SAP work process that is causing a CPU load of 30% over several minutes. At the same time, the SAP Work Process Overview shows a long-running background program. You should try to see if the background program could be run at a time when the dialog load is lower.

Memory requirement of individual programs

You can identify programs with high memory requirements that may be causing a main memory bottleneck in a way similar to the method described above for the CPU bottleneck. See also Chapter 5.

Minimize file system cache

Operating systems normally administer their own *File System Cache*. This cache is located in the main memory, where it competes for memory space with the SAP system and the database. If the cache is too large, it causes high paging rates despite the fact that the physical main memory is more than large enough to accommodate both the SAP system and the database. SAP recommends reducing this cache to between 7% and 10% of the physical memory.

UNIX

The operating system parameters for configuring the file system cache include *dbc_max_pct* for HP-UX, *ubc-maxpercent* for Digital UNIX and *maxperm* for AIX.

Windows

To reduce the size of the file system cache for Windows NT: from the NT screen (symbol: **Network**) in the control panel of your NT operating system, choose the **Services** tab, the **Server** service, and the **Properties** button. In the following screen, under the screen area **Optimization**, select the **Maximize Throughput for Network Applications** option and confirm by clicking on **OK**. You have to reboot the computer to activate the file cache's new settings.

A main memory bottleneck can give rise to excessive paging which in turn requires more CPU and can lead to a CPU bottleneck. Removing the cause of excessive paging usually makes the CPU bottleneck disappear.

Analyzing Read/Write (I/O) Problems

In the Operating System Monitor (transaction code ST06) under

Detail analysis menu · Disk

you will find, among other things, information on hard disk load and—if the operating system makes it available—information on the disks' waiting and response times.

Field	Explanation
Disk	Operating system name for the hard disk
Resp.	Average response times of the hard disk (in msec)
Util.	Load on the hard disk (in %)
Queue Len.	Number of processes waiting for I/O operations
Wait	Wait time (in msec)
Serv	Service time (in msec)

Table 2.2 Columns in the Hard Disk Monitor

By double-clicking a row in the Hard Disk Monitor, you can display an overview of the average response times over the previous 24 hours for the selected hard disk.

I/O bottleneck

In the Hard Disk Monitor, a heavy load on an individual disk is signified by a value greater than 50% in the column **Util.** this may indicate an *I/O bottleneck*. However, to perform a more detailed analysis, you need the tools provided by the hardware manufacturer.

An I/O bottleneck is particularly critical if it is on the hard disk where the operating system's paging file resides. Monitoring is particularly recommended for the disks of the database server. To prevent bottlenecks during read or write operations to the database, use the

Database Performance Monitor and the Hard Disk Monitor. For further details on these problems, please see the section "Identifying Read/Write (I/O) Problems" on page 90.

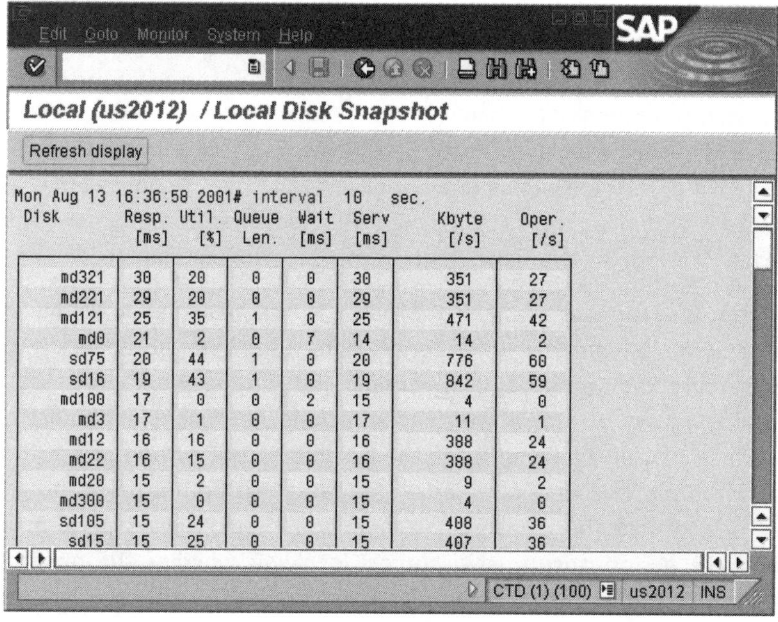

Disk	Resp. [ms]	Util. [%]	Queue Len.	Wait [ms]	Serv [ms]	Kbyte [/s]	Oper. [/s]
md321	30	20	0	0	30	351	27
md221	29	20	0	0	29	351	27
md121	25	35	1	0	25	471	42
md0	21	2	0	7	14	14	2
sd75	20	44	1	0	20	776	60
sd16	19	43	1	0	19	842	59
md100	17	0	0	2	15	4	0
md3	17	1	0	0	17	11	1
md12	16	16	0	0	16	388	24
md22	16	15	0	0	16	388	24
md20	15	2	0	0	15	9	2
md300	15	0	0	0	15	4	0
sd105	15	24	0	0	15	408	36
sd15	15	25	0	0	15	407	36

Figure 2.2 Monitor for evaluating hard disk work load

Other Checks With the Operating System Monitor

Parameter changes

For UNIX operating systems, the SAP system logs all operating system parameter changes. To display the log of all such changes, from the Operating System Monitor, choose:

Detail analysis menu • Parameter changes

Place the cursor over the name of a server and select the **History of file** button. This log lets you determine whether the start of performance problems can be linked to the time when particular parameters were changed.

LAN check

With the **Detail analysis menu • Lan Check by Ping** tool you can carry out a quick test on the network. You can select any database server, application server or presentation server and test the network connection, for example response times or to see whether there was any data loss. An example for an analysis with this tool can be found in Chapter 7 in the section "Analyzing and Optimizing the Performance of GUI Communication" on page 223.

Summary

Performance problems may be indicated if

- The average idle CPU capacity is less than 20% every hour
- More than 20% of the physical main memory is paged every hour
- Utilization of individual hard disks is more than 50%

Excessive utilization of the hard disks, particularly on the database server, can cause systemwide performance problems. To check whether the high CPU load or the high paging rate significantly damages response times in the SAP system or the database, use the Workload Monitor (see the section "Performing Workload Analysis" on page 132 in Chapter 3).

Figures 2.3 and 2.4 show the procedure for analyzing a hardware bottleneck. A common solution for resolving a hardware bottleneck is to redistribute the workload (for example, by moving work processes). Possible causes of a CPU bottleneck include: inefficient applications, which can usually be identified in the Database Process Monitor and the Work Process Overview or external processes that do not belong to an SAP instance or the database instance. You should always perform a complete performance analysis before deciding whether the existing hardware is sufficient for the demands made on the SAP system.

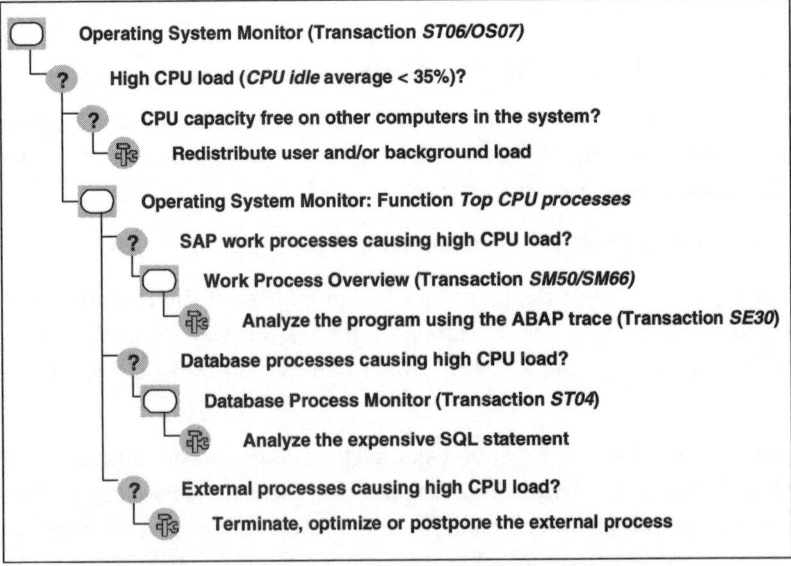

Figure 2.3 Procedure roadmap for analyzing a hardware bottleneck (CPU)

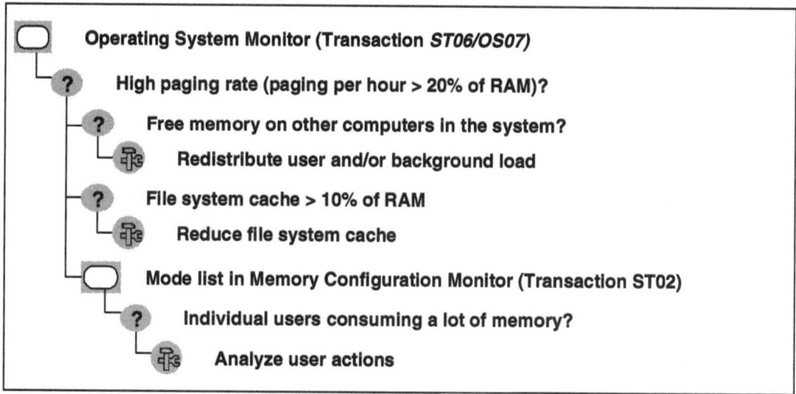

Figure 2.4 Procedure roadmap for analyzing a hardware bottleneck (main memory)

The roadmaps in Figures 2.3 and 2.4 show the procedure to be followed in the event of a hardware bottleneck. They refer to monitors and analyses described later in this book. Throughout this book, you will find similar procedure roadmaps. A collection of all the roadmaps and an explanation of the symbols used in them can be found in the appendix.

Monitoring the Database

The SAP system currently supports seven different relational database systems, each of which has a different architecture. Many performance problems, however, occur independently of the type of database system implemented. To help customers analyze and tune their databases, the SAP system has its own Database Performance Monitor with basic functions that work independently of the database system used. The Database Performance Monitor collects performance data from two sources:

- The monitor relies on performance data collected by the relevant database system. Analytical functions are also used. Every database user has access to these analytical functions in a stand-alone database and the results are only displayed in the SAP system. Functions which have been developed by SAP or partner companies for monitoring the performance of the SAP system can also be used to a certain extent.
- A portion of the performance data is entered and collected directly by the SAP system—for example, in the database interface for the SAP work processes.

This book covers the basic functions of the Database Performance Monitors, which can be used with all database systems. Examples of analyses performed using this monitor for different database systems are

included. A summary of menu paths for all database systems can be found in the appendix.

The Database Performance Monitor can be started as follows:

Tools · Administration · Monitor · Performance · Database · Activity

The **Database Performance Analysis: Database Overview** screen appears.

Analyzing the Database Buffer

Every database has various *buffers* that enable user data (data from tables) and administrative information from the database to be stored in main memory and as a result, reduce the number of accesses to the hard disk. Accesses to these buffers in main memory are normally 10 to 100 times faster than accesses to the hard disk. If the buffers are made too small, the data volume is too large for the buffer. Data is then forced out of the buffer and has to be reread (reloaded) from the hard disk. For this reason, monitoring buffer activity is an important element of performance analysis. Information needed for monitoring the buffer can thus be found in analyses of all databases.

The most important buffer in a database is the *data buffer* or *data cache*, which stores parts of the most recently read database tables and their indexes. The data in the database tables is not read directly from the hard disk and sent to the user's SAP work process. Rather, it is first stored temporarily in the data buffer. The data buffer is divided into *blocks* or *pages*, which can be 2 KB to 32 KB in size, depending on the database system and the operating system. Data is read from the hard disk in blocks or pages and then stored in the data buffer.

The following values characterize the quality of data buffer accesses:

- **Physical read accesses**
  Number of read accesses to the hard disk. This value indicates how many blocks or pages must be loaded to satisfy the user queries being processed in an SAP work process.
- **Logical read accesses**
  Total number of read accesses. This figure indicates how many blocks or pages are read from the buffer *and* the hard disk.

- ▶ **Buffer quality** or **hit ratio**
  This value is given by the following relation:

  Buffer quality = (logical accesses—physical accesses) ÷ logical accesses × 100%.

The smaller the number of physical accesses in relation to the number of logical accesses, the higher the buffer quality. A buffer quality of 100% is ideal, and means that no database tables are read from disks. Instead, all required objects reside in the main memory of the database instance.

If the database instance has just been started, the buffer will just have been loaded, and the hit ratio is low. Therefore, when you evaluate the buffer quality, ensure that the database has already been running for several hours. In production systems, the size of the data buffer normally varies between 100 MB and 500 MB, depending on the size of the database. However, for large installations, the data buffer can be significantly larger.

The different memory areas for the example of a DB2 database (DB2 UDB for UNIX and Windows) are explained below. Information on other types of database systems can be found in the appendix.

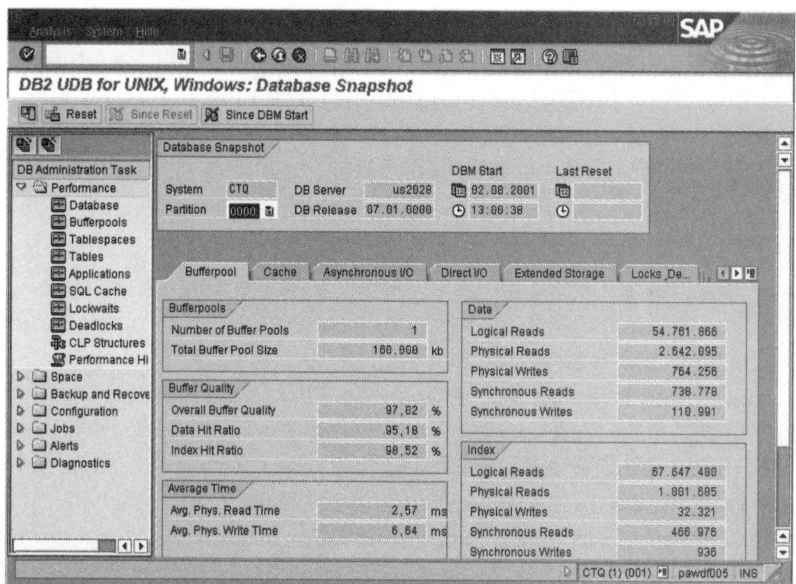

Figure 2.5 Main screen of the Database Performance Monitor (DB2 UDB for UNIX and Windows)

Memory management using the example of a DB2 UDB database (DB2 Universal Database for UNIX and Windows)

Memory allocated by a DB2 UDB database installation is made up of two parts: the *Database Global Memory*, allocated in the shared memory of the database server; and the *Agent Private Memory*, the memory for the individual database processes, which in DB2 UDB are referred to as *Agents*. For every SAP work process (at least) one Agent is started and as a result the total memory requirement is calculated as follows:

Total memory = Database Global Memory + Agent Private Memory × number of SAP work processes

The most important elements of the Database Global Memory are:

- The *Buffer Pool*, which buffers tables and index pages
- The *Database Heap*, a memory area for internal control structures
- The *Lock List*, an area of the memory in which database locks are administered
- The *Package Cache*, which buffers the run schedules for already executed SQL statements
- The *Catalog Cache*, which buffers the database's data dictionary information

The Agent Private Memory includes, for example, the *Application Support Layer* and the memory area for sorting result quantities of SQL statements *(Sort Heap)*. It should be noted that most memory areas are only really allocated when they are actually used. Exceptions to this rule are the buffer pool, the lock list and the application support layer, which are allocated right from the start of the database instance.

buffer pool

You can create several *buffer pools* for a single DB2 UDB database instance. Allocating which data will be contained in which buffer occurs at the table spaces level. The block size of data pools and the associated table spaces is identical. Blocks can be between 2 and 32 KB in size. The size of DB2 UDB buffer pools is set using the parameter *buffpage* or with the command "Alter Bufferpool". Logical read accesses to the data pool are executed in the Database Performance Monitor (transaction code ST04), separated according to table and index pages. Logical accesses to table pages can be found in the **Data Logical Reads** column and logical accesses to index pages in the **Index Logical Reads** column. Similarly, the physical read accesses can be seen in the **Data Physical Reads** and **Index Physical Reads** columns. Under **Performance · Database** you will find a global overview and under **Performance • Bufferpools**, you find the same information separated according to buffer pool.

Database system	Name of buffer	Key figures and assessment	Parameter
DB2 Universal Database	buffer pool	overall buffer quality = 96%	buffpage, dbheap
	Package cache	Package cache quality = 98%	pckcachesz
	Catalog cache	Catalog cache quality = 95% Catalog cache overflows ~ 0 Catalog cache heap full ~ 0	catalogcache_sz
	Lock list	Lock escalations ~ 0	locklist

Table 2.3 Key figures for evaluating the performance of database buffers (DB2/UDB for UNIX and Windows)

Summary

The key figures to be considered when evaluating database buffers for different database systems in the SAP environment are listed in the appendix. Poor buffering normally has two possible causes:

- *Expensive SQL statements* are the main cause for poor buffering in the buffer pool. They should be identified and dealt with as a high priority. Proceed with the next section in the present chapter and analyze your system to find expensive SQL statements.
- The other main cause is that the *buffer pool is too small*. If your database server still has sufficient main memory reserves, you can increase the respective buffer—for example, by 25%. Check whether the quality of buffering significantly improves as a result. If it does, you can try increasing the size of the buffer yet again. However, if this initial increase to the buffer has no effect, you need to look elsewhere for the cause of the poor buffer quality.

Please note that these buffer quality values are only guideline values. In some cases, a database instance can still run well with an apparently low buffer quality. Before investing time and energy in buffer optimization, perform a workload analysis to check the database response times.

Checkpoints and Savepoints

The buffer pool of a database instance not only reduces the time required by database read accesses, it also speeds up database change operations. When a record is in the buffer, a database change operation initially involves only changes to the respective data block in the buffer pool. These changes are saved to the hard disk asynchronously—that is, at a later point in time. This means that several change operations can be collected on a data block in the buffer before that block is saved to the hard disk. However, the database instance must write *all* the changed data blocks to the hard disks within a certain interval, defined by a *checkpoint* or *savepoint*.

For all database systems, you can strategically define the frequency of checkpoints or savepoints by setting certain parameters. To find out which parameter defines the checkpoint for your specific database system, consult the online help documentation for the Database Performance Monitor. SAP's default parameter settings should be changed only after consulting SAP.

Number of database processors

For some database systems, you can specify the maximum number of processors that can be used by the database instance. For SAP DB, for example, the parameters are MAXCPU, and for INFORMIX, NUMCPUVPS. It is important that these parameters have the correct setting, because if this parameter is set too small, there will not be enough CPU capacity available for the database instance, even if CPU resources are actually still free.

Suppose an SAP installation has a total of five computers. On the database server, there are four available processors. Both the database instance and the central SAP instance with enqueue and dialog work processes are located on the database server. The Database Profile parameter, which limits the number of processors that the database instance can use, is set to 1. Thus, the database instance can use only one processor. Let us assume that the central SAP instance also requires only one processor. The Operating System Monitor (Transaction ST06) shows that there is an average CPU utilization of 50%, so there are no bottlenecks. However, you may see high database times with this configuration because one processor is normally too little to process database queries in a system with five computers.

If the Database Profile parameter that limits the number of processors used by the database instance is set too large, this can also limit performance.

Suppose the Database Profile parameter is set to four, and that the database instance thus has all of the processors to itself. The operating system and the SAP instance with the enqueue work process would then suffer from a CPU bottleneck, causing the enqueue queries of all the SAP instances to be processed very slowly.

On computers with more than two processors, the maximum number of processors that can be used by the database instance is normally smaller than the number of the physically available processors. Chapter 5 provides guidelines on how many processors you should reserve for the database instance in an SAP System.

Identifying Expensive SQL Statements

Expensive SQL statements are long-running statements and are one of the main causes of performance problems. In addition to causing long runtimes in the programs in which they are called, they also indirectly cause performance problems for other transactions.

Expensive SQL statements can have the following effects on the entire system:

- They cause a high CPU utilization percentage and a high I/O load. This can lead to an acute hardware bottleneck on the database server and reduce the performance of other programs.
- They block SAP work processes for a long time. This means that user requests cannot be processed immediately and have to wait for free work processes. This can mean waiting in the SAP dispatcher queue.
- They read many data blocks into the data buffer of the database server, which displaces data required by other SQL statements. This data must then be read from the hard disk. As a result, the execution times of other SQL statements also increase.

It is not uncommon for a few expensive SQL statements to cause more than half of the entire load on the database server. Identifying these statements is therefore an important part of performance analysis.

Analyzing currently running SQL statements

First we will present a strategy to help identify expensive SQL statements that are currently being executed. All database systems have a monitor for analyzing SQL statements currently being processed on the database: the *Database Process Monitor*.

- For a DB2/UDB database select **Applications** on the main screen of the Database Performance Monitor (transaction code ST04). The **Application Snapshot** screen is displayed. This monitor displays the currently active database processes, which may have different names, depending on the database system: agents in DB2, shadow processes in ORACLE or threads in INFORMIX. If you select the **Only active** option, only those database processes currently carrying out a task will be included.
- Double click on a process in the list of database processes to select it. In this screen, the tab page **Application** displays, among other things, the process ID (PID) of the corresponding operating system process, along with the process ID (PID) and application server of the corresponding SAP work process. Select the **Statement** tab page to display the SQL statement that is currently being executed.

Figure 2.6 shows that the SQL statement **SELECT * FROM »DSVASRESULTSATTR« WHERE ...** from the database process number 86 (**Application Handle** field) is currently being executed.

Open a second user session and start the system-wide work process overview parallel to the Database Process Monitor (see the section "Analyzing SAP Work Processes" on page 107 in this chapter). To identify long-running SQL statements, you must continually refresh the monitors in both user sessions. Since both monitors display the application server and the PID of the related SAP work process for the respective database processes, you can see which database process corresponds to which SAP work process. From the two monitors, you can determine:

- Program name and transaction code of the executed program (from the Work Process Overview)
- Table name (from the Work Process Overview and the Database Process Monitor)
- The user who started the program (from the Work Process Overview)
- WHERE conditions of the SQL statement (from the Database Process Monitor)

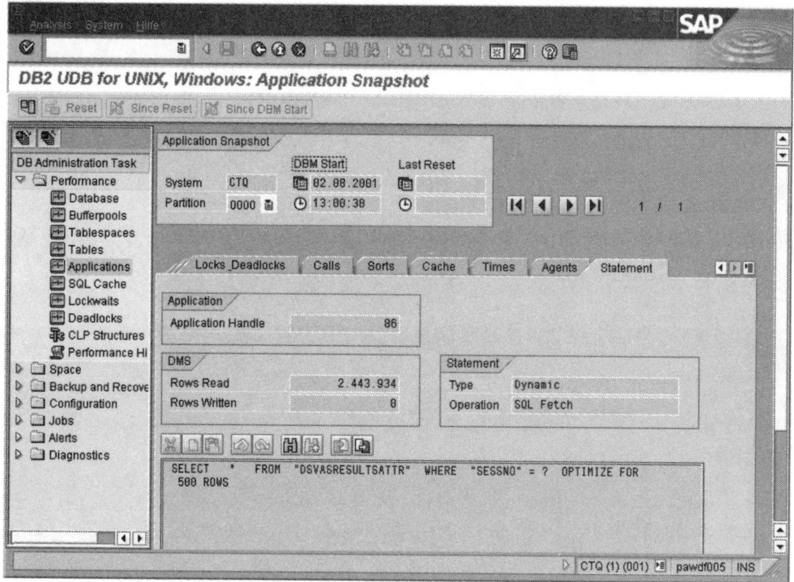

Figure 2.6 Database Process Monitor (DB2 Universal Database)

- From the database performance monitor it is also possible to create an execution plan for the SQL statement, using the **Explain** function. More details can be found in Chapter 11.

This is all of the information that you require to perform a detailed analysis of an SQL statement.

Analyzing previously executed SQL statements (Shared SQL Area)

For almost all database systems, you can display various types of *statistics on previously executed SQL statements*. These statistics cover, for example, the number of times an SQL statement is executed, the number of logical and physical read accesses for each statement and the number of lines read. For some database systems, these statistics are collected from the time the database was started; for other database systems, you must explicitly switch on these statistics. These are the statistics to use when analyzing expensive SQL statements. For Oracle databases, monitoring statistics on previously executed SQL statements is commonly referred to as monitoring the *Shared SQL Area* (also referred to as the *Shared Cursor Cache* or the *Shared SQL Cache*). In this book, Shared SQL Area is also the collective term used for the previously executed SQL statements in database systems other than Oracle.

To monitor the Shared SQL Area (Transaction ST04) from the main Database Performance Monitor screen, choose:

- for Oracle: **Detail analysis menu · SQL request**
- for INFORMIX: **Detail analysis menu · SQL Statement**
- for other database systems: see Appendix B

In the dialog box that appears, change the automatically suggested selection values to zero and choose **OK**.

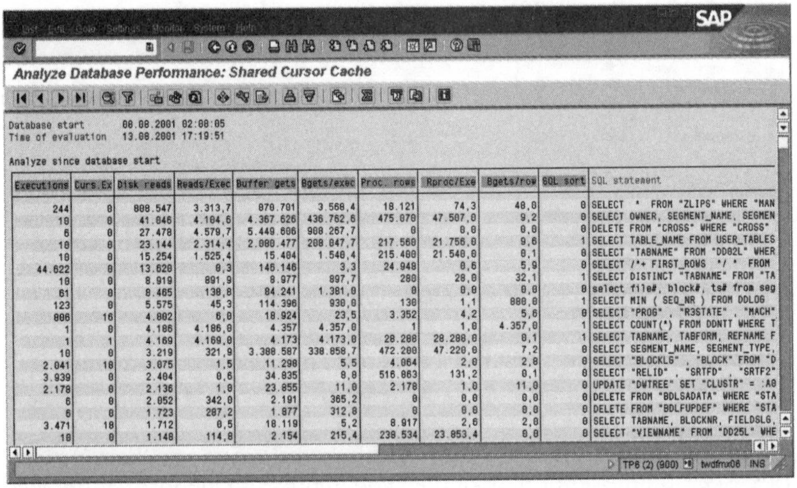

Figure 2.7 Shared SQL Area (Oracle)

A list appears containing all SQL statements for which the database has statistics. Ideally, these are all the statements that have been executed since database startup. The initial part of the SQL statement is located on the right-hand side of the screen. To view the complete SQL statement, double-click the appropriate row. For each SQL statement the list contains the following details, among other things:

Field	Explanation
Total Execution (ORACLE and INFORMIX)	Number of times the statement has been executed since the start of the database
Disk Reads (ORACLE) or Page/Disk Reads (INFORMIX)	Number of physical read accesses required for all the executions of the statement

Table 2.4 Fields in the Shared SQL Area (ORACLE/INFORMIX)

Field	Explanation
Reads/Execution (ORACLE) or Pg Reads/Execution (INFORMIX)	Number of physical read accesses required on average for one execution of the statement
Buffer Gets (ORACLE) or Buffer Reads (INFORMIX)	Number of logical read accesses required for all the executions of the statement
Gets/Execution (ORACLE) or Buf.Read/Execution (INFORMIX)	Number of logical read accesses required on average for one execution of the statement
Records processed (ORACLE)	Number of rows read for all the executions of the statement
Estimated Costs (INFORMIX)	Estimated cost for the execution of the statement
Estimated Rows (INFORMIX)	Estimated number of rows read for execution of the statement

Table 2.4 Fields in the Shared SQL Area (ORACLE/INFORMIX) (contd.)

Expensive SQL statements

Expensive SQL statements are indicated by a high number of logical read accesses and physical read accesses. Logical read accesses place a load on the CPU of the database server; physical read accesses place a load on the I/O system. To get the highest numbers of accesses at the top of the list, sort the list according to the number of "Buffer Gets" (Oracle), "Buffer Reads" (Informix), "Disk Reads" (Oracle), or "Page/Disk Reads" (Informix). This organizes the expensive SQL statements in the order in which they require analysis and possible optimization.

The following information can also be obtained from the Monitor:

- Table name
- WHERE conditions of the SQL statement
- Procedure roadmap of the SQL statement

Shared SQL Area analysis

The *Analyze Shared SQL Area* is a powerful tool for performance analysis. However, considerable experience is required when it comes to deciding which of the expensive SQL statements can be optimized.

To identify the most expensive SQL statements, compare the indicated number of read accesses of a particular SQL statement with the number of read accesses for the entire database. To do so, proceed as follows:

1. Sort the shared SQL area by the "Buffer Gets" column (Oracle database).
2. Open a second user session and start the main screen of the Database Performance Monitor. The "Buffer Gets" in the Shared SQL Area

correspond to the "Reads" in the main screen of the Database Performance Monitor; similarly, the "Disk Reads" in the Shared SQL Area correspond to the "Physical Reads" in the main screen of the Database Performance Monitor.

3. To calculate the percentage of all logical accesses made by an SQL statement, divide the number of "Buffer Gets" in the Shared SQL Area by the "Reads" in the main screen of the Database Performance Monitor. Similarly, to calculate the percentage of all physical accesses made by an SQL statement, divide the "Disk Reads" in the Shared SQL Area by the "Physical Reads" in the main screen of the Database Performance Monitor.
4. If there are SQL statements that are causing more than 5% of the total logical or physical accesses on the entire database, tuning these statements normally improves database performance significantly.

For the detailed analysis and optimization of SQL statements, see Chapter 11. Before entering into a detailed analysis, however, you should look for SAP Notes on the particular expensive SQL statements you have identified. Search for notes using the search term "performance" and the respective table name.

SAP also has monitors for the Shared SQL Area of database systems other than Oracle and Informix. Further information can be found in the appendix.

A further way of identifying expensive SQL statements is the SQL trace, which is discussed in Chapter 4.

Identifying Read/Write (I/O) Problems

To achieve optimal database performance, I/O activity (read accesses and write accesses) should be evenly distributed on the hard disks of the database. For the Oracle and Informix database systems, there are monitors that display the I/O workload distribution at the file system level. You can start this Monitor from the main screen of the Database Performance Monitor (Transaction ST04) as follows:

- for Oracle: **Detail analysis menu · Filesystem request**
- for Informix: **Detail analysis menu · Chunk I/O Activity**

The number of write and read operations is displayed for each file. For Oracle, the write and read times are also listed, provided you have switched on the time statistics in the database. Using this monitor, you can identify frequently used data files and ensure that they are located on different data mediums. This prevents the I/O requests for these objects from directly competing with each other.

For Oracle, to display statistics about wait situations on the file system level, choose **Goto · Statistics · Filesystem waits**.

I/O bottleneck

In the Operating System Monitor of the database server (Transaction ST06), under **Detail analysis menu · Disk**, you will find information about the load on the hard disks as well as wait times and response times for I/O operations on these disks. There is a risk of an I/O bottleneck if individual disks show a very high level of utilization (**Util.** > 50%), if frequently accessed data files reside on these disks or if wait situations occur when you access these files.

You can resolve an I/O bottleneck by improving the table distribution on the file system (see previous section). In particular, ensure that the disks with a high load contain no additional frequently accessed files that could be relocated. The components listed in the table below are some of the most frequently accessed database objects. As a general rule, these objects should not reside on the same hard disk as the data files of the database, nor should they reside on a hard-disk array such as a RAID-5 system.

Database System	File or Database Object
Independent	Operating system swap space (high priority)
SAP DB	Log Area, System Devspace
DB2 Universal Database	Online log directory (high priority) Offline log directory (medium priority)
Informix	Dbspaces ROOTDBS, PHSYDBS and LOGDBS
Oracle	Redo log files (high priority) Tablespace PSAPROLL (medium priority) Directory for the offline redo log files (SAPARCH) (medium priority)
SQL Server	Transaction log (high priority) Tempdb (medium priority)

Table 2.5 Examples of files and database objects with large amounts of read/write-activity

However, only limited information about I/O problems can be gained from the SAP system. For a more detailed analysis the hardware manufacturer's tools are necessary.

Other Checks on the Database

Exclusive Lockwaits

An exclusive database lock occurs when a user locks a row in a table, for example, with the SQL statement **update** or **select for update**. If another user also tries to lock this row, that user has to wait until the first user releases the row. This wait situation is called an *exclusive lockwait*.

All database systems have a Monitor for displaying exclusive lockwaits. These Monitors can be called as follows:

> **Tools · Administration · Monitor · Performance · Database · Activity · Detail analysis menu · Exclusive lockwaits**
>
> or
>
> **Tools · Administration · Monitor · Performance · Database · Exclusive lockwaits**
>
> or enter the transaction code DB01.

The following information is displayed for both the process holding the lock and the process waiting for the lock:

- ID of the database process
- Client host and client PID: Name of the application server and the process ID of the related SAP work process. This helps you find the related SAP work process in the SAP Work Process Overview and thus identify the program and the user holding the lock.
- Database-specific information, such as the time from which a lock is held and information about the locked row, etc.

Exclusive database locks

Refresh this monitor several times to observe the progress of wait situations brought about by database locks. With the help of the fields **Client host** and **Client PID** in the Work Process Overview you can determine which programs and users hold locks.

The following is a checklist for the elimination of exclusive database locks:

- If the Work Process Overview shows that the lock is being held by a database process that is not related to an SAP work process, you can use operating system tools to terminate the database process. This applies if, for example, an external program that is not related to the SAP system is holding a lock, or if an error caused an SAP work process to terminate and the related database process is not properly closed.

- If a program holds a lock for several minutes, you can contact the user who started the program. Together with the user, check whether the program is still working properly. If not, end the program after consulting the user.
- Determine whether the lockwait is due to users using programs in parallel, in a way that ultimately causes the programs to lock the resources from each other. In this case, the user should study the documentation of the affected program and modify the way they are using the program, so they can avoid causing lockwaits in future.
- If none of the previous points apply, check whether there are other database performance problems that prevent SQL statements from being processed quickly and cause relatively long holds on database locks. After resolving the other database performance problem, check whether the database locks are released more quickly.

Database locks are absolutely necessary to safeguard data consistency on the database. For this reason, short wait situations due to database locks should not be regarded as a performance problem. The situation becomes critical if locks are held for a long time and the wait situation cannot be resolved. This leads to a chain reaction where more and more users have to wait because of locks. More detailed information on database locks can be found in Chapter 10.

Database error log file

Database error or message files contain important information on errors and the general condition of the database. The log should be checked regularly. It can be viewed as follows:

Tools · Administration · Monitor · Performance · Database · Activity · Detail analysis menu · Database message log
or **Database alert log**

For more detailed information about the error messages, refer to the manuals for your specific database.

Parameter changes

The SAP system logs all changes made to database parameters. The change log can be viewed as follows:

Tools · Administration · Monitor · Performance · Database · Activity · Detail analysis menu · Parameter changes

Select the **History of file** button. From the dates of parameter changes indicated, you may be able to detect correlations between parameter changes and subsequent performance problems.

Update statistics for the database optimizer

All database systems that can be used in conjunction with the SAP system use a *cost-based optimizer*. The only exception is the Oracle database system, for which the rule-based optimizer is normally active up to SAP R/3 3.1. To change the default setting, use the Oracle profile parameter OPTIMIZER_MODE to decide which optimizer is to be used (see also **Detail analysis menu · Parameter changes** in the Data Base Performance Monitor). If the entry "OPTIMIZER_MODE = CHOOSE" is displayed, the cost-based optimizer is activated; if the parameter is set to "RULE", the database uses the rule-based optimizer. For R/3 Releases prior to 4.0, this Oracle parameter must be set to "RULE". As of R/3 Release 4.0, it must be set to "CHOOSE". You should not use other settings unless expressly advised to do so by SAP.

If your database uses a cost-based optimizer, up-to-date statistics on the size of tables and indexes must be generated regularly. The optimizer needs these statistics to create the correct access plans for SQL statements. The administrator should regularly schedule the relevant update-statistics program. If these statistics are missing or obsolete, the optimizer creates ineffective access paths, which can lead to serious performance problems. Update statistics do not need to be generated for a rule-based optimizer.

To check whether the relevant update-statistics program has been scheduled, open the DBA Planning Calendar by selecting:

Tools · CCMS · DB administration · DB scheduling

If the update-statistics program is scheduled, you will regularly see the entry "AnalyzeTab" (for Oracle), "Update sta0" (for Informix), or "Update Statistics" (for SQL Server). View the logs regularly to check that the runs of the update-statistics program were successful.

To generate update statistics it is essential that you use the SAP tools from CCMS or the program **SAPDBA**. The statistics generated through these tools are specifically adapted to the SQL statements that are used by the SAP system.

For more information about the different optimizers and update statistics see Chapter 11, "Optimizing SQL Statements", and the notes listed in the appendix.

Missing database indices

Missing database indices can lead to a significant reduction in system performance. To check the consistency of the indices between the ABAP Dictionary and the database, from the initial screen of the Database Performance Monitor, choose:

> **Tools · Administration · Monitor · Performance · Database · State on disk**

or enter the transaction code DB02. Then choose **Missing indices**. A screen appears that displays indices that are defined in the ABAP Dictionary but are missing from the database.

The display of the missing indices is divided into primary and secondary indices. If a primary index is missing, the consistency of the data is no longer ensured. There is a danger that duplicate keys can be written. Furthermore, a missing primary index causes ineffective database accesses; in cases of large tables, this can then lead to massive performance problems. This status is critical for the system and requires immediate intervention by the database administrator. For instructions on creating indices, see the section "Administration for Indexes and Table Access Statistics" on page 349 in Chapter 11.

Database not responding

If the database instance no longer responds, before long this will cause the SAP system to stop responding. The database instance stops responding particularly when critical memory areas of the database are full, such as the file system, or *log areas* such as the redo log files (for Oracle) or the transaction log (for SQL Server). Database errors that can cause the database to stop responding are especially likely to occur when a large volume of data is updated on the database—for example, when data transfers or client copies are performed. Consider the following examples of how an error situation on the database can cause the SAP system to stop responding.

Example 1: Database and SAP system not responding because of fully used-up log areas:

1. Because of an administration error or incorrect capacity planning, the log areas of the database are full (for example, the redo log files for Oracle). As of this moment, no further database operations are possible. In the Oracle environment, this situation is called *Archiver Stuck*. The database instance writes an error message in the database error log file, such as "All online log files need archiving" (Oracle).
2. Every SAP work process that tries to execute a database change operation will be unable to complete it. You can view this process in the Work Process Overview.
3. Soon, there are no more SAP work processes available. The SAP system stops responding. All users who send a request to the SAP system must wait.
4. Normally, the error situation can be resolved without having to stop the SAP system or the database. The data in the log area must be archived.
5. After archiving, the database instance can resume work and process the accumulated requests.

Example 2: Database file overflow:

1. While attempting to write data into a database table through an **INSERT** operation, an error occurs in the database because a database file is full or the hard disk is full. The database instance then returns an error message to the SAP work process that called it, and the error message is normally written to the database error log file.
2. If the error occurs during an SAP update, the work process deactivates the entire SAP update service. As of this moment, SAP update requests receive no response. To determine whether the update service has been deactivated, display update records. To do this, use the following menu path:

   Tools · Administration · Monitor · Update

   or use the transaction code SM13. Determine whether the field **Status** displays the message "Updating by system deactivated". If so, to find the associated error message and user, check the SAP system log (Transaction SM21).
3. Once updates are no longer being completed, dialog work processes, which are waiting for the updates to finish, will gradually stop responding. You can view this process in the Work Process Overview.

4. Normally, the error situation can be resolved without having to stop the SAP system or the database. First resolve the database error—for example, by expanding the file system. Then, activate the SAP update service manually. To do this, choose:

   Tools · Administration · Monitor · Update · Update records · Update · Activate

5. Now the SAP update service can resume work and process the accumulated requests.

The update service was stopped to enable the database administrator to correct a database error without terminating the updates. If the update service were not stopped, other update work processes would also be affected by the same database error. If the database error is not found quickly enough, many hundreds of terminated updates may result, all of which must then be individually updated by the users.

Ensuring that the database remains operational is a database administration task rather than a matter for performance optimization, and is therefore not explicitly covered in this book. Refer to the literature on database administration and set up a contingency plan tailored to your company that, for example, provides procedures to:

- Ensure that a potential overflow of the log area or file system is detected well in advance.
- Determine which database error has occurred if the SAP system is not responding. Explain how to locate the database error log file and which error messages are critical.
- Determine what must be done if an error occurs and whether the R/3 System or the database must be restarted. Simulate error situations and response procedures in a test system.

Summary

Performance problems in the database instance affect the performance of the entire SAP system. Performance monitoring for this instance therefore has a high priority and consists of the following tasks (listed in order of priority):

- *"Keep your database engine running!"*—The database is the heart or engine of your SAP system. If the database instance does not respond, this soon causes the SAP system to stop responding. Regularly monitor the fill level of the file system or the *database log area* (e.g. the redo log files for Oracle or the transaction log for SQL-Server).

- Ensure that the database server has sufficient CPU and storage capacity. More than 20% CPU should be idle and the paging rate should be low.
- If your database system has a profile parameter that limits the maximum number of physical processors that the database instance can occupy, check that the setting of this parameter is neither too small nor too large.
- Ensure that individual hard disks are not showing more than 50% utilization.
- Check whether the configuration and performance of the database buffers is adequate, as outlined above.
- Identify any SQL statements that are putting a heavy load on the database server. An "extremely expensive" SQL statement is one that takes up more than 5% of the entire database load in the shared SQL area (measured in "reads" or "gets").
- Remove the causes of frequent exclusive lockwaits.
- Ensure that update statistics for the cost-based optimizer are updated frequently, and regularly check the consistency of the database and look for missing indices.

Analyzing SAP Memory Management

To start the SAP Memory Configuration Monitor for the SAP instance you are currently logged on to, use Transaction ST02, or, from the initial screen, choose:

> **Tools · Administration · Monitor · Performance · Setup/Buffers · Buffers**

The main **Tune Summary** screen appears, as shown in Figure 2.8.

The main screen of SAP Memory Configuration Monitor displays information on the configuration and utilization of the SAP buffer, the SAP extended memory and the SAP heap memory. All data shown correspond to the period since the last startup of the SAP instance in question.

Analyzing SAP Buffers

Details of the various SAP buffers can be found in the **Buffer** section of the SAP Memory Configuration Monitor. Table 2.6 explains the columns corresponding to these buffers.

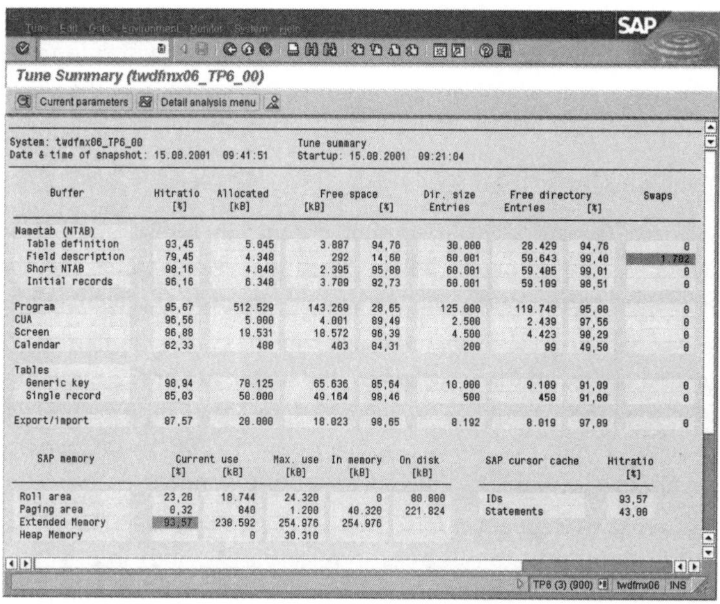

Figure 2.8 Main screen of the Memory Configuration Monitor (Tune Summary)

Field	Explanation
Hitratio	The definition of the SAP buffer hit ratio is identical to that given for database buffers.
Allocated	Memory space allocated to the respective buffer. Every SAP buffer is normally characterized by two parameters: the size of the buffer and the maximum number of buffered entries.
Free space	Currently unoccupied memory space in the respective buffer
Dir. Entries	Maximum number of entries that can be stored in the buffer
Free directory entries	Difference between the current number of objects stored in the buffer and the maximum possible number of objects
Swaps	Number of buffer objects displaced from the buffer
Database accesses	Number of database accesses (which is also the number of data transfers from the database into the buffer)

Table 2.6 Fields in the SAP Memory Configuration Monitor

As with the database buffer, the SAP buffer also has to achieve a minimum buffer quality to ensure smooth operation of the SAP system. If the buffers are too small, data is displaced, and the database has to be unnecessarily accessed to reload the data. When an object is loaded into the buffer and the free space in the buffer is too small to completely store the object, other objects have to be displaced from the buffer to make space available. For example, the number of swaps for the Field description buffer can be seen in Figure 2.7 in the **Swaps** column.

When monitoring the SAP buffers, consider the following guidelines:

- The hit ratio for the SAP buffers should generally be 98% or better. (Exception: for the program buffer, the single record buffer and the export/import buffer, lower hit ratios can be regarded as acceptable.)
- There should be no swaps (displacements) in the buffers of a production system. If there are swaps, the buffer size or the maximum number of entries should be increased. Here again, the exception is the program buffer, for which approximately 10,000 swaps per day represents an acceptable number of buffer displacements.
- To help avoid subsequent displacements, ensure that each buffer has sufficient memory (indicated as "Free space") and free entries (indicated as "Free directory entries")

Buffer settings

If, in the Memory Configuration Monitor, you see that there have been displacements in an SAP buffer, proceed as follows:

1. First of all check whether the buffer is too small (**Free space** field) or whether the maximum number of possible buffer entries is too small (**Free directory entries** field).
2. Depending on the results of these checks, either increase the buffer size or the maximum number of allowed entries by 10 to 50%. To find out the relevant SAP profile parameters, choose **Current parameters** from the main screen of the Memory Configuration Monitor as described below. Before increasing the buffer size, ensure that the computer still has sufficient main memory reserves; otherwise, you run the risk of a memory bottleneck.

Displacements and invalidations

Do not confuse *displacements* (Swaps) with *invalidations*, which are not indicated in the **Swaps** column. Invalidation is when a buffered object such as a program or table is declared invalid because it has been changed. The effect of invalidations is to lower the hit ratio and cause objects to be reloaded from the database, but they cannot be identified with this Monitor. Invalidations can occur when programs or customizing settings have been transported into a production system or have been changed in production operation. Therefore, it is recommended that transports be scheduled one or two times per week when the system load is low. Tables that are too large for buffering can also lead to problems with table buffers. This subject is dealt with in Chapter 9, "SAP Table Buffering".

All SAP buffers and the related SAP profile parameters are listed in the appendix. The current settings can be viewed in the SAP Memory Configuration Monitor by selecting the **Current parameters** button.

Parameters for buffer settings

Analyzing SAP Extended Memory, SAP Heap Memory and SAP Roll Memory

The **SAP Memory** section of the SAP Memory Configuration Monitor (Figure 2.8) lists data on the SAP memory areas **Roll area**, **Paging area**, **Extended Memory** and **Heap Memory**. An explanation of these fields is given in Table 2.7.

Field	Explanation
Current use	Amount of memory currently in use in the respective memory area, given in KB and %
Max. use	Maximum amount of this memory area that has been used since the SAP instance was started (also known as the High Water Mark)
In memory	The amount of main memory allocated to this area at system startup. For the "Roll area" and the "Paging area" this space corresponds to the SAP roll buffer and SAP paging buffer.
On disk	For the "Roll area" and the "Paging area" SAP roll files and SAP paging files are located on the hard disk of the application server. The size of these files is indicated here.

Table 2.7 Fields in the SAP Memory Configuration Monitor

When monitoring the SAP memory areas, consider the following guidelines:

- For **Roll area** the **Max. use** value should not exceed the corresponding amount in the **In memory** column. In other words, the role file should not be used.
- For **Extended Memory** the **Max. use** value should be at least 20% smaller than the corresponding value in the **In memory** column. This ensures that there will continue to be sufficient free extended memory.

In Figure 2.8 you will see that almost 100% of the SAP extended memory is in use. In addition, more roll memory is being used than is available in the roll buffer; **Max. use** in the **Roll Memory** column is greater than the corresponding amount in **In memory**.

Should you detect the problem that the roll memory or the SAP extended memory requires all of the memory allocated to these areas at SAP instance startup, you can increase the values in the SAP profile parameters *rdisp/ROLL_SHM* or *em/initial_size_MB* (provided there is sufficient physical memory on the computer). Check whether this solves, or at least eases, the problem. If the problem persists see Chapter 8 for further information on SAP memory management.

Experience shows that performance is dramatically reduced when SAP extended memory is full, making it impossible to work productively in the SAP instances. *Therefore, high priority should be given to monitoring the SAP extended memory.* You can generally afford to allocate extended memory generously. Unused extended memory is swapped out by the operating system. As a rule of thumb, (a) around 6–10 MB of extended memory is allocated for each user and (b) approximately 70–120% of the physical main memory can be allocated as extended memory. These guidelines do, of course, depend on the release and the application module. Ensure that the swap space on the operating-system level is large enough. Ensure also that the operating system can administer the desired memory size. More details can be found in Chapter 8.

Parameters for memory area configuration

To display the current system settings, choose **Current Parameters** in the **Roll, extended and heap memory** section. The appendix lists all the relevant SAP profile parameters for memory area configuration.

Zero administration memory management

With R/3 Release 4.0, SAP introduced *Zero Administration Memory Management* which made manual settings unnecessary. Zero Administration dynamically allocates memory based on the hardware available to the SAP instance, and adapts memory management settings automatically.

For R/3 Release 4.0, Zero Administration Memory Management is available for Windows NT (see SAP Note 88416) on the Online Service System (OSS). Other operating systems will follow. Zero Administration Memory Management requires only one SAP profile parameter: **PHYS_MEMSIZE**. This parameter defines how much of the computer's main memory should be used for the SAP instance. If no value is entered in the instance profile for **PHYS_MEMSIZE**, the full amount of physical main memory is automatically set for this parameter. All other SAP memory management settings are automatically calculated on the basis of **PHYS_MEMSIZE**.

After an upgrade to R/3 Release 4.0 or higher, all the SAP profile parameters for memory management should be deleted from the instance profiles. For instances on the same computer as the database, set the parameter **PHYS_MEMSIZE** to limit the memory use of the SAP instance appropriately. In R/3 Release 4.0, Zero Administration Memory Management only covers SAP extended memory, SAP heap memory, SAP roll memory, and SAP paging memory. The SAP buffers still have to be set manually.

Displaying the Allocated Memory

In order to analyze performance, it is important to have an overview of current memory allocation. To do so, choose:

> **Tools · Administration · Monitor · Performance · Setup/Buffers · Buffers · Detail analysis menu · Storage**

The **Storage Usage and Requirements** screen appears. Figure 2.9 shows an example of this screen and Table 2.8 explains the meanings of key figures in this screen.

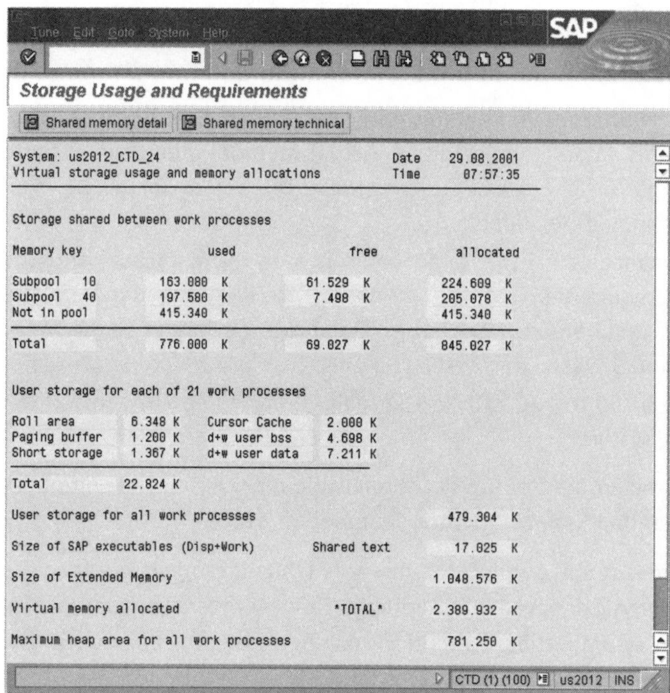

Figure 2.9 SAP memory configuration monitor (detail view)

Field	Explanation
Storage shared between work processes	The value for "allocated" column in the "total" row shows the total memory allocated to the SAP buffers. (For UNIX operating systems, this section also displays the values for the allocated, used, and free memory space for each Shared Memory Pool.)
User storage for all work processes	This value is the size of the memory allocated for the SAP work processes.
Size of Extended Memory	This value is the size of the memory allocated to the SAP extended memory.
Virtual memory allocated	This value is the size of the total memory allocated at instance startup to the SAP buffer, SAP work processes, and extended memory. This is the critical value for assessing whether main memory bottlenecks are likely to occur.
Maximum heap area for all work processes	This value is the size of the SAP heap memory that can be allocated as local memory by the SAP work processes, if required. This value corresponds to the parameter **abap/heap_area_total**.

Table 2.8 Fields for determining allocated memory

Allocated and physical memory

To ensure that the total memory allocated by SAP is not significantly disproportionate to the physically available main memory, compare allocated and physical memory. Begin by calculating the allocated memory as follows:

- Obtain the amount of memory allocated by an SAP instance since startup. This value is indicated as **Virtual memory allocated**. If there are multiple instances on the computer, the values for all the SAP instances should be added.
- If the instance is on the same computer as the database, add the memory requirement of the database. To find out the database memory requirement, see the Database Performance Monitor (Transaction ST04).
- Add around 50 to 100 MB for the main memory requirements of the operating system.

To find out the amount of physically available memory on the computer, see the Operating System Monitor (Transaction ST06).

Normally, the amount of allocated memory is significantly larger than the amount of physically available memory. However, as a general rule of thumb, we assume that no critical paging should occur when the allocated memory is more than 50% larger than the physically available memory. If this limit is exceeded, use the Operating System Monitor to check the paging rates and the Workload Monitor to analyze the response times to determine whether there is a memory bottleneck.

You can also use the Memory Configuration Monitor to determine whether there is sufficient swap space at the operating-system level. First, calculate the maximum memory that can be allocated by the SAP system—add the values of **Virtual memory allocated** and **Maximum heap area ....** When added to the memory requirements of any other systems on the same computer (such as a database, the operating system, and possibly other systems), the maximum allocatable memory area should be smaller than the sum of the physically available main memory and the swap space. Otherwise system failure may occur.

Other monitors in the Memory Configuration Monitor

SAP parameter changes

The SAP system logs all changes to SAP parameters. The change log can be viewed as follows:

> **Tools · Administration · Monitor · Performance · Setup/Buffers · Buffers · Detail analysis menu · Parameters**

Mark an application server and choose **History of file**. Note that very recent changes may not yet appear in the log. This monitor enables you to check for parameter changes that are linked to performance problems.

Other monitors

In the **Detail analysis menu** of the SAP Memory Configuration Monitor you can call other monitors on the allocation of the SAP buffers using the buttons **Call statistic** and **Buffer synchron**. These Monitors are discussed in greater detail in Chapter 9.

Summary

When you set the profile parameters for SAP memory management, you define how much virtual memory can be allocated by an SAP instance. You can allocate more virtual memory than is physically available.

The SAP Memory Configuration Monitor enables you to monitor the size and usage of the SAP memory areas. Displacements should not occur in the SAP buffers (with the exception of the program buffer, which may have up to 10,000 displacements each day). Ensure that neither the extended memory nor the roll buffer become full.

Make it a top priority to monitor the extended memory. If this memory is fully used up, production work ceases, and immediate action is required to solve the problem. One solution is to increase the size of the extended memory. You should also check whether there are programs with excessive memory consumption that can be terminated or improved (see Chapter 8).

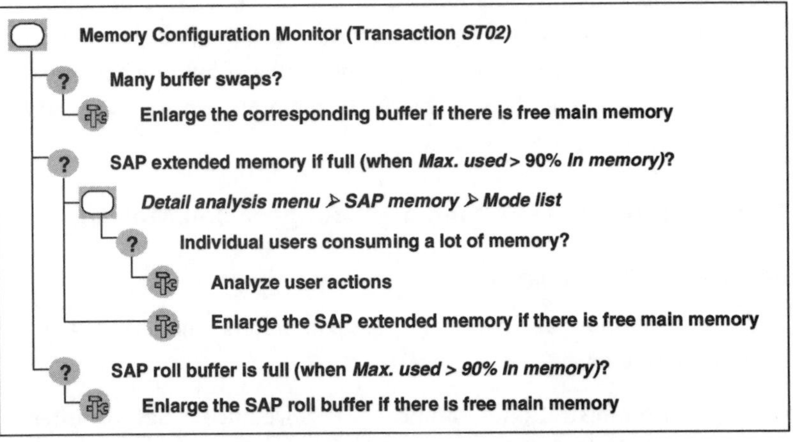

Figure 2.10 Procedure roadmap for analyzing SAP Memory Configuration

If you detect displacements in the following buffers, adapt the corresponding parameters with medium priority (that is, within a few days):

- TTAB, FTAB, SNTAB and IRDB buffers
- Roll buffers, program buffers and table buffers

The settings of the following buffers have a somewhat lower priority:

- CUA buffer and screen buffer
- SAP paging buffer

Note that the size of allocatable memory is affected by operating system-specific limitations such as the maximum size of allocatable shared memory and the maximum address space. If you change the memory configuration, check whether the new parameters allow the SAP instance to start without error (see Figure 2.10).

Analyzing SAP Work Processes

To display data on the SAP work processes active on a particular application server, log on to that server and call the SAP monitor known as the Local Work Process Overview. From the SAP initial screen, choose:

> **Tools · Administration · Monitor · System monitoring · Process overview**

or enter the transaction code SM50. The **Process Overview** screen is displayed.

To display the work processes of any application server, call the server overview as follows:

> **Tools · Administration · Monitor · System Monitoring · Server** (Transaction SM51)

Place the cursor on the desired application server and choose **Processes**.

To see a systemwide overview of all the work processes in the SAP System, start the Systemwide Work Process Overview with

> **Tools · Administration · Monitor · Performance · Exceptions/Users · Active users · All processes**

Alternatively, you can enter the transaction code SM66. The **Systemwide Work Process Overview** screen is displayed.

If a given performance problem has escalated to such an extent that the Work Process Overview can no longer be called from the SAP system, you can start the auxiliary program **dpmon** on the operating-system level instead. The work process overview can also be found under menu option **l**.

Fields in the Work Process Overview

Table 2.9 describes the various columns that appear in the Local Work Process Overview.

Field	Explanation
No.	Work process number (unique for each SAP instance). This number and the SAP instance name (or the computer name and the process ID) uniquely identify an SAP work process in an SAP system.
Type	DIA: Dialog, BTC: Background, UPD: update, ENQ: enqueue, SPO: spool
PID	Process ID for the operating system (unique for each computer). Using this number, the process can be dealt with using operating system commands (e.g. terminated).
Status	This field displays the status of a work process. Status "waiting" shows that the process is available for a user request. Normally there should always be sufficient work processes displaying this status; otherwise, users will experience poor response times. Status "running" means that the work process is processing a user request. To determine which action the work process is currently executing, look in the column "Action/Reason for waiting". Status "ended" means that the process was terminated because of an error in the SAP kernel. Status "stopped" means that the process is waiting for a message.
Reason	For work processes with the status "stopped", this column explains the reason for the wait time. An overview of the most important reasons for waiting and their causes can be seen in the appendix.
Start	This column tells you whether, for a given work process, the dispatcher is set to restart the work process if the work process terminates.
Err	Number of times the work process has been terminated
Sem	Number of the semaphore: A number with a green background shows that this work process is holding a semaphore. A number with a red background shows that the work process is waiting for the semaphore.
CPU	The CPU time used by the work process so far in *minutes : seconds*
Time	The elapsed processing time for the current request (in seconds).
Clie	Client
User	Name of the user whose request is currently being executed.
Report	Name of the report currently being executed.
Action / reason for waiting	For work processes with the status "running", this field displays the current action.
Table	The database table that was last accessed by the work process

Table 2.9 Fields in the Work Process Overview

The combination of computer and *process ID* enables you to clearly identify an SAP work process in an SAP system. The process ID is also used in the following monitors:

Process ID

- Process Overview in the Operating System Monitor (Transaction ST06):

  Detail analysis menu · Top CPU processes

  This monitor enables you to determine how much CPU load a specific work process is currently generating.

- Database Process Monitor (Transaction ST04):

  Detail Analysis Menu · DB/2 Applications (for DB2/Universal Database)

  This monitor enables you to determine which SQL statement is currently being processed by a work process.

- Database Lock Monitor (Transaction ST04):

  Detail Analysis Menu · Exclusive lockwaits

  This monitor enables you to determine whether a work process is currently holding a database lock or waiting for a lock to be released.

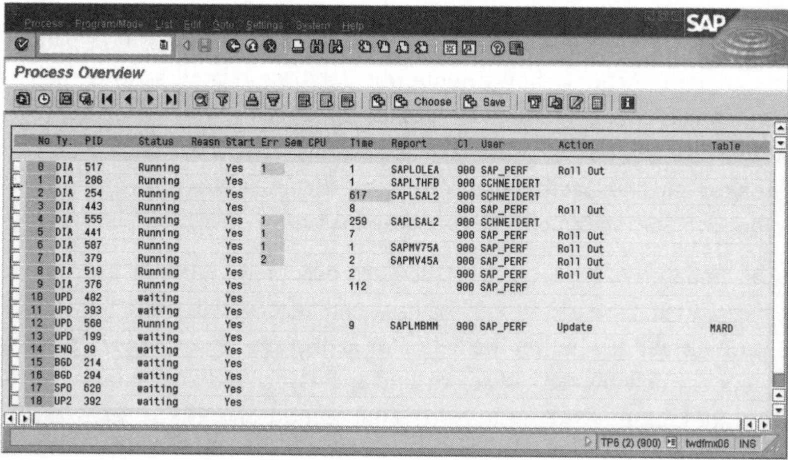

No	Ty.	PID	Status	Reasn	Start	Err	Sem	CPU	Time	Report	Cl.	User	Action	Table
0	DIA	517	Running		Yes	1			1	SAPLOLEA	900	SAP_PERF	Roll Out	
1	DIA	286	Running		Yes				1	SAPLTHFB	900	SCHNEIDERT		
2	DIA	254	Running		Yes				617	SAPLSAL2	900	SCHNEIDERT		
3	DIA	443	Running		Yes				8		900	SAP_PERF	Roll Out	
4	DIA	555	Running		Yes	1			259	SAPLSAL2	900	SCHNEIDERT		
5	DIA	441	Running		Yes	1			7		900	SAP_PERF	Roll Out	
6	DIA	587	Running		Yes	1			1	SAPMV75A	900	SAP_PERF	Roll Out	
7	DIA	379	Running		Yes	2			2	SAPMV45A	900	SAP_PERF	Roll Out	
8	DIA	519	Running		Yes				2		900	SAP_PERF	Roll Out	
9	DIA	376	Running		Yes				112		900	SAP_PERF		
10	UPD	482	waiting		Yes									
11	UPD	393	waiting		Yes									
12	UPD	560	Running		Yes				9	SAPLMBMM	900	SAP_PERF	Update	MARD
13	UPD	199	waiting		Yes									
14	ENQ	99	waiting		Yes									
15	BGD	214	waiting		Yes									
16	BGD	294	waiting		Yes									
17	SPO	620	waiting		Yes									
18	UP2	392	waiting		Yes									

Figure 2.11 Work process overview. All work processes are occupied and almost all are on "roll out".

A combination of the information contained in these four monitors—the Work Process Overview, the Process Overview in the Operating System Monitor, the Database Process Monitor, and the Database Lock Monitor—provide you with an extensive overview of the current situation with regard to work processes in your SAP system.

Semaphores

Every application server has resources that can be used by only one work process at a time. If a work process wants to use these resources, it sets a *semaphore*. If other processes also require this resource, they have to wait until the process that is holding the semaphore has completed its action. If, for example, an entry in an SAP buffer needs to be changed, a semaphore is set because only one process can perform changes in the buffer. If several processes are waiting for a semaphore, this is called serialization. Another operation for which a semaphore must be set is "roll in" or "roll out". This means that only one process at a time can perform a roll in or roll out. A complete list of SAP semaphores can be obtained using **F1** help on the **Sem** field.

Analyzing Work Processes

If you watch the Work Process Overview for several minutes and repeatedly choose the **Refresh** button to update the display, you can usually determine whether there is a current performance problem related to work processes in the SAP instance, and if so, you can roughly estimate its cause. The main indication of a performance problem for work processes is that all the work processes of a particular type (such as dialog or update) are occupied.

Problem: long database response times

There is a problem in the database area if the Work Process Overview in the column "Action" shows numerous database-related actions such as Sequential Read, Direct Read, Update, Commit, or Waiting for DB Lock. In this case, start two additional user sessions. Start the Database Process Monitor and the Database Lock Monitor (*Exclusive Lockwaits*) to look for expensive SQL statements or database locks.

Problem: deactivated update service

If all update work processes (UPD) are occupied you have a problem. Check to see if the update service has been deactivated, using Transaction SM13. Establish whether the field **Status** displays the message "Updating by system deactivated". If so, to find the associated error message and user, look at the SAP system log (Transaction SM21). As soon as the underlying problem is resolved—for example, a database error—you can reactivate the update work process in Transaction SM13.

Problems with SAP memory management

Problems with SAP memory management are often indicated in the Work Process Overview as follows:

- The **Action/Reason for waiting** field frequently displays "Roll In" or "Roll Out" (accompanied by a semaphore of type 6).

- Many work processes are in PRIV mode (**Status** field displays "stopped", **Reason** field displays "PRIV").

Figure 2.8 and Figure 2.11 are screenshots that were taken at the same time, and indicate how a performance problem can become evident. The problem is more evident in the Local Work Process Overview (Figure 2.11). We can see that almost all the work processes are in the "roll-out" phase. Furthermore, the Memory Configuration Monitor (Figure 2.8) shows that the cause for the wait situation is that both the SAP extended memory and the roll buffer are completely full. Increasing the size of the extended memory (parameter **em/initial_size_MB**) is likely to solve the problem in this case.

Stopped work processes

If a work process listed in the Local Work Process Overview has the status "stopped", the cause is indicated in the column **Reason**. To obtain a list of the possible reasons, call up the Help for this column.

Normally, it is not a problem if some work processes have the status "stopped" for short periods of time. However, if the number of work processes that are stopped for the same reason exceeds 20%, or if these work processes continue to have the status "stopped" for a long time, you should analyze the situation in detail. A single ineffective or defective work process often starts a chain reaction that stops other work processes. You can often assume that the work process with the longest runtime (indicated in the column **Time**) caused the problem. If the problem is acute, consider manually terminating the defective work process.

Completed processes

In the Local Work Process Overview, if you detect numerous terminated work processes (indicated as "complete" in the column **Status**), and find that you cannot restart them, it is likely that there is a problem with the SAP kernel or with logging on to the database. Examine the relevant trace file by marking the appropriate work process and choosing **Process · Trace · Display file**. As the trace file will be overwritten when the work process is restarted, save the trace file to a local file to enable subsequent troubleshooting. Look for SAP Notes referring to the problem in the Online Service System (OSS), or consult SAP.

Problem: nonoptimal workload distribution

In a distributed system with several computers, you may find that all work processes on one or more computers are busy and are keeping users waiting, while other computers have idle work processes. Check how many users are logged on to each SAP instance. On the workload monitor you can also check how many dialog steps have been executed on each individual server. If you discover a very unevenly distributed load, your logon distribution should be optimized. Use the Transaction Maintain Logon Group (Transaction SMLG) to check whether all the servers are available for logon distribution, or whether there are any relevant error messages. Proceed to reorganize the logon distribution.

For an overview of current user distribution, see the logon group distribution:

> **Tools · Administration · Configuration · Logon groups**
> (Transaction SMLG)
>
> **Goto · Load distribution**

Problem: too few work processes

As you can see from the variety of work-process problems described above, there are many reasons why all work processes of a given type may be occupied. If you have ruled out all the problems discussed so far, yet still have a work-processes bottleneck, it may be that you have not configured enough work processes. In this case, you should increase the number of work processes. However, before doing so, you should check whether the computer has sufficient CPU and main memory resources. If the CPU is already being 80% utilized, an increase in the number of work processes will probably not increase, but more likely decrease, performance still further.

Further information

Table 2.10 summarizes the parts of this book that explain how to deal with the problems that can be identified through the Local Work Process Overview.

Problem	Chapter	Section Title
Long database response times	2, 11	Identifying expensive SQL statements
	2, 3, 4, 10	Exclusive lockwaits
	11	Optimizing SQL statements
SAP memory configuration	2	Analyzing SAP memory configuration
	8	Memory area configuration
Nonoptimal load distribution, too few work processes	5	Workload distribution

Table 2.10 References to problems that can be detected using the Work Process Overview

Systemwide Work Process Overview

To monitor a system with multiple SAP instances, use the Systemwide Work Process Overview (Transaction SM66). Navigating with the → button, the following fields are also shown in the systemwide work process overview:

For a dialog work process:

- Tcod: Code for the transaction that is currently running
- CUA Rep.: Name of the program from which the currently running transaction was started by the user (also known as the main program)
- Scre: Name of the screen last processed
- Fcod: Code for the last function called in the current program

For a background work process:

- Job: Name of the executed background job

For both cases:

- Ext. Mem: Current extended memory utilization
- Priv. Mem: Current heap memory utilization

In the Systemwide Work Process Overview the following options can be changed.

Using the **Settings** button:

- **Display connections and status in the status line**
  Selecting this option displays the current server connection or other status issues in the status line at the bottom of the screen. This is helpful if, for example, the connection is problematic or takes a long time. By default, this option is not selected.
- **Display only abbreviated information, avoid RFC**
  Selecting this option means that the Systemwide Work Process Overview gets its information from the message server rather than from each application server (through RFC). Given that the application servers report the status of their work processes to the message server only after a delay, the message server is not always up to date. By deselecting this option, an RFC connection is established to each application server to check on the current status of the work processes. The information is thus up to date; however, this takes more time. By default, this option is selected, i.e. only abbreviated information is

displayed. If you require a complete overview of work processes for a performance analysis, deselect this option and refresh the display frequently.

- **Do not take personal work processes used for analysis into account**
  For a complete analysis (see next point) an RFC connection is made to each server, each of which occupies one work process. These work processes are not displayed if this option is selected. By default, this option is selected.
- **Do not look for exclusive database locks**
  With this option the Monitor program looks for exclusive locks on the database and if it finds any, displays them in the **Action/Reason for waiting** field ("Stopped DB Lock" or "Waiting for DB Lock").

Using the **Select process** button:

- A specific group of work processes can be found and displayed. This is particularly necessary for large installations with hundreds of work processes. Thus for example, by default, waiting work processes are not shown.

Monitoring the Dispatcher Queue

Occasionally, it may be useful to monitor the dispatcher queue. Statistics on dispatcher activities can be seen by selecting in the Server Overview,

> **Tools · Administration · Monitor · System Monitoring · Server** (Transaction SM51).

Then mark an SAP instance with the cursor and select **Goto · Queue Info**. A list appears, showing information for each work process type on the requests currently waiting, the maximum number of user requests since the SAP instance was started, the maximum possible number of user requests for each queue and the number of requests read and written.

The information about the dispatcher queue is especially important when the system is not responding because the number of requests in the queue is much larger than the number of work processes. In this situation, the SAP system does not have any more work processes available to perform an analysis. To obtain the queue data you can use the auxiliary program **dpmon**.

Summary

To monitor the actions of the SAP work processes, use the Local Work Process Overview, referring in particular to the columns **Time**, **Status**, **Reason**, **Action/Reason for waiting** and **Table**. The following should be noted:

- Are there enough work processes of all types available (status "waiting") for each SAP instance?
- Is there a program that occupies a work process for too long (Field **Time**)? If this is the case the user should check this program and see if it has any errors. A detailed program analysis may also have to be carried out.
- Check the fields **Status**, **Reason**, **Action/Reason for waiting** and **Table**, to see whether more than 20% of the work processes are performing the same action. The main problems with this can be:
  - If more than 20% of the work processes are in PRIV mode or in the roll-in or roll-out phase, this indicates a problem with SAP memory management.
  - If more than 40% of work processes are performing a database action, such as "sequential read", "commit" etc., this indicates a database problem.
  - If more than 20% of work processes are reading the same table at the same time, this means that there may be a problem with an expensive SQL statement or exclusive lockwaits in the database.

You can call the Local Work Process Overview on the operating system level with the **dpmon** program. This is particularly necessary if the performance problem is so massive that no work processes can be used for the analysis.

Figures 2.12 and 2.13 show the analysis procedure for the SAP work processes.

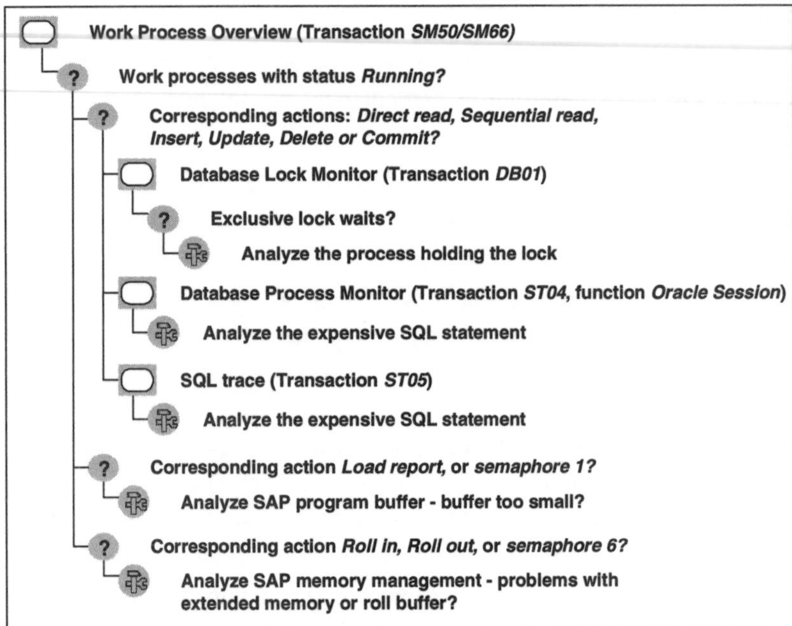

Figure 2.12 Procedure roadmap for analyzing SAP work processes (I)

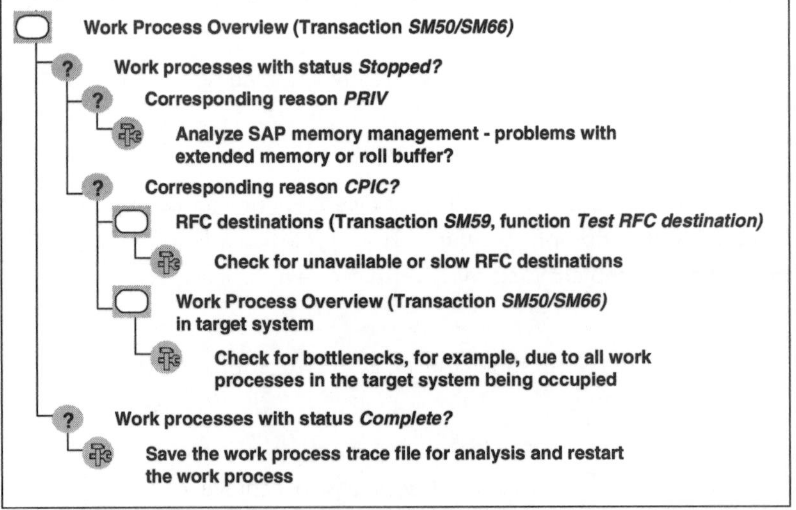

Figure 2.13 Procedure roadmap for analyzing SAP work processes (II)

Summary

You will find a summary at the end of each section in this chapter.

Important terms in this chapter

After studying this chapter you should be familiar with the following terms:

- Hardware bottleneck
- Logical and physical database read accesses ("Buffer Gets" and "Disk Reads")
- Expensive SQL statements
- Exclusive database locks
- Allocated and physical memory
- SAP work process bottleneck
- Semaphores

Questions

1. Which of the following can cause a CPU bottleneck on the database server?
   a) External processes that do not belong to the database or an SAP instance are running on the database server.
   b) The SAP extended memory is configured too small.
   c) Work processes that belong to an SAP instance running on the database (e.g. background or update work processes) require CPU capacity.
   d) There are expensive SQL statements—for example, those that account for 5% or more of the entire database load in the Shared SQL Area.
   e) The database buffers are set too small, so that data must continuously be reloaded from the hard disks.
2. Which of the following are necessary to achieve optimal database performance?
   a) Update Statistics must be regularly scheduled.
   b) The number of SAP work processes must be sufficiently large so that there are enough database processes to process the database load.
   c) The database buffers must be sufficiently large.

d) You should regularly check whether expensive SQL statements are unnecessarily occupying CPU and main memory resources.

e) The database instance should be run only on a separate computer without SAP instances.

3. Which points should you take into consideration when monitoring SAP memory configuration?

   a) The total memory allocated by the SAP and database instances should not be larger than the physical main memory of the computer.

   b) The extended memory must be sufficiently large.

   c) If possible, no displacements (swaps) should occur in the SAP buffers.

4. In the Local Work Process Overview, the information displayed for a particular work process over a considerable time period is as follows: "Running", "Sequential Read", and a specific table name. What does this tell you?

   a) There may be an expensive SQL statement accessing the indicated table, that can be analyzed more closely in the Database Process Monitor.

   b) There may be a wait situation in the dispatcher, preventing a connection to the database. The dispatcher queue should be analyzed more closely.

   c) There may be an *exclusive lockwait*, that can be analyzed in the Monitor for exclusive database locks.

   d) There may be a network problem between the application server and the database server.

3 Workload Analysis

Workload analysis gives reliable data on throughput, load and response times for the SAP system and its components. As described in the Introduction, an experienced performance analyst begins by using a workload analysis to reveal areas of the SAP system that have noticeable performance problems, and then proceeds with a more detailed top-down analysis.

Example: Assuming that you have systematically performed the analyses explained in the last chapter and have discovered several problems both in the database area and in SAP memory configuration. How can you determine which problem is the most serious and requires the most urgent attention? The workload analysis can provide the answer.

Workload analysis examines the various response times measured by the system. The kinds of performance problems identified by workload analysis are those that negatively affect throughput and response time and are known as *bottlenecks*. Bottlenecks can critically affect production operation and therefore require speedy removal. Workload analysis can also be used to prioritize performance problems.

In addition, workload analysis reveals the load distribution for each application's programs or transactions and indicates which of these are placing the greatest load on the SAP system. Workload analysis should therefore be the starting point for a detailed application analysis.

The first section of this chapter explains the basic concepts of workload analysis. After an introduction to the Workload Monitor, there is an explanation of which statistics are measured in units of time by the SAP system and how you can use these measurements to identify performance problems The second section of the chapter provides recommendations on how to monitor your system performance regularly.

When should you read this chapter?

Read this chapter when you want to monitor, analyze, and interpret the response time of the SAP system or of individual programs and transactions. If you want to technically monitor and optimize the performance of the SAP system, you can read Chapter 3, "Workload Analysis", either before or after Chapter 2, "Monitoring Hardware, Database and SAP Basis". If you want to monitor and optimize the performance of programs and transactions, you should read this chapter and then read Chapter 4, "Performance Analysis for ABAP-Programs". Understanding workload analysis is a precondition for successful performance optimization.

The Workload Monitor

This section describes the Workload Monitor. First we will deal with the functions and availability of the Workload Monitor, then we will describe how to work with the Monitor and, finally, we shall look at the technical settings.

Functions and Availability

The Workload Monitor (transaction code ST03) has formed a part of SAP software since the first release of SAP R/3 (in the Computer Center Management System CCMS). With SAP Basis 4.6C the Workload Monitor is now available with a completely reworked interface, in EnjoySAP format (transaction code ST03N). In the latest version of the (central) Workload Monitor it is possible to display statistical data from all mySAP.com components in complex system landscapes (even from "non-R/3" systems) (transaction code ST03G). The statistical data from remote components can be accessed using RFC. The central Workload Monitor is available with SAP Basis 6.10. The system to be monitored must be at least SAP Basis 4.0 with corresponding support packages.

In the following section we shall refer to the mapping and menu paths in SAP Basis 4.6C and higher. Menu paths for older versions of Basis are also given.

Working With the Workload Monitor

Statistics such as response times, memory use, and database accesses are collected and stored for all transaction steps for all mySAP.com components. These statistics are organized in load profiles that can be displayed in the Workload Monitor. The Workload Monitor enables you to obtain a comprehensive overview of load distribution within a mySAP.com component.

To access the initial screen of the Workload Monitor, use transaction code ST03N. The main screen of the Workload Monitor appears, **Load Analysis in System X**, as can be seen in Figure 3.1. The main screen is divided into three windows:

In the window on the upper left you will first of all find a button (in the top left-hand corner), with which you can choose a role. There are three roles:

- **Administrator**
  This is the standard user mode. It offers fast access to the system load statistics of the current day and gives an overview of system load distribution. In addition, in this mode you can also display the functions related to the data collector.
- **Service Engineer**
  This mode gives you the system load statistics for the current day and for the previous week as well as an overview of the history and distribution of the workload and a detailed analysis of system load. By default, the system displays all of the statistics for all application servers.
- **Expert**
  This mode gives users all functions available in Transaction ST03N. You can display all available data on system load (daily, weekly and monthly data).

Furthermore, in the window in the upper left you can choose the SAP instance you wish to analyze or "Total", if you want to analyze the entire SAP system. You can also select the period of time to be included in the analysis.

You will find administration information in the top part of the window on the right. The **Instance** field displays the name of the SAP instance or "Total", if you are analyzing the entire SAP system. Using the data for **Period**, **First record** and **Last record** you can check to see if the collection and compression of data in the selected time period has been done accordingly.

Further down you will see statistical data on the performance of the SAP system and information on possible causes of performance problems. If you select the **Workload overview** analysis view in the window in the lower left, you will see a breakdown of statistics on response times and throughput, according to different task types. For the most part, the task types correspond to the *work process types* "Dialog", "Update", "Update2", "Background" and "Spool". The "Dialog" work process type is further subdivided into the task types "Dialog", "RFC", "AutoABAP" and "Buffer Sync".

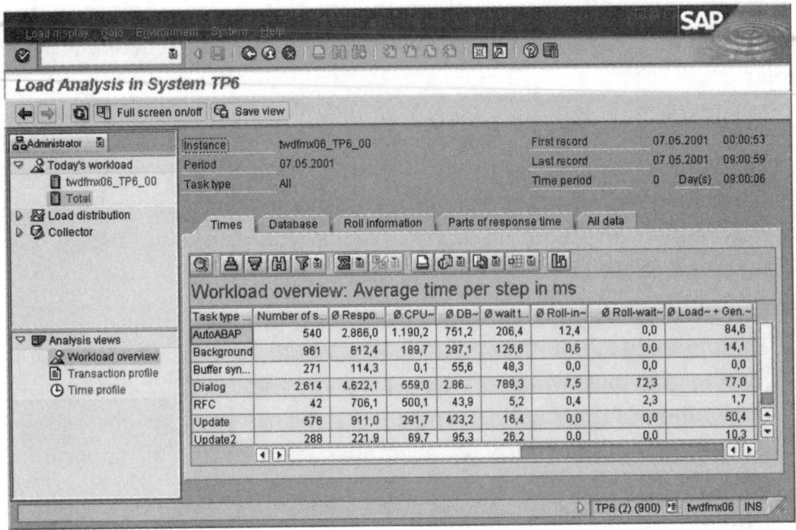

Figure 3.1 Main screen of the Workload Monitor

Transaction step

The first important values are the number of *transaction steps* (**Number of steps** column) and the average response time (**Av. Response time**). In a dialog task, a transaction step corresponds to a screen change—that is, to a request that is executed for a user by the mySAP component. The term "dialog step" may be somewhat misleading, as dialog steps used in the Workload Monitor are performed not only in dialog tasks (immediate responses to input from online users), but also in background tasks, update tasks, and spool tasks. Processing an update request or a spool request is counted by the Workload Monitor as one dialog step. Similarly, a background program may involve one or more dialog steps. To avoid ambiguity, this book will use the term *transaction step* for the processing steps referred to in the Workload Monitor as dialog steps, to differentiate them from background dialog steps. The number of transaction steps per unit of time will be referred to as *system activity* or *throughput*.

Response time

The *average response time for a transaction step* in a dialog task (**Av. Response time**) is seen by many SAP users as the criterion for the acceptable performance in a mySAP.com component. Another generally accepted rule of thumb is that good performance in SAP R/3 is indicated by an average response time of 1 second or less. As we will see in this chapter, however, a broad generalization of this kind is not accurate when you consider the variety of different mySAP.com components and the demands made on each.

In addition to the average response time, there are many other statistics, such as database time, CPU time, and so on, that enable you to understand performance problems and their possible causes. These statistics are explained in the next section.

Using tabs in the menu interface you can select other screens with information on database accesses etc. Using the **Save view** function you can save user-specific views. The next time you call up Transaction ST03N, the system automatically displays the view saved.

Load profiles, or analysis views, enable you to perform a detailed analysis of load distribution and response times. Apart from the **Workload overview** already mentioned, in the lower left window you can select other analysis views: Transaction profile and Time profile, which we will discuss in greater detail in later sections.

Older versions

For older SAP Basis versions, enter transaction code ST03. The initial screen of the Workload Monitor appears, **Workload: Analysis of SAP System SID**. From this initial screen, you can access the main screen. First, choose the **Performance database** button. In the dialog boxes that appear you can select data for a specific server or for the entire system ("TOTAL") and a period to be analyzed. You are then shown the main screen of the Workload Monitor, **Performance: Workload summary of server**.

If you are interested in the current statistics for the server you are connected to, from the initial screen of the Workload Monitor choose **This application server · Last minute load**. Then specify over how many minutes the response times should be given (e.g. the last 15 minutes). You are then brought to the main screen of the Workload Monitor, **Performance: Recent Workload for Server**.

The main screen of the Workload Monitor is divided into three sections. The first section, **Instance**, contains administrative information. The fields **SAP System**, **Server** and **Instance no** show the name of the mySAP.com component and the name of the server selected (or "Total", if you are analyzing the entire mySAP.com system). Using the data for **First record** and **Last record** you can check to see if the collection and compression of data in the selected time period has be done accordingly. The lower section, **Task types**, tells you which task type you have chosen (**Current** field), and the buttons that enable you to choose other task types. The central section of the screen (**Workload**) contains the statistical data.

From the main screen of the Workload Monitor you can go to the load profile by selecting **Goto · Profiles**. There, you can select profiles for the technical analysis, such as Task Type Profile, Time Profile, Computer Profile and Memory Profile and profiles for the application analysis, such as Transaction Profile, User Profile, Client Profile and Accounting Profile.

Technical Settings for the Workload Monitor

To ensure that individual statistical records, generated and recorded for each transaction step, are regularly collated in profiles, the `RSCOLL00` program must be scheduled to run every hour as a background job (generally under the name SAP_COLLECTOR_FOR_PERFORMANCE). You can display and modify the parameters affecting the creation of profiles in the Workload Monitor. In the "Expert" role, select

Collector & Perf. Database · Parameter & Reorg · Collector & Reorg

Under **Standard statistics** you can enter the retention periods for profiles—that is, the time before they are automatically deleted. Under **Time comparison data** you can enter the retention period for data displayed under the Workload Monitor menu option **Load history**. The **Cumulate server statistics to a systemwide total statistics** option determines whether or not a systemwide statistic should be generated. This option should always be selected. With the **Delete seq. statfile after ...** and **Max. number of records...** parameters you can specify when the individual statistical records are deleted and also the maximum number of records that are to be collated in each run of the `RSCOLL00` program.

Protocols are set for each run of the `RSCOLL00` program which you can use for troubleshooting. You can see the protocols in the Workload Monitor by selecting **Collector & Perf. Database · Perf. Monitor Collector · protocol** or **Collector & Perf. Database · Workload collector · protocol**. Explanations of the functions and settings of the data collector may be found in SAP Online Help and in the SAP Notes listed in the appendix.

Workload Analysis

To examine Workload Analysis more closely, in this section we will discuss the sequence of events in a transaction step and the times measured during it, with the help of Figures 3.2 and 3.3.

Course of a Transaction Step

Once an SAP user completes an entry, the presentation server sends the request to the dispatcher on the application server. The response time (**Av. response time**) is measured from the moment when the request from the presentation server reaches the dispatcher in the application server (step 1 in Figure 3.2). The response time ends when the request is processed and the last data is sent back to the presentation server.

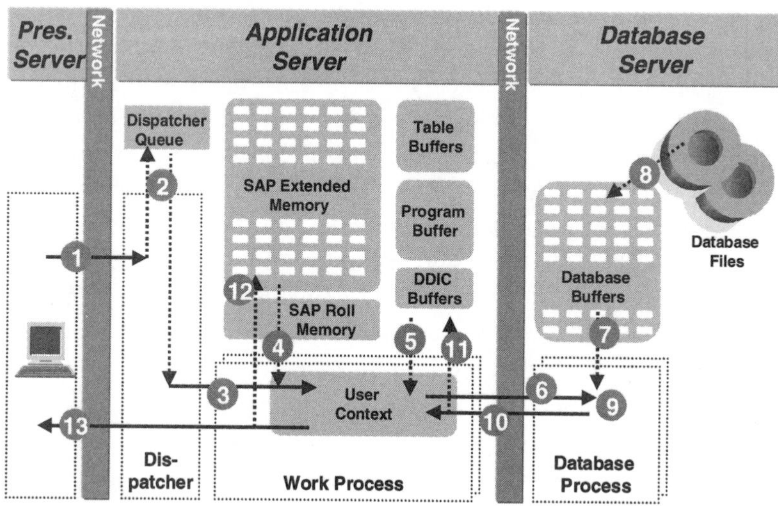

Figure 3.2 Course of a transaction step

Dispatcher wait time

When the dispatcher receives a processing request, it looks for a free SAP work process of the required type (dialog, update, and so on) and then sends the request to this work process, which begins the processing work. If all SAP work processes of the required type are busy when the request initially reaches the dispatcher, the request is placed in the dispatcher queue (2).

In the dispatcher queue, the request waits until a work process of the required type is free. As soon as a work process is free, the dispatcher sends the request to it (3). The time the request spends in the dispatcher queue is indicated as the **Av. wait time**. Note that there are many other kinds of wait time involved in the processing — for example, waiting for RFC calls, locks, CPU access, database access, and so on. To differentiate the wait time discussed here from others, it should be referred to as *Dispatcher wait time*.

Roll in, roll out An SAP transaction normally extends over several transaction steps (screen changes). During these steps, data such as variables, internal tables, and screen lists is built up and stored in the main memory of the application server. This data is known as *User context*. Different transaction steps are normally processed by different dialog work processes. For example, the first transaction step may be processed by work process number 3, the second transaction step by work process number 4, and so on. At the beginning of a transaction step, the user context is made available to the appropriate work process. This procedure is called *Roll in* (4). The technical processes comprising a roll in, such as copying data into the local memory of the work process, are described in detail in Chapter 8. The analogous process of *Roll out* saves the current user-context data to the virtual memory at the conclusion of a transaction step (12). The duration of the roll in is referred to as *Roll-in time* and the duration of the roll out is known as the *Roll-out time*. The average roll times are indicated as **Time per roll in** or **Time per roll out** in the Workload Monitor in Release 3. To obtain the average roll times in Release 4, divide the values **Roll-in time** or **Roll-out time** by the number of "roll ins" or "roll outs" respectively. Please note that the roll out time is *not* part of the response time of a transaction step. At roll out, when the user context is copied from the local memory of the work process to the roll memory, the processed data has already been returned to the presentation server.

Load time All ABAP programs and screens that are required and are not yet available in the application server buffers must be loaded and possibly generated. The time it takes to do this is indicated as **Av. load+gen time**. Loading a program also entails accesses to database tables storing the ABAP programs—for example, the tables D010S and D010L.

Database time When data is read or changed in the database, the time required is known as *database time* and is indicated as **Av. DB request time**. Database time is measured from the moment of sending the database request to the database server and runs until the moment at which the data is returned to the application server (6–10). Because database time is measured by the application server, database time includes not only the time required by the database to produce the requested data, but also the time required for the network transfer of that data. Thus, a network problem between the database and the application server results in a greater database time.

Before accessing the database, the database interface of the work process checks whether the required data is already in the SAP buffers. If the data is already in the buffers, the buffers are accessed directly because using buffers is up to 100 times faster than a database access (5, 11). Buffer accesses do not contribute to database time.

Roll wait time

Roll wait time occurs in connection with Remote Function Calls (RFC), in other words, when there is communication between software components or, from SAP Basis 4.6 on, when there is communication with the presentation level.

GUI time

Up until SAP Basis 4.5 the duration of communication between the presentation and application servers (network transfers and the creation of images on the presentation server) was not included in the workload analysis data. Since SAP Basis 4.6, these times are included in the response time, for the main part at least, as *GUI time*. Roll wait time and GUI time are explained in Chapters 6 and 7, "Interfaces", and "SAP GUI and Internet Connection".

Enqueue time

Enqueue time, indicated as **Av. enqueue time**, is the time during which a work process sets an enqueue request.

Processing time

Processing time is the total response time minus the sum of all times mentioned above (except GUI time).

CPU time

All the statistics discussed above concern actions that form part of an SAP work process; that is to say, whenever the action in question runs, it is timed. With **Av. CPU time** on the other hand, at the end of a transaction step, the SAP work process asks the operating system how much CPU time has expired during that step. CPU time is not determined by the operating system. CPU time is not an additive component of transaction response time (like the times mentioned above), but is consumed during load time, roll time, and processing time (see Figure 3.3).

Interpreting Response Times

To analyze response times for dialog processing, use the guideline values in Table 3.1.

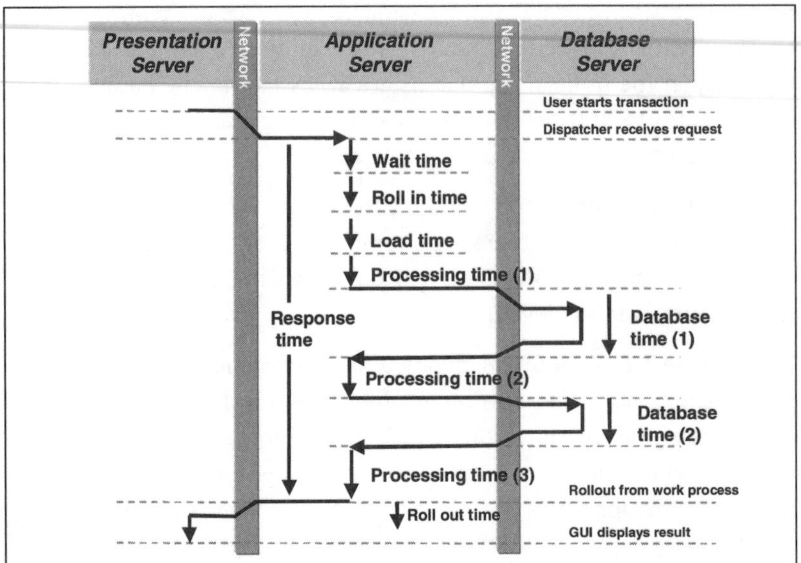

Figure 3.3 Response time and its components: dispatcher wait time, roll-in time, roll wait time, load time, database time, processing time and CPU time

Time	Guideline value	Problem indicated	See chapter
Dispatcher wait time (»Wait time«)	< 10% of response time; < 50 ms	General performance problem with many possible causes	
Load time (Load+gen time)	< 50 ms	Program buffer too small or CPU bottleneck	2
Roll-in time, Roll-out time (in Release 4.0: "Roll-in time" / "Roll Ins"; in Release 3.0/3.1: "Time per roll in" etc.	< 20 ms	SAP roll buffer, SAP extended memory too small or CPU bottleneck	2, 8
Roll wait time	< 200 ms	Problem with frontend communication (together with higher GUI time) or with communication with external component	4, 6, 7

Table 3.1 Guideline values for analyzing the average response times for task type dialog. In the task type update the value can be around 50% higher. The "Problem indicated" column specifies what problem may arise if the given guideline values are significantly exceeded.

Time	Guideline value	Problem indicated	See chapter
GUI time	< 200 ms	Problem with frontend communication (together with higher roll wait time)	4, 6, 7
Enqueue time	< 5 ms	Problem with enqueue, network problem	4
Processing time CPU time	Processing time < 2 ×CPU time	CPU bottleneck or communication problem	5
Database time ("DB request time")	< 40% of (response time minus dispatcher wait time); Guideline value: 200–600 ms	Database problem, network problem or CPU bottleneck	3, 4, 11
Time per DB request	< 5 ms	database problem	3, 4, 11
Direct reads	< 2 ms	database problem	3, 4, 11
Sequential reads	< 10 ms	database problem	3, 4, 11
Changes and commits	< 25 ms	database problem	3, 4, 11

Table 3.1 Guideline values for analyzing the average response times for task type dialog (contd.)

If the values you observe in the Workload Monitor are *significantly* outside the guideline range indicated here, there may be a performance problem in the relevant area (e.g. on the database). Note that these values are based on standard situations and may differ in some mySAP.com components.

"Lost time"

In addition to comparing your statistics with the guideline values, you should perform the following analysis, which could be referred to as the "search for time lost". As mentioned above, there are two different sources of time statistics. All times, apart from CPU time, are measured from the perspective of the SAP work process, whereas CPU time is measured from the perspective of the operating system. The lost time analysis aims to check whether the two statistics can be brought together. To do so, from the total average response time, subtract all times for which the SAP work process does *not* require any CPU time—namely, dispatcher wait time, database time, enqueue time and roll wait time. (As of Release 4, to find the average roll wait time from the Workload Monitor, divide the "Roll wait time" by the "Dialog steps".)

For the most part, programs are processed during processing time and as a result, CPU capacity is normally "consumed" during this time. As a result, processing time and CPU time should be more or less the same. As a rule of thumb, the difference between processing time and CPU time should not be more than 100%. Greater "lost times" indicate performance problems.

What are the possible causes for a significant difference between processing time and CPU time?

- The first possible cause is a CPU bottleneck. This would mean there is not enough CPU capacity available for the SAP work processes, which must therefore wait until CPU becomes available. In this case, processing time is being measured in the work process while no CPU time is used, and this processing time is considerably larger than CPU time.
- Another reason for a difference between processing time and CPU time concerns wait times in the SAP work process. Whenever the SAP work process has a status "stopped", processing time is measured without CPU time being used. This type of wait situation can be identified in the Work Process Overview.

Activity, Throughput and Load

Activity, throughput

The concepts of system activity, throughput and load can best be explained using the **Workload overview** analysis view (see Figure 3.1): The number of transaction steps can be seen in the second column (**Number of steps**). The number of transaction steps per unit of time can be defined as *system activity* or *throughput*. In our example we can see the highest level of activity (2,614 transaction steps) corresponds to dialog processing, that is to say that the user has performed 2,614 screen changes in dialog processing mode during the period of time in question.

Load

If two users have each executed 100 transaction steps in a given time period, they have created equal activity. This does not mean, however, that they have both produced the same *load* on the system. If, for example, the first user has entered 100 financial documents and has executed 100 transaction steps with an average response time of 500 ms, this user has occupied the system for 50 seconds. If a second user has created auditing reports and performs 100 transaction steps with of an average response time of 5 seconds, this user has occupied the system for

500 seconds. Evidently the second user has created a system *load* that is 10 times greater, with the same amount of *activity*. As can be seen from this example, the product of the number of transaction steps and the average response time is a way of measuring the load generated. (To be more exact, subtract dispatcher wait time and roll wait time from the total response time, because a request does not create system load while it waits in the dispatcher queue or while it waits for an RFC to be carried out.) Similarly, the database load created by the different task types can be determined using the total database time (transaction steps by average database time). CPU load on the application server can also be measured in this way. The distribution of times (database time, CPU time and so on) thus reflects the distribution of load on the system better than just the number of transaction steps.

Active users

The simplest and most graphic measure for the size of a mySAP.com component is the number of users. Unfortunately, the "number of users" is also an imprecise expression, and its meaning varies according to context. It can mean, for example, the number of licenses or the number of user master records, to mention just two possible meanings. For components that are mainly characterized by background or interface load, the number of users is no longer relevant as an indication of size.

To avoid confusion, this book distinguishes three types of users, as follows:

- **Occasional user**
  On average a user of this type performs fewer than 400 transaction steps (screen changes) per week. For a 40-hour work week this corresponds to an average of one transaction step every 6 minutes. This is typically a user who only uses the mySAP.com component now and again.
- **Transactional user**
  On average a user of this type performs up to 4,800 transaction steps per week. This corresponds to less than one transaction step every 30 seconds. These are users who use the mySAP.com component regularly and continuously.
- **Data entry/telesales/high volume "power user"**
  Power users perform more than 4,800 transaction steps per week. They use the mySAP.com component regularly and at a high volume.

In this book, *active users* are users who correspond to either the "transactional user" or the "power user" categories.

The user profile gives information about the activities of users. You can call the user profile in the Workload Monitor under **Load distribution • Users per instance**.

Older versions For older versions of SAP Basis call the user profile from the main screen of the Workload Monitor by choosing: **Goto • Profiles • User profile**. The profile provides information on the users logged on during a particular period of time and their activities.

Performing Workload Analysis

In general, the first input for performance analysis comes in the form of observations made by the users. The Workload Monitor helps you to verify the subjective comments of users and narrow down the causes of performance problems. We can distinguish between two types of problem:

- **General performance problems**
  A *general performance problem* results in poor response times and unsatisfactory throughput in *all transactions*. A problem of this type can have a negative impact on business processes and lead to financial loss.
- **Specific performance problems**
  If the throughput or response time of *individual transactions* is unsatisfactory, then we can speak of *specific performance problems*. Specific performance problems can have a negative impact on business processes if the transaction in question is one of the key transactions in the business process (such as goods issue).

With the help of the seven questions included in the following sections, you can further limit performance problems. Guideline values and examples are provided to help you to answer these questions. You should, however, bear in mind that a simple yes or no answer is not always possible.

Analyzing General Performance Problems

Is there a general performance problem?

The users can usually identify a general performance problem. You can use the Workload Monitor to verify the users' observations and check whether response times affecting all transactions are high. The following criteria, which apply to dialog tasks, may help you to decide:

- Dispatcher wait time >> 50 ms: A significantly large dispatcher wait time always affects all transactions. It implies that programs are too slow and are blocking work processes for lengthy periods — or that too few work processes have been configured.
- Database time >> 40% (response time—dispatcher wait time) and database time > 400 ms: A high database time slows performance for all transactions.
- Processing time > 2 × CPU time: High processing time slows performance for all transactions. This can be caused by a CPU bottleneck or a problem with communication between systems.
- Average response time > system-specific guideline value: Average response time for a dialog task is seen by many SAP users as the decisive criterion for acceptable performance in a mySAP.com component. A guideline value must be defined for each individual mySAP.com component. A generally accepted rule of thumb is that good performance is indicated by an average response time of 1 second or less. A broad generalization of this kind is not always valid for all the different requirements of mySAP.com components.

With SAP Basis 4.6 the repsonse times displayed in the workload monitor include, for the first time, time data regarding communication between application and presentation levels (as part of GUI time, as time for network transfer and processing in the presentation server). This means that time elements are created that were not included in measurements in older versions. Due to the change in measuring techniques, as a rule of thumb the workload monitor for an SAP R/3 4.6 displays average response times of around 100 to 200 milliseconds higher than in the older versions, even though performance has not changed from the user's point of view. This should be borne in mind when negotiating service level agreements.

Is the performance problem temporary or permanent?

After verifying that there is a general performance problem, try to find out how frequently the problem occurs. The following questions may help:

- Is the problem permanent or temporary?
- Does this problem occur at regular time intervals—for example at particular times of the day?
- Is it a non-recurring problem?

- What times (database time, CPU time or processing time) are high when the problem occurs?
- Does the problem occur following only specific system activities—for example, when background programs run on the system?

To examine these questions more closely, compare the workload statistics of recent days with each other.

In Workload Monitor expert mode, in the upper left window, select **Load history and distribution · Load history · Total**. Compare the performance values for several days to find out if the performance problem only occurs on certain days (see Figure 3.4).

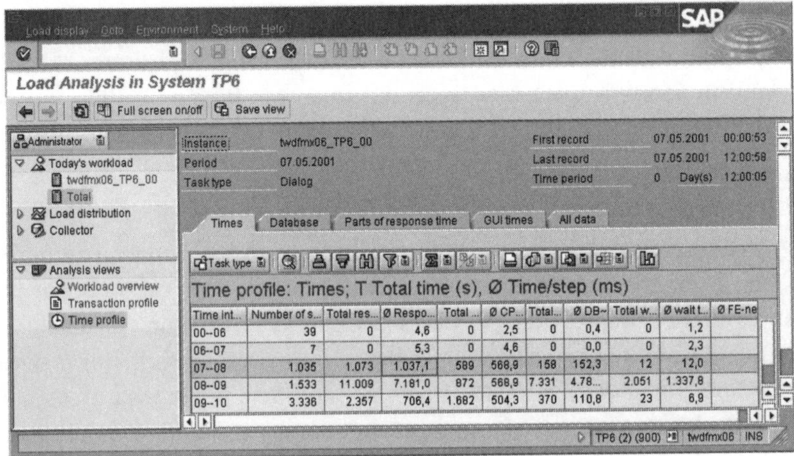

Figure 3.4 Time profile for dialog processing

Then generate the *day or time profile* by selecting the **Time profile** analysis view in the window in the lower left of the Workload Monitor. In a day or time profile the transaction steps and response times for all of the hours in one day are presented.

Using the time profile, you can analyze the daily loads on the system. If you find that the average response time increases dramatically only at particular periods of high load, you can infer that your system is overloaded at these times. If the average response times are also unsatisfactory at times of low system load, the performance problem is load-independent.

Example: You can diagnose a general performance problem using the workload analysis. By comparing the workload data for different days you can narrow the problem down to a particular period of time. In this period of time there are conspicuously high database times, especially *Changes and Commits*. On closer examination of the error log file in the database it emerges that an *Archiver stuck* occurred over night. (An *archiver stuck* occurs in an Oracle database if the directory for redo log files is full. This means that no further redo information can be written; the database and the SAP instances stop responding. Once the problem has been eliminated the database and SAP instances continue working without error.) The problem is resolved by the database administrator the next morning. In the middle of the day the *Archiver stuck* leads to higher database times for this day (especially for *Changes and Commits*). In an analysis on the Workload Monitor, this would suggest a poor database performance, although the performance is actually good, as becomes evident once this problem has been eliminated.

Dialog load vs. background load

The time profiles enable you to determine whether excessive background processing during periods of peak system load has a negative impact on dialog processing. To create time profiles for dialog processing and background processing, using the **Task type** button, select the task types **Dialog** or **Background**. Use the **Total Response time (s)**, **Total CPU time total (s)** and **Total DB time total (s)** fields to determine at what time of the day the dialog or background load occurs. These profiles enable you to determine whether excessive use of background processing during periods of peak system load has a negative impact on dialog processing. You should try to ensure that the background processing load remains low during these peak periods, particularly if there are performance problems.

You may also find it helpful to compare the time profile per day in the Workload Monitor with the time profile per day for CPU load and for paging (both indicated in the Operating System Monitor). This comparison enables you to determine whether deteriorating response times correlate with a large CPU load or a high paging rate. If so, a temporary hardware bottleneck is indicated (see the next question below).

Older versions

For older versions of SAP Basis, in the initial screen of Workload Monitor select the **Performance database** button.

Then select **TOTAL**, **Previous Days** and one of the preceding days. Repeat this procedure for several days to find out if the performance problem only occurs on certain days.

Then create the *day or time profile*, by using the following menu path in the main screen of the Workload Monitor:

Goto · Profiles · Time profile

Is there a hardware bottleneck?

A CPU bottleneck or main memory bottleneck can be detected as follows:

1. Find out if the hourly averages for the CPU load or paging rate are large. As a rule of thumb the risk of a hardware bottleneck is regarded as high when the hourly average of free CPU capacity (indicated as "CPU idle") is less than 20%, or the paging rate per hour exceeds 20% of the physical main memory. See also the section "Analyzing a Hardware Bottleneck (CPU and Main Memory)" on page 71 in Chapter 2.
2. In a second step, check whether the large CPU load or high paging rate really does negatively affect mySAP.com component response times.
   - To check whether there is a hardware bottleneck on an application server, look at the processing time. If the processing time is much greater than double the CPU time, this indicates that the work processes are waiting for CPU. (However, an increased processing time may have other causes. See the section "Workload Analysis" on page 124.) A further indication of a hardware bottleneck on the application server is given by increased load times, roll-in times, and dispatcher wait time.
   - To check whether there is a hardware bottleneck on the database server, establish whether the database time is too large. Compare, for example, the average database times in the daily time profile at times of high and low load.
3. To check whether there is a main memory bottleneck, compare whether the virtually allocated memory is significantly greater than the physically available main memory. As long as the virtually allocated memory is smaller than 1.5 times the physical main memory, there is normally no risk of a main memory bottleneck. (See the section "Displaying the Allocated Memory" on page 103 in Chapter 2, for more on this subject).

Only if all three of these checks (the first two apply to CPU and memory, the final one only to memory) indicate a hardware bottleneck, can you be fairly certain that there is, in fact, a hardware bottleneck.

The three possible causes of a hardware bottleneck are as follows:

- **Poor load distribution**
  The load is not optimally distributed across the servers. There may be servers with free CPU or main memory capacity. Alternatively, load distribution may become nonoptimal at certain times of the day, for example, when several background processes are run in parallel during periods of peak system load. You should be able to reschedule these programs to run at times of low system load.
- **Individual processes causing a high CPU load:**
  Individual processes with a high CPU load may be running at times of high system load. Such processes may include database processes (with expensive SQL statements), SAP work processes (with programs running as background jobs), or processes external to SAP. To improve performance, you may be able to tune, reschedule, or (in the case of external processes) cancel these processes.
- **Insufficient hardware capacity**
  If the two previously mentioned causes of a hardware bottleneck do not apply, the hardware capacity may be too small for your system load.

If you have correctly identified a hardware bottleneck, proceed as described in Chapter 2 in the section "Analyzing a Hardware Bottleneck (CPU and Main Memory)" on page 71.

Is there a general database performance problem?

A general database performance problem is indicated by increased database times. The following guideline values for dialog tasks in the Workload Monitor indicate a general database performance problem:

- Database time >> 40% (response time minus dispatcher wait time); and
  database time > 400 ms
- Direct reads >> 2 ms
- Seq. Reads >> 10 ms
- Changes and Commits >> 25 ms

A database performance problem has many possible causes. Proceed as described in Chapter 2 in the section "Monitoring the Database" on page 79.

Is load distribution optimal?

A performance problem caused by nonoptimal load distribution can be detected by comparing the CPU load and the paging rates for the various servers (in the Operating System Monitor). You should also compare the response times for the various application servers in the Workload Monitor.

To display the *server profile* from the initial screen of the Workload Monitor, use the following menu path:

> **Goto · Performance database · Analyze all servers · Compare all servers.**

You can then enter the desired period of analysis with the menu option **Edit · Choose period type** and the buttons **Period+** and **Period-**.

The server profile shows the transaction steps and related response times for each server. If there are several SAP instances on one application server, the statistics indicated for the server are the totals for all instances on that server. To obtain details of the task types on individual servers, double-click a row in the list of servers.

Dispatcher wait time

In the server profile, check the load distribution across your servers. For example, if the *dispatcher wait time* occurs only on one server or on a small number of your servers, this implies either that too many users are working on these servers or that too few work processes are configured on these servers.

CPU time

Total CPU time (indicated as **CPU time total**) on all application servers should be roughly equal if all servers have the same CPU capacity. If you have servers with different CPU capacities, CPU time should differ proportionately.

One cause of a poor load distribution may be a nonoptimal configuration of log-on groups or work processes. To optimize load distribution, see Chapter 5, "Workload Distribution".

database time

If the average *database times* (indicated as **DB time avg.**) for the various servers differ greatly, this may indicate a network problem. You can assume that application servers are configured with the same work processes and that users on the various application servers are, on average, using the same transactions. Thus, there is no obvious reason, apart from a network problem, as to why the database should serve one application server more slowly than another application server. This argument applies only to servers that are configured with the same work processes. For background servers, update servers or servers mainly used for reporting, the average database time will be greater than that for dialog servers.

For older versions of SAP Basis, to display the *server profile* from the initial screen of the Workload Monitor, use the following menu path:

Older versions

Goto · Performance database · Analyze all servers · Compare all servers.

You can then enter the desired period of analysis with the menu option **Edit · Choose period type** and the buttons **Period+** and **Period-**.

Is there a performance problem caused by SAP memory management?

Performance problems caused by SAP memory management (see the section "Monitoring the Database" on page 79 in Chapter 2) may be the result of SAP buffers or SAP extended memory being too small. These problems would be seen in the Workload Monitor as follows:

- If the program buffer, CUA buffer or screen buffer are too small, there is an increase in average load time (average load time >> 50 ms).
- If the extended memory or the roll buffer are full the roll-in or roll-out times may increase (average roll-in or roll-out times >> 20 ms).

These guideline times apply to dialog tasks.

You should also monitor the *memory profile*. Up to SAP Basis 4.6, in the old Workload Monitor (transaction code ST03) this could be found under:

Memory profile

Goto · Profiles · Memory profile

The memory profile shows memory usage per program. Utilization of extended memory and heap memory (**Priv. mem.**) are indicated. The monitor also shows how often work processes entered PRIV mode (in the column **Workproc. Reservations**) and how often a work process was restarted after its use of heap memory exceeded the value of the parameter **abap/heaplimit** (indicated in the column **Workproc. Restarts**). If you notice higher roll or load times, proceed with the analysis in Chapter 2 in the section "Analyzing SAP Memory Management" on page 98.

With SAP Basis 6.10 the main memory profile is integrated in the new Workload Monitor (transaction code ST03N).

Analyzing Specific Performance Problems

The Workload Monitor is an analysis tool used for both technical analysis and application analysis.

Is there a performance problem with a transaction?

The *Transaction profile* is of primary importance for application analysis. To change over to the transaction profile, in the lower left window of the Workload Monitor, under **Analysis views**, select **Transaction profile**.

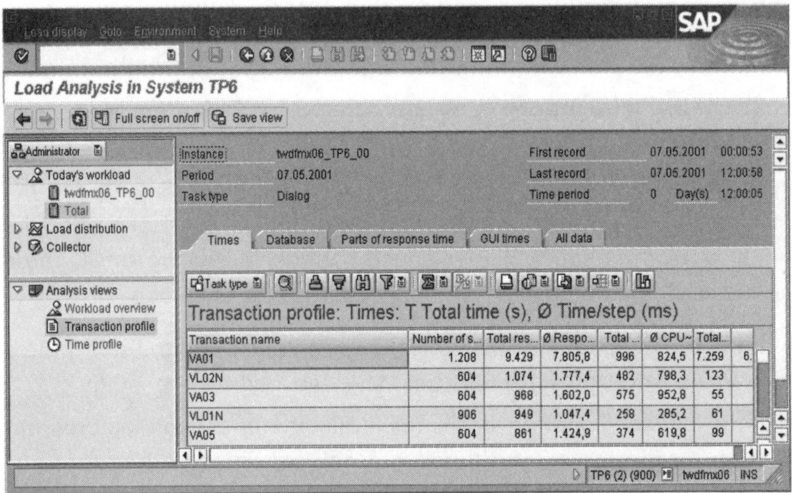

Figure 3.5 Transaction profile

The transaction profile contains a list of all transactions (or programs) started in the selected period. The number of transaction steps for each transaction is recorded (**Number of steps**), which is a measure of the activity of a transaction. Other columns in the transaction profile show the total response times and the average response times, as well as the proportion of CPU time, dispatcher wait time and database time. Using the tab pages in the menu interface you can select other screens with information about database accesses and so on.

System activity

From the number of transaction steps (**Number of steps**) you can estimate how frequently the transaction was executed if you know how many transaction steps (screen changes) each regular user requires on average per procedure. For example, if a regular user requires around 5 transaction steps to create a sales order (transaction code VA01) and the transaction profile shows 100,000 transaction steps for the selected time period, you can calculate that around 20,000 sales orders were created. If you wish to see which transaction had the most activity, sort by the column **Number of steps**.

The column **Total response time** provides a measure for the entire load on the system. (See the section "Activity, Throughput and Load" on page 130.) To find out which transactions produced the most load on the system, successively sort the list by the columns **Total response time**, **Total CPU time** and/or **Total DB time**. After each sort, the programs at the top of the list are likely candidates for performance optimization.

load

In Figure 3.5, Transaction VA01 is executed twice as often as Transaction VA03 (1,208 steps compared to 604); however, due to the higher average response time, Transaction VA01 generates 10 times as much load as Transaction VA03 (9,429 seconds compared with 968 seconds).

Average response time

For users, the *average response time* of the transactions they use is an important index of performance. Monitor and create guideline values for the average response times of core transactions—that is, transactions whose performance is central to business operations.

In general, when analyzing the transaction profile, consider the following questions:

- Sort the transaction profile according to **Total DB time**. Which transactions cause the greatest database load?
- Sort the transaction profile according to **Total CPU time**. Which transactions cause the greatest CPU load?
- Are there transactions for which the proportion of database time or CPU time is significantly higher than 60% of the total response time? Analyze these transactions using an SQL trace or ABAP trace. The procedure for analyzing individual programs and transactions is described in Chapter 4, "Performance Analysis for ABAP-Programs".
- Are there any customer-developed programs or transactions that produce a large load?

Monitor and save a copy of the transaction profile at regular intervals. This enables you to determine whether the response times of individual transactions grow continuously over time, or whether there is a sudden worsening of response times following a program modification. By recognizing such trends in the transaction profile *early*, you can initiate a detailed program analysis *before* a program causes a bottleneck for an entire process chain, or worse, reduces the performance of the entire mySAP.com system through large CPU or database loads.

Table 3.2 provides explanations and guideline response times for common system transactions.

Transaction/ Program	Description/Comment	Acceptable response time
MainMenu	Actions in the menu. "MainMenu" frequently appears near the top of the list if sorted according to "Dialog Steps".	< 100 ms
Login_Pw/ Logoff	logon or logoff screen	
AutoABAP	The Auto ABAP runs periodically in the background and executes actions such as those required by Alert Monitor	< 1,000 ms
Buf.Sync	buffer synchronization	< 1,000 ms
Rep_Edit	Actions in the ABAP editor	
(B)SCHDL	The batch scheduler runs periodically and checks whether background programs are due to be started.	
RSCOLL00	The performance collector runs periodically and collects data on performance. If you sort the transaction profile according to "Response time total", this program is often near the top of the list. However, the columns **CPU time total** and **DB time total**, indicate that this program produces little CPU or database time. Most of the response time for this program occurs when this program is waiting in work processes to receive performance data.	
RSM13000	The update program is used to summarize all update module statistics that cannot be ascribed to a transaction.	< 3,000 ms

Table 3.2 System programs in the transaction profile. In general these programs can be ignored during performance analysis.

Older versions

For older versions of SAP Basis, transaction profiles are generated as follows:

1. Start the Workload Monitor (Transaction ST03), select

   Performance database

   and then select **Total** (or a server) and a period of time.
2. You are then brought to the main screen of the Workload Monitor. Using the buttons **Total, Dialog** and so on, located in the lower part of the screen, select the task type you require.
3. Then use the **Transaction profile** button to create the transaction profile.

Application Monitor

Another important instrument for workload analysis is the Application Monitor (transaction code ST07), which you can use to create a load profile for each SAP module. To call this monitor, select:

> **Tools · Administration · Monitor · Performance · Workload · Application · Application monitor**

All screens of the Application Monitor show performance-relevant data according to SAP application module. The Monitor takes advantage of the fact that each transaction, each program and each table can be found in the SAP component hierarchy. For example, you can see statistics on the transaction "Create Sales Order" (transaction code VA01) under the SAP hierarchy branch → "Sales & Distribution" → "Sales" → "Create sales order". (To see an outline of the full SAP component hierarchy structure, use Transaction HIER.) Many screens in the Application Monitor show data that is also displayed in other monitors, such as the Workload Monitor, the SAP Storage Configuration Monitor (transaction code ST02), the Table Call Statistics (transaction code ST10), and so on. The advantage of using the Application Monitor is that the data is grouped according to the SAP application component hierarchy; from an initial overview, you can descend to an increasingly detailed view of the particular modules, sub-modules and transactions that are consuming the most system resources.

User Profile

The initial screen of the Application Monitor shows the current number of users for the different SAP modules. The user profile for each listed application consists of the numbers of logged on users, active users, and the users currently waiting for a request to be processed. To descend to a lower level of the SAP application component hierarchy and thus see the user profile for a more specific area, successively double-click the appropriate modules.

For example, double clicking on the **Sales & Distribution** module displays the distribution of users in the sub-modules "sales", "shipping", "billing" and "basic functions". A subsequent double click on **Sales** shows the user profile for transactions belonging to Sales, such as "VA01", "VA02".

Looking at the user profile in the Application Monitor is a convenient way of finding out the number of logged on and active users. An "active" user is one who has performed a transaction step in the last 30 seconds. You

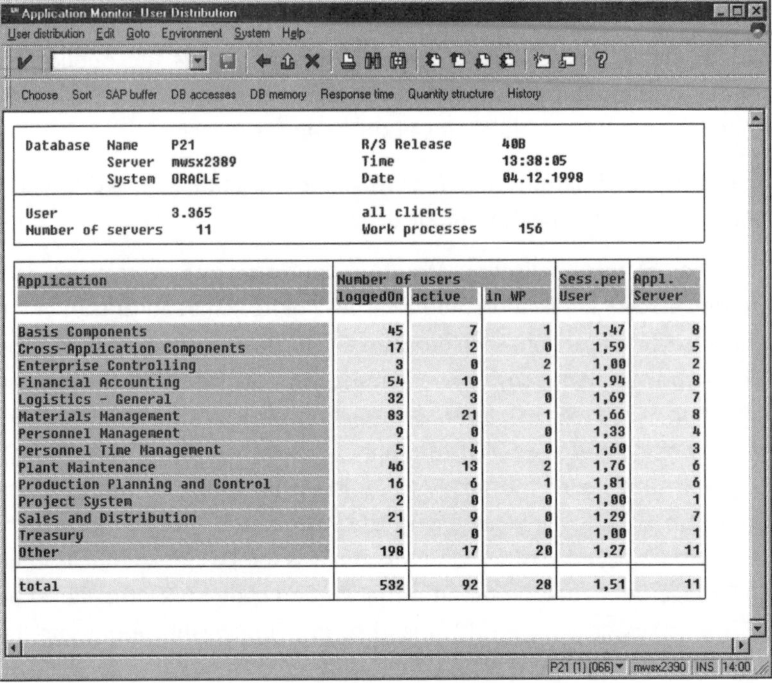

Database	Name	P21	R/3 Release	40B
	Server	mwsx2389	Time	13:38:05
	System	ORACLE	Date	04.12.1998
User		3.365	all clients	
Number of servers		11	Work processes	156

Application	Number of users loggedOn	active	in WP	Sess.per User	Appl. Server
Basis Components	45	7	1	1,47	8
Cross-Application Components	17	2	0	1,59	5
Enterprise Controlling	3	0	2	1,00	2
Financial Accounting	54	10	1	1,94	8
Logistics - General	32	3	0	1,69	7
Materials Management	83	21	1	1,66	8
Personnel Management	9	0	0	1,33	4
Personnel Time Management	5	4	0	1,60	3
Plant Maintenance	46	13	2	1,76	6
Production Planning and Control	16	6	1	1,81	6
Project System	2	0	0	1,00	1
Sales and Distribution	21	9	0	1,29	7
Treasury	1	0	0	1,00	1
Other	198	17	20	1,27	11
total	532	92	28	1,51	11

Figure 3.6 The user profile in the Application Monitor

can change this time period by selecting the menu option **User distribution • Change active time**. To analyze the user distribution on the application servers, select **User distribution • Choose app. server**. The user profile in the Application Monitor is especially useful when you wish to check whether logging on with logon groups is functioning correctly, so that users are logged on to application servers independently of one another.

Load per SAP Application Module

1. From the Application Monitor initial screen choose **Response time** to display the load profile for each SAP application module.
2. In the dialog boxes that appear, specify the relevant server and time period—similar to the Workload Monitor.

The data on this screen matches that in the transaction profile and includes transaction steps, response times per transaction step and CPU times, wait times and database times. Use the **Total?↔Avg** button to toggle between the average response times per transaction and total response time for all transaction steps. All data on this screen is grouped according to SAP application module. By successively double-clicking the appropriate module, you can descend to statistics on more specific component areas.

You can use the Application Monitor in the same way as you used the transaction profile in the Workload Monitor. The advantage of using the Application Monitor is that the data is grouped according to the SAP application component hierarchy; from an initial overview, you can descend to an increasingly detailed view of the particular modules and sub-modules that are consuming the most system resources.

In the Application Monitor, you can create graphs and diagrams illustrating load distribution. Use the button **Total?↔Avg** to show total response times (that is to say, "Resp. time total (s)", "CPU time total (s)" and so on) and then choose the **Graphic** button. The resulting pie charts illustrate the distribution of transaction steps and the response times according to SAP application module. The distribution of transaction steps on the module corresponds to the activity distribution, the distribution of total response time corresponds to the load distribution in the entire mySAP.com components, and distribution of database time corresponds to load distribution on the database and distribution of CPU time corresponds to load distribution on the application servers.

SAP Buffers

From the initial screen of the Application Monitor use the **SAP buffer** button to access an application of the SAP buffer, differentiated according to SAP modules (program buffer, CUA buffer, screen buffer and table buffer for generic buffering and single record buffering). To access statistics for more specific areas within an SAP application module (following the SAP component hierarchy), successively double-click on the appropriate rows in the Application column, drilling down to individual programs and tables.

Summary

The Workload Monitor enables you to make detailed statements about the distribution of response times not only across different system components, such as the database, hardware, and SAP Basis components, but also across different transactions and programs. By performing a workload analysis, you can determine the system areas in which you require further analysis and tuning. Always remember to compare the results of your workload analysis with the observations of users. This helps you avoid jumping to the wrong conclusion if a superficial analysis of the Workload Monitor indicates a performance problem where, in fact, there is no real problem. It also avoids the opposite situation of not noticing that the Workload Monitor is indicating a performance problem that is readily apparent to users.

Figure 3.7 summarizes a workload analysis for a general performance problem. You can find the corresponding detailed analyses for hardware, database, and SAP memory configuration in Chapter 2 in the sections "Monitoring Hardware" on page 70, "Monitoring the Database" on page 79, and "Analyzing SAP Memory Management" on page 98.

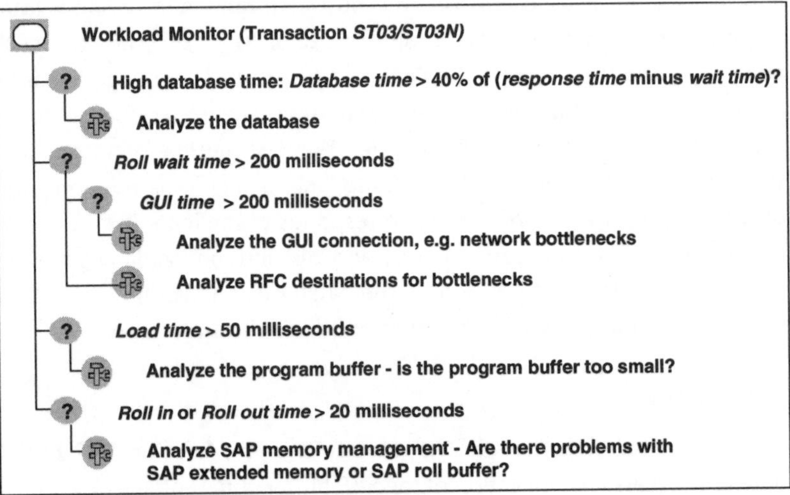

Figure 3.7 Summary of the most important steps of a workload analysis

Important terms in this chapter

After studying this chapter you should be familiar with the following terms:

- Dispatcher wait time, load time, database time
- Roll-in time, Roll-out time
- Processing time and CPU time
- Activity, throughput and load

Questions

1. Which of the following statements are correct?
   - CPU time is measured by the operating system of the application server.
   - Database time is measured by the database system.
   - High network times for data transfers between the presentation server and the application server are reflected in an increased response time in the Workload Monitor.
   - High network times for data transfers between the application server and the database server are reflected in an increased response time in the Workload Monitor.
   - The roll-out time is not part of the response time because the roll out of a user occurs only after the answer has been sent to the presentation server. Nevertheless, it is important for the performance of the mySAP.com components to keep the roll-out time to a minimum, as during the roll outs, the SAP work process remains occupied.
2. How is the term "load" defined in this book?
   - "Load" is defined in this book as the amount of load on the CPU of a computer, expressed as a percentage. It can be monitored in the Operating System Monitor (**CPU utilization**).
   - In this book "load" means the sum of response times, that is to say that the term "total load" refers to the total response time (**Response time total**), CPU load refers to the total CPU time (**CPU time total**) and database load refers to total database time (**DB time total**).
   - The term "load" in this book refers to the number of transaction steps per unit of time.
3. The Workprocess Monitor displays increased dispatcher wait times ("Av. wait time" >> 50 ms). What does this tell you?
   - There is a communication problem between the presentation servers and the dispatcher of the application server—for example, a network problem.
   - There is a general performance problem—for example, a database problem, a hardware bottleneck, or insufficient SAP extended memory; or there are too few SAP work processes. This statement does not provide enough information to pinpoint the exact problem.

- An increased dispatcher wait time is normal for a mySAP.com component. It protects the operating system from being overloaded, and can be ignored.

4 Performance Analysis for ABAP-Programs

This chapter explains how to perform a detailed performance analysis for programs and transactions you have already identified as expensive. That is, you have performed a workload analysis and consulted users, and discovered that the performance of these programs is not satisfactory.

To begin the analysis, examine the *single statistical records*, which will help give you an overview of the response times of a transaction. For more in-depth analysis use the SAP Performance Trace for detailed analysis of database accesses, RFCs and lock operations (enqueues). If, after using these methods, the problem still cannot be found, you can try with the ABAP trace and the ABAP debugger.

When should you read this chapter?

You should read this chapter if you have identified a program or a transaction as being critical for performance and now wish to make a detailed analysis of it.

Single Record Statistics

For every transaction step executed in the SAP system, a *record with statistical information* is generated and saved in files on the application servers. This statistical information includes response times, memory requirements, database accesses and so on. These records are collected hourly by the collector program `RSCOLL00` and are deleted after approximately one day (see also the section "Technical Settings for the Workload Monitor" on page 124 in Chapter 3).

From SAP Basis 4.6 on, the *statistical records* can be displayed using transaction code STAD—provided they have not been deleted. (For versions older than SAP Basis 4.6 the single statistical records can be viewed using the transaction code STAT). The single-record statistics in SAP Basis 4.6 are much more complete than in earlier versions, and as a result it is now possible to evaluate all SAP application servers (up to this it was only possible to get an overview of the server to which one was logged on). The statistical records can be grouped and evaluated according to transaction and the values displayed can be personalized. You will find further information on these options below.

1. Once you have called Transaction STAD, a dialog box appears, in which you should specify a user, transaction or program name and the period of time you wish to analyze. In the selection mask you can also establish how the single statistics will be presented. Choose between the options **Show all statistic records, sorted by start time** (standard option), **Show all records, grouped by business transaction** or **Show business transaction sums**.
2. A screen with the statistical records that match your selection criteria will then be displayed. Using the button **Sel. Fields** you can select which statistical values you wish to be displayed in the list.

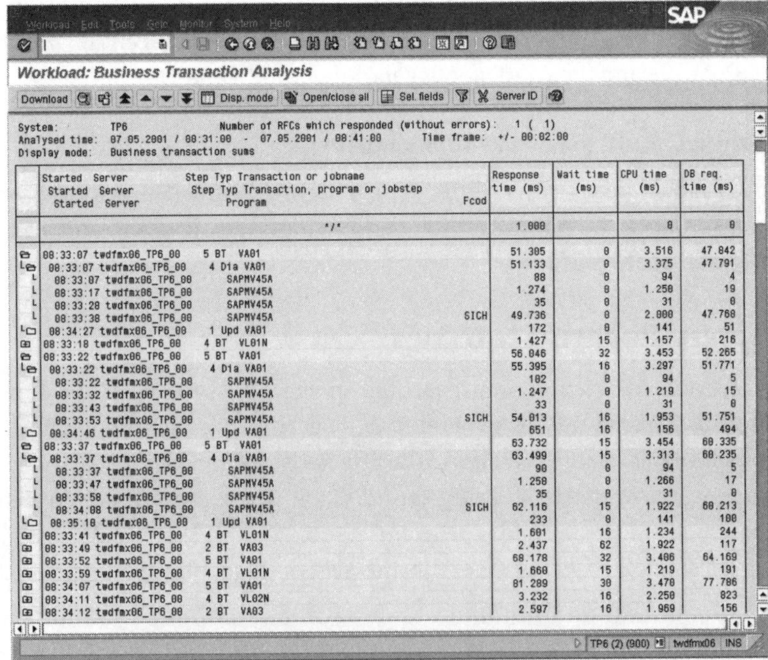

Figure 4.1 Single statistical records (in this example for transactions VA01, VL01N and so on)

Figure 4.1 shows an example of statistical records relating to a user's SD transactions. **Show business transaction sums** has been selected as the presentation mode, which means that all records belonging to one transaction are grouped together. Under Transaction VA01 you can see a sequence of four dialog steps and one update step.

The single-record statistics mean that you can identify problems that might not be visible in the average values of the transaction profile. For example, single records enable you to determine whether the response times for all transaction steps are equally high, or whether they are generally low but occasionally extremely high (in which case, the averages would be deceptively high). For example the **Fcod** column, which displays the function code within a transaction, helps to determine whether observed high response times are always associated with a particular transaction screen. In the example in Figure 4.1, the response times for the transaction are generally less than 1 second in the first three steps, but the last transaction step in the dialog task (marked with function code "SICH") displays high response times of 49 to 62 seconds. These records should be examined in greater detail.

3. To display more details on an individual record, double-click on it, choose record and choose the **All details** button, to display all details of a single record, as can be seen in the example in Figure 4.2.

The following list provides an overview of typical problems that you can recognize with the help of single-record statistics:

- High database times ususally indicate a database problem that can be analyzed using an SQL trace. Using the values for **KB transferred** (Figure 4.1) or **Database rows** (Figure 4.2), two types of database problems can be distinguished:
  - Database time is high despite the fact that relatively little data is transferred. Figure 4.2 shows a single statistic for which 47,684 ms are needed for 219 records (in the area **Sequential read**) which implies an average read time of 217.7 ms per record. According to the classification of SQL statements presented in Chapter 11, this represents an expensive SQL statement of type 2.
  - Database time is high because the quantity of data transferred is large but the data transfer speed is optimal. An optimal rate of data transfer is around 1 ms per record. This observation indicates an expensive SQL statement of type 1 according to our classification.

  For more information on the interpretation and analysis of database times and other analyses, see the section "Evaluating an SQL Trace" on page 155, and Chapter 11, "Optimizing SQL Statements".
- If you find high database times only sporadically, check individual records to see whether the message "Note: Tables were saved in the table buffer" is displayed. This entry means that tables that have been transferred from the database, have been saved in the table buffer. If the SAP system has been running for some time, with a high load since the start, all necessary tables should be located in the table buffer and

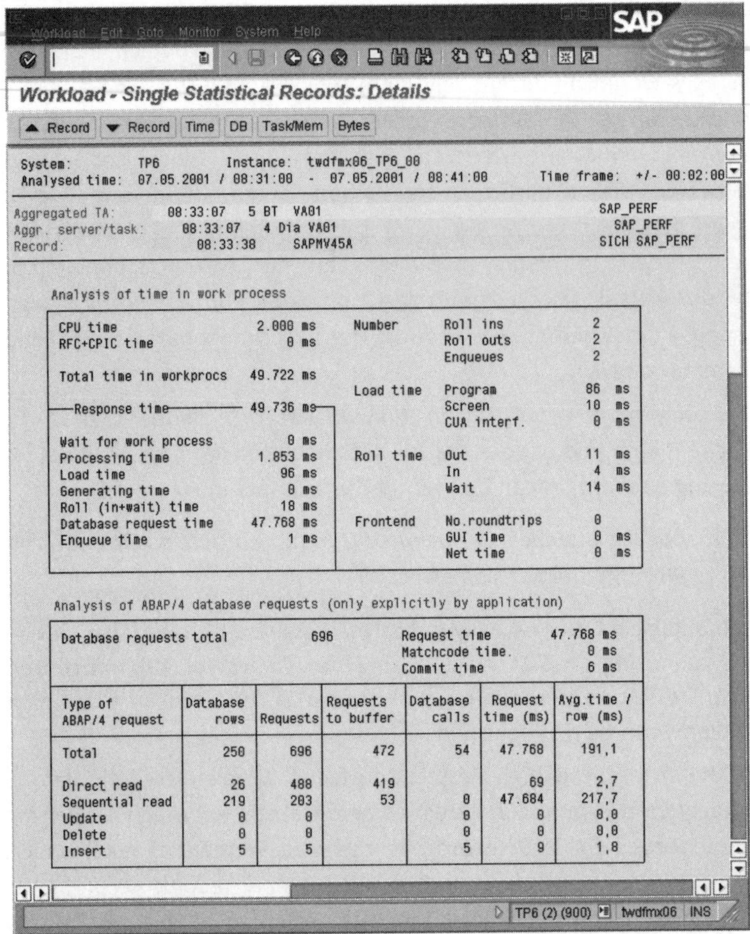

Figure 4.2 Single statistical records with a high database time due to a high read time per data record ("Avg. time / row (ms)" = 217.7 for "sequential read"). Optimal read time would be 1 msec per data record for "Sequential read".

do not have to be reloaded. If this entry occurs frequently in production operation, this indicates problems with displacements or the invalidation of table buffers. In this case, proceed with the analysis in Chapter 9, "SAP Table Buffering".

- High roll wait times and high GUI times indicate problems with communication. These problems can be analyzed with the RFC trace. We will discuss the analysis of such problems in greater detail in the section "Evaluating an RFC Trace" on page 161, and in Chapters 6 and 7, "Interfaces" and "SAP GUI and Internet Connection".

- High CPU times indicate either time consuming calculations in the ABAP coding or frequent access to table buffers. Programs with over 50% CPU time can be examined in greater detail with the ABAP trace or with the ABAP debugger.
- Other problems that can be located using single statistics include those with program buffer load procedures, SAP lock administration (enqueue) or RFC calls.

Performance Trace

Performance trace is a powerful tool for analyzing the run time of ABAP programs. This tool means that you can record the runtime for a program for the following operations: Database access, that is to say, SQL statements of a user, RFC calls (from SAP Basis 4.0), enqueue operations (from SAP Basis 4.0) and access to SAP buffer (from SAP Basis 4.5). The Performance Trace tool is developed by SAP and it is therefore identical for all database systems, even including fine details.

To enter the initial screen of Performance Trace, select

System · Resources · Performance Trace

or use transaction code ST05. On this screen you will find buttons to start, stop and evaluate Performance Trace. You also find check boxes for selecting the trace modes *SQL trace, Enqueue trace, RFC trace* and *Buffer trace*. In the default setting only the SQL trace is activated. For standard analysis we recommend that you check the SQL trace, Enqueue trace and RFC trace.

Activating a Performance Trace

You can start and stop a Performance Trace using the buttons **Trace on** and **Trace off**, which you will find in the above mentioned screen. Only one Performance Trace per application server can be created at a time. In the **State of Trace** field you can read whether or not a trace is already being processed and which user has activated the trace. When you start a trace a selection screen appears in which you can enter users for whom the trace should be activated. The name under which you have logged on is normally the user name entered here. Change the name if you wish to trace the actions of a different user. The user who activates the trace does not have to be the same user whose actions are to be traced.

The following points should be borne in mind when generating a trace:

- Ensure that the user whose actions are to be recorded only carries out one action during the trace, otherwise the trace will not be clear. You should also ensure that there are no background jobs or update requests running for this user.
- A performance trace is created in the application server. For each database operation, data is written to a trace file in the file system on the application server. You must therefore ensure that you have logged on to the same application server as the user to be monitored. This is particularly important if you want to record an update request or a background job and are working in a system with distributed updating or distributed background processing. In this case you do not know where the request will be started and as a result, you must start the trace on all application servers with update or background work processes.
- The SQL trace only displays accesses to the database. SQL statements that can be satisfied from the data in the SAP buffer do not appear in the trace. Should you wish to analyze buffer access, activate the SAP buffer trace.
- However, the buffer load processes are also recorded in the SQL trace. Since you are normally not interested in recording the buffer load process in the SQL trace, you should first execute a program once without activating the trace to allow the buffers to be loaded (that is, the SAP buffers and database buffers). Then run the program again with the SQL trace activated and use the results of this trace for evaluation.
- During the trace, look at the following monitors: the Work Process Overview (for general monitoring), the Operating System Monitor of the database server (for monitoring possible CPU bottlenecks on the database server) and the Database Process Monitor for direct monitoring of the executed SQL statements. It makes no sense to look at these monitors during the trace if you are logged on as the user being traced. The SQL statement of the monitors would appear in the trace.
- The default trace filename is set with the SAP profile parameter **rstr/file**. In the initial screen you can assign a different name to the trace file. Writing to the trace file is cyclical in the sense that, when it is full, the oldest entries are deleted to make room for new entries. The size of the trace file in bytes is specified by the SAP profile parameter **rstr/max_diskspace**, for which the default value is 16,384,000 bytes (16 MB).

Evaluating an SQL Trace

To evaluate a performance trace, in the trace initial screen select **List trace**. A dialog box is displayed and in the **Trace Mode** field you can specify which part of the trace you wish to analyze. In this section and subsequent ones we will first discuss the evaluation of an SQL trace, followed by those of an RFC trace and of an Enqueue trace respectively. (In practice, you can of course analyze all three trace modes together.) Table 4.1 lists other fields that you can use to restrict the analysis of the SQL trace.

Field	Explanation
Trace Filename	Name of the trace file. Normally this name should not be changed.
Trace Mode	The default trace mode setting is SQL trace. To analyze an RFC trace or Enqueue trace, activate the corresponding check boxes.
Trace Period	Period in which the trace runs
Username	The user whose actions have been traced
Objectname	The names of specific tables to which the display of trace results is to be restricted. Note that by default, the tables D010*, D020*, and DDLOG are not shown in the trace results, as these tables contain the ABAP code of the program being traced and the buffer synchronization data.
Duration	This field is used to restrict the display to SQL statements having a certain execution time.
Operation	This field is used to restrict the trace data to particular database operations.

Table 4.1 Fields in the dialog box for evaluating a trace

Then choose the **Execute** button. The Basic SQL trace list is displayed. Figure 4.3 shows an example of a basic trace list; Table 4.2 explains the columns displayed in an SQL trace.

Field	Explanation
Duration	Runtime of an SQL statement, in microseconds. If the runtime is more than 150,000 ms, the corresponding row is colored red to identify that SQL statement as having a "long runtime". However the value 150,000 is a somewhat arbitrary boundary.
Object	The name of the database table or database view

Table 4.2 Columns in an SQL trace. The last three columns are displayed only if you select the button More Info.

Field	Explanation
Oper	The operation executed on the database, for example "Prepare: preparation ("parsing") of a statement, Open: open a database cursor, Fetch: Transfer of data from the database and so on.
Rec	The number of records read from the database
RC	Database-specific return code
Statement	Short form of the executed SQL statement. The complete statement can be displayed by double clicking the corresponding row.
hh:mm:ss.ms	Time stamp in the form *hour: minute: second: millisecond*
Program	Name of the program from which the SQL statement originates.
Curs	Database cursor number

Table 4.2 Columns in an SQL trace. The last three columns are displayed only if you select the button More Info. (contd.)

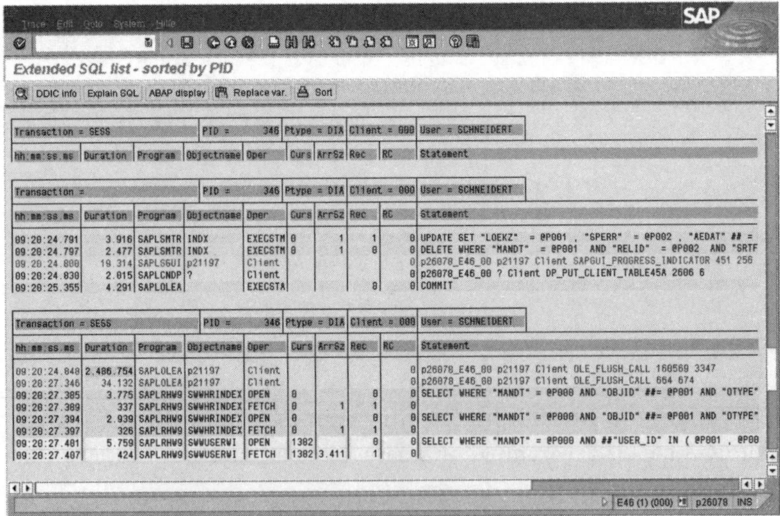

Figure 4.3 Basic performance trace list with entries from the SQL trace and the RFC trace

Direct read One SQL statement that appears in Figure 4.3 accesses the table SWWHRINDEX. The fields specified in the WHERE clause are key fields in the table. The result of the request can therefore only be either one record (Rec = 1) or no record (Rec = 0), depending on whether a table entry exists for the specified key or not. SQL statements that use the "equals" (=) sign to specify all key fields of the respective table are called *fully qualified accesses* or *direct reads*. A fully qualified database access should normally not last longer than 2–10 ms. However, in individual cases, an access may last up to 10 times longer, for example, when blocks cannot be found in the database buffer and must be retrieved from the hard disk.

The database access consists of two *database operations*, one **OPEN/REOPEN** operation and one **FETCH** operation. The Reopen operation transfers the concrete values in the **WHERE** clause to the database. The Fetch operation locates the database data and transfers it to the application server.

Sequential read

A second object accessed in Figure 4.3 is table SWWUSERWI. With this access not all key fields in the **WHERE** clause are clearly specified. As a result, multiple records can be transferred. However, in our example only 1 record was transferred (Rec = 1). The data records are transferred to the application server in packets, in one or more **FETCHES** (*array fetch*). An array fetch offers better performance than transferring individual records in a client/server environment.

The maximum number of records that can be transferred in a **FETCH** operation is determined by the SAP database interface as follows: Every SAP work process has an input/output buffer for transferring data to or from the database. The size of this buffer is specified by the SAP profile parameter **dbs/io_buf_size**. The number of records transferred from the database by a **FETCH** is calculated as follows:

Number of records = dbs/io_buf_size ÷ length of one record in bytes.

The number of records per **FETCH** depends on the **SELECT** clause of the SQL statement. If the number of fields to be transferred from the database is restricted through a **SELECT** clause, more records fit into in a single **FETCH** than when a "SELECT *" is used. The default value for the SAP profile parameter **dbs/io_buf_size** is 33,792 (Bytes) and should not be changed unless recommended by SAP.

Guideline response times for optimal array fetches are under 10 ms per selected record. The actual runtime depends strongly on the **WHERE** clause, the index used and how well the data is stored.

Changes

Two operations in Figure 4.3 show how changes have been made to the INDX table, with the help of **EXECSTM** operations.

Declare, Prepare, Open

Other database operations that may be listed in the SQL trace are **Declare, Prepare** and **Open**. The **Declare** operation defines what is known as a *cursor*, to manage the data transfer between ABAP programs and a database and also assigns an ID number to the cursor. This cursor ID is used for communication between SAP work processes and the database system.

In the subsequent *prepare* operation, the database process determines the access strategy for the statement. In the **Statement** column, instead of the correct values of the **WHERE** clause, a variable is indicated (**INSTANCE** =:A0, not shown in Figure 4.3). **PREPARE** operations can be time consuming. To reduce the need for them, each work process of an application server retains a certain number of already parsed SQL statements in a special buffer (SAP cursor cache). Each SAP work process buffers the operations **Declare**, **Prepare**, **Open** and **Exec** in its SAP cursor cache. Once the work process has defined a cursor for a **DECLARE** operation, the same cursor can be used repeatedly until, after a certain time, it is displaced from the SAP cursor cache due to the limited size of the latter.

The database does not receive the concrete values of the **WHERE** clause (for example Mandt ="100" etc) until the **Open** operation is used. A **Prepare** operation is only necessary for the first execution of a statement, as long as that statement has not been displaced from the SAP cursor cache. Subsequently, the statement, which has already been prepared (parsed), can always be re-accessed with an **Open** or **Reopen**.

Figure 4.3 shows the SQL trace for the second run of the same report. Given that the **Declare, Prepare** and **Open** operations are executed only in the first run of a report, in our example only the **Open** operation can be seen.

Network problems

If, through an SQL trace, you identify an SQL statement with a long runtime, you should perform a second and third SQL trace to deepen your analysis. It is useful to perform the trace at a time of high system load and again at a time of low system load. If you find that the response times for database accesses are high only at particular times, this indicates throughput problems in the network or in database access (for example an I/O bottleneck). If, on the other hand, the response times for database access are poor in general (not only at particular times), the cause is probably an inefficient SQL statement, which should be optimized.

When evaluating database response times, remember that the processing times of SQL statements are measured on the application server. The runtime shown in the trace comprises not only the time required by the database to furnish the requested data, but also the time required to transfer data between the database and the application server. If there is a performance problem in network communication, the runtimes of SQL statements increase.

Network problems between the database and the application server may best be recognized by comparing traces as follows: Execute the same SQL trace at least twice; once on the application server that is on the same computer as the database and directly connected to the database, and once on an application server that is connected to the database through the TCP/IP network. Compare both SQL traces. If there are significantly higher response times (greater by 50% or more) on the application server connected through the network, you have a network problem. Perform this test at a time of low system load, and repeat it several times to rule out runtime differences due to the buffer load process on the database and the application servers. This test functions only when your application server is connected to the database through IPC.

Other Tools in the SQL Trace

Summary

Using the **Summary** function of the SQL trace you can get an overview of the most expensive SQL accesses:

Goto · Summary · Compress

A list appears, which displays the columns explained in Table 4.3 for every table. Sort the list according to the runtime of the SQL statements. The SQL statements with the longest runtimes should be optimized first.

Field	Explanation
SQL op	Database operation: Select, Update, Insert or Delete
Accesses	Number of accesses per table
Records	Number of records read per table
Time	Runtime per table in ms
Percent	Runtime per table in percent

Table 4.3 Fields in the compressed summary of an SQL trace

Identical selects

Programs that reduce performance often read identical data from the database several times in succession. To identify these identical SQL statements, the SQL trace offers the following functions:

Goto · Identical selects

A list of identical selects is displayed that tells you how often each identical select was executed. By using this function in conjunction with the compressed data, you can see roughly how much of an improvement in performance you stand to gain by optimizing the programming for identical SQL statements.

Other functions

After this preliminary evaluation using the SQL trace, you have all information necessary for a more detailed analysis:

- *Program name and transaction code* of the executed program.
  Using the **ABAP Display** button in the trace list you can jump directly to the code location that executes the SQL statement.
- *Table name.* The **DDIC Info** button gives a summary of the most important dictionary information for this table.
- *WHERE clause* in the SQL statement
- Detailed analysis of the SQL statement—for example using the *explain* function.

  For more information on these functions, see Chapter 11.

For customer-developed ABAP programs, perform at least the following checks as a form of program quality control:

1. For each customer-developed ABAP program, perform an SQL trace either on the production system or on a system with a representative volume of test data.
2. From the basic trace list display, create a compressed summary to find the SQL statements with the longest runtimes:

   Goto · Summary · Compress
3. Display a list of identical accesses to find SQL statements that are executed several times in succession.

   Goto · Identical selects
4. Use these lists to decide whether the program should be approved or whether it needs to be improved by the responsible ABAP developer.
5. Save a copy of the lists together with the program documentation. If program performance later diminishes (whether due to a modification or due to the growing data volume), perform a further SQL trace and compare it to the earlier one. Monitor performance in this way after each significant program modification.

These measures can be used not only to monitor customer-developed programs, but also to regularly monitor frequently used standard SAP transactions that are critical for performance. If the runtime of particular SQL statements grows over time, you may need to archive the corresponding table.

Evaluating an RFC Trace

Table 4.4 lists the columns displayed in an RFC trace.

Field	Explanation
Duration	RFC runtime in microseconds.
Object	Name of the recipient, for example, the SAP instance called
Oper	If "Client" is entered: RFC sent, this means that the instance on which the trace is executed is the Client (sender); If "Server" is entered: RFC received, this means that the instance on which the trace is executed is the Server (recipient)
Rec	Not used
RC	Return code (for successful execution: 0)
Statement	Additional information on the RFC, including the name of sender and recipient, name of the RFC module and amount of data transferred. You can view all information on the RFC by double-clicking on the corresponding row in the RFC trace.
hh:mm:ss.ms	Time stamp in the form *hour: minute: second: millisecond*
Program	Name of the program from which the RFC originates.
Curs	Not used

Table 4.4 Fields in an RFC trace. The last three fields are only displayed if you select the button More Info or Extended List.

As with the SQL trace, different detail analysis functions are available with the RFC trace:

- By double-clicking on a row in the RFC trace or using the **Details** button you can view the complete information on the RFC, including the name and IP addresses of the sender and recipient, the name of the RFC module and the amount of data transferred.
- Using the **ABAP Display** button you can view the source text of the corresponding ABAP program.

Evaluating Enqueue Traces

Table 4.5 contains the fields that are displayed in an RFC trace and explains their meaning. You can find more detailed explanations on the SAP enqueue concept in Chapter 10, "Locks".

Field	Explanation
Duration	Runtime of the enqueue/dequeue statement in microseconds
Object	Name of the enqueue object. To see details on the object, call the ABAP dictionary (using transaction code SE12) and enter the object name in the field under **lock objects**. To view the features of the objects, select **Display**.
Oper	**ENQUEUE** operation: Enqueue(s) set. **DEQUEUE** operation: Individual enqueues are released. **DEQ ALL** operation with specific object entry in the **Object** column: All enqueues for the object in question are released. **DEQ ALL** operation with no object entry in the **Object** column (entry "{{{{{{{{{"): All enqueues for the transaction in question are released (end of a transaction).
Oper	**ENQPERM** operation: At the end of the dialog part of a transaction, enqueues are passed on to update management.
Rec	Number of enqueues that are set or released
RC	Return code (for successful execution: 0)
Statement	More detailed information on the enqueue: Enter "Excl" or "Shared": Exclusive or "shared" locks; name of locked unit, (such as "MARC 900SD000002": In table MARC, in client 900, material SD000002 is locked). The entries in this row correspond with the features of the enqueue object defined in the ABAP dictionary (see above)
hh:mm:ss.ms	Time stamp in the form *hour: minute: second: millisecond*
Program	Name of the program from which the SQL statement originates.
Curs	Not used

Table 4.5 Fields in an SQL trace. The last three columns are only displayed if you select the button More Info.

Performance Analysis With ABAP Trace (Runtime Analysis)

You should use an ABAP trace when the runtime of the programs to be analyzed comprises mainly CPU time. An ABAP trace measures not only the runtime of database accesses (**SELECT, EXEC SQL** and so on), but also the time required by individual modularization units (such as **MODULE,**

PERFORM, CALL FUNCTION, SUBMIT), internal table operations (**APPEND, COLLECT, SORT, READ TABLE**) and by other ABAP statements.

The functions and ergonomics of runtime analysis are significantly expanded in SAP Basis 4.6.

Activating an ABAP Trace

1. Use the following menu path to access the initial screen of the ABAP trace:

   System · Resources · Runtime analysis · Execute

   or select transaction code SE30.
2. In the upper part of the screen, under **Measure**, enter a transaction code, a program name or a function module and select **Execute** to start the measuring process.
3. The system starts to measure the runtime and creates a file with the resulting measurement data.
4. When you wish to return to the initial runtime analysis screen, simply exit the program, function module or transaction in the normal way or start the runtime analysis again. The initial screen for runtime analysis shows the newly created **measurement data file** in the lower part of the screen.

When activating an ABAP trace, you can use filter functions which enable you to restrict the trace to a particular function module or a particular group of ABAP statements or to adjust an aggregation. In the section "Using Function Variations" on page 165 we will explain how to use these options.

When you activate an ABAP trace you should bear the following points in mind, which are similar to those that apply to an SQL trace:

- Since you are normally not interested in recording the buffer load process in the trace, you should first execute a program once without activating the trace to allow the buffers to be loaded (that is, the SAP buffers and database buffers). Then run the program again with the ABAP trace activated and use the results of this trace for evaluation.
- Perform the trace at a time of high system load and again at a time of low system load. Ensure that the measured times are not influenced by a temporary system overload (for example, a CPU overload).

To enable you to perform runtime analysis, the system requires the SAP profile parameters **abap/atrapath** and **abap/atrasizequota**. These parameters are set when the system is installed. For more information on these parameters, see the parameter documentation in Transaction RZ11.

Evaluating an ABAP Trace

To display the results of an analysis, select the desired file. In the initial screen of the runtime analysis, select the **Analyze** button to display an overview of the analysis. There are different views of the results, which the runtime analysis presents in the form of lists:

- Using the **Hit list** button you can view a list which displays the execution time in microseconds for each statement. This list is sorted in decreasing order of the gross times.
- The **hierarchy** is a chronological procedure of your transaction or program.
- Other buttons will display specific analyses which, for example, categorize database tables or modularization units.

If you have generated an ABAP trace, first of all display the hit list. Sort the hit list according to net time, to get an overview of statements with the highest net runtimes.

gross and net time

The runtime analysis establishes the gross and/or net times of individual program calls in microseconds. Gross time is the total time required for the call. This includes the times of all modularization units and ABAP/4 statements in this call. The net time is the gross time minus the time required for the called modularization units (**MODULE, PERFORM, CALL FUNCTION, CALL SCREEN, CALL TRANSACTION, CALL DIALOG, SUBMIT**) and separately specified ABAP statements. For "elementary" statements such as **APPEND** or **SORT** the gross time is the same as the net time. If the gross and net times for a call differ from one another, this call contains other calls or modularization units. If, for example, a subroutine shows a gross time of 100,000 ms and a net time of 80,000 ms, this means that 20,000 ms are used for calling the routine itself and 80,000 ms for assigning further statements to the routine.

The runtime analysis involves a lot of work, that is to say, generating the analysis can as much as double the runtime of a program (compared to a program run without runtime analysis activated). The runtime analysis takes this into account and displays correspondingly adjusted runtimes in the lists. However if you look at the statistical record created while the runtime analysis was active, you will see that in comparison to a program run without runtime analysis, it is clearly distorted. (In comparison, letting a performance trace run simultaneously does not involve much extra load; experience shows that the additional load is less than 5%).

Using Function Variations

The ABAP trace function offers variants with which you can adjust how the trace is carried out. It is particularly advisable to try out such options when analyzing a complex program, because data quantities of several MB can be generated very quickly, much of which is often completely irrelevant to the analysis. Using variants you can determine more precisely what it is that you want to analyze.

The currently selected variants can be seen in the initial screen of the runtime analysis in the screen section **measurement restrictions**. Two variants are already set in the system; **DEFAULT** and **TMP**. You can save your personal settings as your own variant.

The button **Display variants** or **Change variants** brings you to the screen in which you can enter the settings for a variant:

- On the tab page **Program parts** you can set which parts of the program you wish to analyze. Entries in the table enable you to limit the trace to selected function modules, form routines and other modularizing units.
- The settings in the **Statements** tab page determine which operations will be monitored in the runtime analysis. Tip: If you wish to analyze operations on internal tables such as **Append**, **Loop** or **Sort**, you should activate the check boxes **Read operations** and **Change operations** under **Int. Tables**. These settings are not activated in the default variant.
- In the **Duration + type** tab page, among other things, you can set the type of aggregation. Aggregation is always relevant when a statement is called numerous times in a program. We could use an SQL statement within a loop as an example. If aggregation is not activated, an entry will be written to the trace measurement file for each time the SQL statement is called. If aggregation is activated, only one entry will be recorded in which the runtimes for each execution are added together. On the tab page **Duration + type** you are offered three options:
  - **No aggregation**
    An entry is written to the measurement file each time the statement is called.

- **Full aggregation**
  The runtimes for individual executions of a statement are added together in one entry; thus, one entry is written to the measurement file for each statement.
- **Aggregation according to call location**
  The runtimes for individual executions of a statement are added together in one entry. However, if a statement appears several times in a program at several locations in the program text, one entry is written for each time it appears in the program text.

In general, activating aggregation dramatically reduces the size of the measurement file and in many cases an analysis of long program flows is only possible with aggregation. When you use aggregation, the hierarchy list is lost and is therefore no longer available for evaluation. In SAP Basis 4.6C full aggregation is set as default.

How should you carry out an analysis of more complex programs? We recommend that first of all you carry out an analysis of the entire program with aggregation and without analyzing operations on internal tables, as set in the default variant. The objective of this analysis is to find the modularization units with the highest runtimes. After this initial analysis, sort the hit list according to net times and identify the modularization units or statements with high runtime.

If you cannot deduce recommendations for optimizing the program from this first analysis, proceed to perform a more detailed analysis, setting variants to limit the analysis to these modularization units. Simultaneously, activate the trace for operations from internal tables and deactivate the aggregation.

Performance Analysis With the ABAP-Debugger

Apart from expensive SQL statements, one of the most important causes of performance problems are internal tables with many entries. Large internal tables consume large amounts of memory and CPU, for example during copy, sort or search operations.

The ABAP debugger can show a list of all internal tables built by a particular program. The ABAP debugger is actually a tool for performing functional troubleshooting in programs. More detailed descriptions of the debugger can be found in SAP literature on ABAP programming. "Performance analysis" using the ABAP debugger is not a standard procedure and is best performed by an ABAP developer.

The following advice should be taken into account when working with the ABAP debugger: When working with the ABAP debugger, the ABAP program being debugged may terminate and display the error message "Invalid interruption of a database selection" or the system may automatically trigger a database commit. In both cases, an SAP logical unit of work (LUW) has been interrupted, which may lead to inconsistencies in the application tables. Therefore, you should only debug on a test system or in the presence of someone who is very familiar with the program being analyzed and who can manually correct the inconsistencies in the database tables if necessary. See "Debugging Programs in the Production Client" in SAP Online help for the ABAP debugger.

- Begin performance analysis with the debugger by starting the program to be analyzed. Then open a second session where you can monitor the program to be analyzed in the Work Process Overview (transaction code SM50). Enter the debugger from the Work Process Overview by choosing **Debugging**. By using the debugger several times in succession, you can identify the parts of the program that cause a large CPU consumption. Often these sections consist of **LOOP ... ENDLOOP** statements affecting large internal tables.
- To display the current memory requirements, from the menu, choose:

  Goto · Other screens · Memory use

  Check for cases of unnecessary memory consumption that may have been caused by a nonoptimal program or nonoptimal use of a program. As a guideline value, bear in mind that a program being used by several users in dialog mode should not allocate more than 100 MB. Background programs (for example, billing runs at night on a dedicated application server) should not require more than 1 GB. With the current 32-bit architecture, program termination typically results when 1 GB to 3 GB of memory are required.
- To create a list of the internal tables of the program in the debugger, first choose

  Goto · System · System areas

  and in the area field, enter **ITAB**. The **FILL** column shows the number of rows in the respective table. To calculate the memory requirements for the listed tables, multiply the number of rows by the width of the header line (indicated in the **Leng** column).

Experience shows that there are two common programming errors that cause large memory or CPU requirements for programs:

- Missing **REFRESH** or **FREE** statements: The ABAP statements **REFRESH** and **FREE** delete internal tables and release the memory that was allocated to them. If these statements are missing, memory resources may be unnecessarily tied up.
- Reading in internal tables: The ABAP statement **READ TABLE ... WITH KEY ...** means that it is possible to search in internal tables. If you use this statement by itself for a standard table, the search is sequential. For large tables, this is a time-consuming process. You can significantly improve search performance by adding the statement **... BINARY SEARCH** thus specifying a binary search. However, the table must also be sorted (see ABAP help on the statement **READ TABLE**).
- As of SAP Basis 4.0, you can optimize the performance of operations on large tables by using sorted tables (through the **SORTED TABLE** statement) or hash tables (through the **HASHED TABLE** statement).

Further information is available on SAP online help for the ABAP programming environment.

Summary

The following monitors allow a detailed analysis of individual ABAP programs.

Analyzing *single statistical records* lets you narrow down the causes of the performance problems of individual programs to one of the following problem areas:

- Problems due to inefficient table buffering
- Problems due to expensive SQL statements
- Problems due to high CPU consumption

The *SQL-Trace* is the recommended tool for analyzing expensive SQL statements in ABAP programs. Evaluating the trace enables you to identify network problems or throughput bottlenecks in the database. You will find further information on optimizing SQL statements in Chapter 11.

The RFC trace can be used to analyze the performance of sent and received RFCs. For further information on this subject, see Chapters 6 and 7, "Interfaces" and "SAP GUI and Internet Connection".

The Enqueue trace is the means of selecting analyses of lock operations (Enqueue/Dequeue operations). You will find further information in Chapter 10, "Locks".

For problems of high CPU consumption, use the *ABAP trace*. In contrast to the SQL trace, this enables time measurements for operations on internal tables such as **LOOP**, **READ**, and **SORT**. Alternatively, CPU-consuming programs can be monitored using the *ABAP debugger*, which can be called up from the Work Process Overview. This form of analysis should only be performed by ABAP developers.

Figure 4.4 summarizes the procedure for analyzing a single program or transaction.

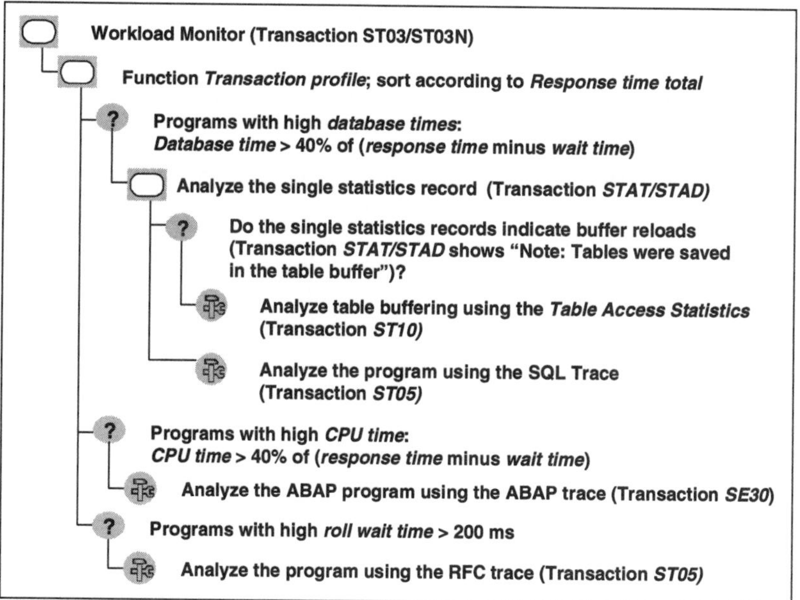

Figure 4.4 Performance analysis procedure for an ABAP program

Questions

1. What do you have to consider when you perform an SQL trace?
   a) There is only one trace file for each SAP system. Therefore, only one SQL trace can be performed per SAP system.
   b) The user whose operations are being traced should not run multiple programs concurrently.
   c) You should perform the SQL trace on a second execution of the program because the relevant buffers are then already loaded.
   d) SQL traces are useful on the database server, but not on application servers, which yield inexact results due to network times.
2. When should you perform an ABAP trace?
   a) You should perform an ABAP trace if a problem occurs with the table buffer.
   b) An ABAP trace should be performed for programs with high CPU requirements.
   c) An ABAP trace is useful for analyzing I/O problems on hard disks.

5 Workload Distribution

To achieve optimal performance it is necessary to distribute the SAP system load across the CPU resources of all available servers. This helps the CPU resources to cope with the demands on the system—for example, with the number of users and user activities, as well as with the number of background programs. In addition to improving performance, optimizing workload distribution also protects performance critical processes and gives these processes priority in accessing resources.

The sections in this chapter describe how to use the tools for optimizing workload distribution and explain the relationship between the expected demands on the mySAP.com solution, the logical services and the demands they will make on physical resources.

Driven by the quickly developing hardware market—at the time this book goes to press, hardware partners for SAP installations offer servers with up to 128 processors and 128 GB of main memory—many projects now involve installing several SAP systems on one server. We shall examine the trend known as *server consolidation* in this respect. You will also find information on SAP Standard Application Benchmarks in this chapter.

When should you read this chapter?

You should read this chapter if you want detailed suggestions for optimizing workload distribution within the SAP system.

SAP Services

An important task of an SAP system is the creation and processing of business documents, such as sales orders or financial documents. There are four ways to differentiate how documents should be found and/or processed in the system:

- **Processing by dialog (or online) users**
  Users logged on to the SAP system create or process documents in dialog mode. An example of this type of processing is a call center, where employees take orders from customers over the telephone and enter them directly into the system.
- **Processing by background programs**
  With this type of processing, documents are created or processed by programs which work without continuous communication with dialog users (hence the term "background"). In this way, for example, with

the multiple processing of delivery notes, all existing sales orders are analyzed and deliveries are automatically created for these orders within the specified time. A second example of a background program is automatic salary calculation, based on personal master data stored on the system and time data entered by employees. Background processing is therefore characterized by the fact that the corresponding program reads data that is already in the system and uses this information to create new documents (in our examples, delivery notes and pay slips).

- **Background input processing (batch input)**
  In many cases the data needed for the SAP system to create documents is already in electronic form, for example as existing files. It would make absolutely no sense for dialog users to manually enter this data again. Rather, with the SAP system you can import this data into the system using interface programs that run in the background. This type of processing is also referred to as *batch input* and is a special type of background processing. It is often used as a communication interface between the SAP system and external DP systems. Let us take the example of a project in which sales orders are created and saved in decentralized computers with local software. When required, these computers send their orders in a file to a central office, where they are imported into the SAP system in "batch input".

- **Processing using interfaces**
  An SAP system can not only communicate with another IT system indirectly via files, as described above; there can also be direct data exchange. This takes place via *Remote Function Calls* (RFCs). RFCs can be exchanged between SAP systems but also between an SAP system and an external system, once the external system is RFC enabled. With this type of processing an external DP system can transfer data into the SAP system and remotely execute a program in the SAP system and vice versa. With RFCs, for example, a warehouse management system can be linked to the SAP system. The SAP system creates the transfer orders for stock movements and sends this transfer order to an external system via RFC. Once the warehouse management system has carried out the transfer order, it executes a transaction by RFC to inform the SAP system of the movement of goods.

The SAP basis system provides logical services for processing the ensuing workload: dialog service, background service, update service, spool service, dispatcher service, enqueue service, ATP service, gateway service and message service. Only the dialog service and background service can be directly accessed by the SAP user. All other services are accessed by these two as required. These services are carried out by what are known as *work processes*, which correspond to operating system processes (with a Windows operating system they are known as *threads*) (Note: Gateway service and Message service are always separate processes).

The services listed in Table 5.1 exist on the application level of an SAP Basis system.

Service	Number of processes per SAP system	Number of processes per SAP application instance
Message	1	0 or 1
Enqueue	≥ 1	0 or ≥ 1
Dialog	≥ 2; ≥ the sum of non-dialog WPs	≥ 2
update (U1 and U2)	≥ 1	≥ 0
Batch	≥ 1	≥ 0
Spool	≥ 1	SAP Basis 3.1: 0 or 1 SAP basis 4.0 and higher: ≥ 0
Dispatcher	1 per SAP application instance	1
Gateway	1 per application server	1

Table 5.1 Rules for the type and number of SAP processes on the application level

Message service and enqueue service

Within an SAP Basis system there is one *Message Server*, located on one computer of the SAP Basis system. The message server is a logical unit; it controls communication between the different instances of an SAP Basis system and places free process resources on the SAP instance level.

The *enqueue service* manages the SAP locks (*SAP enqueues*). It is provided by one SAP instance. The instance containing the enqueue service is often called the *Enqueue Server*. Since the release of R/3 4.0, the *availability check using ATP logic* can be executed centrally on just one SAP instance. This instance is known as the *ATP server*. An SAP instance can fulfill several functions. An instance can be a message, enqueue and an ATP server all at the same time. You will find further details on SAP enqueues and the ATP server in Chapter 10.

Dialog, update, background, spool

Similar to the enqueue service, *dialog, update, background* and *spool services* are provided by one or several SAP work processes. Dialog, update, background and spool service can be distributed over several SAP instances. If update or background processing takes place on only one SAP instance, this is referred to as central update or background processing. If they are located on more than one SAP instance, we speak of distributed update or background processing. The service provided by each SAP work process is determined by the *dispatcher* of the corresponding SAP instance. The dispatcher is a selected process that coordinates the work of the other work processes, and hence, the services they offer. Each SAP instance has exactly one dispatcher. The dispatcher coordinates the work done within each SAP instance, while the message server manages communication between the SAP instances.

SAP services and hardware landscape

How should the *SAP services* be represented in a *hardware landscape*? In a *central installation* the database instance and all SAP services (in particular message, enqueue, dialog, update, background and spool services) are configured on a single computer. This type of installation is typically found in development, testing and small production systems (with up to around 100 active users).

In a *distributed installation* the services are distributed over several servers. The following sections describe how this should be done as regards the *high availability* of the SAP system and as regards performance.

The Workload Monitor (transaction code ST03N or ST03), the Logon groups Monitor (transaction code SMLG) and the Work Process Overview (transaction code SM66 or SM50) are the tools available for monitoring workload distribution. In the sections "Analyzing SAP Work Processes" on page 107 (Chapter 2), and "Analyzing General Performance Problems" on page 132 (Chapter 3) you will find a description of the analyses you can use to check whether or not the work load is optimally distributed over the system. If you find a bottleneck in the distribution of workload, redistributing work processes can be an effective means of solving the problem. In the following sections you will find detailed recommendations for distributing work processes.

Distributing Message, Enqueue and ATP Services

Message, *enqueue* and *ATP services* work together closely. For reasons of performance, they should always be run on the same instance. The corresponding SAP profile parameters are:

- **rdisp/mshost:** <Server>
- **rdisp/enqname:** <Server>_<Instance>_<Nr>
- **rdisp/atp_server:** <Server>_<Instance>_<Nr>

From the point of view of *system availability* (*High Availability*) the critical points in an SAP system are the message, enqueue and ATP services and the database instance (called "single points of failure" or SPOFs). In general, these services cannot be distributed over several servers. If a server with one of these services goes down, then the entire SAP system goes down. Therefore, mainly for reasons of availability, the database instance and the central SAP instance (with message, enqueue and ATP service) should be operated on the same computer and should be specially protected by a *Failover solution*, of the kind offered by almost all hardware providers. For large installations, however, the database instance and the central SAP instance should be configured on separate servers for reasons of performance.

If you use the *ATP server* (from SAP R/3 4.0) or the *locking with quantity* (from SAP R/3 3.0) in the availability check, you should configure at least five dialog work processes on the enqueue server, even if there are no dialog users working on this server. More detailed information on locking with quantities and the ATP server can be found in Chapter 10 in the section "ATP Server" on page 325.

Distributing Dialog, Background and Spool Work Processes

In a distributed SAP system, *dialog*, *background* and *spool services* are distributed to the application server. In practice, the error is frequently made that although the dialog work processes are configured on separate application servers, the background work processes are kept on the database server. The following observations explain why you should not run background work processes on the database server:

- Experience shows that the load generated by background programs can fluctuate greatly from one time to another (for example, because of background programs that run on particular days or that run at the close of the month). This may result in a temporary CPU bottleneck on the database server if several background programs are started at the same time. By distributing the background work processes on the application server these high load peaks can be controlled more easily.

- Dialog and background load often complement each other, which means that dialog work load is usually heaviest during the day while background load should be scheduled to run over night. In this way, an application server, on which dialog work processes are configured, remains unused at times of low dialog load, while at the same time there may be a CPU bottleneck caused by background programs running parallel to each other.
- System administrators sometimes find that background programs run a lot faster on the database server than on the application server which is occasionally said to be only half as fast or less. However, this is not a valid argument for leaving background work processes on the database server. Rather this points to a network problem between the database and application servers, which must be resolved. (The problems with the TCP/IP connection between SAP instances and an Oracle database, as described in SAP Notes 72638 and 31514 are one example of this.)

Distributing Users and Work Processes Over CPU Resources

How many work processes should be configured in an SAP system and how should they be distributed over the application servers? Two ratios are relevant here:

- *Number of users / number of dialog work processes*
- *Number of work processes / number of processors*

The first ratio is calculated from the *think time* and the *response time*:

> *Number of users / number of dialog work processes = (think time + response time) / response time.*

The *response time* is the average time that the SAP system requires to process a user request. The *think time* is the time one user takes to enter data to the presentation server and to interpret it—pauses by the user are also included. It is difficult to provide a general rule for these activities. They depend on the user's activities, the SAP applications and modules installed, the SAP release and the CPU type (that is to say, the power of the processors installed), which all vary from on SAP system to another.

Please note that in this formula, response time to the presentation server is included. In the Workload Monitor, however, we measure response time of the application server. The difference between these times is the network time that is needed for transferring data between the application server and the presentation server. This network time should be low (< 10% of the response time of the application server).

The optimal ratio of *number of work processes / number of processors* should also be determined for each SAP system individually. There is no one general guideline value valid for all SAP systems. The ratio of the *number of work processes / number of processors* is determined from the *Response time* and the *CPU time*:

Number of work processes / number of processors = response time / CPU time

In a certain system, if one assumes that the CPU time should be at least 20%, or one fifth, of the response time, then a maximum of five work processes should be configured per CPU.

Dispatcher wait time

What favours the configuration of more or fewer work processes? The argument for a high number of work processes is obvious: If users have to wait in the SAP dispatcher queue for work processes, then the temptation to make more work processes available is strong, in the hope that in doing so more users can work at the same time. This is the case if work processes are being blocked by wait situations, which actually incur no CPU load, for example, when work processes are running in PRIV-Mode or are often blocked by lock situations on the database. On the other hand, "pumping up" the number of work processes may help little if resources are scarce at some lower level. Adding more work processes only eases the symptoms, but generally does not really resolve the performance problem.

Having too few SAP work processes leads to *dispatcher wait times*, which are indicated in the Workload Monitor. However, the reverse does not apply: A dispatcher wait time does not automatically mean that there are too few work processes. A comprehensive bottleneck analysis must first be carried out to find out if other performance problems are blocking the work processes.

CPU wait time

A high number of SAP work processes makes it possible to process many user requests at the same time. If the number of processes that you wish to work on simultaneously is significantly higher than the number of processors, then this causes wait situations in the operating system queue. Because work processes receive CPU time more or less simultaneously (or, to be more precise, in time slices), the number of context switches on the operating-system level increases with the number of work processes. (*Please note:* Here we are talking about the rotation of process contexts in the processor, from one SAP work process to the next. This should not be confused with the SAP context switching, that is to say, the roll in and roll out of user context in SAP work processes.) Each context switch increases the load on the operating system by consuming processor time and memory for context information. However, waiting in the SAP dispatcher queue does not use up any CPU resources. Taking all of this into consideration, we can see that if all available CPU resources are in use, it is better to tolerate dispatcher wait times and let user requests be processed by fewer work processes, than to burden the operating system with too many work processes and the numerous context switches that this would involve. Benchmark measurements in fact show that if all available CPU resources are in use, reducing the number of work processes actually improves performance.

The *CPU wait time* is not explicitly indicated in the Workload Monitor. However, high CPU wait time leads to increased processing time. By comparing processing time and CPU time you can determine if there are wait situations on the CPU. See also the more detailed description in Chapter 3 in the section "Workload Analysis" on page 124.

Other situations that suggest reducing the ratio of work processes to CPU processors include:

- In contrast to UNIX, with Windows NT the context switch puts considerable load on the operating system. Therefore, particularly for Windows NT, it is recommended that you have a small number of work processes per CPU processor (see also SAP Note 68544).
- Reducing the number of work processes also reduces the number of database processes and the need for main memory. This is of particular advantage for databases in which each SAP work process has only one database process assigned to it.

Therefore, you should only increase the number of SAP work processes if neither the CPU nor the server memory are being fully consumed. If there is already a CPU or main memory bottleneck together with a high processing time on an application server, reducing the number of work processes can improve performance.

Dynamic User Distribution (Logon-Groups) and Operation Modes

Once a user has logged on to an SAP system, he or she works on a particular SAP instance until logging off. There is no feature enabling a dynamic, load-related switch to another SAP instance during a user session.

The dynamic distribution of dialog users over the SAP instances is therefore only possible during logon. To achieve this you can set up logon groups (or work groups), to which you can allocate one or more SAP instances. The user chooses a particular logon group when logging on to the SAP system. From among the allocated SAP instances, the system automatically selects the one with the best performance statistics or the least users.

Configuring Dynamic User Distribution

Use the following transaction to set logon groups (transaction code SMLG).

Tools · CCMS · Configuration · Logon groups

Further information on this transaction is available in SAP online help.

The simplest variant is to set one logon group over all SAP instances, to achieve a uniform distribution of users. Alternatively, you can distribute users according to the following criteria:

- **Logon groups according to SAP application**
  You can set logon groups such as "FI/CO", "HR", "SD/MM" and so on. The advantage of this method of procedure is, for example, that only the programs of the assigned SAP applications are loaded in the program buffer of a particular instance. As a result, the program buffer requires less memory space and this helps to avoid displacements.
- **Logon groups according to language, country or company division**
  If you operate an SAP system for several countries or languages, you can set up the logon groups "France", "Germany" and "Canada", for example. In this way, only texts and data relating to one country are loaded into the buffers of the corresponding SAP instances. With this method of procedure less memory space is required in the table buffer.
- **Logon groups for certain user groups**
  You can set up a special logon group for employees in telesales, for example, because their work is particularly performance critical. The corresponding SAP instances should operate with a particularly high level of performance (for example, with no background or update work processes, with few users per server, very fast processors, or a dedicated network). Another example of a user-specific logon group is one for employees in controlling, who draw up time-consuming reports in dialog mode. For this group you should assign an SAP instance for which the SAP profile parameter **rdisp/max_wprun_time** (which limits the runtime of an ABAP program in dialog mode) is set

particularly high. In addition, setting a low value for this parameter on all other instances means that these lengthy reports will not be run on those instances, where they could cause performance problems for other users. In this way you can separate performance-critical applications (such as order entry in telesales) from less critical, albeit resource-intensive applications (such as controlling).

- **Logon groups for SAP Internet Transaction Server**
  SAP ITS can be logged on to the application level using either a dedicated SAP application instance (with data on the application server and the instance number) or with a logon group (data on the message server and a logon group). For optimal availability and workload distribution, you should use the second option. It makes sense to set up a separate logon group for logons via the SAP ITS.
- **Logon groups for ALE/RFC**
  Asynchronous RFCs are used to run applications in parallel. If the degree of parallelizing is not limited, it can result in a snowballing of RFCs, which can bring the application level to a standstill for the user (all work processes are busy). To avoid such situations it can be useful to define specific SAP instances with a special logon group for incoming RFC load, so that work processes for RFCs are kept separate from work processes for online users and the users are not restricted in their work.

When setting up logon groups you should bear the following guidelines in mind:

- After assigning instances to logon groups, check to see if the instances are evenly distributed or if any group has too many or too few resources assigned to it.
- If there are temporary load peaks, for example increased activity in the "FI/CO" group towards the close of the month or the financial year, bottlenecks may occur on the corresponding instances. On the other hand, this can be useful or desirable to ensure that resources will be available for other users, such as those in telesales.
- If an application server hangs or if you temporarily disconnect an application server, the users must be redistributed.
- Bearing all of the above in mind, at least two SAP instances should be assigned to each logon group.

To sum up: Setting up logon groups involves extra administration and monitoring work. You should therefore not set up unnecessarily large numbers of logon groups.

Limit resources per user

Using SAP profile parameters, you can limit the resources available to users on the SAP application instances. These include:

- Automatic logoff of inactive users (the time after which an inactive user is logged off should be at least one to two hours, otherwise the frequent logging on can itself generate unnecessary load)
- Limiting the runtime of programs (this should not be less than the default value of 300 seconds; it should also be possible to execute longer running programs on some instances)
- Apportionment of memory consumption (a more detailed description can be found in Chapter 8; if you want to put strict limits on memory use for some instances, you should configure individual instances so that programs with a high memory use can also be finished on them.
- Limiting multiple logon and the use of parallel sessions (this should not normally be used)

You will find the profile parameters with which you can enter the corresponding settings in Appendix C.

The resources available to users should only be limited to the extent that this is useful. The main focus of your work should be on optimizing the programs, tuning instances and in training users in the correct use of programs. An over-zealous limiting of resources obstructs users in their work and is often perceived by them as spoon-feeding, which can lead to user dissatisfaction.

Planning Operation Modes

The demands made on an SAP system vary over the course of 24 hours: During the day, for example, there are many dialog users working with the system, while the demands made on the system by background programs usually increases at night. To adapt the number of SAP work processes to meet the changing demands, the SAP system offers the possibility of defining different operation modes for daytime and night-time operation. A certain number of work processes of a certain type are assigned to an operation mode. The operation mode is automatically changed by the SAP system according to the time.

You can define operation modes by means of the following transaction:

Tools · CCMS · Configuration · OP modes and servers

You can set the times for changing the operation mode using the following transaction:

Tools · CCMS · Configuration · OP modes timetable

You will find more detailed information on setting and monitoring operation modes in SAP online help.

Update Processing

If changes need to be made to a database table in an SAP transaction, they are first collected in the main memory and once the transaction is completed, they are bundled and asynchronously "updated". Figure 5.1 shows the steps involved in an update. "DIA" denotes a dialog work process, "UPD" indicates an update work process and "MS" is the message service. In our example the characteristics of a material need to be changed. For this, a change is necessary in table MARA—among other things. In the dialog part of the transaction, however, the MARA table is not directly changed in the database; rather the information to be changed is temporarily stored in special database tables—known as update tables. This can be seen in step one in Figure 5.1, which shows an insert operation (ins) in the update table VBMOD, which in the diagram also represents other update tables VBHDR and VBDATA. On completion of the dialog part of the transaction the dialog work process selects an application server with update work processes and sends a message to the message server (2). This in turn forwards the update request to the corresponding dispatcher of the application server (3). The latter allocates the request to an update work process (4). The update work process reads the information from the update tables ("select" in step 5) and finally changes the application table with an update operation—the MARA table in Figure 5.1 ("update" in step 6). This process is known as an *asynchronous update*.

In an SQL trace you can identify the end of the dialog part of a transaction with the help of insert statements on the VBMOD, VBHDR and VBDATA tables. The start of an update step is indicated by **SELECT** statements on this table.

Monitoring Update Requests

If update processing is terminated (status "Err"), you must manually restart or delete the request. If the processing of an update request could not be started (because, for example, the update process was deactivated or because, as a result of an error, there is no application server with

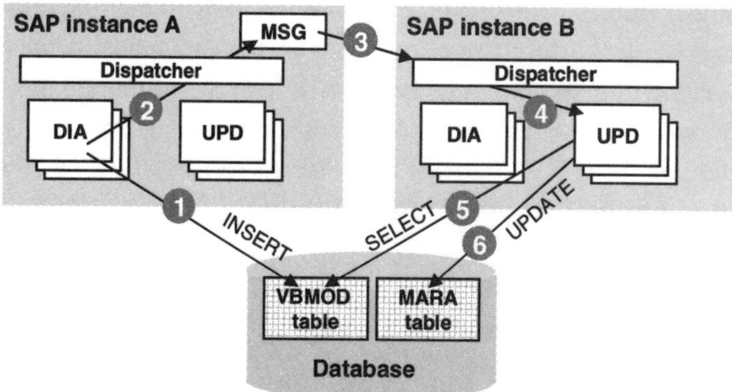

Figure 5.1 The course of an update step

update work processes), the requests remain in the status "Init". If the SAP profile parameter **rdisp/vbstart** is set at 1 (default setting), when the SAP system is restarted the update request will be tried again. Each application instance only updates the update requests that were assigned to it when it stopped. If **rdisp/vbstart** <> 1 or if the repeat fails to update the request, you must manually restart or delete the update.

Interrupted or unexecuted updates lead to a situation where documents entered or changed by users are not finally saved in the corresponding application table and are thus "non-existent" for the user. The daily checking of updating tasks is therefore an important task of the SAP system administrator. If interrupted updates are not investigated immediately, once a few days have passed there is little chance of finding the cause of the error.

A monitor is available for controlling update records:

Tools · Administration · Monitor · Update

Alternatively, you can enter transaction code SM13.

If an update request is correctly completed, the corresponding entries in the update tables are deleted. The update tables should therefore be empty (including erroneous requests and requests currently being processed). If the update tables grow considerably because of erroneous, incorrectly processed update requests, this will lead to a massive performance problem in the medium term.

VBMOD, VBHDR, VBDATA

The update tables VBMOD, VBHDR and VBDATA are among the most frequently modified tables in the SAP system. If bottlenecks arise with hard disk access to these tables, it may be helpful to partition, or distribute, these tables over several hard disks. For some database systems it can be useful to change the order of the key fields in these tables. However, this should only be carried out by someone with specialist knowledge of database and SAP tuning or based on recommendations from SAP. Further information can be found in the documentation on the SAP profile parameter *rdisp/vb_key_comp* or in SAP Notes on this parameter.

Distributing Update Work Processes

In small SAP installations the update work processes, together with database instances, message, enqueue and ATP services, are all configured on a single machine. In medium and large SAP installations, updates should not be configured centrally on the database server. In this case, there is some debate as to whether or not a central update server should be set up (an SAP instance dedicated solely to updates) or if the update tasks should be distributed symmetrically over all application servers. Some good reasons why you should use a distributed arrangement are as follows:

- The failure of a central update server would cause system activity to come to a standstill. With distributed update work processes this problem would not occur.
- A symmetrical configuration of application servers enables you to add or remove application servers to or from the SAP system without needing to readjust the workload distribution.
- Distributed update work processes can handle temporary load peaks better than a single server.

Therefore, for a large SAP installation, there are good arguments for distributing not only background work processes but also update work processes equally over the application servers.

Dispatching update requests

Dispatching update requests is activated by setting the SAP profile parameter **rdisp/vb_dispatching** at 1 in the default profile. The SAP system ensures that all instances receive update requests proportional to the number of update work processes configured on them. This normally guarantees a balanced workload distribution. However, the system does not actually check the load distribution. If for example, an SAP instance has only one update work process, which is taken up by a very long-running update request, the dialog work process continues to send update requests to this instance despite the free update work processes available on other instances. It is recommended, therefore, that you never configure only one update work process on an instance. You should configure at least two.

Update dispatching as described here is the standard solution for all applications. Only in special cases and on the express recommendation of SAP should you use the methods of local update or update multiplexing. These methods are not explained in this book.

As a rule of thumb you can configure update work processes in a ratio of 1:4 to dialog work processes, based on the total of all SAP instances.

Selecting Types of Update

V1, V2 and V3 updates

To enable you to prioritize update requests (and in so doing, distribute the workload over time), there are different types of update. We differentiate between asynchronous V1, V2 and V3 updates and the synchronous and local updates. In general, the type of update is set by SAP when your software is delivered. You only have to decide on update type yourself in certain individual cases and in the case of customer developments. A V1 update is the "normal" type of update, as described above.

V2 function modules are different from the VI type in two aspects: First, they are processed without enqueue locks (for more information on locks see Chapter 10, "Locks") and second, they are given lower priority. The following rule applies for deciding on priority between V1 and V2 updates:

- The standard update work processes (task type "Upd"), process V1 modules with complete priority, which means that no V2 module will be processed as long as there are V1 modules waiting to be processed (if V2 update work processes have been configured).
- This workload distribution rule can mean that in extreme situations there are absolutely no V2 functions being processed. This obstructs V2 type update work processes, which are processed as V2 functions. To ensure that V2 functions are also processed during times of high workload, you should also always configure V2 update work processes. As a rule of thumb you should allow a ratio of one V2 update work process to every four V1 update processes.

Modules that are absolutely necessary for operation are classified as V1 modules. Modules can be classified as V2 if they can be processed in times of lower workload and without the protection of enqueue locks (such as updating statistics).

Interfaces for the maintenance of statistic systems, such as the SAP Logistic Information System (LIS) are generally carried out by V2 function modules (however, in customizing you can select between V1, V2 and V3).

V3 function modules are also processed without enqueue locks. As with V1 and V2 modules, at the end of the dialog part of the transaction, entries are written to the update tables; however, the update is not started. The update requests remain in the update tables until a background job processes them explicitly. This background job is application-specific. It may contain its own application logic, which could be, for example, to accumulate update requests in the main memory and only write the prepared data to the database afterwards. For tables in which the values are frequently changed, this can mean a considerable reduction in database changes. The decision whether or not a business processes can be updated in V3 can be found in the corresponding documentation or in customizing.

With V3 updates you can separate the update workload from the dialog workload, as regards processing time, by starting updates during times of low dialog activity. Yet because no locks are held with V3 updates, their use is limited. One case where V3 updates can be used is in maintaining the SAP Business Information Warehouse interface.

The type of update can be seen in the Function Builder (transaction code SE37) on the **Characteristics** screen. Under **Process type**, **Update module** either the entry **Start immediately** or **Do not start immediately, update later** (or: V1 update), **Start delayed** (V2) or **Collective processing** (V3) is activated. A change to this characteristic is considered an object modification.

Synchronous update

As described above, updates in update work processes are usually asynchronous, which means that the dialog work process does not wait until the update task has concluded its work. Rather, once the data has been temporarily stored in the update tables, the user is informed that the transaction has been completed, so that they can continue with their work, although the update task is still running. However, synchronous updating is also possible, by which the dialog work process waits for the update work to finish. (In the Work Process Monitor, transaction code SM50 or SM66, this situation is displayed with the status "stopped" and reason "Upd".). Synchronous updating is activated with the **And Wait** clause for the ABAP statement **Commit Work**.

However, *synchronous updating* has hardly any advantages and is therefore practically never used. Rather, in cases where immediate updating is necessary, local updating is used, as described below.

Local update

The third type of updating is to carry out the update directly in the dialog or background work process, which means that no update work process is enlisted. This method is known as *local update*. With this method the update data is not stored in update tables in the database; rather, it is stored in the main memory of the application server. The update is executed directly after completion of the dialog part of the transaction in the dialog work process (or in the background work process, if it is a background process). Local updating is activated in the program called up using the ABAP statement **SET UPDATE TASK LOCAL**.

What are the advantages of local updates? The concept behind asynchronous updates is that the total response time for processing a transaction is divided into a dialog response time, which the user sees directly, and an update time, which runs without the user being aware of it. To achieve this, additional work is involved, that is, writing and reading the update tables. With local updates both parts of the transaction occur one after the other, but the additional work of writing to the update tables is spared. Local updates are mainly used for background processes with mass updates and for interface programming with massive parallel asynchronous RFCs. In both cases the advantage lies in the fact that entries do not have to be written to the update table. This is an advantage with mass updates because bottlenecks can occur in I/O channels to the update tables. Furthermore, the updates are started immediately and as a result they are not affected by potential overloading of the update work processes.

Update type	Method	With enqueue	Advantage	Limitations	Examples of use
Asynchronous V1	Asynchronous in update WP	Yes			standard
Asynchronous V2	Asynchronous in V2 update WP	No	Prioritizing because V2 work processes configured	No locks	statistical data (can be selected for LIS interfaces)
Asynchronous V3	Started by background job, then asynchronous in V2 update WP	No	Prioritizing because V2 work processes configured; load distributed over time because of update planning; performance advantage because of accumulation of changes in background program	No locks	statistical data (can be selected for LIS interfaces, standard for SAP BW interfaces)
Synchronous	Synchronous in update WP (dialog or background WP stops)	Yes	Reliable confirmation to user	Longer dialog response time	None
Local	Directly in dialog or background WP	Yes	Reliable confirmation to user; no entries in VB tables, resulting in lower database workload	Longer dialog response time	Background processing, tRFC, qRFC processing

Table 5.2 Overview of update types (Abbreviations: WP for work process, LIS for SAP Logistic Information System, SAP BW for SAP Business Information Warehouse)

Hardware Sizing

Whereas the previous sections dealt with the logical configuration possibilities of SAP services, we shall now deal with questions related to how services are distributed on hardware. In this and the following section we shall discuss the hardware sizing process and describe how SAP systems, instances and processes should optimally be distributed on hardware.

Calculating what hardware is necessary for an SAP system, that is to say, the required CPU power, size of main memory and hard disk, is referred to as *hardware sizing*. Sizing for SAP systems follows clear guidelines, which are worked out between SAP and their certified hardware partners and are constantly being improved. A study by the Gardner Group, comparing the sizing procedures for leading ERP software producers, showed the sizing procedure for SAP products to be better than the competition in all of the criteria evaluated.

Sizing decisions must draw on detailed figures, gained through experience about the CPU and memory requirement of users and transactions. Because these values quickly become outdated, in this section we do not endeavor to describe exactly how to do the sizing for your SAP system. Furthermore, this is not necessary because sizing is done by the hardware partners' experts—in consultation with SAP experts if necessary. However, as project leader or employee, you will need basic understanding of the sizing process, in order to competently compare and evaluate different sizing offers and reports and to understand all the possibilities, risks and limits of a sizing report. In this section, we would like to present the background necessary for this understanding.

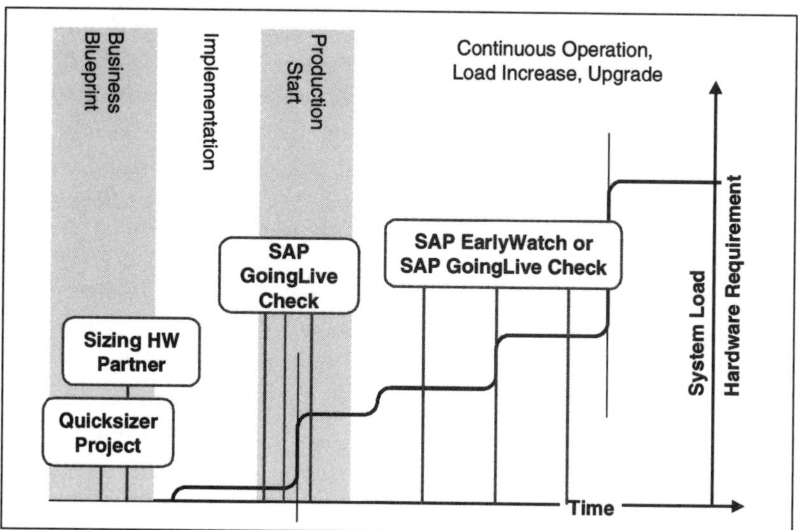

Figure 5.2 Hardware sizing in the lifecycle of an SAP project

Figure 5.2 shows the steps involved in the sizing process. On the horizontal axes you can see the phases of a project. Important milestones include going into live production operation, subsequent update releases, and production operation starts for additional functions or users. The bold black curve shows the growing workload on the system and with it, the growing demands made on the hardware.

Initial sizing is done before live operation begins. It involves both hardware partners—with their corresponding sizing offers—as well as SAP—with SAP Quick Sizing and the SAP GoingLive Check. The hardware requirements for a system can grow even after the initial start of production operation—because of a new release or the inclusion of additional functions or users, for example. As a result, planning for additional capacity planning is also necessary during these phases. SAP assists you in this capacity with the service program, and hardware partners may offer re-sizing.

Planning Initial Sizing

Calculation of the hardware necessary in initial sizing is done on the basis of data about users (user-based sizing) and/or transactions (document-based sizing).

Data about the number of users in different SAP applications serves as sizing input. Using detailed values based on past experience of how SAP applications consume memory and CPU capacity the CPU and memory requirements are calculated for each application (the product of the number of users and application-specific load factors). Then the total CPU requirement and total memory requirement are calculated as a sum of the individual requirements of each application. User-based sizing always delivers reliable data if the main system load is created by dialog users and if the SAP standard has not been changed significantly.

Input for document-based sizing can be data about what is referred to as the quantity structure. This includes data on the number of business operations that need to be processed within particular time frames. This could be, for example, the number of sales orders, deliveries and production orders, or printed documents. The advantage of this method is that data transfer in background processes (for example in batch input or ALE) and the distribution of the document throughput over the day are taken into consideration. The document-based approach should always be selected if a considerable amount of the load is created by background processes or interfaces. Examples for this are mySAP retail solutions (transfer of sales data in Point-of-Sale Inbound Processing) as well as banking, utilities or telecommunications solutions. In practice, a combination of both forms of sizing is usually carried out.

SAP Quick Sizer

Since 1997, SAP offers the *SAP Quick Sizer* in the SAP Service Marketplace. This tool gives you an approximate idea of the size of the hardware needed (CPU, main memory and disk capacity) and is based on published benchmark results, carried out with SAP Standard Application Benchmarks. Using detailed values, based on experience, regarding the memory and CPU consumption of different SAP applications, SAP Quick Sizer calculates the necessary main memory, the CPU capacity and the hard disk sizes. SAP Quick Sizer also gives a value for minimum and optimum main memory structure for the database and for all SAP instances together.

Hardware-independent details on the forecast resource requirements can be found in the SAP-specific unit *SAPS*. The SAPS unit is a measure for the performance of hardware in an SAP Standard Application Benchmark. SAPS stands for *SAP Application Benchmark Performance Standard*. 100 SAPS correspond to: 2,000 fully processed order items per hour, 6,000 dialog steps (screen changes) with 2,000 updates or 2,400 SAP SD transactions. The SAPS data is specific to the version of the mySAP.com component being tested. For each benchmark, the hardware is classified at the SAPS figure achieved. The SAPS data is therefore an effective means of comparing different manufacturers' hardware.

The *Quick Sizing* program can be found in SAP Service Marketplace under `www://service.sap.com/sizing`. Apart from documentation about SAP Quick Sizing, you will also find information here on sizing for mySAP.com solutions.

Sizing by the hardware partner

As a project proceeds you will receive one or several offers from *hardware partners*. The hardware partners are ultimately responsible for the hardware sizing of a project, because only they can guarantee the performance of their hardware. Where necessary, the hardware partners can gain support from SAP sizing experts via their SAP Competence Center

To simplify the sizing process, SAP has defined the following standard procedures:

1. Compile a sizing plan for your implementation project in SAP Quick Sizer in the SAP Service Marketplace. Enter the data necessary for sizing there, too.
2. Next, any hardware partners from whom you wish to receive a sizing offer should be given access to this sizing plan in the SAP Service Marketplace by giving them the password for the plan. You will also find the links to the Websites of hardware partners in the SAP Quick Sizer.

3. Finally, on the basis of the data you have entered, the hardware partners can create a concrete hardware offer.

If you wish to receive offers from several hardware partners, do not forget to check the data on hardware performance in SAPS. Only in this way can you compare offers from different manufacturers. You should also ask about the benchmark certificates of the hardware offered (these can also be called up on the Internet).

SAP GoingLive Check

As part of their software maintenance contract (TeamSAP Support), SAP offers all customers an *SAP GoingLive Check*. To carry out this service, employees of SAP or their service partners log on to your system remotely at several different times (sessions) and check the system. This service is carried out within a period of two months after the start of production operation. The SAP GoingLive Check contains a Sizing Plausibility Check. This does not involve a new sizing plan; rather, it gives a rating as to how the already installed or planned hardware can deal with the estimated load. Three different ratings can be given:

- *Green:* Based on the results of the SAP GoingLive Check and data on the hardware and forecast load, there is no fear of any hardware bottlenecks occurring.
- *Amber:* Based on the results of the SAP GoingLive Check and data on the hardware and forecast load, the hardware complies with the minimum requirements. Thus, bottlenecks are possible, or even probable, in situations of high workload.
- *Red:* Based on the results of the SAP GoingLive Check and data on the hardware and forecast load, the hardware will not be able to cope with the workload. Performance bottlenecks will probably occur. SAP recommends that you do not go into production operation with the existing hardware.

In the event that the evaluation gives a red signal, a follow-up on the case is automatically triggered, by which SAP informs the hardware partner in question of the result of the analysis and requests a response and follow-up.

You can find further information on the SAP GoingLive Check in the SAP Service Marketplace, under `www://service.sap.com/goinglivecheck`.

Summary of the initial sizing

Why do hardware partners and SAP offer their customers this three-fold security? To put it another way, what are the strengths and limitations of this three-step sizing? The advantages of the SAP Quick Sizer are the constant availability and ease of use by project employees. However, as only standard applications are accounted for, this procedure soon reaches its limits.

A hardware offer from a manufacturer can clearly examine the individual requirements of a project in greater detail. For example, an experienced sizing consultant can estimate the additional investment necessary to deal with interfaces, individually developed functions and requirements of availability or down time and performance, even in situations of high workload. The disadvantage is that individual sizing offers are costly and can therefore not be repeated as often as you wish.

The SAP GoingLive Check takes into account the same influencing factors as the sizing done by the hardware partners. While the hardware partner's sizing can often be several months old, the SAP GoingLive Check is done immediately before the start of production. As a result, any changes that have been introduced to the project plan and the latest knowledge can be included in the analysis. In addition, if necessary the service employees can analyze business-critical transactions in detail. In this way, for example, it is possible to see if inefficient customizing or customer enhancements (user exits) cause additional load—something not taken into consideration in standard sizing.

In order to be able to generate a sizing report, the experts need information about project-specific key values which will determine the sizing. These include, in particular, the software versions used, the expected number of users and the expected number of transactions (throughput) in the different applications. In the SAP Quick Sizer you will, first of all, find questionnaires on these key values. Later, relevant questionnaires will be sent to you by hardware partners as part of the SAP GoingLive Check. You should adopt the following rules when working with these questionnaires:

- Treat these questionnaires as very important. Only if the data is entered correctly in the questionnaire can you be sure that you will receive reliable sizing information.
- Constantly evaluate the figures as the project proceeds. If changes are made to the project plan during the implementation phase and data in the sizing questionnaire is changed, you should inform your hardware partner immediately and you can discuss the possible effects on the planned hardware.

The authors of this book know from experience that incorrect sizing and the resulting conflicts usually occur because of imprecise forecasts on the expected number of users and documents. Taking responsibility for the quality of these forecasts is the project leader's most important task in the sizing process. The corresponding experts with the hardware partners are available to offer advice on this matter.

SAP Standard Application Benchmarks

To what extent do *SAP Standard Application Benchmarks* help in the hardware sizing process and in the subsequent distribution of processes over the hardware? Figure 5.3 shows the CPU requirement of dialog, update and database services for the SAP applications FI, WM, MM, SD, PS and PP. The diagram is the result of numerous SAP Benchmark Tests (SAP Standard Application Benchmarks). Let us assume that one processor is needed for a certain number of FI users, thus, around 9% of CPU capacity is necessary for database requests (Database), 13% for updates and the remaining 78% is needed to cover dialog activities. How many FI users can be served by one processor depends mainly on the processor build type and the SAP release, and cannot be ascertained from the graphic. The bar chart level for the FI application is therefore standardized at one, just as a reference point.

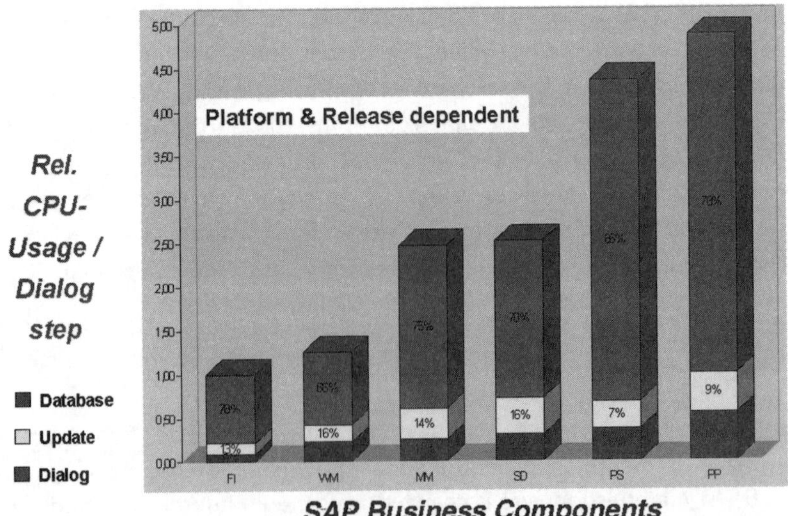

Figure 5.3 CPU requirement for dialog, update and database services for different SAP applications.

From this chapter, we can draw the following conclusions with regard to the SAP Standard Benchmarks:

- SAP Standard Benchmarks provide cutoff values on CPU requirements for different SAP applications. The height of the individual bars in Figure 5.3 shows the drastic difference in the CPU requirements of different applications. We can see that a PP application user needs five times more CPU capacity than an FI user. Accordingly, the number of work processes to be configured also depends strongly on the applications running on the corresponding SAP instance.
- In addition, the SAP Standard Benchmarks give information on the CPU requirement of individual services. The lower part of the bars in Figure 5.3 shows the CPU requirement of the database instance. According to the SAP application, this accounts for between 10 and 15% of the CPU requirement of the entire SAP system. The middle section of the bars shows the CPU capacity required by update services, also accounting for around 10 to 15% of the entire requirement. The remaining 70 to 80% corresponds to the requirements of the dialog service. The ratio of dialog work processes to update work processes can also be estimated.

Simulations with SAP Standard Benchmarks provide useful results that help configure real SAP systems. However, there are some points that SAP Standard Benchmarks cannot take into consideration.

An SAP Standard Benchmark cannot take into consideration that you may do more transaction processing (OnLine Transaction Processing, OLTP) or more reporting (OnLine Analytical Processing, OLAP) than normal. The SAP Standard Benchmark mainly takes OLTP activities in the SAP system into account, as these are generally critical to performance. (Posting sales orders, deliveries and invoicing is more important than the reporting on these processes). Reporting activities normally place a high load on the database. As a result, in real SAP systems the database workload would normally be higher in relation to the dialog and update load; the share of the database instance would typically be between 10 and 30%. The ratio of dialog work processes to the number of update work processes depends on the actual requirements of the system.

The Benchmark shown in Figure 5.3 does not take any background workload into account. However, in a real system the bars shown in Figure 5.3 as "dialog" would be split into a dialog segment and a background segment. The relationship between the dialog workload and background workload therefore depends on the actual implementation of the business process.

In the SAP Standard Benchmark for the SD application, sales orders, deliveries and invoices are generated in dialog mode. In your SAP system, however, perhaps only sales orders are created in dialog mode, while deliveries and invoices are created in background mode by what is referred to as collective processing for delivery notes and invoices. If you should wish to create a workload profile for this example and compare it with the profile of the SAP Standard Benchmark in Figure 5.3, the relationship between database workload and update workload would not change. The part marked "dialog" would, however, be divided into a dialog section and a background section.

You will find comprehensive documentation on benchmarks in *ideas international* (`http://www.ideasinternational.com`) and, for information on the SAP Standard Application Benchmark in particular, also in the SAP Service Marketplace (`http://service.sap.com/benchmark`).

Planning Hardware Capacity to Deal With Increased Workload, Change of Release or Migration (Re-sizing)

Only very rarely do large projects go live with one "big bang". More often, a SAP system is brought up in several stages. Before workload is increased, you should always carry out a review of capacity planning. The same applies for a change in version of the SAP software (upgrade) or migration to a different hardware or database platform.

Before a planned increase in workload, you should make use of an SAP service that determines current hardware load and evaluates the effects of the planned increase in workload. SAP recommends that you use the SAP EarlyWatch Service for planned workload increases of up to 30% and the SAP GoingLive Check for bigger increases in workload. Special SAP GoingLive Checks are also available for changes in SAP release or changing database or hardware platform (see Table 5.3).

SAP service	Project
SAP GoingLive Check	Start of production operation (initial start or start for additional users or functions)
SAP GoingLive Functional Upgrade Check	Change of SAP release
SAP GoingLive Migration Check	Change of database platform or hardware platform (changing operating system or manufacturer)
SAP EarlyWatch, SAP EarlyWatch Alert	Continuous monitoring of capacity

Table 5.3 Services in the area of sizing

These services measure and evaluate the current load on hardware is measured and evaluated. The additional hardware requirements are determined on the basis of data on the planned project steps. Previously planned changes to the hardware landscape are included in the evaluation. Should the evaluation indicate a risk of a hardware bottleneck, the hardware partner's corresponding service center is contacted and on the basis of the report of the GoingLive Check, the service center works out recommendations for optimizing the hardware landscape.

The free, automatic SAP EarlyWatch Alert service also determines the current hardware workload and presents it in a summary report.

New Challenges Arising From the Internet

When sizing for Internet applications, the number of users and throughput at times of peak workload can only be estimated very roughly in advance.

We will illustrate this problem with the help of some current, concrete examples.

- **Internet sales**
  A German soccer team, very successful both nationally and internationally, uses the SAP Online Store (SAP R/3 4.5) to sell merchandise on the Internet. A German-American automobile group also uses the SAP Online Store to sell merchandise related to their Formula-1 team on the Internet. A Japanese entertainment group uses the Internet sales scenario, as part of mySAP CRM, to sell their game console and the games that go with it.

- **Internet portal**
  A financial services company (one of the market leaders in Germany) runs its Internet portal for a planned 120,000 customers and potential customers with mySAP Workplace 2.11. Customers and potential customers can access up-to-date information related to their investments and in addition, they can also access operative applications such as account balance and online brokerage.
- **Managing donations on the Internet**
  A large German charity organization manages incoming donations with a specially developed application based on SAP R/3. In the future, potential benefactors can make their donations directly over the Internet.

These three business scenarios share a common problem as regards hardware sizing. On a few specific days of the year there are peak workload times, on which the number of users can be outstandingly high. If for example, the Internet address of the team shop appears before the eyes of millions of television viewers during a large sporting event, the site will be in great demand. The entertainment group would expect peak load times when a new version of the console appears or popular games are launched with a strong media campaign. The financial services provider will expect high access rates to the Internet portal when there are spectacular movements on the stock and financial markets or if initial offerings of a well-known firm come onto the market. The charity organization has mainly designed its Internet connection to deal with donations coming in as a result of a benefit event on television.

Obviously, these demands occur only during a few peak periods in the year, yet they are of prime importance for the business process holder. If their applications are not available and performing well at these times, they may suffer grave consequences:

- For the one thing, there is *financial damage*, because after unsuccessful attempts, many potential customers will not try again.
- *Image damage*, because many unsuccessful potential customers may feel that the Web site operator is incompetent and the application is unsafe.
- And possibly, even *legal damage*: For example, a bank's home pages and call centers must be available to all customers using online banking at all times. In fact, in Germany the federal authorities have warned banks that they are obliged to make reasonable access available continuously if they offer online banking services.

In all of the cases described, there would be several thousand users at peak workload times. Given that benchmark results are available (for example, for the SAP Online Store), hardware sizing to meet peak demand can be carried out by the relevant people at the hardware partner's company.

Unfortunately, however, the hardware necessary for times of peak workload will be lying around unused for maybe 350 days of the year. In future there will be more and more business scenarios of this type for which active capacity management is required. In large server centers, for example, this can be done by a hardware performance service provider. Unfortunately, creative solutions are an exception here.

Planning the System Landscape

After hardware sizing—or even in connection with hardware sizing—comes the question of how software instances (database, SAP applications and so on) are to be distributed on the server.

In particular, with the introduction of mySAP.com the project team is faced with the challenging task of not letting the amount of work involved in the maintenance and administration of hardware, databases, SAP instances and other software explode. Against this backdrop, many projects strive for consolidation, which means reducing the software instances to a few powerful computers. Hardware partners support this consolidation with innovative concepts in technology and marketing.

In this context, this section aims to address the following approaches:

- **Server consolidation**
  - Consolidation of SAP instances: Over how many SAP instances and servers should the SAP application level be distributed? Can the number of SAP instances be reduced by designing larger instances?
  - Hardware consolidation (consolidating SAP systems): Can the use of several production systems on the same server help to reduce the number of servers?
- **Database consolidation**
  Since 2001 it is possible to run several SAP systems on one database. Because this can also enable reductions in database administration, this alternative should also be checked out.

Apart from the main objective of this section, there is the closely linked matter of system consolidation, or harmonization, which is mainly a matter of business consulting.

System consolidation or harmonization: Over how many SAP systems should business processes be distributed? Can business processes that are currently running in several systems be merged into one system? How many production clients should be set up in an SAP system?

Distribution of SAP Instances

Over how many SAP instances and servers should the SAP application level be distributed?

Basically, you should not set up too many servers and instances, because each additional server and each additional instance brings with it increased administration and monitoring work. The following line of reasoning, however, supports the setting up of several instances:

- If one server or instance goes down, the remaining servers or instances have to absorb the additional workload. The fewer servers or instances configured, the more severe the effects will be.
- As we have seen before, logon groups are an important way of distributing workload. However, logon groups can only be implemented if several instances have been configured.
- Some older arguments in favor of distributing the application level of a system over many SAP instances have since been dealt with by enhancements in the SAP kernel. Nevertheless we would like to address the following points here:
  - With SAP Basis 3.x, additional instances were often set up because only one spool work process can be set up per instance. With SAP Basis 4.0, this limitation has been removed.
  - With 32-bit technology the physical main memory cannot be correctly addressed—because of operating-system-specific limitations—and as a result cannot be used, or at least not optimally used. This limitation has been eliminated with the introduction of 64-bit technology. For further details on this matter, see Chapter 8, "Memory Management".
  - With very large instances, the dispatcher, roll administration or buffer administration can become performance bottlenecks. However, each of these possibilities must be checked individually.

You can, however, assume that with 64-bit technology it is possible to have instances for 500 users or more.

Therefore, for distributing the application level over instances, the rule of thumb should be: install as many instances as necessary, but as few as possible.

Hardware Consolidation

Server consolidation—the concentration of all services on a few, very powerful servers—has been, without a doubt, an important trend in the IT market in recent years. The benefits which hardware partners promise customers include lower hardware costs; however, these often result less from procurement than from reduced hardware maintenance costs, after production begins. The technology developed by SAP supports this trend in many respects.

Notwithstanding, deciding whether or not server consolidation is the best approach for a project does not depend on the costs of hardware procurement and maintenance. Consolidation can give rise to costs in other areas of the production operation, which must be taken into account.

- Maintenance schedules (for example, for upgrades) have to be accepted by many different user groups. A maintenance level may have to be applied for a system, which implies downtime for all systems.
- To achieve high availability in a consolidated landscape, the server must be configured in high-availability clusters. This means that if one server goes down the various services are automatically started in other servers (failover recovery). These recovery scenarios have to be configured and tested.
- The awarding of resources to different systems has to be defined and monitored. Training and use of the corresponding software for resource management, offered by the manufacturers of UNIX operating systems, must also be taken into account.

Benchmark studies of various hardware manufacturers show that running several SAP systems on one server is possible without any problems as regards performance. In practice, however, the question of resource management remains to be resolved. A discussion of the possible solutions offered by hardware partners in this respect goes beyond the scope of this introduction. You can, however, evaluate the different solutions using the following check list:

- Do the different applications (SAP instances, database instances, etc.) run in different operating system instances (windows), that is to say, are they virtually disconnected?
- Can the CPU, main memory and disk I/O resources be administered using the methods of the operating system manufacturer?
- Can resource management be regulated with a fixed allocation of CPU, main memory and disk I/O or by prioritizing requests?
- Can resources be dynamically re-distributed (that is to say, without having to restart the operating system) to adapt to current requirements?

Up-to-date information from SAP on these matters can be found in SAP Note 21960. If you wish to run several SAP systems on a single server, this should be done in close collaboration with your hardware partner, and a corresponding consultancy project should also be agreed with your hardware partner.

Several SAP Systems on one Database

Since 2001 it is possible to run several SAP systems on one database. This allows for savings in the area of database administration. You can find further information on the SAP Service Marketplace (`http://service.sap.com/onedb`) and in SAP Note 388866.

Summary

The most important method for optimizing workload distribution in an SAP system is the *configuration of SAP work processes*. The number of work processes to be set up depends on the demands made on the SAP system and the CPU resources available. Important considerations are: Is the system to be used mainly for OLTP (Online Transaction Processing) or for OLAP (Online Analytical Processing) applications? Will there be more dialog processing or more background processing?

The following guidelines should be taken into account:

- Around 10–30% of the CPU requirement of the entire system is normally consumed by the *database service*. Ensure that any SAP instances residing on the database server do not consume too much

CPU capacity. Too many SAP work processes on a database server can lead to a CPU bottleneck, which in turn leads to higher database times and inconveniences all users.

- Around 10-20% of the CPU requirement of the entire SAP system is normally consumed by the *SAP update service*.

We would recommend the following procedure for distributing work processes on the instances:

- Message, enqueue and ATP services should be on one SAP instance (known as the central SAP instance). There should be at least five dialog work processes on this instance. For small and medium installations this central SAP instance is configured on the database server. For large installations it is located on a separate application server.
- Dialog, background, update and spool work processes should be equally distributed on the remaining application servers in a symmetrical manner. The CPU capacity of individual servers must be taken into account when configuring the work processes. If you configure the update service on one instance, at least two update work processes should be configured there.

Additional techniques for system load management include:

- Central update server and background server
- Update types (V1/V2/V3 and local update), dedicated updates and update multiplexing
- Logon groups for dynamic user distribution

However, please note that these techniques involve higher administration and monitoring effort. The rule of thumb is that the system should be configured as symmetrically as possible and as asymmetrically as necessary.

Hardware planning is strongly recommended before start of production operation and migrations. SAP and their hardware partners offer you clearly defined processes and services (SAP GoingLive Check). The quality and results depend largely on the quality of project planning (planned users and throughput figures). You can get continuous statistics on the workload of your hardware using the SAP EarlyWatch Alert Service.

There is no rule as to how many *SAP work processes per processor* can be configured. A guideline value is around 5–10 work processes per processor. Often SAP administrators and consultants make the mistake of increasing the number of work processes to solve any type of performance problem. In our experience this can lead to a problem that is as serious as before and in some cases even worse.

Important terms in this chapter

After studying this chapter you should be familiar with the following terms:

- Sizing methods (user, document and workload based)
- Workload distribution
- Logon groups
- Update distribution
- Update: V1, V2, V3 and local updates

Questions

1. Where should background work processes be configured?
   a) Background work processes should always be configured on the database server. Otherwise the runtime of background programs will be negatively affected by network problems between the database server and the application server.
   b) If background work processes are not configured on the database server, thy must all be set up on a dedicated application server known as the background server.
   c) Background work processes can be distributed evenly over all the application servers.
2. How should you configure and monitor dynamic user distribution?
   a) By setting the appropriate SAP profile parameter, for example **rdisp/wp_no_dia**
   b) By using Transaction SM04, "User Overview"
   c) By using Transaction SMLG, "Logon Groups"

6 Interfaces

Interfaces represent a significant factor when considering performance. In the first section of this chapter we will give a general introduction to RFC technology—which is the basis for almost all interfaces. The second section deals with the configuration and monitoring of interfaces to external systems.

When should you read this chapter?

In this chapter you will find information on configuring and monitoring RFC interfaces to external systems.

The Fundamentals of RFC

Remote Function Calls (RFCs) allows one program to execute another program "remotely" (that is to say, "in a different location").

Concepts

RFCs are used for the following purposes:

- For communication between different systems, be it between two SAP systems or between an SAP system and an external system
- Within an SAP system:
  - For communication between application instances or between the application level and the presentation level (GUI communication)
  - For parallelizing processes: Given that one program after another can start several RFCs asynchronously, without waiting for processing to finish, RFCs are used to parallelize processes and dynamically distribute workload over the different servers within an SAP system.

With RFCs, SAP systems (such as SAP R/3, SAP APO, SAP BW) of different versions can be linked, or SAP systems can be linked with external systems, for example an SAP R/3 system with an external warehouse management system, where the SAP R/3 system creates the transfer orders for stock movements and sends them to an external system via RFC. Once the warehouse management system has carried out a transfer order, it executes a transaction using RFC to inform the SAP R/3 system of the movement of goods.

How the business processes of an enterprise are distributed over different mySAP.com components is of critical importance for the subsequent administration of the system. It can be said in favor of a distributed, linked system landscape, that the individual system parts can be handled more flexibly in all contexts (build, upgrade, administration, organization and so on). With interfaces, which have to be built and operated, the total expense for build and administration (and hardware requirements) is greater than in a large integrated system.

With RFCs the system can be linked in two ways; we differentiate between:

- What is known as *"hard" coupling*, in which one system relies on the partner system being available. If communication is interrupted, for example as a result of a network malfunction or because the partner system is not working, the other system can continue working; however, the functions that use the RFCs will be terminated with an error.
- *"Soft" coupling* does not require this reciprocal availability of the systems. Rather, the systems exchange data periodically. If one system is temporarily unavailable, the other system can continue to work without any problems. An example of a "soft coupling" is ALE (Application Link Enabling) coupling.

We call the process that starts the RFC the Sender or Client, and the process in which the RFC is executed is the Recipient or Server. We differentiate between four types of RFCs: synchronous, asynchronous, transactional and queued.

- A *synchronous RFC* is characterized by the fact that the sender waits while the RFC runs in the recipient process.
- With an *asynchronous RFC*, the sender does not wait until the RFC recipient process has been completely processed. Rather, once the RFC has started, the sender can continue working. As a result, a sender can start several asynchronous RFCs at the same time. (With a synchronous call on the other hand, only one RFC can run at a time, because the sender has to wait until processing has finished.)
- A *transactional RFC (tRFC)* is an asynchronous RFC that runs under "special security conditions". Details on this can be found later in this chapter.
- A *queued RFC (qRFC)* is a transactional RFC for which the sequence of processing in the destination system complies with the call sequence in the source system (for all qRFCs in a particular queue).

ABAP coding

You can recognize an RFC in an ABAP program by the syntax **CALL FUNCTION <function name> DESTINATION <connection name>** ... The variable **<connection name>** contains the name of the RFC connection, also called the Destination.

If the function call contains the clause **STARTING NEW TASK**, it is an asynchronous RFC; the clause **IN BACKGROUND TASK** indicates a transactional RFC. If the call only contains the clause **DESTINATION**, but neither **STARTING NEW TASK** nor **IN BACKGROUND TASK**, then the RFC is started as a synchronous RFC.

The following code starts the functional module Z_BC315_RFC synchronously, asynchronously and transactionally. (**DESTINATION 'NONE'** here means that the destination and source systems are identical.)

```
* Synchronous RFC
CALL FUNCTION 'Z_BC315_RFC'
     DESTINATION 'NONE'
     EXCEPTIONS
          argument_error = 1
          send_error     = 2
          OTHERS         = 3.

 * Asynchronous RFC
CALL FUNCTION 'Z_BC315_RFC'
     STARTING NEW TASK task
     DESTINATION 'NONE'
     EXCEPTIONS
         communication_failure = 1
         system_failure        = 2
         RESOURCE_FAILURE      = 3.

* Transactional RFC
CALL FUNCTION 'Z_BC315_RFC'
            IN BACKGROUND TASK
            DESTINATION 'NONE'.
COMMIT WORK.
```

All RFCs, whether synchronous, asynchronous or transactional, are started in dialog work processes. Therefore, you should not be deceived by the syntax **IN BACKGROUND TASK**; this has nothing to do with background work processes. Transactional RFCs are also executed in dialog work processes. A detailed introduction to the programming of RFCs can be found in ABAP online help under the statement **CALL FUNCTION**.

Course of an RFC

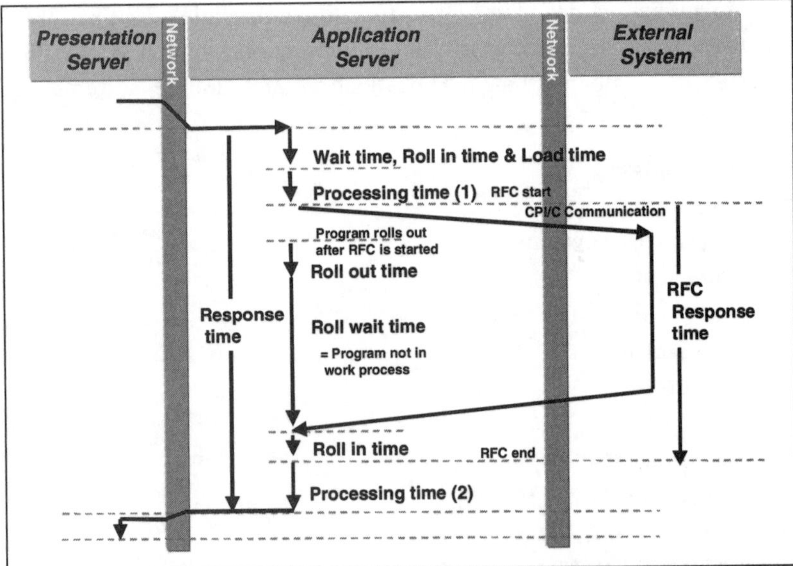

Figure 6.1 Course of a transaction step with synchronous RFC and the times measured during it.

When an RFC is executed the following process is launched:

1. First the sender (the work process that wishes to start the RFC) creates a connection with the recipient system. This connection is realized using the gateway services of the two systems involved (initializing phase). The dispatcher on the recipient system looks for a free dialog work process that can execute the RFC. In the work process overview (Transaction SM50 or SM66) the sender work process is in "stopped" status during this time, with "CPIC" as the reason. The "Action/Reason for waiting" column shows the entry "CMINIT".

2. Once the connection between the sender work process and the recipient work process has been set up, the data necessary for executing the RFC is transferred. Now, in the Work Process Overview for both the sender work process and the recipient work process, the status "stopped" is displayed, with "CPIC" as the reason and "Action/Reason for waiting" is "CMSEND". After the entry CMSEND there is a number. This is known as the communication ID.
3. After this point synchronous and asynchronous RFCs are treated differently. Once all necessary data have been transferred and the RFC has been started on the recipient side, in asynchronous RFCs the connection is broken and the program on the sender side continues working, without waiting for the end of the RFC. This type of processing means, for example, that another RFC can now be started which will then run parallel to the first.
4. With synchronous RFCs the sender side waits until the RFC has finished processing. During the wait time the user context on the sender side is rolled out of the work process, so that it is available to other users. In the Work Process Overview, on the sender side, there is nothing to be seen of the running RFC and the waiting program. On the sender side, the waiting program can only be seen as a session in the User Monitor (Transaction SM04) and as an open communication connection in the Gateway Monitor (Transaction SMGW). On the recipient side, the running RFC creates a status entry of "running" in the Work Process Overview. In the User Monitor (Transaction SM04) the RFCs coming from outside can be identified by the terminal entry "APPC-TM". From SAP Basis 4.6 on, there is a special column in the User Monitor for user type (**Type** column). For an RFC connection you will see the entry "RFC".
5. Once the recipient side has closed the processing of the synchronous RFC, the waiting context on the sender side has to be "awakened", that is to say, rolled in to a work process. During the subsequent data transfer from recipient to sender, in the Work Process Overview, both work processes display the status "stopped" with "CPIC" as the reason and "CMRECEIVE" as "Action/Reason for waiting".
6. Finally the connection is closed, the recipient work process is free once again and the sender work process continues with its work.

In this procedure the creation of the connection (the CMINIT phase) should only last a few milliseconds. If you find this status often in the Work Process Overview, there may be an overload in the recipient system (further details on this will be given in the next section). The duration of the CMSEND and the CMRECEIVE phases depends mainly on the amount of data to be transferred and the speed of the network. No time data can be given for these phases.

Figure 6.1 illustrates the course of a synchronous RFC and the times measured during it, which are displayed in the single record statistics (transaction code STAD or STAT) and in the Workload Monitor (transaction code ST03 or ST03N).

roll wait time While the sending program is waiting for the response to the synchronous RFC, the user context is rolled out of the work process to make it available for other users. Once the RFC has ended in the recipient system, there is a roll in to a work process and the transaction step is continued. During an RFC call the response time for the calling program is still growing. In an analysis of the "lost time" (see the section "Workload Analysis" on page 124 in Chapter 3) the *roll wait time* has to be subtracted from the total response time, because during this time the calling system does not require any CPU resources. In a single statistical record for a transaction step with a synchronous RFC, a roll wait time is also listed. (However, for very short RFCs with a response time of less than 500 ms, there is no roll out.) You will find no roll wait time for an asynchronous RFC (because with an asynchronous RFC the program is not rolled out; rather, it continues working).

RFC time In the field **RFC+CPIC Time** of the single statistical record and the Workload Monitor appears the total time for the RFC. For asynchronous RFCs this includes phases 1 to 3 of the above list. As a rule of thumb, the *RFC time* here should not be longer than 50 ms per call. For synchronous RFCs, the RFC time includes phases 1 to 6. It is clear that the RFC time here must be greater than the roll wait time.

SAP R/3 3.1 The Workload Monitor for SAP R/C 3.1 presents no information on the RFC and roll wait times. The average response times for RFCs in called systems can be found in the transaction profile (**Transaction Profile** button) as the program **CPIC/RFC**.

Interfaces to External Systems

In this section we shall discuss the performance aspect of interfaces between SAP systems or between SAP systems and external systems.

Configuring and Testing RFC Destinations

RFC connections (also called destinations) can be set in the transaction **Display and maintenance of RFC destinations** (transaction code SM59). You can access this transaction via the menu as follows:

Tools • Administration • Administration • Network • RFC destinations

In this transaction all available RFC destinations are first presented in a tree structure. Table 6.1 describes the four possible types of RFC destination.

Destination type	Description
Internal destination	RFC connections to all SAP application instances on the same SAP system. These connections are automatically generated when you install your SAP system in the form <server name>_<SAP system name>_<instance number>. Here, you will also find the destination "NONE" which always indicates the current instance.
R/3 destinations	RFC connections to other SAP systems, such as connections in the form TMSADM@<System 1>.DOMAIN_<System 2>: These are needed by the Transport Management System (TMS) and are generated during the build.
TCP/IP destinations	These are connections to non-SAP systems. Many standard destinations are already pre-configured here.
Destinations via ABAP/4 drivers	Not of interest here

Table 6.1 RFC destination types

Double click on a destination to select it and you are brought to a screen with details on this destination. The layout of this screen will differ according to the destination type. Figure 6.2 shows one example.

Apart from the details on the configuration of the RFC destination, in the list of buttons you will find the function **Test connection**. You should execute this function now if you anticipate problems with a connection. It logs on to the recipient system and transfers some test data. Then it shows the response time for the data transfer, or an error message if the logon was not successful.

The response time for the transfer of the test data depends on the network used. Ideally, the response time should be between 10 and 100 milliseconds. If you execute the connection test at times of high and low system load, you can determine whether the connection has a capacity

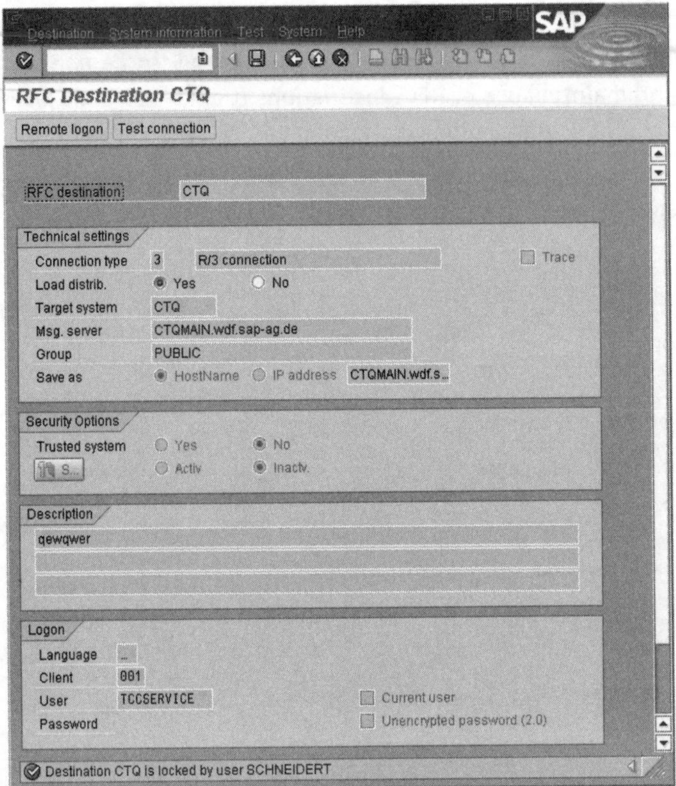

Figure 6.2 Configuration of an external RFC connection (transaction code SM59)

overload at times of high workload. High response times can be due to three things:

- The network connection is generally slow or overloaded.
- The recipient system is physically overloaded.
- There are too few processes configured in the recipient system to receive RFCs.

Destination type	Connection test result	Measures to be taken
R/3	Error message "TCP/IP Timeout"	The recipient system cannot be contacted. Check the availability of the recipient system and the network connection
	High response times (> 100 ms) for a connection to an SAP system	1. Check the network connection to the external system with the help of the Ping command or using the network provider's tools. Optimal ping response times are around 20 to 50 milliseconds. 2. Logon and performance test on the recipient system. Are all work processes busy?
TCP/IP	Error message "Partner program not registered"	Begin the corresponding recipient process
	Error message "TCP/IP Timeout"	Check the network connection between the SAP Gateway Process in question and the other side. If the gateway needs to be maintained, view information on it using the **Gateway** button. If this is not the case, the local Gateway of the SAP application server will always be used. If you still wish to change subsequent Gateway settings, do so using the menu **Destination • Gateway options**. (This is always done on both sides.)
	High response times (> 100 ms) for a connection to an external system	1. Check the network connection to the external system with the help of the Ping command or using the network provider's tools. Optimal ping response times are around 20 to 50 milliseconds.
		2. Check to see how many parallel recipient processes are started on the other side to receive the Idocs. In the event high load develops on the recipient side, it can be useful to increase the number of processes. 3. Please see SAP Notes 63930 and 44844 on RFC connections with Gateway registration.

Table 6.2 Sources of problems with setting up connections

SAP system as recipient

Depending on the recipient system, different parameters can be configured for the connection. If the recipient system is an SAP system, first of all you must decide if logon to the recipient system should be done via logon groups or directly via a set application server. This choice can be made by setting the option **Load distribution**. If the load distribution is activated, the message server and the corresponding logon group have to be reported to the recipient system; if the connection is made without load distribution, the data on application server (**Target machine** field) and instance number (**System number** field) are requested.

You should choose to log on using a logon group. This procedure has two advantages over direct logon to a dedicated application server:

- Several application servers can be assigned to a logon group. If one server is down, another server can process the in-coming RFCs (high availability aspect).
- There is logon balancing, that is to say that workload is distributed among the instances, which averts a capacity overload (performance optimization aspect).

Monitoring Inbound and Outbound Load

The inbound and outbound workload created by RFCs can be monitored in the RFC profile in the Workload Monitor. You will find this in SAP Basis 4.6 (from Basis support package 22) in the new Workload Monitor (transaction code ST03N), or in the old Workload Monitor (transaction code ST03) under:

Goto · Profiles · RFC profile

The profiles under menu points **Clients** and **Client destinations** correspond to the in-bound RFCs (the local system is the recipient or server); under **Server** or **Server destinations** you can see the load created by out-bound RFCs (the local system is the sender or client). Tables 6.3, 6.4 and 6.5 show the different RFC profiles (**Client Destinations, Server Destinations, Clients** and **Server**) of the performance indicators and the different views specified in the RFC profiles.

Profile	Description
Client destinations and Server destinations	The single record statistic writes total statistics records to each transaction step, with data on everything that has been executed for each RFC destination. In these profiles you will find the total workload generated by RFCs. Please note: Data on the function module name and the corresponding view (see Table 6.5) is of no significance (and is no longer output in the new Workload Monitor).
Clients and Server	The single record statistics write the function module name of the five (this can be changed using the parameter **stat/rfcrec**) most expensive function modules in a transaction step to the statistical record. In these profiles you will find the workload of these five expensive function modules. These statistics are particularly useful for an introduction to application analysis, because with them you can see which functions create the highest workload.

Table 6.3 RFC profiles

Field	Explanation
Quantity	Number of Remote Function Calls (RFCs)
Call time	Response time for the RFCs, measured in the sender system. The difference between "Call time" and "Execution time" is the time it takes to make the connection and transfer data between the sender system and the recipient system. As a rule of thumb this time should not be more than 20% of the "Call time". If this value is exceeded, look for a bottleneck in the connection between sender and recipient.
Execution time	Response time for the RFCs, measured in the recipient system. The "execution time" is the net time for the execution of the RFCs in the recipient system.
Sent Data	Quantity of data sent
Received Data	Quantity of data received

Table 6.4 Fields in the RFC Profile in the Workload Monitor (transaction code ST03/ST03N)

View	Button	Remarks
Transaction codes	Transaction code	
User names	User names	This view is useful if a user name is associated with a particular transfer channel (for example you can set up your RFC connection in such a way that sales orders are sent in your system under a user RFC_SALES).
RFC function modules	Function modules	This view is suitable mainly for application analysis, because in it you can identify the functions that create the highest workload. This view is of no consequence in the profiles **Client Destinations** and **Server Destinations**.
External RFC destinations	Remote destinations	SAP instances of remote systems can be entered as remote destinations, for example, or as names of servers that run programs with which the local SAP system communicates via RFC.
Local RFC destinations	Local destinations	Distribution of the RFC load over the instances in the local SAP system.

Table 6.5 Views in the RFC profile of the Workload Monitor

To evaluate the RFC profile, proceed as follows:

1. Sort the RFC profile according to the **Call time** column. The functions or destinations with the longest processing time are at the top of the

list. (Note: In some SAP kernel versions, for software imports (program **tp**) incorrect times are calculated for "call time", so that extremely high times are given for the server from which the software import was started. However, in the profile these can be recognized immediately.)

2. Compare the value given for **Call time** with that given for **Execution time**. As a rule of thumb the difference between them should not be greater than 20%. If you do this comparison in the different views, you can identify destinations, function modules or users for which there may be a problem with the communication between the sender and recipient. Analyze the connection and the data transfer by testing the relevant connection, and generate an RFC trace for the corresponding program.
3. You can then sort the RFC profile according to **Execution time**, **Sent Data** and **Received Data** in order to identify the function modules with the highest workload.

Configuring the Parallel Processes with Asynchronous RFCs

As we have already seen, *asynchronous RFCs* are used to parallelize applications, because the sender side does not have to wait for an RFC to be finished, but can send other RFCs straight away. If the degree of parallelizing is not limited, however, it can result in a snowballing of RFCs, which can bring the application level to a standstill for the user (all work processes are busy).

There are two ways to avoid this situation: You can create your own SAP instances with a dedicated logon group, as explained in Chapter 5 in the section "Configuring Dynamic User Distribution" on page 179. In addition, the resources for RFC processing can be limited for each SAP instance. In this way a certain share of the resources can be reserved for dialog applications. For asynchronous RFCs (ABAP keyword **STARTING NEW TASK <Taskname> DESTINATION IN GROUP <Group>**) the load information is evaluated on the recipient side. As many aRFCs are sent to each application instance as there are resources available. If an application instance has no more free resources available, then no more aRFCs are sent to it. The request for resources is repeated until all aRFCs have been processed.

Resources available for aRFC processing are set in profile parameters. With the help of the program **RSARFCLD** the quotas can be configured dynamically. You can find further information on the profile parameters in Appendix C, "Performance Parameters", and in SAP Note 74141.

Monitoring Data Transfer With Transactional RFCs

A transactional RFC is an asynchronous RFC that runs under "special security conditions". Transactional RFCs (tRFCs) are not executed immediately; rather, the calls are first gathered in an internal table. On the next **COMMIT WORK** statement all calls are processed in order of sequence. If update records are also generated before the **COMMIT WORK** statement, then the transactional RFCs are only executed if the update modules can be processed without any errors. The transactional RFCs of a transaction form a Logical Unit of Work (LUW) for each destination.

All tRFCs are displayed on the sender side in the tables ARFCSSTATE and ARFCSDATA. Each LUW is identified with a universally unique ID. On **COMMIT WORK**, the call bearing this ID is executed on the corresponding target system. If an error occurs with a call, all executed database operations from the previous calls are revoked (**ROLLBACK**) and a relevant error message is written to the ARFCSSTATE table. If an LUW is successfully executed on the target system, this is confirmed in the target system. The corresponding entries in the ARFCSSTATE and ARFCSDATA tables are deleted on the sender side. Error messages regarding tRFCs can be evaluated with the help of Transaction SM58.

Interrupted or un-executed tRFCs lead to inconsistencies between systems and thus impair the business process considerably. The daily checking of errors in interface processing (Transaction code SM58) is therefore an important task of the SAP system administrator.

Dealing with tRFC errors

If the target system cannot be reached, because, for example, the connection is currently not active, by default a background job is planned for each failed tRFC, so that the tRFC will be started again at regular intervals (Report RSARFCSE with the ID of the tRFC as a parameter).

If a lot of tRFCs are transferred for a particular connection, which is then interrupted, it may occur that the sending SAP system is inundated with background jobs, which will continue to try sending the tRFCs to the unavailable system, with no success. This can lead to considerable performance problems in the sender system if the recipient system is not available over a certain period of time. We therefore recommend that for connections in which more than 50 tRFCs have to be transferred each day, you deactivate the scheduling of background jobs in the event of error. To do this, select the destination in question in Transaction SM59. Select **Destination · TRFC options**. In the next screen activate the option

Suppress batch job in the event of communication error and confirm your entry with the function **Continue**. Now, in the event of error, no background jobs are created and processed for the tRFC. Instead of these individual jobs, you must now schedule the report RSARFCEX to run regularly (around every 30 minutes) with the destinations in question and with the current date as the variant (explicit parameter for variants). This program now searches the ARFCSSTATE table sequentially for tRFCs that have not yet been sent and tries to send them. This adjustment should only be carried out and tested by an experienced system consultant.

Reorganization of tRFC tables

If errors occur when sending tRFCs, the corresponding entries in tables ARFCSSTATE and ARFCSDATA are not deleted. As a result, these tables have to be reorganized at regular intervals. For this purpose you should schedule **RSARFC01** to run at least once a week as a background job. Otherwise you may experience performance problems with the tables ARFCSSTATE and ARFCSDATA. Further notes on undeleted tRFC protocol entries can be found in SAP Note 375566, "Many entries in the tRFC and qRFC tables".

Summary

Interfaces are a core element of mySAP.com technology. Remote Function Calls (RFCs) constitute the most important interface technology.

Performance problems in the area of RFC interfaces can be proactively eliminated with the appropriate configuration of the RFC connection and the recipient instance. If performance problems occur even after this, good analysis tools that you can use include the Work Process Overview, the RFC Profile in the Workload Monitor, the Single Record Statistics, the Performance Trace (RFC trace) and the transaction for configuring RFC connections.

Important terms in this chapter

After studying this chapter you should be familiar with the following terms:

- Remote Function Call: RFC, aRFC, tRFC, qRFC
- Roll wait time, RFC time
- RFC profile in the Workload Monitor

Questions

You will find questions at the end of Chapter 7, "SAP GUI and Internet Connection".

7 SAP GUI and Internet Connection

SAP is supplying a revision of its software with the EnjoySAP Initiative (SAP R/3 4.6). The interface included with this revision is more intuitive and easier for users to learn and use than the previous versions. The new interface is based on a new type of interaction between the presentation and application level, referred to as the controls. The first section of this chapter is devoted to the performance aspects of controls.

More and more users are now using a Web browser to log on to SAP systems rather than the classical SAP GUI for Windows and Java environments, the advantage being that no special GUI programs need to be installed on the desktop computers. Communication between the Web browser and the SAP application level is handled by a Web server and the SAP Internet Transaction Server (SAP ITS). The second section looks at configuration and performance monitoring of the SAP ITS.

When should you read this chapter?

This chapter provides administrators with an introduction to configuration and monitoring for SAP GUI interfaces (from SAP Basis 4.6) and the SAP Internet Transaction Server. You should have read the section "The Fundamentals of RFC" on page 205 in Chapter 6 before reading this chapter.

SAP GUI 4.6

With the EnjoySAP initiative (SAP R/3 4.6), SAP presents a revision of its software. In concrete terms, SAP R/3 4.6 is characterized by three new features.

- A new visual design
- A new interaction design
- Increased personalization of functions

Technically, the new design is based on a completely new interaction model for communication between the presentation and application levels—the Controls.

All three GUI variants that are available for accessing the SAP system, the SAP GUI for HTML, the SAP GUI for Windows or the SAP GUI for Java support the use of controls. In other words, they are "Enjoy-abled"!

Interaction Model and Performance Measurement

EnjoySAP and controls

Controls are interface elements that allow application developers to adapt their user interfaces more precisely than before to the needs of the respective users and also allow them to integrate a greater number of elements into one screen. Typical controls include:

- ABAP List Viewer Control (ALV Control)
- Tree Control
- Textedit Control
- HTML Control

You will find examples of controls on your SAP system under **Tools · ABAP Workbench · Development · ABAP Editor · Environment · Control Examples** (transaction code DWDM).

Controls are not screen elements in the traditional sense; rather, they are software components that run independently in the SAP GUI program and have their own functionality, which operates at the GUI level and requires no communication with the application level.

In a traditional list or traditional tree structure (prior to SAP Basis 4.6), for example, each scroll operation or each collapse or expansion of a branch in the tree represents a communication step between the GUI and application levels. Where the new List Viewer Control or Tree Control is used, a larger volume of data is transferred the first time the list or tree is constructed. Consequently, the list or tree can be navigated independently in the GUI without referring back to the application level. Functions such as "Find" and "Replace" are further examples of actions that can be processed directly in the GUI in the case of some controls.

The new interaction model therefore results in fewer communication steps, on average, between the presentation and application level. This is a distinct advantage for users who call up a screen once and then navigate it frequently. On the other hand, however, the network load increases the first time the screen page is constructed. The new interaction model is therefore a disadvantage if you only call up a complex screen once and then exit immediately. In general, tests show that the average network load in Release 4.6 is higher in comparison with previous versions (SAP Note 164102).

Without being familiar with the actual programming, it is not possible to say which actions require a communication step with the application level.

Application developers are required to transfer data to the GUI in logical batches. Lists or trees that are only a few pages long are transferred completely, while very long lists or trees are transferred in batches (for example in the case of trees, a fixed number of nodes in advance). The new interaction model therefore clearly involves extra responsibility for application developers, since they can decide in their programs how much data to send to the GUI and in how many batches.

Roundtrip, roll wait time and GUI time

Several interactions may be necessary in a transaction step between the application level and the GUI in order to construct a screen. Such interactions are referred to as *Roundtrips*. Data is transferred in a roundtrip on the basis of a synchronous RFC from the application level to the GUI. The entire duration of communication with the GUI within a transaction step is referred to in the statistics record as *GUI time*. The program is rolled out from the work process as it waits at the application level for the GUI to respond. This wait time is referred to in the statistics record as the *Roll wait time*. In general, you will notice that the roll wait time and the GUI time are approximately the same in a statistics record for a transaction step in which controls are constructed and no RFC is issued to an external system. If controls are constructed and external RFCs are started in a transaction step, the roll wait time will be greater than the GUI time because the roll wait time includes the time for issuing the RFCs to the GUI and the time for the external RFCs.

Transferred data volume

The *volume of data transferred* between the application level and the GUI can be calculated from the fields **Terminal out-message** (application level to GUI) or **Terminal in-message** in the statistics record.

Figure 7.1 illustrates the times measured in a transaction step with controls.

Analyzing and Optimizing the Performance of GUI Communication

Single record statistics

If you suspect that your system is having problems with GUI communication in terms of constructing controls, you should first call up the *single record statistics* (transaction code STAD, see the section "Single Record Statistics" on page 149 in Chapter 4).

1. You should restrict your search in the selection screen, for example, to the user who reported the problem or to a transaction or program name as well as a time period.

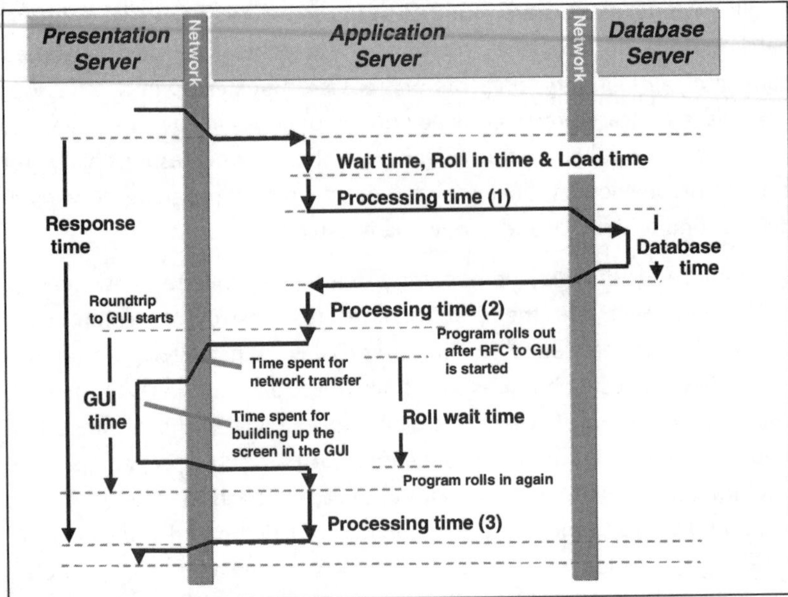

Figure 7.1 Course of a transaction step with controls and the times measured during it

2. You then access the overview screen. Use the **Select Fields** function to choose the fields that primarily indicate problems with GUI communication: **Roll wait time, No. of roundtrips, GUI time, Terminal in-message** and **Terminal out-message**.
3. Now scroll the list and search for transaction steps with a high GUI time or a high data transfer volume (**Terminal out-message**). The following guidelines can be followed here:
   - You should aim at achieving an average rate of 1 KB per 100 ms for transferring data to the GUI. 1 second for 1 KB would be the slowest acceptable rate. If these guide values are exceeded frequently, it can only be assumed that there is either a problem in the network or a hardware bottleneck on the presentation server.
   - In addition, it is also possible that the transfer rate is okay and the GUI time is still high because too much data is being transferred. As a guide value, a transaction step should not transfer more than 5 to 8 KB on average. Even a complex screen layout should not require more than 50 KB of data. If these guide values are exceeded frequently, the problem lies in the program or in the way it is being used.

The *performance trace* (transaction code ST05) is a further tool that can be used to analyze performance problems with the GUI.

Performance trace

1. Activate the performance trace (SQL trace, Enqueue trace and RFC trace) for the user activity being investigated and then list the trace result.
2. Search for RFC modules in the trace that are intended for your presentation server. To do this, search for the name of your presentation server in the **Object** column. Typical function modules for transferring data to the GUI include SAPGUI_PROGRESS_INDICATOR and OLE_FLUSH_CALL (see also Figure 4.3 in Chapter 4).
3. Add up the response time for these function modules and check whether this accounts for a significant portion of the overall response time.
4. Compare the response times and the volume of data transferred for each function module. The response time in microseconds for an RFC is shown in the **Duration** field in the basic trace list. Double-click the relevant line in the trace list to establish the volume of data transferred and take the value from the **Bytes sent** field. Compare the values with the guide values specified above.

The Automation Queue Trace is a developer tool for analyzing the performance of controls. It can be activated via the SAP GUI. You will find information in this regard in the SAP Note 158985.

High GUI time despite moderate volume of data

If you discover that the *GUI time* is high despite a relatively small volume of data, this can have two causes: a hardware bottleneck on the presentation server or a network bottleneck. Often the simplest way to analyze this further is to try to extract just those users from the single record statistics who typically experience these problems.

The **Terminal out-message** (in the single record statistics) and **Bytes sent** (in the performance trace) fields indicate the uncompressed volume of data for the screen layout or RFC. This data is compressed before being sent over the network so that, in effect, a much smaller volume of data is sent.

Figure 7.2 shows an example of a statistics record with extremely slow GUI communication. Of the 27.5 seconds the transaction step takes, 22.5 seconds can be attributed to GUI time. The volume of data transferred (**Terminal out-message** field; not shown in screen extract) is 17 KB in this case. At 1.5 seconds per KB, the transfer rate does not meet our expectations.

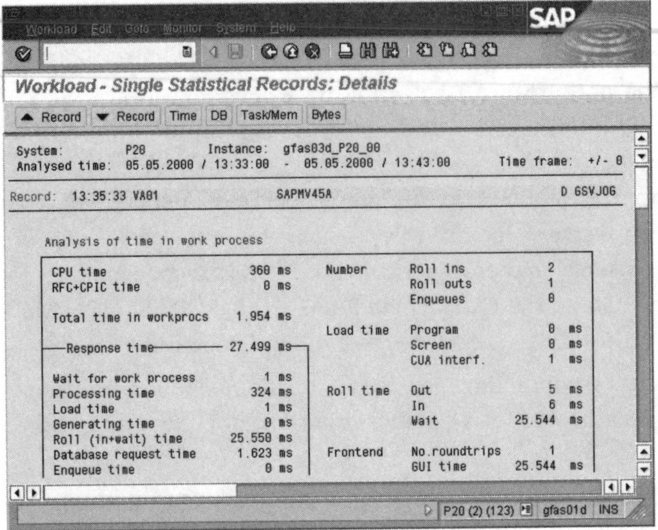

Figure 7.2 Example of a statistics record (transaction code STAD) with extremely slow GUI communication. Of the 27.5 seconds the transaction step takes, 22.5 seconds can be attributed to GUI time.

In a subsequent analysis step we will look closely at the network between the presentation and application levels. The **LANcheck by Ping** function is provided for this purpose on the Operating System Monitor.

1. On the Operating System Monitor (transaction code ST06), choose the **Detailed Analysis Menu · LANcheck by Ping** function. Then choose the **Presentation Server** function.
2. You will then see a list of all logged-on presentation servers. Select the presentation server you want to analyze (or choose ten presentation servers arbitrarily) and select the respective server using the **Pick** function. Then start the network analysis with the **10 x Ping** function.
3. You will find an example of the analysis result in Figure 7.3. Ten presentation servers were selected in this example, whose names and IP addresses are shown in the **Server Name** and **Server IP** columns. The minimum, average and maximum runtime for a Ping command (columns **Min/ms, Avg/ms** and **Max/ms**) is shown on the screen for each of these servers as well as the number of Pings that were not answered (in the **Loss** column). Typical response times for a Ping with a packet size of 4 KB are as follows:
   - In a Local Area Network (LAN): < 20 milliseconds
   - In a Wide Area Network (WAN): < 50 milliseconds

- For modem connections (for example, a 56-KB modem): < 250 milliseconds
- There should be no "losses" of data packages.

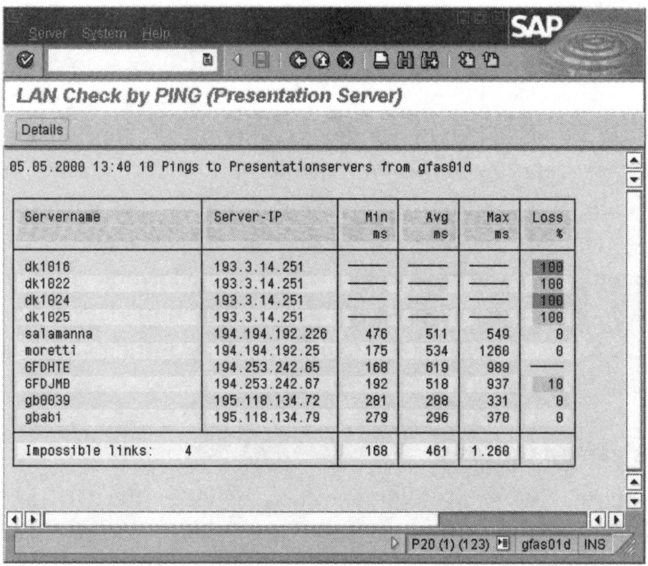

Servername	Server-IP	Min ms	Avg ms	Max ms	Loss %
dk1016	193.3.14.251	—	—	—	100
dk1022	193.3.14.251	—	—	—	100
dk1024	193.3.14.251	—	—	—	100
dk1025	193.3.14.251	—	—	—	100
salamanna	194.194.192.226	476	511	549	0
moretti	194.194.192.25	175	534	1260	0
GFDHTE	194.253.242.65	168	619	989	—
GFDJMB	194.253.242.67	192	518	937	10
gb0039	195.118.134.72	281	288	331	0
gbabi	195.118.134.79	279	296	370	0
Impossible links: 4		168	461	1.260	

Figure 7.3 Example of an analysis of a network between the application and presentation levels (transaction code ST06). The timeouts and slow response times indicate a major communication problem.

This screen image is taken from the same SAP system as in Figure 7.2. The analysis shows a completely corrupt network with major communication problems. No connection can be set up to some of the presentation servers while others respond with a turnaround of 300 to 500 milliseconds. This explains the poor GUI times we witnessed in the statistics record in Figure 7.2. Nothing more can be done here at the moment from the point of view of the SAP system. As a next step, the network must be analyzed using the respective vendor's tools and the network must then be repaired.

Large volume of data

The second case described above occurs if the transfer rate (on average 100 ms per KB or better) is good but problems arise because too much data is transferred in a transaction step. This problem can only be resolved by transferring less data in each step. This can be done by simplifying the screen. In many cases, the screens supplied as standard by SAP clearly contain more information than individual users need for their work.

Transaction variants allow the screens to be adapted to the current needs of users and at the same time allow the performance to be improved. For a description of how to use transaction variants to optimize performance, refer to SAP Note 332210 and the example of a transaction to create a sales order (VA01). If the problem still cannot be resolved, the developer of the relevant transaction must perform a detailed analysis.

You should be able to solve the problem easily if the response time of the SAP_GUI_PROGRESS_INDICATOR module represents a considerable proportion of the overall response time in the performance trace. The module simply updates the status message in the footer of your GUI during a dialog step. For example, the module sends messages, such as "Data being loaded" and updates the small clock in the lower left corner of the screen window, which displays the progress of an operation. You can disable this status display easily at user level by setting the user parameter SIN to the value "0".

Other optimization options

Low speed connection

We recommend that network communication between the GUI and application level be switched to a *low speed connection* in WAN (Wide Area Network) environments. This will reduce the volume of data transferred per dialog step (see SAP Note 164102). The low speed connection can be activated in the SAP logon window by selecting the entry for an SAP system and choosing the menu option **Low Speed Connection** under **Properties · Advanced**.

New visual design

SAP has given its user interface a completely *new visual design* with SAP GUI V4.6, which places more stringent requirements on the hardware of the presentation server. If your presentation server does not meet the hardware requirements described in SAP Note 26417, high GUI times may result because the presentation server's CPU is too slow or because the presentation server pages heavily because of main memory shortage. Performance can be increased in this case by switching locally from the new GUI design supplied with SAP GUI 4.6 to the old SAP GUI design. You can use the **SAP Visual Settings** icon on the desktop to switch between the new and old design. The setting becomes active for the next session you start.

Functionality is not restricted by enabling the low speed connection or disabling the new visual design. Controls are still displayed as usual. The enabling of the low speed connection is independent of the disabling of the new visual design. The first action is helpful if the network connection is slow, while the latter makes sense if there is a hardware bottleneck on the presentation server. Disabling the new visual design only allows performance to be increased if old PCs are used, which do not comply with the requirements of SAP GUI 4.6. There is no benefit to be gained by switching to the old design if the PC hardware is adequate.

SAP Easy Access Menu

The *SAP Easy Access Menu* is used in SAP Basis 4.6 instead of the familiar SAP default menu as the entry point for users. Users are presented with a personalized menu that has been assigned to them on the basis of their respective role. This personalized menu only contains the transactions users actually need for their work. Alternatively, you can of course also use the global SAP menu. You should make sure the SAP Easy Access Menu builds efficiently, as there is nothing more frustrating for users than having to wait for their initial screen after they log on. The most important recommendations include avoiding unwieldy background images in the SAP Easy Access Menu (these should be no larger than 20 KB) and restricting the number of transactions in a role (ideally to 1,000 or fewer). SAP Note 203924 provides you with the necessary information for efficiently customizing the menu.

SAP Internet Transaction Server (SAP ITS)

Since SAP R/3 3.1, the SAP application level can be accessed directly from a Web browser via the SAP Internet Transaction Server (SAP ITS) and a Web server. Possible Web servers here include the Microsoft Internet Information Server or the Netscape Enterprise Server.

ITS Fundamentals

AGate and WGate

The ITS comprises two components, the *WGate* and the *AGate*. The WGate sets up the connection to the Web server. Its task is to recognize and forward Web server queries that are directed at the ITS. On the NT platform, the WGate is a DLL that is incorporated in the Web server. The AGate is the portal to the SAP application level and handles the main work on the ITS. It reads the input data from the HTTP query from the Internet/Intranet and sends it to the SAP application level; the incoming SAP screens then convert it to HTML pages.

Various techniques are available to application developers for implementing Web applications for their mySAP.com solutions. The most important of these are:

- The SAP transaction screen is converted generically by the AGate to HTML in the SAP GUI for HTML. This means that every SAP transaction can be executed in the browser with the SAP GUI for HTML (with a few minor restrictions). HTML-specific programming is not necessary.
- Easy Web Transaction (EWT), which replaces the former Internet Application Components (IACs). An EWT comprises a transaction in the SAP system and HTML templates on the ITS AGate. If an EWT is invoked from the browser, the AGate starts the respective transaction in the SAP system. The AGate logs on here via the DIAG protocol and behaves like a Windows GUI to the application server. The AGate reads the screen contents from the screen returned by the application server, including the field contents, table contents, buttons, and so on, and inserts these in the HTML template at the appropriate places.
- The dialog flow is exported to the ITS in the case of Easy Web Transactions (EWTs) with flow logic in other words, program text in the ITS (so-called flow logic files) determines which screen will be processed next. Only the data retrieval then takes place at the application and database level, generally via RFCs.
- HTML preparation takes place at the application level with a Web RFC. If a Web RFC query is executed in the browser, the WGate and AGate forward this query directly as an RFC to the application level. The data is then retrieved at this level and the complete HTML page is generated and transferred via the RFC interface. The AGate and WGate send the completed HTML page to the browser.

The Web application techniques can be classified according to which part of the transaction is executed at the application level and which part on the ITS. Table 7.1 provides a detailed list of the steps that are executed by the different Web applications.

	EWT without flow logic	**EWT with flow logic**	**SAP GUI for HTML**	**Web RFC**
Logon at SAP application level	DIAG protocol	RFC protocol	DIAG protocol	RFC protocol
Business logic (data retrieval, updating and calculation)	Application and database level			

Table 7.1 Programming modules for Web applications with the SAP ITS

	EWT without flow logic	EWT with flow logic	SAP GUI for HTML	Web RFC
Generation of HTML page	AGate (from HTML template and SAP screen)		AGate (generically from SAP screen)	Application level
Flow logic (dialog flow)	Application level	AGate (with flow logic file)	Application level	

Table 7.1 Programming modules for Web applications with the SAP ITS (contd.)

Before we discuss configuration and tuning options for the ITS, let us examine in detail how a dialog step is executed in a Web application.

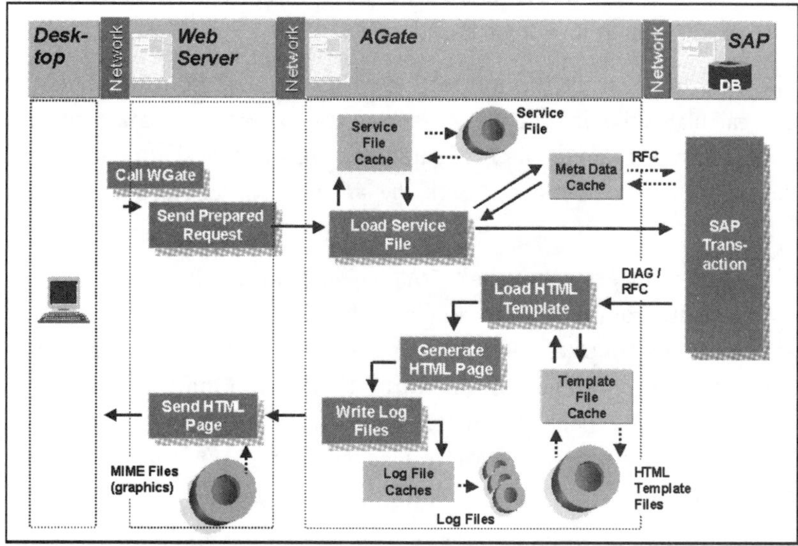

Figure 7.4 Transaction step on the SAP ITS

Logging on to the application server

If you want to invoke an Easy Web Transaction via the Internet, you will typically enter an URL such as this one: `http://<sapWeb-Server>.<company.com>/scripts/wgate/<tcode>/!`

This URL can be interpreted as follows: `<company.com>` stands here for your Internet address and `<sapWeb-Server>` for the name of the Web server belonging to your SAP system. The `/scripts/wgate` suffix indicates to the Web server that this query is to be forwarded to the WGate. The WGate then forwards the query directly to the ITS AGate.

The AGate interprets `<tcode>` as the name of a service file `<tcode>.srvc` and searches for the relevant file in the directory that contains its service files. Among other information, the AGate finds the name of the SAP transaction being called in this file. According to naming conventions, the name of the service file should comply with the transaction code.

Typical Web transactions include transactions from the SAP Online Store (transaction code VW01, WW10) or from the Human Resources department (Employee Self Services such as time recording on the Web, CATW, travel accounting on the Web, PRWW). In accordance with the naming convention, the associated service files would then be `vw01.srvc`, and so on.

The AGate logs on to the application level with the information from the service file, via the DIAG protocol in the case of EWTs without flow logic and the SAP GUI for HTML and via the RFC protocol (see Table 7.1) in the case of EWTs with flow logic and the Web RFC.

The data retrieval for the transaction reads the data from the database and calculates the defined dependencies. If necessary, the data entered is checked and changed in the database. Data retrieval, updating and calculation are performed essentially at the application and database level.

Generating HTML pages

The AGate now generates the HTML page from the SAP screen returned to the AGate from the application level. In the case of an EWT, the AGate searches in its templates directory for the HTML template that belongs to the relevant service and fills this with the data from the SAP screen. The generated HTML page is sent to the WGate, which supplements the HTML page with integrated MIME files (graphic, audio files) and sends it to the browser.

SAP GUI for HTML

This is how you invoke the *SAP GUI for HTML*: `http://<sapWeb-Server>.<company.com>/scripts/WGate/webgui/!` This activates the `webgui.srvc` service in the AGate. You are initially shown a logon screen when you enter the above address. Once you have logged on to the application level, the web gui service translates all transactions to HTML. You can therefore work with your browser as with your SAP GUI for Windows or SAP GUI for Java.

Web RFC

You can use the following syntax to start a *Web RFC query*: `http://<sapWeb-Server>.<company.com>/scripts/WGate/webrfc/!?_function= <function module> &<_variable1>=<value> ...` The first thing you notice from the address is that the webrfc.srvc service is invoked. This is followed by the name of the RFC module to be called and the variables to be passed to the module, separated in each case by question marks. An example of calling the "WWW_GET_REPORT" module with the REPORT = "RSCONN01" variable is as follows: http://<sapWeb-Server>.<company.com>/scripts/WGate/webrfc/!?_function= www_get_report&_report=rsconn01. The complete HTML page is already generated at the application level in the case of the Web RFC. The AGate and WGate then simply forward this to the browser.

Each of these transactions has its advantages and disadvantages. When you start a Web development project you have to decide which technique best suits the functional requirements for the project. The different techniques impact the sizing, configuration and performance of the ITS, which we want to look at in the next sections.

Planning a Web Connection

As explained at the outset, all SAP applications are Web-enabled, apart from a few applications such as graphical planning tools. This means that a company can opt strategically for the SAP GUI for HTML as a single GUI solution. The alternative would be to implement a double-track solution, deploying the SAP GUI for HTML as the GUI for some users and the classical SAP GUI for Windows for other users. In this section, we hope to clarify which arguments you should be guided by in this respect.

Web applications

First of all, there are some SAP applications that essentially only run with the SAP ITS; these include all solutions for the Internet or Intranet, for example SAP Employee Self Service (SAP ESS), SAP Online Store, Enterprise Buyer Professional (E-Procurement). The decision for a Web solution has, in essence, already been taken with these applications. These applications are optimized to the requirements of the Web.

The situation is somewhat different for many classical SAP R/3 transactions. These run both with the SAP GUI for HTML and with the SAP GUI for Windows. You should consider performance when making your decision in this case.

Performance of the HTML GUI and Windows GUI

Essentially, additional work is required to use the *SAP GUI for HTML* (CPU time and data transfer), which can mean delays in comparison with *SAP GUI for Windows*. The following individual aspects should be considered.

- The CPU time required by the ITS for converting the SAP screens to HTML pages.

- The higher data transfer between the ITS and browser (in comparison with data transfer between the application level and the SAP GUI for Windows).
- The generation time in the Web browser; this is higher than the processing time in the SAP GUI for Windows.

The extent to which the response time is faster for a user using the SAP GUI for HTML in comparison with the SAP GUI for Windows depends ultimately on the functions used and the hardware. Around one extra second can be calculated for the CPU time on the ITS and the frontend. The following can be assumed in the case of a higher volume of traffic. SAP rightly refers to its SAP GUI for Windows as an "ultra-thin client" because the data traffic between the application level and GUI is very low, some 1 to 2 KB per screen switch for SAP R/3 4.0 and some 3 to 5 KB per screen switch for SAP R/3 4.6 for transactions with controls. The Internet standard on the other hand is many times higher. Between 20 and 200 KB are typically transferred to construct HTML pages. SAP products are at the lower end of the scale here in terms of data traffic, with some 20 to 40 KB. This increased data traffic is barely noticeable in terms of turnaround in a high bandwidth LAN. However, this difference can seriously impair the performance of the SAP GUI for HTML in comparison with the SAP GUI for Windows in a low bandwidth WAN. We therefore recommend that evaluation measurements be performed, as described in the section "Performing Runtime Analyses in the Web Browser" on page 240.

Configuring ITS

The ITS can be scaled almost arbitrarily because of its architecture. This section shows how to adapt the ITS optimally to your load requirements.

In the case of a development, test or small production system without special high-availability requirements, it is possible to install all levels of the mySAP.com technology (presentation level, Internet level, application level, database level) on one computer.

If availability and throughput requirements then change, it makes sense to distribute the individual levels over a number of computers. (Security aspects also play a role here, as explained in more detail below).

The first step in scaling is to provide separate computers for the Internet level (ITS and Web servers) and to hence separate these from the SAP application level and the database level.

Configuration of ITS instances

ITS instances

The ITS, like the application level, is also organized in instances. This means, therefore, that several *ITS instances* can be installed on one computer, which are administered separately. Theoretically, it is possible for the different ITS instance services to point to different SAP systems. However, for administration reasons, this is not recommended for productive use. You should set up your system landscape such that an ITS instance always points to one SAP system.

Logon via a logon group

The ITS instance can be logged on to the application level using either a dedicated instance (with specification of the application server and instance number) or via a *logon group* (with specification of the message server and a logon group). For optimal availability and workload distribution, you should use the second option. This setting is made in the service files on the AGate.

Scalability of ITS instances

Depending on the throughput requirements, you can run several *ITS instances* (possibly pointing to different SAP systems) on one computer. Alternatively, you can also run several ITS instances for one SAP system and distribute these to different computers. In order to ensure optimally high availability, at least two computers are needed for the Internet level, each of which runs one ITS instance, each of which points to at least two SAP instances via a logon group, which in turn are configured on different computers.

Firewall between AGate and WGate

For security reasons, access to the AGate file system must always be protected, because anyone who has access to the AGate can define a service and hence execute all function modules released for Internet usage on the application server. The best way to protect the AGate is to set up a *firewall* between the AGate and the WGate, because the data flow is then the responsibility of SAP and can be properly monitored. According to security experts, a firewall around the Web server (WGate) is much less reliable. The best configuration is to operate a Web server (with WGate) and AGate on different computers and to separate these via a firewall. This configuration is mandatory if the ITS connects your SAP system with the Internet. It must be decided whether this high standard of security is also appropriate in the case of Intranet projects.

An ITS configuration that is optimized in terms of availability, performance and security therefore comprises a dual Web server configuration (with WGate), ITS AGate and SAP instance, so that if one computer fails, the load can be taken over by the remaining computer. In parallel, the database and the application level should be protected with the enqueue server using a suitable high-availability solution at operating system level (switch-over solution).

Configuration of work processes, sessions and caches

Work processes and sessions

Queries from the dispatcher (mapping manager process) are assigned within an ITS instance to an ITS work process (work thread). The ITS work process copies the query data to a specific memory area, the so-called user session. The number of ITS work processes and sessions can be defined on the ITS. You will find an overview of performance-related ITS parameters in Appendix C.

The ITS architecture is therefore similar to that of an SAP application instance, which likewise has a dispatcher and several work processes that access global user contexts (sessions). However, the ITS does not have a dispatcher queue. If all ITS work processes are reserved, the dispatcher sends back an error message to the browser (while an application instance "parks" the query, in this case in the dispatcher queue).

Cache mechanisms

The ITS uses *cache mechanisms* to optimize performance. This means, for example, that service files, interfaces from SAP function modules invoked by the ITS, HTML templates, module calls (when using flow logic) and log entries are stored in the main memory. These cache mechanisms can be enabled and disabled via parameters (Appendix C).

Performance-limiting factors

The following factors can limit the performance of the ITS:

- Hardware bottlenecks, in other words, CPU or main memory bottlenecks (high paging activity).
- The number of work processes and user sessions: If too few of these are configured, error messages are issued because the ITS can no longer edit the queries being sent to it.
- Restriction on the addressable memory: In the Windows NT architecture, the addressable memory is restricted to 2 GB per AGate process. If the AGate process requests additional memory beyond this limit during runtime, error messages are issued that can be monitored in the AGate and operating system log files.

▶ Restrictions caused by network connections: The AGate process can set up a maximum of 4,096 user sessions with the application level. This restricts the maximum number of logged on users per AGate and SAP application instance. This means, therefore, that several AGate and SAP application instances may have to be configured.

▶ Incorrect configuration of the cache mechanisms: If the cache mechanisms are not activated correctly, too much file traffic will be generated unnecessarily.

In order to avoid hardware bottlenecks in advance of an installation, you should have your hardware partner draw up a sizing proposal before productive startup. You will find information on ITS sizing in the SAP Service Marketplace under `http://service.sap.com/sizing`. Recommended settings for work processes, sessions and cache mechanisms can be found in Appendix C.

If bottlenecks arise at runtime, these can be localized using analysis tools. You will find a description of the tools and associated methods in the next sections.

ITS Administration Tools

There are several options for administering and monitoring an ITS instance. On the one hand, you can do this using the ITS administration instance, which you start from a browser from the following URL address: `http://<sapwebserver>.<company.com>:<portnumber>/scripts/wgate/admin /!`, where `<company.com>` stands for an Internet address, `<sapwebserver>` for the ITS Web server and `<portnumber>` for the TCP port, which the administration instance listens to.

You can use the administration instance to:

▶ Start and stop ITS instances

▶ Change ITS parameters

▶ Evaluate the ITS log files (error and performance logs)

▶ Establish the current performance and capacity utilization

The log files that you can monitor are the AGate log (AGate.trc), the dispatch log (Mmanager.trc), the performance log (PERFORMANCE.LOG), the workload distribution log (LOADSTAT.LOG) and the access log (ACCESS.LOG).

Global CCMS alert monitor

All performance data that you find in the proprietary ITS administration tool is also integrated in the central CCMS Alert Monitor (transaction code RZ20). The main advantages offered by using the CCMS Alert Monitor to monitor the ITS instances are that you have all performance data in one tool and the entire functionality of alert monitoring and administration is at your disposal. SAP Note 418285 provides details on how to integrate ITS instances into the CCMS Alert Monitor. Figure 7.5 and Table 7.2 show the ITS performance data and an explanation.

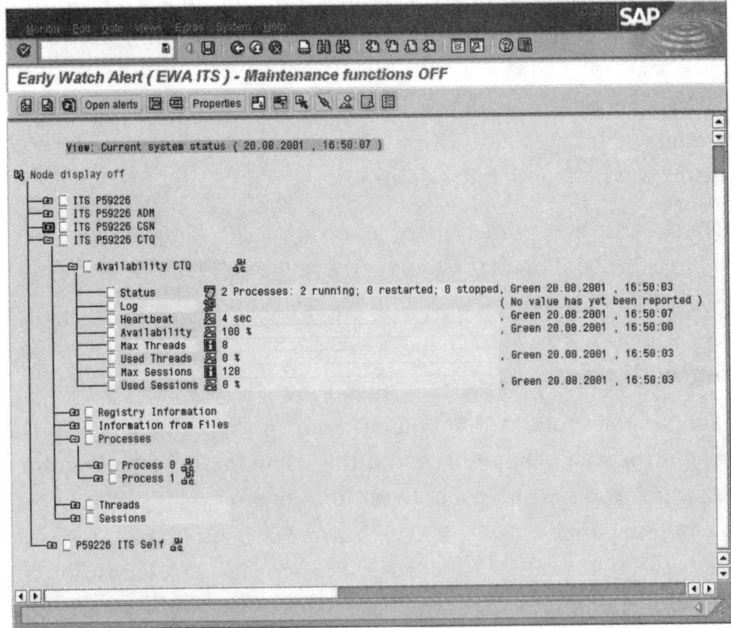

Figure 7.5 ITS performance data in the central CCMS Alert Monitor

Entry in the central CCMS alert monitor	Explanation
Status	Information on the initiated AGate processes
Log	AGate instance number
Heartbeat	"Sign of life" of SAP ITS
Availability	Availability of ITS instance in the last 15 minutes

Table 7.2 ITS performance data in the central CCMS Alert Monitor. The values indicated by an asterisk are not shown in Figure 7.5; you will find these in the branch under "Processes".

Entry in the central CCMS alert monitor	Explanation
Max. Threads	Total number of available ITS work processes (work threads)
Used Threads	Number of used ITS work processes (as a percentage)
Max. Sessions	Total number of available sessions
Used Sessions	Number of used sessions (as a percentage)
Hits*	Number of accesses (hits) per second
Hits A*	Number of currently opened accesses to the application server
TAT*	Turnaround time: Average response time for accessing the application server and generating the HTML page
Up time*	Time since ITS instance started
User time*	User's CPU share on the ITS server
Kernel time*	System's CPU share on the ITS server (as a percentage)

Table 7.2 ITS performance data in the central CCMS Alert Monitor. The values indicated by an asterisk are not shown in Figure 7.5; you will find these in the branch under "Processes". (contd.)

Global Operating System Monitor

You can monitor more detailed data on the hardware utilization of the ITS server from an SAP system using the *global Operating System Monitor* (transaction code OS07) (see also Section 2.2). To do this, you have to start the data collector programs `SAPOSCOL` and `RFCOSCOL` as well as an SAP gateway on the computers on which ITS instances are running. You will find details about the installation in SAP Note 202934.

Performing a Bottleneck Analysis for the ITS

Problem: All ITS work processes are busy

If the number of free *ITS work processes* is close to zero, error messages are issued because the ITS can no longer process the queries sent to it. In this case, it must be checked whether the problem can be resolved by increasing the number of ITS work processes. Essentially, the same rule applies here as for the application level: the number of ITS work processes should only be increased if there are still hardware resources free. However, the problem of work processes being occupied can also be caused by a programming error, which means that either the program on the AGate (business HTML or flow logic) or the program on the application server (ABAP) was programmed inefficiently and requires an unnecessary volume of resources (or in extreme cases gets caught up in an endless loop).

Problem: Insufficient addressable memory

You can use the display of freely addressable (virtual) memory to check whether this will cause a bottleneck. Overall, 2 GB can be addressed on Windows NT per AGate process. Once this limit is reached, you can resolve the problem by starting several AGate processes for each ITS instance. A bottleneck in the addressable memory also causes an error entry to be written to the AGate log (AGate.trc).

Problem: Hardware bottleneck

You will recognize a *hardware bottleneck* by a high level of CPU utilization and a high paging rate (see also next section).

Problem: Shutdown because of insufficient disk space

The ITS hangs if there is no further disk space available. This may happen, for example, if log files are not reorganized as recommended over a longer period or if you forget to reduce the trace level after creating a detailed runtime analysis.

Performing Runtime Analyses in the Web Browser

If users complain about the poor performance of their Web application and if you cannot identify an acute bottleneck in the application server, database server and ITS, problems on the presentation server or in the network may be a further possible cause. To verify this suspicion, you can perform a trace on the presentation server using an analysis tool from the respective operating system.

The following analysis is not limited to the SAP ITS; you could also use this method to analyze the Web applications in your online base, for example, if they appear to you to be too slow. We describe the analysis on Windows NT below with the **PERFMON** program; the **SYSMON** program is available for Windows 95 and offers practically the same functionality.

1. Start **PERFMON** on your Windows NT presentation server, for example by choosing **Start · Run · PERFMON**. (If **PERFMON** does not exist, you can install it by choosing **Start · Settings · Control Panel · Add/Remove Programs**.)
2. Set up **PERFMON**:
   - You have to measure the CPU utilization on your presentation server. Enter the following in the **PERFMON** menu: **Edit · Add to Chart**. Choose the value "Processor" from **Object** and the value "%Processor Time" for **Counter**.

- You then need the transferred data for your analysis: Choose the value "Network Interface" for **Object** and the value "Bytes Received/sec" for **Counter**. Note: Depending on the type of network connection, the **Category** and **Item** name may differ from the examples given above. You may have to start processes at the NT level to monitor the network traffic.

3. Start your analysis: To do this, call the Web application you want to test. In the **PERFMON** screen, observe how quickly the network and CPU utilization increase on the presentation server after the application is started.

The evaluation of the analysis provides information in relation to:

- The browser generation time (also referred to as the rendering time): This is the time during which your browser is busy generating the HTML page. You will see from the upper screen in Figure 7.6 that during rendering the CPU utilization is practically 100%.
- The network transfer time: This is the time during which the data is transferred to the browser. You will see from the lower screen in Figure 7.6 that the network transfer rate levels off at 8 KB/sec. This is the bandwidth of the ISDN line, which is used to connect the computer in this example. You can save the measurement data with the **File • Export Chart** function and transfer it to a spreadsheet program. You can then establish how much data is transferred by adding up the values in the **Bytes Received/sec** column.
- The "residual time": If you neither measure the CPU activity on your presentation server nor the network activity, although you can see the hourglass in the browser, you can assume that you have to search for the time on the server (in our case at the ITS, SAP application or database level).

You can estimate the optimization potential as follows using this simple analysis:

- The browser generation time is high: In this case, you have to consider whether the PC being used is perhaps not powerful enough. You can tell immediately whether an investment in new hardware would increase performance.
- The network transfer time is high: In this instance you can also immediately calculate to what extent a faster network connection would result in a faster response.

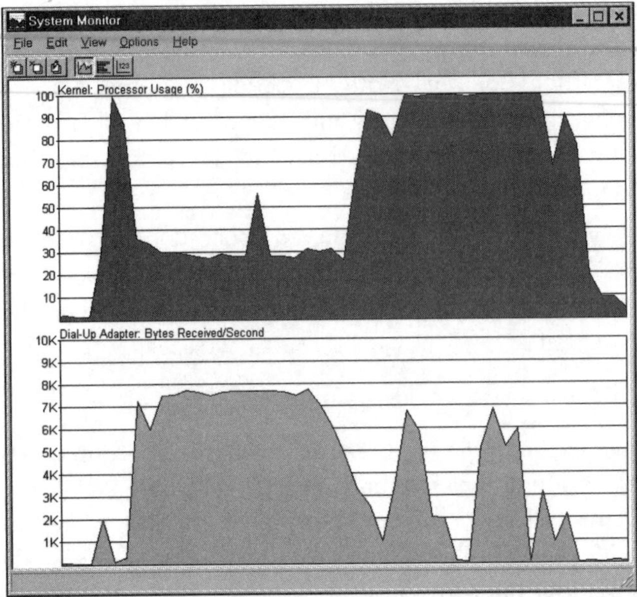

Figure 7.6 Analysis of a Web application with SYSMON on a presentation server with Windows 95 as operating system and an ISDN network connection with a bandwidth of 8 KB/sec.

- Performance could of course also be increased in both cases by optimizing the application, in other words, by transferring less data. The most important points in this regard include:
  - Fewer images
  - Simplification of screen contents in SAP GUI for HTML applications using transaction variants (already described in the section "Analyzing and Optimizing the Performance of GUI Communication" on page 223)
  - Analysis of HTML text with regard to superfluous coding, for example coding transferred unnecessarily in Includes
- The "residual time" is high: You should perform a performance analysis at the ITS and SAP application level in this case. In particular, you should evaluate the statistics records in the SAP system, which you can access via the transaction codes STAD (from SAP Basis 4.6) or STAT (up to SAP Basis 4.5) (see also Chapter 4). You have to specify the user name and the measurement period in order to display the statistics records. These statistics records will tell you the response time in the SAP system, the CPU time in the SAP system, the database time and other details.

Monitoring Web Applications Continuously

Many vendors now offer tools for monitoring URLs. The following Internet page provides a summary of such monitoring products: `http://dmoz.org/Computers/Software/Internet/Site_Management/Monitoring/`.

At the time this book goes to print, SAP is developing its own URL monitoring tool for integration in the central CCMS Alert Monitor.

Such tools allow the availability of strategically important Web pages to be monitored centrally, regardless of which server supplies the pages. The tools also offer a content check; in other words, they can check whether the correct contents are displayed. You can also define other URL transactions, that is to say, sequences of HTML pages, which are to run periodically. (You have to make sure here, of course, that no real documents are created.)

URL monitoring ideally complements the ITS "internal monitoring" described above. URL monitoring is easy to start up and generic; in other words, it is independent of the server technology that generates the HTML pages (SAP ITS, Java Application Server or simple Web server). However, if an alarm is set off, possibly indicating the failure of a Web application, it provides no further insight for analyzing the cause of the error. It is also not proactive, in the sense that it only reacts after errors have occured; whereas, for example, the monitoring of work processes in the ITS could trigger an alarm if a certain utilization level is exceeded but the end user has not yet detected any problem.

Summary

Starting with SAP Basis 4.6, RFCs have been used for communication between the SAP application level and the SAP presentation level so as to set up screen elements known as controls (and they are being used increasingly in the framework of the EnjoySAP Initiative). Tools such as the single record statistics, the performance trace (RFC trace) and the network check are available in the Operating System Monitor for analyzing possible performance problems (for example, in the network to the presentation servers).

A number of points are relevant in relation to the performance of the Web connection with the SAP Internet Transaction Server. First of all comes the selection of the correct GUI. The SAP GUI for HTML is not the obvious choice for some user groups. In some cases, it makes sense to continue using the SAP GUI for Windows (or Java). The ITS configuration involves the redundant installation of WGate and AGate, the configuration of the ITS work processes (threads), sessions and caches as well as the creation of logon groups for logging on to the SAP system. Finally, you should be familiar with ITS performance monitoring and analysis. The central CCMS alert monitor provides constant monitoring, while analyses with the ITS administration tool provide assistance in the event of performance problems.

The final method described for analyzing the performance of HTML pages using operating system tools (for example, **PERFMON**) is generic and can be used not only for Web pages, which have been generated by the SAP ITS, but also for those generated by the SAP Web Application Server or a Java Application Server.

Important terms in this chapter

After studying this chapter you should be familiar with the following terms:

- Roll wait time, RFC time, GUI time
- Controls and frontend communication
- Choosing the "correct" GUI: SAP GUI for Windows, SAP GUI for HTML, SAP GUI for Java Environment
- SAP Internet Transaction Server: WGate, AGate, thread and session concept, caching on the ITS
- Performance analysis with **PERFMON**

Questions

1. Which statements characterize a high roll wait time?
   a) A high roll wait time is a unique indication of a problem with GUI communication (for instance, in the network between the presentation and application servers).
   b) A high roll wait time is a unique indication of a problem with RFC communication with external SAP or non-SAP systems.
   c) A high roll wait time is a unique indication of a problem with GUI communication or with RFC communication.
   d) A high roll wait time can also be caused by a poor-performance network between the application and database level.

2. A transaction that uses controls is processed in a transaction step, though no external RFC is invoked. Which statements apply?
   a) GUI time is greater than roll wait time.
   b) RFC time is greater than roll wait time.
   c) Roll wait time is always greater than zero.
   d) Roll wait time is generally greater than zero but can also be zero.
   e) Roll wait time is always equal to zero.
3. A program is processed in a transaction step that uses no controls and no synchronous RFCs, although asynchronous RFCs are invoked. Which statements apply?
   a) GUI time is greater than the roll wait time.
   b) RFC time is greater than roll wait time.
   c) Roll wait time is always greater than zero.
   d) Roll wait time is generally greater than zero but can also be zero.
   e) Roll wait time is always equal to zero.
4. A Web application implemented using the ITS and an SAP system is too slow. Which analyses will you perform?
   a) Use the ITS administration tool or the central CCMS Alert Monitor to check whether all work processes (threads) or sessions on the ITS are busy or whether the CPU is constantly busy.
   b) Use the work process overview for the connected SAP system to check whether all work processes are occupied.
   c) Use a performance trace and the single record statistics on the connected SAP system to analyze the response time on the SAP system and compare this with the response time measured by the user on the presentation server.
   d) Use an analysis tool on the presentation server (**PERFMON**, for example) to check the volume of data transferred to the browser and the render time for the HTML page in the browser; then compare the time needed with the overall response time.

8 Memory Management

This chapter describes the SAP memory areas that have to be configured for an SAP instance: SAP buffer, SAP roll memory, SAP extended memory, SAP heap memory (variable local memory of SAP work processes), SAP paging memory and the fixed local memory of the SAP work processes.

The chapter is divided into two sections: The first section explains the concept and function of the individual memory areas as well as their influence on the performance of the SAP system. The second section contains important implementation information for different operating systems and gives concrete recommendations with respect to configuration.

The key factors influencing the configuration are as follows:

- **Physical main memory (RAM)**
  Are the physically available main memory and the virtually allocated memory in a proper ratio to one another? Which memory areas most urgently need attention when resources are low?
- **Operating system options and restrictions**
  Do these permit the desired configuration? What do I have to look out for on systems with 32-bit and 64-bit architectures?

When should you read this chapter?

You should read this chapter if you want to re-configure SAP memory management following a re-installation, an upgrade or a system expansion or if you have discovered performance problems in relation to memory management.

Basics of Memory Management

Before we begin to explain the memory areas of an SAP instance, some key terms will be introduced in a preliminary section.

Basic Terms

Physical and virtual memory

More memory can be allocated virtually in all operating systems than is physically available. The term "memory" always refers to *virtual memory*, which is managed by the operating system either in the *physical main memory* or in the *swap space*. The maximum amount of virtual memory that can be allocated is limited by two variables:

- All processes together cannot allocate more memory than the sum of the physical main memory and the available swap space. This limit is a result of physical hardware restrictions.
- Each individual process cannot allocate more memory than the maximum addressable memory area (*address space*) permitted by the operating system. This logical limit is imposed by the architecture of the operating systems. The address space is theoretically 4 GB (2^{32}) for 32-bit architecture; the memory that can be addressed is far below this (between 2 and 3.8 GB depending on the operating system). This is a serious restriction in terms of the practical configuration. The address space restriction is not relevant in practical terms any more in the case of 64-bit operating systems.

Local memory and shared memory

The operating system manages two types of memory, *local memory* and *shared memory*. Local memory is always allocated precisely to one operating system process, in other words only this one process can write to or read from this memory area. Shared memory, on the other hand, is accessible to multiple operating system processes. Thus, for example, all SAP buffers lie in the shared memory because all SAP work processes of an SAP instance have to write to and read from the SAP buffer. In addition, local memory is created for every SAP work process. (The local memory of an SAP work process includes, for example, the SAP cursor cache and the I/O buffer for transferring data from and to the database, as described in Chapter 4 in the section "Evaluating an SQL Trace" on page 155.) The virtually allocated memory is the sum of the local memory and the shared memory.

If there are several SAP instances or one SAP instance and one database instance on one computer, the processes of one instance can always only access the shared memory of "their own" instance but not the shared objects of other instances.

32-bit and 64-bit technology

In the *32-bit technology* used up to now, a process can theoretically address a maximum of 4 GB of memory. Because in practice a large percentage of memory cannot be used because of fragmenting, the memory actually available to an SAP work process is much smaller in real terms. The restrictions for the different operating systems are outlined in SAP Note 146528.

These problems have been solved with *64-bit technology*. An address space of several terabytes is available to the work process in this case. In order to use 64-bit technology, you need a 64-bit operating system, a 64-bit version of your database software and a 64-bit version of the SAP kernel. The 64-bit SAP kernel has no new functionalities compared with the 32-bit version. There is no difference in handling, either for users or for administrators. Memory management is simplified considerably by the use of the 64-bit SAP kernel compared with the 32-bit version. You will find details in SAP Note 146289.

64-bit SAP kernels are released on UNIX operating systems for SAP Basis 4.0 and higher and on Solaris from SAP Basis 4.6. The restriction with respect to the 32-bit architecture continues to apply on Windows platforms. You will find information on released 64-bit products in SAP Notes for the component XX-SER-SWREL or in the SAP Service Marketplace under `http://service.sap.com/platforms`.

Language is the source of misunderstandings—this applies to an extreme extent in the case of SAP memory management: For example, the same terms are used at the operating system level and at the SAP system level to describe different things: We distinguish between operating system paging and SAP paging, context switching at operating system level and context switching at SAP level, and so on. Even the term "heap" is duplicated. At the operating system level, it is used to refer to the local memory allocated by an operating system process. At the SAP level, on the other hand, it describes a special local memory area, in other words the SAP heap memory is only a small part of the "heap" referred to at operating system level.

In order to limit confusion, we prefix the SAP terms explicitly in this book with "SAP", for example SAP heap memory or SAP paging memory, to distinguish them from other operating system terms. If you are reading secondary literature or information in the SAP Service Marketplace, clarify on the basis of the context whether the author is referring to the SAP term or the operating system term.

SAP Roll Memory, SAP Extended Memory, SAP Heap Memory

We will introduce the terms *user context, SAP roll memory, SAP extended memory* and *SAP heap memory* in this section.

User context

An SAP transaction generally extends over several transaction steps or screen switches. Data such as variables, internal tables and screen lists are generated during these steps and stored in the application server memory. This data is referred to as *user context*.

Session

If you open a new session by choosing **System · Create session**, a new user context is also created. The data from the transactions that you execute in the two sessions is hence stored independently in different memory areas. Sessions that are opened explicitly by users in this way are called *external sessions*. An ABAP program can also open a new session implicitly from another program for which a new user context is then likewise created. The ABAP commands in this case are **SUBMIT, CALL TRANSACTION, CALL DIALOG, CALL SCREEN, CALL FUNCTION IN UPDATE TASK, CALL FUNCTION IN BACKGROUND TASK and CALL FUNCTION STARTING NEW TASK**. Sessions opened implicitly by the program are called *internal sessions*.

User contexts are stored in the *SAP roll memory*, the *SAP extended memory* or the *SAP heap memory*. You can set parameters to influence which memory area will be used.

SAP roll memory

The initial part of the user context is stored in the *local SAP roll area of the work process*. Because this is local memory, each SAP work process can only access its own roll area. Figure 8.1 illustrates two SAP work processes with their local roll areas. At the end of the respective transaction step, the user exits the work process so that another user can also use this work process. The content of the local work process roll area used by the user has to be backed up. To this end, the local roll area is copied to the *shared SAP roll area*. The shared roll area is either a memory area in the shared memory of the application server (what we call the *SAP roll buffer*) or a file on the application server's hard disk (the *SAP roll file*) or a combination of the two. The shared roll area is accessible to all of an instance's work processes. The process of copying the local roll memory to the shared roll area is called *roll-out* (see also Chapter 3, "Course of a Transaction Step" on page 125). If the user is assigned a different work process in the next transaction step, the user context is copied from the shared roll area to the local roll area of the new work process. The user can then continue working with his/her old data. This procedure is called *roll-in*. The roll buffer and the roll file are shown in Figure 8.1. The two arrows in the diagram symbolize the copy process for a roll in and roll out.

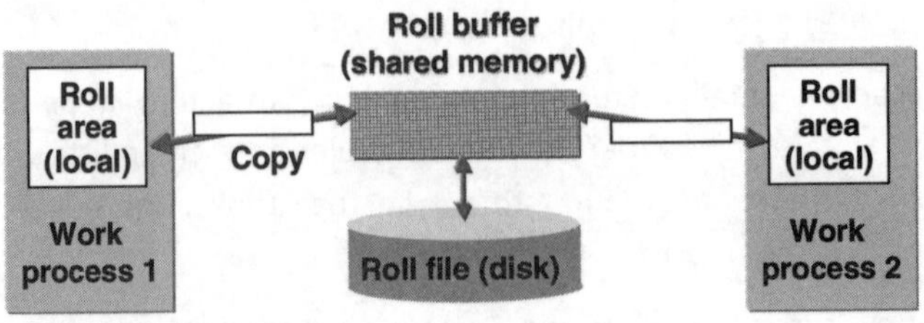

Figure 8.1 Roll memory

You can use the following SAP profile parameters to configure the size of the SAP roll memory.

ztta/roll_area, rdisp/roll_SHM, rdisp/roll_MAXFS

- **ztta/roll_area** establishes the size of the local SAP roll area in the work process. This parameter applies equally for all work process types.
- The size of the SAP roll buffer is established by the SAP profile parameter **rdisp/ROLL_SHM**.
- The size of the entire shared SAP roll area (i.e. roll buffer plus roll file) is defined by the **rdisp/ROLL_MAXFS** parameter.

SAP extended memory

User contexts are stored mostly in the *SAP extended memory* from SAP Basis 3.0. The SAP extended memory is allocated as shared memory: Consequently, all SAP work processes of an SAP instance can edit the stored user contexts directly. Hence, not the entire user context is copied in the roll in to the local memory of the work process, rather only the addresses indicating where the user context is located in the SAP extended memory, in other words, the pointers. The volume of data copied in a roll in or roll out is reduced considerably by using the SAP extended memory, which makes the roll process much faster overall. The SAP system is generally configured in such a way that most user context data is stored in the SAP extended memory.

em/initial_size_MB, em/block_size_KB, ztta/roll_extension

The SAP extended memory is allocated as shared memory.

- The size of the SAP extended memory allocated when the SAP instance starts up is defined by the SAP profile parameter **em/initial_size_MB**.
- The SAP extended memory is split internally into blocks of size **em/blocksize_KB**. The default block size is 1,024 KB and must not be changed unless explicitly recommended by SAP.
- The SAP profile parameter **ztta/roll_extension** defines the maximum size of a user context in the SAP extended memory. This measure prevents an individual user from occupying the entire SAP extended memory with a highly memory-intensive transaction and leaving no memory for the other users.

SAP heap memory

The third memory area where user contexts can be stored is the *SAP heap memory*. Whereas the roll area allocation is already fixed as local memory by a work process at startup, the SAP heap memory is allocated variably as local memory as required, in other words, when the user context exceeds a certain size. The memory is released again when the transaction has ended.

abap/heap_area...

- The SAP profile parameters **abap/heap_area_dia** and **abap/heap_area_nondia** define the quotas of SAP heap memory that a dialog work process or a non-dialog work process can allocate.
- **abap/heap_area_total** specifies how much SAP heap memory can be allocated in total by all work processes.
- The maximum possible value for the **abap/heap_area...** parameter is 2,000,000,000 (2 GB) or, more precisely, $2^{31}-1$.

abap/heaplimit

Once a transaction is complete, an SAP work process that has allocated SAP heap memory must release this memory again. This is achieved in technical terms by the work process restarting as soon as the allocated memory exceeds the value **abap/heaplimit**. If the work process allocates less SAP heap memory, the memory is released in the ABAP (i.e. it can be used again by the next transaction) but not at operating system level. It is therefore highly desirable in this case for the work processes to be restarted. The corresponding entry in the SAP SysLog (transaction code SM21) should therefore not be understood as an error message but simply as information.

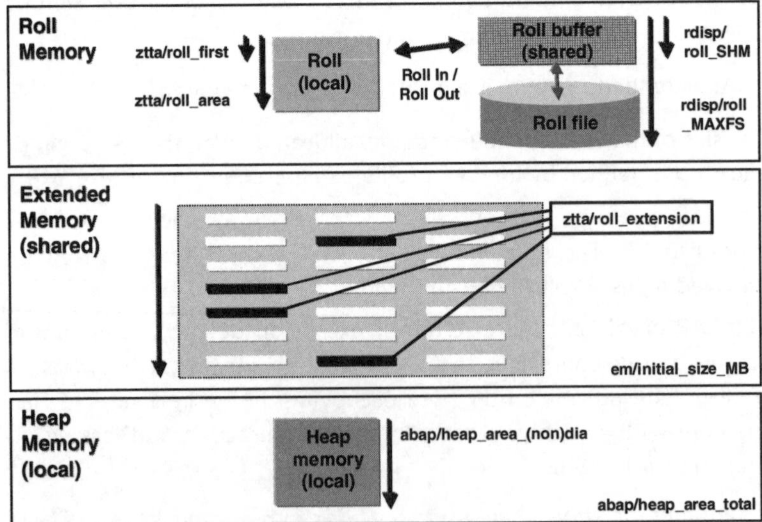

Figure 8.2 SAP memory areas and the associated SAP profile parameters

Sequence in which memory is allocated

User context data is stored by dialog work processes in the following order:

ztta/roll_first

1. When a transaction is started, the user context is stored in the local roll area of the work process up to a size of **ztta/roll_first**. **ztta/roll_first** should be set to 1 (byte). This means that absolutely no SAP roll memory should be reserved initially. (However, administrative data up to 100 KB in size is always stored in the local roll area of the work process for technical reasons, even if **ztta/roll_first** = 1.)
2. If the size of the user context exceeds the value **ztta/roll_first**, the data is stored in the SAP extended memory.
3. If the SAP extended memory is used up or if the user context reaches the **ztta/roll_extension** quota, the remainder of the local roll area is used up to a size of **ztta/roll_area**.
4. If the context continues to grow and if the memory requirement also exceeds this value, the work process allocates SAP heap memory as required. The disadvantage of using the SAP heap memory is that this memory is local and also cannot be copied (rolled)—as with the SAP roll memory—to a shared memory area. If a process allocates SAP heap memory, the context can no longer be transferred to another work process. The work process remains assigned exclusively to one user. This state is referred to as *Private Mode*. This status is documented in the work process overview in the **Status** and **Reason** columns by the values "stopped" and "PRIV".
5. If the value **abap/heap_area_dia** is reached for one work process or the value **abap/heap_area_total** for all work processes, the program will terminate.

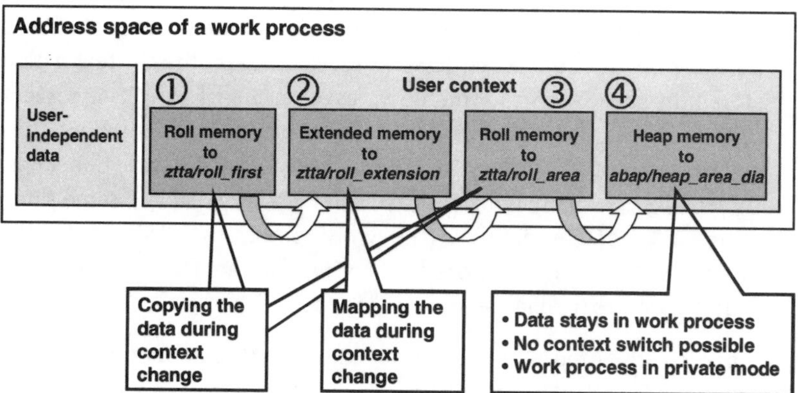

Figure 8.3 The order in which memory is allocated for SAP work processes

Figure 8.3 shows the memory areas that are accessed by a dialog work process: initially, these are memory areas for user-independent objects, for example the SAP buffer. The user-dependent objects (user contexts) are stored by the work processes in the SAP roll memory, SAP extended memory or SAP heap memory.

Performance aspects

SAP extended memory full

In order to ensure optimum performance, the copying of data during a context switch should be kept to a minimum, in other words, as little SAP roll memory as possible should be used. It is therefore recommended for all operating systems with SAP Basis 4.0 to set **ztta/roll_first** = 1.

What happens if the *SAP extended memory* is fully occupied? Two scenarios are possible here, neither of which is optimal in terms of performance:

- Because the SAP extended memory is fully occupied, user contexts up to a size of **ztta/roll_area** are stored in the local roll area (see Figure 8.3 and Table 8.1). It may therefore be necessary with every context switch to repeatedly copy (roll) data of several MB in size; this typically leads to wait times in roll management, particularly if the roll buffer is full and data has to be written to the roll file. Experience shows that if this happens in the case of large application servers with more than 100 users, performance abruptly collapses, with catastrophic effects. An example of such a situation is described in Chapter 2 in the section "Analyzing SAP Work Processes" on page 107.
- The local roll area (**ztta/roll_area**) can be reduced in order to help remedy this situation. If the SAP extended memory is fully occupied, only a small amount of roll memory is used and the volume of data to be copied with a context switch is reduced. Instead, the context data is stored in the SAP heap memory, as a result of which the work processes cease rolling and switch to PRIV mode, in other words, they remain assigned exclusively to one user between the transaction steps. If there are too many work processes in PRIV mode at the same time, there will not be enough free work processes available to the dispatcher. This can therefore lead to high dispatcher wait times and thus likewise to a collapse in performance.

It is particularly important to ensure that the SAP extended memory is large enough and can be further enlarged if necessary. In an ideal scenario, the SAP extended memory would be infinitely extensible and the SAP roll and SAP heap memory could be completely done without.

However, this has not been possible to date because operating system restrictions limit the size of the SAP extended memory. There are therefore mechanisms in the SAP system that can be used to reduce the need for SAP extended memory.

Non-dialog work processes

For example, memory is requested in the following sequence for *non-dialog work processes* in SAP Basis 3 for all operating systems and in SAP Basis 4.0 for UNIX operating systems.

1. The user context is stored initially in the local roll memory of the work process until it reaches a size of **ztta/roll_area**.
2. If additional memory is required, the work process allocates SAP heap memory as required until a value of **abap/heap_area_nondia** is reached or until the entire SAP heap memory (**abap/heap_area_total**) is used up.
3. If one of these limits is exceeded, the work process reserves SAP extended memory until the **ztta/roll_extension** quota is reached or until the SAP extended memory is used up.
4. If these limits are also exceeded, the program terminates.

While dialog work processes essentially use the shared SAP extended memory (as described above), non-dialog work processes should primarily use local heap memory. The sequence in which memory is allocated by dialog and non-dialog work processes, as summarized in Table 8.1, is hence quite complementary. The reason for the different implementations is that non-dialog work processes do not have to exchange their user contexts because background, update and spool requests are always executed fully by one work process; in other words, there is no user switching in non-dialog work processes. It is therefore intended that non-dialog work processes essentially use local SAP heap memory in order to reserve the shared SAP extended memory for dialog work processes.

In more recent versions of the operating systems it is possible to allocate considerably more shared memory. This is why some operating systems (for example Windows NT) in SAP Version 4.0 no longer distinguish between memory management of dialog and non-dialog work processes. As soon as the respective operating system version can provide sufficient shared memory for the SAP extended memory, the memory allocation sequence for non-dialog work processes will be adapted gradually to that of dialog work processes.

	Dialog work processes	Non-dialog work processes (to date)
1	Local SAP roll memory up to **ztta/roll_first**	Local SAP roll memory up to **ztta/roll_area**
2	SAP extended memory until **ztta/roll_extension** is reached or until the SAP extended memory is used up.	SAP heap memory until **abap/heap_area_nondia** is reached or until the SAP heap memory is used up.
3	Local SAP roll memory up to **ztta/roll_first**	-
4	SAP heap memory until **abap/heap_area_dia** is reached or until the SAP heap memory is used up.	SAP extended memory until **ztta/roll_extension** is reached or until the SAP extended memory is used up.
5	Program termination	Program termination

Table 8.1 Sequence in which memory is allocated for dialog and non-dialog work processes

Zero administration memory management

SAP has included Zero Administration Memory Management with SAP Basis 4.0 under Windows NT. The aim of this initiative is to reduce the number of SAP profile parameters and to simplify administration considerably. Zero Administration Memory Management does not require any manual settings and adjusts dynamically to the memory requirements of the user. Even hardware changes (for example memory extension) are recognized and the parameters set accordingly.

PHYS_MEMSIZE

The SAP profile parameter **PHYS_MEMSIZE** defines how much of a computer's total physical main memory should be used for the SAP instance. The default value for **PHYS_MEMSIZE** is the size of the physical main memory. All other memory area configuration parameters are calculated on the basis of the **PHYS_MEMSIZE** parameter.

The dynamically extensible SAP extended memory forms the basis for Zero Administration Memory Management. The memory extends until the set limit of the SAP profile parameter **em/max_size_MB** is reached or until the address space in the NT paging file is full. Because **em/max_size_MB** is set to the default value of 20,000 MB, only the size of the NT paging file represents the actual limit for extending the SAP extended memory.

The SAP heap memory has become less important in SAP 4.0 under Windows NT because non-dialog work processes, like dialog work processes, first allocate SAP extended memory and this memory is available in unlimited volumes. The SAP profile parameter **abap/heap_area...** is therefore superfluous now and is set to 2,000,000,000.

The SAP profile parameter **ztta/roll_extension** is likewise obsolete and is set to 2,000,000,000. The quota of SAP extended memory that an individual user context can reserve is defined by the **em/address_space_MB** parameter. The default value of the parameter is 512 MB.

You will find up-to-date information on Zero Administration Memory Management in SAP Note 88416.

Memory management for the IBM iSeries

The implementation of *memory management on the IBM iSeries* can make use of a special feature of this platform—the concept of single-level storage. What is meant by this is that every memory address has a physical representation in an Auxiliary Storage Pool (ASP), in other words, on the installed hard disk memory. The main memory of the machine can hence be regarded in principle as a large data cache. There is no swap space of a defined size.

Memory management on the iSeries has changed considerably since SAP Basis 4.6 compared with the previous versions, where use was made of the benefits offered by the availability of Teraspace. Teraspace avoids the 16-MB limit for shared memory segments at the operating system level, with the result that very large address spaces can be used.

In general, since SAP Basis 4.6, the configuration of memory management for an SAP system on the iSeries is not all that different from a UNIX system. Only the **ztta/roll_area** parameter is still subject to the 16 MB limit, in other words, this parameter must not be set to a value greater than 16 MB (which, in practice, is not done anyway on UNIX systems). The current restrictions for the various SAP profile parameters are listed in the SAP Notes 121625 and 139326.

Because the iSeries uses the concept of single-level storage, no dedicated SAP page or SAP roll file is required. The **rdisp/ROLL_SHM** and **rdisp/ROLL_MAXFS** parameters therefore do not need to be specified. From SAP Basis 4.6 on, the size of the SAP extended memory is defined via the **em/initial_size_MB** parameter, as on other platforms (maximum value is 8 GB). This type of memory was requested dynamically by the system in older versions up to a maximum of 8 GB.

SAP EG Memory and SAP Paging Memory

As previously noted, the user contexts are stored in extended, roll and heap memory. However, memory areas are also required in which data can be stored globally between user contexts. The SAP extended global memory (SAP EG memory) and the SAP paging memory are available for this purpose.

Extended Global Memory (SAP EG memory)

The *SAP EG memory* is used to store data across user contexts. It is only relevant for use since SAP Kernel 4.6D. (This data was previously stored in sub-areas of the SAP roll memory and had to be tediously copied with every context switch.) Use of the SAP EG memory allows fast and copy-free switching based on mapping, as has already been implemented for the actual user contexts in the SAP extended memory since SAP Basis 3.0.

The size of the SAP EG memory is configured using the **em/global_area_MB** parameter. The recommended size for SAP Kernel 4.6D is 10% of the SAP extended memory. (The standard delivery size of 32 KB generally suffices for older versions.) Don't forget, however, that the size of the SAP EG memory has to be subtracted from the size of the SAP extended memory in order to calculate the remaining storage space for the user contexts.

SAP paging memory

One memory area we haven't touched on so far is the *SAP paging memory.* Under no circumstances should the SAP paging memory be confused with the paging memory of the operating system. The SAP paging memory was used in SAP Basis 2.2 for storing internal tables and screen lists. This data is stored in the SAP roll, SAP extended or SAP heap memory from SAP Basis 3.0. The SAP paging memory has therefore lost much of its original meaning. The objects that continue to be stored in the SAP paging memory in SAP Basis Versions 3 and 4 can be divided into three groups.

- ABAP data clusters stored temporarily with the ABAP statement **IMPORT/EXPORT FROM/TO MEMORY**: This data is stored in the SAP paging memory because it is not tied to a user context. The **IMPORT/EXPORT FROM/TO MEMORY** statement exports the data from a user context via the paging memory and then imports it into another context.
- Parameters transferred when programs and transactions are called: A new user context is created when an ABAP program calls another program or another transaction. The variables and lists transferred when the relevant program is called or ended are likewise stored in the SAP paging memory.

- Data extracts created by the ABAP statement **EXTRACT**: Since SAP Basis 4.5, extracts are no longer stored in the SAP paging memory, rather they are stored in a storage buffer for smaller extract volumes or in local files for large extract volumes.

Table 8.2 summarizes the data objects and the associated ABAP statements.

ABAP object	Associated ABAP statement	SAP Basis
Data extracts	EXTRACT	up to 4.0 B
Data cluster	IMPORT/EXPORT FROM/TO MEMORY	Independent
Parameter for calling programs, transactions etc.	SUBMIT REPORT, CALL TRANSACTION, CALL DIALOG, CALL SCREEN, CALL FUNCTION IN UPDATE TASK, CALL FUNCTION IN BACKGROUND TASK, CALL FUNCTION STARTING NEW TASK	Independent

Table 8.2 ABAP objects and statements that use the SAP paging memory

rdisp/pg_MAXFS, rdisp/pg_SHM

The SAP paging memory, like the roll area, comprises a memory area in the shared memory of the application server (the SAP paging buffer) and an SAP paging file on one of the application server's hard disks. The size of the SAP paging memory and the SAP paging buffer is determined by the SAP profile parameters **rdisp/PG_MAXFS** and **rdisp/PG_SHM**. The SAP paging memory is less critical in terms of performance than other memory areas. However, **Rdisp/PG_MAXFS** should be set to a sufficiently large value to prevent program terminations with the errors TSV_TNEW_PG_CREATE_FAILED or SYSTEM_NO_MORE_PAGING. The proposed value of 32,000 (corresponds to 256 MB) should suffice for all normal requirements. If the SAP profile parameter is set to 32,000 and if a program still terminates, there is more than likely a fault in the program itself (see the relevant notes in the SAP Service Marketplace).

Configuring and Monitoring SAP Memory Areas

In optimizing the memory area configuration we are pursuing two main objectives:

- *Performance:* As many users as possible should be able to work efficiently.
- *Stability:* Programs should not terminate because of a memory bottleneck (particularly background programs with a very high memory requirement).

There would be no difficulty achieving these objectives if all SAP memory areas could be set to whatever size needed to prevent both terminations and bottlenecks. Unfortunately, there are two main factors standing in the way of implementing this simple strategy:

- **Physical main memory (RAM)**
  The available physical main memory should be in a sensible ratio to the used memory so that main memory bottlenecks do not arise and the performance of the server does not deteriorate because of excessive paging.
- **Swap space or paging file of the operating system**
  The swap space must be large enough to create the desired memory areas. However, less importance is attached to this factor because the swap space does not play any role in terms of price and can therefore be created to whatever size desired.
- **Operating system restrictions**
  The 32-bit architecture still used on Windows NT and to an extent also on UNIX platforms restricts the memory that can be addressed by processes. This restriction must be taken seriously, particularly in the case of computers with a 2-GB main memory or higher, because the memory areas cannot be made so large as to ensure optimum performance.

Where computers have a small main memory, the different memory areas of the SAP system (and those of the database instance if available on the same computer) compete for the scarce main memory resources. Where computers have a large main memory, the key issue is how large a memory area can be configured without terminations being triggered because of address space restrictions in the operating system. Both issues made it almost imperative in the past to customize the SAP memory management for individual SAP systems if the hardware was to be used optimally in terms of performance.

Now, however, thanks to Zero Administration Memory Management, which was first supplied for Windows NT with SAP Basis 4.0, an initial step has been taken to radically simplify memory management configuration. The problem of address space restrictions has been all but eliminated on UNIX with 64-bit architecture. Memory management configuration has been simplified considerably thanks to these two techniques.

Figure 8.4 and Table 8.3 summarize the different memory areas and their properties.

Memory area	Implementation	Size (MB)	Contents
SAP roll memory	Shared memory (Roll buffer), Roll file	n × 10	User contexts: temporary transaction-based data assigned to a user session
SAP extended memory	Shared memory	n × 100 to n × 1,000	for example screen lists, internal tables, variables, administrative data
SAP heap memory	Local memory	n × 100 to n × 1,000	
SAP buffer	Shared memory	n × 100	Global data that can be accessed by all users, for example program code, table and field definitions, etc.
SAP EG memory	Shared memory (part of SAP extended memory)	n × 10	Temporary data exchanged between user contexts
SAP paging memory	Shared memory (paging buffer), SAP paging file	n × 100	Temporary data exchanged between user contexts; data extracts (up to SAP Basis 4.0)
SAP work processes	Local memory	n × 10 per WP	Executable programs, local data, local roll (ztta/roll_area) and local paging memory (rdisp/PG_local), SAP cursor cache and so on.
Compare:			
Database instance	Shared memory, local memory	n × 100 to n × 1,000	Database buffer and database processes

Table 8.3 The memory areas of an SAP instance and their contents

Monitoring Swap Space

The recommendations in this book are made on the assumption that sufficient swap space is available. "Sufficient" means that the swap space is at least three times the size of the physical memory or at least 3.5 GB overall.

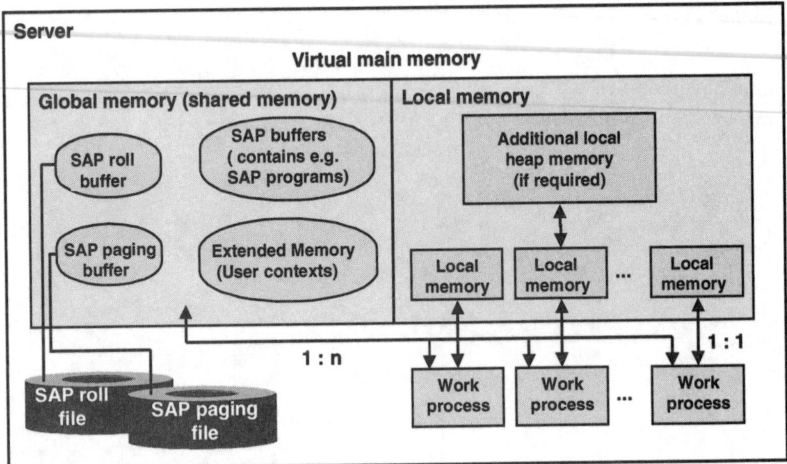

Figure 8.4 Memory areas in the SAP system

You can use the following check to establish whether the swap space is large enough and whether the SAP profile parameter **abap/heap_area_total** is set correctly:

First step: Calculate the available memory

Add the physical main memory of the computer and the available swap space. You will find both values in the Operating System Monitor (transaction code ST06) in the fields **Physical Memory** and **Swap Space**.

Available Memory = Physical Memory + Swap Space

Under Windows NT, the available memory is also referred to as "commit charge limit".

Second step: Calculate the virtual memory required

Call the SAP Memory Configuration Monitor (transaction code ST02) and choose:

Detail Analysis menu · Storage

Add up the following values:

- "Virtual memory allocated" (the memory allocated by the relevant SAP instance at startup)
- "Maximum heap area for all work processes" (the memory that can be allocated temporarily as needed by this SAP instance; this value is equal to **abap/heap_area_total**).
- Add an extra 100 MB for the operating system as a safety margin.

- If there are several SAP instances on the computer, repeat this calculation for each SAP instance.
- If there is a database instance on the computer, add its memory requirement to this. You will find guidelines regarding this in Chapter 2 in the section "Analyzing the Database Buffer" on page 80, or in the appendix.
- If there are other programs running on the computer, calculate their memory allocation and add this on.

Third step: Compare the available memory with the virtual memory required

The following must apply:

virtual memory required < available memory

If this condition is not fulfilled, you have two options:

- Reduce the memory required by, for example, reducing the **abap/heap_area_total**. We recommend, however, that **abap/heap_area_total** be greater than 600,000,000 (600 MB).
- Extend the swap space.

If the available memory is much greater than the virtual memory required, you can increase **abap/heap_area_total** accordingly. The maximum value for **abap/heap_area_total** is 2,000,000,000 (2 GB) for SAP Basis 4.0.

The calculation presented is a good starting point for calculating the size of the swap space, but it does not cover all the eventualities and domains of operating systems (for example fragmenting of memory areas, which can be considerable over time). It is therefore highly advisable to monitor the free swap space.

You should in any case avoid your computer developing a memory bottleneck because the swap space is too small. Because *all* processes are simultaneously affected by such a bottleneck, it is arbitrary which process will terminate first. It may happen that an important operating system or database process will terminate because of a general memory bottleneck. If the swap space is too small, uncontrolled errors and terminations may occur, or even the operating system itself may terminate. See also SAP Note 38052, "System panic, termination because of swap space bottleneck".

Address Space Restrictions (32- and 64-bit Architecture)

To recap: The virtual memory allocated must first be in a sensible ratio to the physical main memory and secondly fit into the available memory (sum of physical main memory and swap space). There is now a third restriction: It must be possible to *address* the memory from the work process.

Address space

Address space is the number of memory addresses a process has at its disposal. The size of the addressable memory is between 1.8 and 3.8 GB ($\leq 2^{32} = 4$ GB) for 32-bit versions of the SAP kernel. All memory areas that a work process has to access must fit into the addressable memory: the local work process memory, the SAP buffer including SAP roll and SAP paging buffer (some 100 MB), the SAP extended memory (some 100 to 1,000 MB) as well as the SAP heap memory (some 100 to 1,000 MB). From this it is clear that if the memory area allocated is too large, there is less address space available for the other memory areas—the memory areas therefore have a reciprocal relationship with one another. See also Figure 8.5.

Let us again summarize the difference between the available memory (definition: see last section) and the available address space: The memory areas of *one* work process (the shared memory of *one* instance and the local memory of *one* work process) must fit in the *available address space*, while the areas of *all* work processes (i.e. the shared memory of *all* instances and the local memory of *all* work processes) must fit in the *available memory*. If several SAP instances or one SAP and one database instance are installed on one computer, the address space only includes the memory areas of one instance (because a work process only has to address the areas of its instance), while the available memory must offer sufficient space for the shared memory areas of all instances.

UNIX operating systems

Figure 8.5 shows the standard implementation of the SAP extended memory on UNIX operating systems: The entire SAP extended memory must be addressed by the work process.

32-bit architecture

If the SAP extended memory is too large, a work process will not be able to address any SAP heap memory. We therefore recommend that the SAP extended memory **(em/initial_size_MB)** is no larger than 2 GB. The maximum possible size of the SAP extended memory is considerably smaller than this on some operating systems. This recommendation only applies for 32-bit architecture.

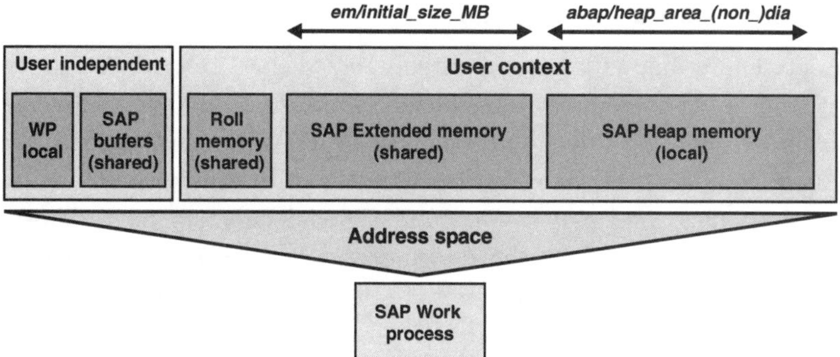

Figure 8.5 Address space allocation of a work process in a standard implementation for UNIX operating systems

The address space of the operating system therefore restricts the size of the memory areas, particularly the size of the SAP extended memory and thus directly the number of users who can work on an SAP instance. One problem that arises in particular on computers with a physical main memory of more than 2 GB is that the main memory cannot be used effectively by an SAP instance because the processes of an instance cannot address this memory. The problem of restricted address space can be circumvented in this case by installing more than one SAP instance on a computer.

64-bit architecture

These problems have been solved with 64-bit technology. An address space of several terabytes is available to the work process in this case. In order to use 64-bit technology, you need a 64-bit operating system, a 64-bit version of your database software and a 64-bit version of the SAP kernel. The 64-bit SAP kernel has no new functionalities compared with the 32-bit version. There is no difference in handling, either for users or for administrators. Memory management is simplified considerably compared with the 32-bit version through use of the 64-bit SAP kernel. You will find details in SAP Note 146289.

64-bit SAP kernels are released on UNIX operating systems for SAP Basis 4.0 and higher and on Solaris from SAP Basis 4.6. The restriction with respect to the 32-bit architecture still applies on Windows platforms at the time of this book's appearing in print. You will find information on released 64-bit products in SAP Notes for the component XX-SER-SWREL or in the SAP Service Marketplace under `http://service.sap.com/platforms`. If a 64-bit implementation is possible for the platform and version you are using, it is recommended that this be used. This applies in particular when using computers with a physical main memory in excess of 2 GB.

Windows operating systems

At present, Windows operating systems only offer a 32-bit address space. In order to work around this restriction in relation to the size of the SAP extended memory, the implementation is different on Windows NT. Figure 8.6 illustrates the implementation using Windows NT as an example: Only one part of the SAP extended memory (**em/address_space_MB**) is addressed by the work process. This implementation has the advantage that the entire SAP extended memory can be larger than the address space of the work process. The overall size of the SAP extended memory is therefore only limited by the size of the swap space.

Note that each work process can in principle access all objects stored in the SAP extended memory, while a transaction step can only access an area the size of **em/address_space_MB**. The SAP profile parameter **em/address_space_MB** thus defines the maximum size that a user context can reserve in the SAP extended memory. The size of the user quota **em/address_space_MB** is 512 MB by default. The SAP profile parameter **ztta/roll_extension** is no longer used by default with SAP Basis 4.0; **ztta/roll_extension** is set to 2,000,000,000.

A comparable implementation of the SAP extended memory as under Windows NT also currently exists for the AIX operating system. See the relevant SAP Note 95454 in this respect.

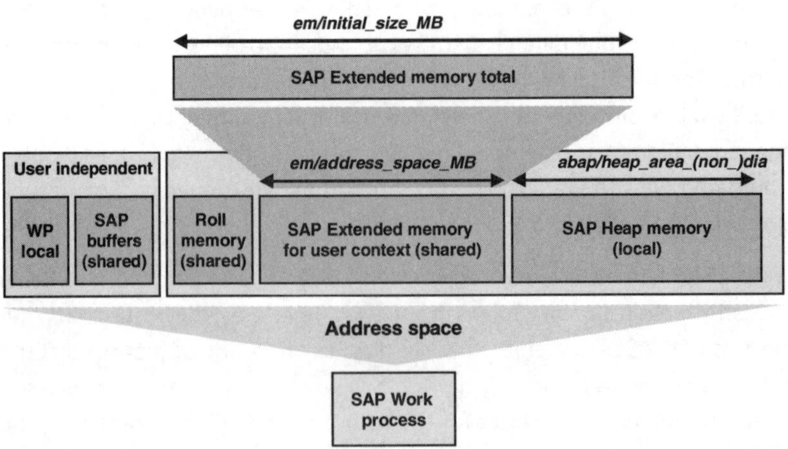

Figure 8.6 Address space allocation of a work process in an implementation for Windows NT

The maximum amount of *SAP heap memory* that can be addressed by a work process is calculated from the size of the address space less the shared memory areas addressed by the SAP work process and the local work process memory (some 10 MB). If a work process tries to allocate more SAP heap memory than there is address space available, the program will terminate with the error STORAGE_PARAMETERS_WRONG_SET. The next section but one, "Assistance with troubleshooting", describes how to deal with this error.

SAP heap memory

Other restrictions

Operating system restrictions can cause the SAP instance not to start or only to start with errors if the memory areas are too large or can also trigger ABAP errors at runtime (e.g. STORAGE_PARAMETERS_WRONG_SET). You will find more detailed information on diagnostics and troubleshooting in the next section but one. The appendix contains a list of notes for the individual operating systems, which describe the restrictions, possible errors and potential solutions. You can also contact your hardware partner or SAP AG for information on the latest restrictions.

memlimits utility

The *memlimits* utility tests the limits of the memory that can be allocated on your operating system. Start the *memlimits* program at operating system level.

The following output, for example, is shown on UNIX systems (excerpt):

UNIX

```
+-------------------------------------------------+
|                  Result (UNIX)                  |
+-------------------------------------------------+
Maximum heap size per process........:   640 MB
Maximum protectable size (mprotect)..:   996 MB
    em/initial_size_MB > 996 MB will not work
Maximum address space per process....:  1252 MB
Total available swap space...........:  1300 MB
```

- **Maximum heap size per process**
  This value indicates how much memory can be allocated locally by a process. This value limits the sum of fixed local memory for SAP work processes and SAP heap memory:

Fixed local work process memory + variable local work process memory (SAP heap memory) < operating system heap (UNIX)

- **Maximum protectable size (mprotect)**
  This value limits the SAP extended memory.

  The *memlimits* program issues the following warning in this case: "em/initial_size_MB > 996 MB will not work". This warning has only limited applicability. On the one hand, it does not guarantee that this size of SAP extended memory can actually be allocated. On the other hand, there are special solutions for large installations for some operating systems that allow more memory to be allocated. You will find further information in this regard in the Notes quoted in the appendix. Your hardware partner will also be able to supply you with information on special solutions.

- **Maximum address space per process**
  Maximum address space per work process. This value limits the sum of all memory areas that can be allocated by a process (SAP buffer, SAP extended memory **em/initial_size_MB**, SAP heap memory and so on).

Windows NT The following result, for example, is shown on Windows NT:

```
+-------------------------------------------------+
|                 Result (Windows NT)             |
+-------------------------------------------------+
Maximum heap size per process........:  1988 MB
Total available swap space...........:  1988 MB
```

- **Maximum heap size per process**
  Maximum memory that can be allocated per process. Because there are no other restrictions under Windows NT 4.0 in relation to shared memory or local memory, this value restricts the sum of all memory areas that can be allocated by a process (SAP buffer, SAP extended memory *em/address_space_MB*, SAP heap memory and so on).

  The "Maximum heap size per process" represents an upper limit in terms of the memory that can actually be allocated. However, because part of the address space can be lost as a result of fragmenting, the real addressable memory is less than this.

Make sure that the SAP system is stopped when executing the `memlimits` program. You will find a description of the `memlimits` program and possible options using the command **memlimits -h**.

Configuring and Monitoring SAP Memory Areas

How do we now configure SAP memory management? In this section, we have put together a list of points to assist you with your configuration, though we cannot guarantee that we have covered every special case.

- **Total main memory requirement**
  Your hardware partners can establish the main memory requirements for your SAP system for you, based on the information you provide with respect to system requirements. In the case of small and medium-sized installations, you can perform the sizing yourself using the SAP Quick Sizer in the SAP Service Marketplace.
- **Number of computers**
  First establish the number of computers. This is generally done in cooperation with your hardware partner because the decision as to the number of computers over which your SAP system should be distributed depends essentially on the chosen hardware platform.
- **Several SAP instances per computer**
  The decision as to whether several SAP instances are configured per computer is likewise made in conjunction with your hardware partner. The following reasons support the idea of configuring several SAP instances on one server for UNIX servers with more than four processors and 2 GB of main memory:
  - The physical main memory cannot be used effectively with an SAP instance because of operating system-specific restrictions (address space, shared memory, and so on.). Since the inclusion of 64-bit architecture, this reason is already obsolete for UNIX operating systems.
  - Additional instances were often set up with SAP Basis 3 because it was only possible to configure one spool work process per instance. This restriction no longer applies with SAP Basis 4.0.
  - Performance problems (wait situations) can arise in the dispatcher as well as in the roll and buffer administration on computers with more than four processors and a corresponding number of SAP work processes. These can be reduced if several SAP instances are configured.

  Basically, the trend is to create a large instance on each computer with many work processes and a large SAP extended memory. We do not recommend creating an unnecessary number of instances because each instance involves administration and monitoring effort. The first two reasons listed, which favor creating several SAP instances on one computer, are already irrelevant or will be in the near future. To what extent the third reason remains valid has yet to be proven in individual tests.

- **SAP buffer**
  The memory requirement of the SAP buffer basically depends on the SAP modules that are being operated on the relevant SAP instance. The largest buffers are the SAP program buffers with a size of 150–400 MB and the SAP table buffer (for generic and single record buffering) with a typical size of 50–120 MB. Overall, there is a typical memory requirement of 250–500 MB for all SAP buffers in SAP Basis 3.1 and 4.0. The memory area for the SAP buffer is allocated for each individual SAP instance. If the SAP system is distributed over multiple instances, each with a few users and work processes, the memory requirement of the overall system will be greater than if the system were distributed over relatively few instances with more users and work processes each per instance. The monitoring of the SAP buffer following productive startup is described in Chapter 2 in the section "Analyzing SAP Memory Management" on page 98.
- **SAP extended memory and roll buffer**
  Zero Administration Memory Management makes the settings for the SAP extended memory and roll buffer automatically on the basis of the SAP profile parameter **PHYS_MEMSIZE**. For SAP systems in which Zero Administration Memory Management is not yet active, you will find information on configuring and monitoring the SAP extended memory and the roll buffer at the end of the section.
- **Memory for SAP work processes**
  The memory requirement for an SAP work process can be estimated at around 7.5 MB. You will find more detailed information on the number of required work processes and their distribution in Chapter 5, "Workload Distribution".
- **Database instance**
  The Quick Sizing program can likewise provide you with recommendations on the main memory requirement of the database instance. As a guide, you can assume some 20–30% of the overall main memory for the database instance, in other words, the sum of the main memory sizes for all computers. You will find further details on the memory areas of the individual database systems and their monitoring in production operation in Chapter 2 in the section "Analyzing the Database Buffer" on page 80, or in the appendix.

SAP extended memory

The requirement for SAP extended memory (**em/initial_size_MB**) depends on the number and the activities of users and is difficult to calculate before actually going live. When setting this SAP profile parameter initially in a non-production system, you can base your estimate pragmatically on the size of the physical main memory. Configure some 70–100% of the physical main memory which is available for the SAP instance as SAP extended memory.

You want to configure a database instance and an SAP instance on a computer with 1,500 MB of physical main memory. You estimate a main memory requirement of 500 MB for the database instance. This leaves 1,000 MB for the SAP instance. You should therefore set the SAP extended memory initially to a size of between 700 and 1,000 MB.

As was explained in the section "Address Space Restrictions" on page 264, you cannot exceed a size of 2,000 MB for the SAP extended memory for most operating systems because of operating system-specific restrictions (32-bit architecture). The maximum size of the SAP extended memory per SAP instance is even less than this on some operating systems.

In a production SAP system, adapt the size of the SAP extended memory to the actual requirement. The monitoring of the SAP extended memory in the SAP Memory Configuration Monitor (transaction code ST02) is described in Chapter 2. If you find that the SAP extended memory is frequently 100% occupied, you should proceed as follows:

- Extend the SAP extended memory. On the one hand you are restricted here by the limits of your operating system, on the other hand, however, the size of the SAP extended memory should not greatly exceed the size of the physical main memory. The latter is not a strict limit however.
- Check which users are taking up an above-average amount of space in the SAP extended memory. To check this, call the *Mode List*:

  In the SAP Memory Configuration Monitor (transaction code ST02) select:

  Detail analysis menu · SAP memory · Mode list

  A screen then opens, which shows you a list of logged on users (**Name** column) and their sessions. If a user has opened several external sessions, his or her name will appear several times in the list. The columns **Ext Mem [kB]** and **Heap [kB]** indicate how much memory the users are occupying in the SAP extended memory or in the SAP heap memory. The lower part of the list contains a history of the users with the highest memory allocation.

You can use this list to identify the users who have an above-average memory allocation. Establish which programs these users are executing at present. Check whether these programs can be optimized.

- If the SAP extended memory cannot be extended because of the previously listed restrictions and if you establish from the mode list that only a few users have a large share of the extended memory, you can reduce the user quota (**ztta/roll_extension**). As a result, the individual user session takes up less memory in the SAP extended memory and uses SAP heap memory instead. This approach has two disadvantages however:
  - Work processes are more likely to switch to *PRIV mode*. The number of dialog work processes may have to be increased in this case.
  - Less memory is available overall to the individual user; in the worst case scenario this can cause programs with a very high memory requirement to terminate.

Assistance With Troubleshooting

An optimum memory area configuration should not just guarantee good performance, but should also prevent a program termination because of memory bottlenecks.

The following errors can arise because of an incorrect memory area configuration:

- The SAP instance does not start because the operating system cannot provide the requested memory areas.
- Session terminations: A dialog window appears on the user's screen with the error message "roll out failure". The session then disappears and the user is logged off.
- ABAP program terminations: You will find the logs for these errors (dumps) in Transaction ST22:

  Tools · Administration · Monitor · Dump Analysis

Four factors come into play with this error:

- There is a program error (for example an endless loop) or the program has been used incorrectly, with the result that an unnecessary amount of memory is requested.

- The SAP profile parameters are set incorrectly.
- The swap space on the operating system is not large enough.
- The configuration parameters of the operating system are set incorrectly or operating system limits have been reached (for example the maximum addressable memory).

ABAP program terminations

The logs of the ABAP program terminations can be viewed with transaction ST22. In relation to the memory area configuration, the following error messages may come up:

- STORAGE_PARAMETERS_WRONG_SET, SYSTEM_ROLL_IN_ERROR, TSV_TNEW_BLOCKS_NO_ROLL_MEMORY, TSV_TNEW_PAGE_ALLOC_FAILED, TSV_TNEW_INDEX_NO_ROLL_MEMORY:
  The memory for user contexts is used up.
- PXA_NO_SHARED_MEMORY or the message "System not ready (PXA_NO_SHARED_MEMORY)" appears when the user logs on to the SAP system.

  The program buffer is the last object that is created by the SAP system in the shared memory. If there is not sufficient shared memory available at this time, the system cannot create the program buffer. The system is then simply started as an "emergency system" with a minimum sized program buffer. The cause of this, generally, is that the allocated areas in the shared memory (particularly SAP extended memory and program buffer) violate the operating system-specific restrictions.
- DBIF_RTAB_NO_MEMORY, DBIF_RSQL_NO_MEMORY
  The program encounters a memory bottleneck during an operation in the database interface.
- EXSORT_NOT_ENOUGH_MEMORY
  The program encounters a memory bottleneck during sorting.
- RABAX_CALLING_RABAX
  This error occurs if the attempt to create an error log also fails after a program has been terminated due to lack of memory. This error is likewise a follow-on error from the one described above.
- SYSTEM_NO_MORE_PAGING, TSV_TNEW_PAGE_ALLOC_FAILED
  The SAP paging memory is used up (see the section "SAP EG Memory and SAP Paging Memory" on page 258).

▶ SET_PARAMETER_MEMORY_OVERFLOW
The memory for the SET/GET parameter (SPA/GPA memory) is used up. This termination is particularly likely with a file transfer to the presentation server (download/upload) and a local execute (SAPLGRAP program). Extend the memory area with the SAP profile parameter **ztta/parameter_area**.

You will find detailed information on how much memory was requested at the time of termination in the error message logs. To do this, compare the two lines below from an error log:

```
extended memory area(EM) 52431655
fixed allocated memory (HEAP) 80004928
```

The following values are critical for analyzing the error:

- **Extended memory area (EM)**
  Amount of the SAP extended memory that was occupied at the time of termination.
- **Fixed allocated memory (HEAP)**
  Amount of the SAP heap memory that was occupied at the time of termination.

Hence, the memory requested for the user context in this example is 52,431,655 bytes + 80,004,928 bytes = 132.5 MB. (Added to this is the SAP roll memory of size **ztta/roll_area**, which is less than 10 MB in size by default.)

To continue the analysis, proceed as follows:

Application error

- First check for cases of unnecessary memory consumption that may have been caused by a nonoptimal program or nonoptimal use of a program. We shall assume, as a reference, that a program that is executed in dialog mode by a number of users should not allocate more than 100 MB. Background programs (for example, billing runs at night on a dedicated application server) should not require more than 1 GB. Depending on the operating system, 1–3 GB is regarded as "conclusive" for the 32-bit architecture in use at the time of this book's appearing in print.
  - If a program terminates with a memory consumption level above this reference value, clarify with the respective user whether the program was used inappropriately or whether the work list can possibly be split into smaller portions and, consequently, a program be executed repeatedly with lower memory consumption.

- If this is not the case, contact the responsible developer, if the program is user-defined, or search the SAP Service Marketplace for information on optimizing the program.

- While searching for application errors, you should also check whether the program has reached the limits defined by the SAP profile parameter. The memory available for a user context is derived from the sum of **ztta/roll_extension** (quota in the SAP extended memory) and **abap/heap_area_dia** or **abap/heap_area_nondia** (quotas in the SAP heap memory). Added to this is the SAP roll memory with a size of less than 10 MB per context (**ztta/roll_area**). The program aborts in the example given above because these quotas are reached. The parameters in this example amount to **ztta/roll_extension** = 52,428,800 (bytes) or **abap/heap_area_dia** = 80,000,000 (bytes). The comparison with the values "extended memory (EM)" and "fixed allocated memory (HEAP)" from the log at the time of termination shows that the program was terminated because it had reached its quotas for SAP extended memory and SAP heap memory. In this case, you should extend these SAP profile parameters.

Quotas reached

- If the problem was not caused by the **ztta/roll_extension** and **abap/heap_area_(non)dia** quotas being reached, use the SAP Memory Configuration Monitor (ST02) to check whether the SAP extended memory or the SAP heap memory was 100% occupied at the time the roll memory terminated. If this is the case, extend the relevant memory areas if possible. The relevant SAP profile parameters in this case are **rdisp/ROLL_MAXFS, em/initial_size_MB** and **abap/heap_area_total**.

Roll, extended or SAP heap memory occupied

- Finally, it is still possible that the SAP kernel requests memory from the operating system but the operating system cannot provide this memory. For example, the STORAGE_PARAMETERS_WRONG_SET error log contains an entry like "The program had already requested 109,890,288 bytes from the operating system via 'malloc' when the operating system reported, on receiving a new request for memory, that it had no more memory available". This could be caused by operating system parameters being set incorrectly or limits being imposed by the operating system architecture or by the swap space being too small. Operating system restrictions can also cause the SAP instance not to start if the incorrect SAP profile parameters are selected.

Operating system limits reached

- In order to exclude the possibility of errors in the *SAP kernel*, make sure that you are using an up-to-date SAP kernel.

Error in SAP kernel

Developer logs ("dev traces")

You will find further information on memory management errors in the *developer logs (dev traces)* for the work processes. To view this information, first call the Work Process Overview (transaction code SM50). Select a work process and choose the following options:

Process · Trace · Display File

If the SAP instance does not start with a profile, you will find the files in the directory **\usr\sap\<SID>\<instance_name><instance_number>\work**. These files must be backed up in any case for a subsequent analysis because they will be overwritten when the work process restarts and an error analysis is then practically impossible.

Checking profile parameter settings

SAP Note 103747 provides recommendations on setting the *profile parameters* that configure memory. Should problems arise despite these recommendations and contrary to expectations, you should check the settings.

You will find an outline of an ABAP report below, which you can use to establish the maximum amount of memory that can be allocated on your system. You can use this ABAP report to test your system's parameter settings.

```
report zusemem.
* Report for checking the limits of the allocatable memory
parameters mb type I.
data itab(1024) type c occurs 0.
data str(1024).
do mb times.
   do 1024 times. append str to itab. enddo.
enddo.
skip.
write: / 'At the moment', mb,
         'MB of this program are being used.'.
```

The ZUSEMEN report allows you to reserve a certain amount of memory. To do this, execute the report in the ABAP editor (transaction code SE38). A selection screen opens with the input parameter **MB**, which prompts for input of the memory size to be allocated by the report. In the ABAP Editor menu, choose **Program · Run** to start the report and allocate the desired amount of memory. Extend the **MB** parameter gradually to establish the limit at which the report terminates.

To check how much memory can be allocated by background programs, create a variant for this report and execute the report in the background.

Monitor the memory allocation of the report in a second mode in the SAP memory configuration monitor or in the mode list described above.

abap/heap_area_dia

If the report is running interactively, you will notice that the program first allocates SAP extended memory to a quota of **ztta/roll_extension** and then SAP heap memory up to a quota of **abap/heap_area_dia**. If the requested memory exceeds the sum of both quotas, the program terminates with the error TSV_TNEW_PAGE_ALLOC_FAILED. We can assume here that the size of **abap/heap_area_dia** was set to such a low value that the SAP extended memory, the SAP heap memory and all other memory areas that the work process must address do not exceed the address space of the work process. Refer also to Figures 8.5 and 8.6 in the section "Address Space Restrictions", starting on page 264. If, on the other hand, **abap/heap_area_dia** is set to such a high value that the requested SAP heap memory exceeds the address space, the report terminates with the error STORAGE_PARAMETERS_WRONG_SET. In Figure 8.5 and Figure 8.6 this would be the equivalent of the rectangle that symbolizes the SAP heap memory extending over the rectangle that represents the address space. With UNIX, you should set **abap/heap_area_dia** so that the STORAGE_PARAMETERS_WRONG_SET error does not arise.

abap/heap_area_nondia

If you start the report in the background, it depends on your operating system and your SAP kernel version whether the report occupies SAP extended memory or SAP heap memory first. If the report occupies SAP extended memory first (as is the case, for example, in SAP Basis 4.0B and Windows NT), the same parameterization as for dialog work processes applies.

If the report allocates SAP heap memory first, note how the allocated SAP heap memory first extends until it reaches the quota of **abap/heap_area_nondia** before the report starts to reserve SAP extended memory. If the **abap/heap_area_nondia** parameter is set too high, that is to say, larger than the maximum permitted by the operating system for the SAP heap memory, the report terminates with the error STORAGE_PARAMETERS_WRONG_SET before switching to the SAP extended memory. In this case, reduce the value of **abap/heap_area_nondia** until the STORAGE_PARAMETERS_WRONG_SET error no longer occurs. As a rule, **abap/heap_area_dia** and **abap/heap_area_nondia** should be set to the same value; in other words, to be safe, set both values to the smaller of the two values calculated. Errors such as DBIF_RSQL_NO_MEMORY, DBIF_RTAB_

NO_MEMORY or EXSORT_NOT_ENOUGH_MEMORY can arise in some cases. These errors occur if the database interface or the sort algorithm in SAP Basis requests additional heap memory from the operating system and the operating system cannot provide this because the SAP heap memory has already used up the available heap memory in the operating system. (Please note: It is important at this point to distinguish between the heap memory at operating system level and the SAP heap memory.) You can generally resolve this problem by reducing the **abap/heap_area_dia** and **abap/heap_area_nondia** parameters in increments of 50 MB until the error no longer occurs. Less SAP heap memory is hence allocated and more memory is available for the database interface or the sort algorithm.

Summary

Six memory areas have to be configured for an SAP instance:

- SAP buffer
- SAP roll memory
- SAP extended memory
- SAP heap memory
- SAP paging memory
- Local SAP work process memory

The aims of configuring the SAP memory are *stability* (avoiding program terminations because of memory bottlenecks) and performance (fast access to the data and fast context switching).

The following factors affect configuration:

- **Physical main memory (RAM)**
  When configuring the memory, more memory can be allocated virtually than is available physically. An optimum main memory configuration would be a ratio of *virtual main memory / physical main memory* $\leq$ *150%*. The *SAP Quick Sizer* in the *SAP Service Marketplace* is a tool you can use to estimate the requirement for physical main memory for small and average-sized installations.
- **Swap space or paging file of the operating system**
  The basis for all recommendations is the assumption that there is sufficient swap space available (some 3–4 × RAM, but at least 3.5 GB).

- **Operating system restrictions**
  If 32-bit architecture is still being used (Windows, older UNIX versions): Do the operating system restrictions, for example the maximum address space, permit the desired configuration?

Zero Administration Memory Management, which is initially being delivered for SAP Basis 4.0 on the Windows NT platform, simplifies the administration of memory management. The *64-bit architecture*, which is available on UNIX, allows computers with large main memories to be configured more easily and used more effectively.

The following SAP profile parameters are relevant primarily for stability (avoiding program terminations):

> **em/initital_size_MB, em/address_space_MB, ztta/roll_extension, rdisp/roll_area, rdisp/ROLL_MAXFS, abap/heap_area_(non)dia, abap/heap_area_total, rdisp/PG_MAXFS, abap/buffersize**

The following SAP profile parameters are relevant primarily for performance:

> **em/initital_size_MB, ztta/roll_first, rdisp/ROLL_SHM, rdisp/PG_SHM** as well as all parameters for configuring the SAP buffer.

Important terms in this chapter

After studying this chapter you should be familiar with the following terms:

- Physical main memory, swap space, virtual allocated memory
- Local memory and shared memory
- User context
- SAP roll memory, SAP extended memory, SAP heap memory
- Address space, 32-bit architecture, 64-bit architecture

Questions

1. Which SAP profile parameters determine which parts (a) of the extended memory and (b) of the heap memory will be held in the physical main memory or in the swap space?
   a) The extended memory is always held completely in the physical main memory and the heap memory is created in the swap space.

b) None! The distribution of memory areas to the physical memory and the swap space (i.e. the page out and page in) is performed automatically by the operating system. There is no possibility of an application program (such as SAP or database program) influencing this distribution.

c) The SAP profile parameter **ztta/roll_extension** determines which part of the extended memory will be held in the physical main memory whereas, similarly, the **abap/heap_area_(non)dia** parameter determines this for the heap memory.

2. Under what circumstances might an SAP instance not start (or only with error messages) after you have changed SAP memory management parameters?

   a) The program buffer (**abap/buffer_size**) cannot be created in the desired size because of address space restrictions.

   b) The physical main memory is not sufficient for the new settings.

   c) The swap space is not sufficient for the new settings.

   d) The extended memory (**em/initial_size_MB**) cannot be created in the desired size because of address space restrictions.

9 SAP Table Buffering

Every SAP instance has various buffers, in which data to be accessed by users is stored. When the data is in the buffer, the database does not have to be accessed, because buffers enable direct reads from the main memory of the application server. There are two advantages to this:

- Accesses to SAP buffers are normally 10 to 100 times faster than accesses to the database.
- Database load is reduced. This is increasingly important as your system grows in size

For each table defined in the ABAP dictionary you can decide if and how the table should be buffered. To enable the buffering of tables, each SAP instance has two table buffers, the *single record table buffer* (also known as *partial table buffer, TABLP*) and the *generic table buffer (TABL)*. The SAP buffers are illustrated in Figure 9.1. When an SAP system is delivered there are default settings on whether a table should be buffered. However, to optimize runtime, it may be necessary to change these settings. For customer-developed tables these settings must, in any case, be established by the developer.

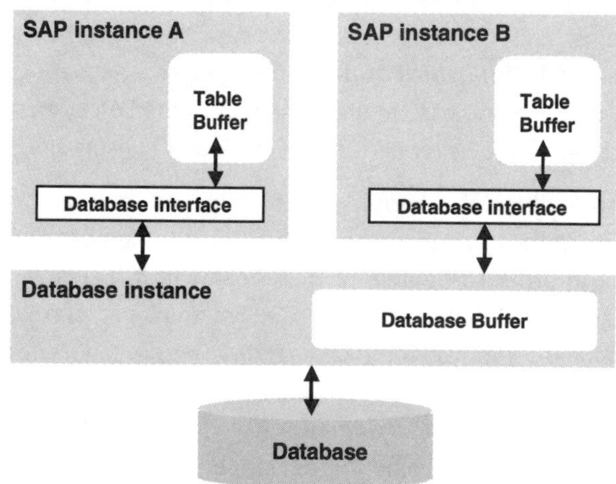

Figure 9.1 SAP buffering

This chapter deals with table buffering on the SAP application level. Table buffering on database level is dealt with in Chapter 11.

When should you read this chapter?

You should read this chapter to help you:

- Get detailed information on the possibilities of SAP buffering
- Monitor and optimize the efficiency of the buffering of SAP tables at regular intervals
- Decide whether customer-created database tables should be buffered
- Decide whether to buffer the condition tables created during customizing for central SAP functions such as price determination or output determination

To better understand this chapter you should have some familiarity with ABAP programming and SQL programming.

Preliminary Remarks Concerning Chapters 9, 10 and 11

The following remarks concern the tuning measures dealt with in Chapters 9 to 11: setting buffering for tables and number ranges and the creation, changing or deletion of database indices. These measures—when correctly implemented—are important techniques for optimizing performance. However, if they are not implemented correctly they can lead to massive performance problems and in some cases to data inconsistencies. Changing the buffer mode for tables and number ranges or creating, changing or deleting database indices, involves changes to the SAP system and should only be carried out by experienced developers or consultants.

Technical analysis—logical analysis

The main aim of the following chapters is to help you to *identify* performance problems in these areas, that is, to find the program or table causing the problem, in order to be able to then deal with it. However, before making any concrete changes to solve the problem, you should perform a *technical analysis* and also a *logical analysis*. The procedure for technical analysis is explained in this book. This type of analysis can be carried out by a system or database administrator, for example. The logical analysis can only be executed by the developer responsible. You should bear the following recommendations in mind:

- For customer developed objects (program, table, index, number range and so on):

  Changes to the buffering status or to database indices should be performed only after careful consultation between the developer and the system or database administrator.

▶ If the objects identified are from SAP standard:

The buffering status and database indices of SAP tables are already preset when the SAP system is delivered. In some cases it may be necessary to change these standard settings. Before you perform a change, you should look in the SAP Service Marketplace for notes on the program name, table or number name which will confirm whether or not you can change the object in question. These notes correspond to the SAP developer's input for the logical analysis. Changes performed without the proper expertise can lead to unexpected performance problems and to data inconsistencies. Take note of the warnings and recommendations provided in the respective sections of this book.

An important part of performance optimization is to *verify* the success of changes that have been carried out and then to *document* the analysis, the changes made and their verification.

Fundamentals of Table Buffering

The following sections deal with the fundamentals of table buffering. This includes types of buffering, how to access buffers, synchronization of buffers and activating buffers. Finally, we will deal with the question of which tables should be buffered.

Buffering Types

We differentiate between three different types of table buffering: single record buffering, generic buffering and full buffering.

Single record buffering

Single record buffering is suitable for accesses that are executed using all table keys—in other words, all fields of the primary index. With single record buffering, each record (a row in a table) that is read from the database for the first time is archived in the buffer. Subsequently, whenever the record needs to be read again, it can be read directly from the buffer.

Let us take an example of a table <tab_sngl>, with the key fields <key1>, <key2> and <key3>. A record is read from the table with the following SQL statement:

```
SELECT SINGLE * FROM <tab_sngl> WHERE <key1> = a1 AND
<key2> = a2 AND <key3> = a3.
```

Assuming that single record buffering is activated for table <tab_sngl>, the single record buffer will be accessed for this SQL statement and not the database.

In order for the buffer to be accessed, the ABAP key word **SINGLE** *must* be contained in the SQL statement. SQL statements in which not all key fields are specified in the **WHERE** clause cannot be processed from single record buffers; instead, the database will be accessed.

On the first attempt to access a table for which single record buffering is activated, if the required record is not in the database, information is stored in the buffer to indicate that the record does not exist. In other words, negative information is also buffered. On a second attempt to access this record, the buffer search recognizes that the record does not exist and thus makes no attempt to access the database. As a result, the number of entries for a specific table in the single record buffer may be larger than the number of actual records in that table in the database.

Full buffering

Full buffering is another way of buffering tables. With fully buffered tables, on the first reading of a table record the entire table is loaded into the buffer. This type of buffering is mainly used for small tables.

Figure 9.2 contrasts the different types of buffering. The buffered records of a table are shown in dark gray. A fully buffered table is shown on the left. Because the table is either completely contained in the buffer or not at all, either all entries will be dark gray or there will be none at all. The right-hand table in Figure 9.2 shows a single-record buffered table. Some individual records are buffered, others are not.

Generic buffering

The third form of buffering is *generic buffering with <n> key fields*. On first read access of a record in a generically <n> buffered table, all records with the same <n> key field values as the targeted record are loaded into the buffer. In Figure 9.2 the table second from the left is a table for which generic buffering is activated and n = 1. For this table all records with the first key value = "002" are stored in the buffer. These records make up what is referred to as a *generic region*. Similarly, in the third column from the left, under "generic buffering, two key fields", the buffer contains generic regions with the first two key fields being the same.

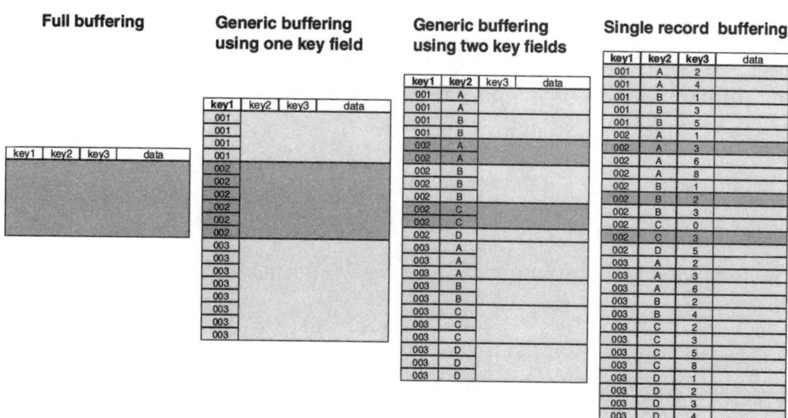

Figure 9.2 Generic regions of a table

For table <tab_gen2> generic 2 buffering has been set. The first two primary key fields are the client (MANDT) and the company code (BUKRS). The table also contains the primary key fields <key3> and <key4>. Let us also assume that the table contains data on the company codes "Poland", "Czech Republic" and "Slovakia". The table is now accessed with the following SQL statement:

```
SELECT * FROM <tab_gen2> WHERE mandt = '100' AND bukrs = 'Poland' AND
<key3> = a3.
```

This statement causes the buffering of all records of table <tab_gen2> that correspond to client 100 and company code "Poland". If your SAP system has the users corresponding to the different company codes working on different application servers, only the data relevant to the company code used on a particular application is loaded in the buffers of that server.

Buffer management is carried out by the database interface in the SAP work process. Single record buffered tables are stored in the SAP single record buffer (TABLP), generic and fully buffered tables are stored in the generic SAP table buffer (TABL). The tables in the buffer are sorted according to the primary key.

Buffer Accessing

Even after a table is stored in the buffer, the database interface does not automatically access the table buffers. As we have explained above, to access a single-record buffered table, all fields of the primary key of the table must be specified in the **WHERE** clause of the SQL statement with an **EQUALS** condition. Similarly, for a generic-n buffered table, the first "n" primary key fields in the **WHERE** clause must be specified with an **EQUALS** condition. Examine the following examples:

For table <tab_gen3> generic 3 buffering has been set. The fields <key1>, <key2>, <key3> and <key4> are the key fields of the table.

The following SQL statements access the SAP buffer:

- `SELECT * FROM <tab_gen3> WHERE <key1> = a1 AND <key2> = a2 AND <key3> = a3`
- `SELECT * FROM <tab_gen3> WHERE <key1> = a1 AND <key2> = a2 AND <key3> = a3 and <key4> > a4`

The following SQL statements cannot be processed with the help of the SAP buffer and require access to the database:

- `SELECT * FROM <tab_gen3> WHERE <key1> = a1`
- `SELECT * FROM <tab_gen3> WHERE <key3> = a3`

The buffer for the generic-3 buffered table is not accessed, because the fields <key1>, <key2> and <key3> are not all specified.

With a fully buffered table the buffer is always accessed, provided that the table in question has been loaded into the buffer.

Table <tab_ful> has full buffering. The fields <key1>, <key2>, <key3> and <key4> are the key fields of the table.

The following SQL statements access the SAP buffer:

- `SELECT * FROM <tab_ful> WHERE <key1> = a1 AND <key2> = a2 AND <key3> = a3`
- `SELECT * FROM <tab_ful> WHERE <key3> = a3`

  Because the second statement does not specify the fields <key1> and <key2> and the table in the buffer is sorted according to these key fields, all the data in the table must be read sequentially. If the table is relatively large (for example with more than 100 records) it will be more effective to optimize table access by not buffering the table but by creating a secondary index on the database using field <key3>.

As this example shows, in some cases access to a database can actually be more optimal than accessing a buffer. We will look at this problem in greater detail at a later stage in the book.

Other exceptions

The following SQL statements do *not* access the SAP buffer:

- SQL statements with the clause **BYPASSING BUFFER**. This clause is used to indicate statements that should deliberately not access the buffer.
- **SELECT FOR UPDATE** statements. These statements set a database lock and as a result they involve a database access.
- SQL statements using the aggregate functions **SUM, AVG, MIN, MAX**
- SQL statements with **SELECT DISTINCT**
- SQL statements containing the operator **IS NULL**
- SQL statements that trigger sorts (except sorts by primary key)
- SQL statements that access views (except projection views)
- Native SQL statements

Buffer Synchronization

If an entry to a buffered table is changed, the corresponding entries in the table buffers of all SAP instances must be updated. This process is referred to as *buffer synchronization*.

First of all we will look at changes to tables executed with an ABAP statement with no **WHERE** clause, that is to say, with the ABAP statements **UPDATE dbtab, INSERT dbtab, MODIFY dbtab** or **DELETE dbtab**. Only one row in the table is changed in this case.

Synchronization in the buffer involves four steps, as illustrated in Figure 9.3. As an example, let us assume that one record is changed in the buffered table T001.

1. On the SAP instance A, the buffered table T001 is changed by the ABAP statement **UPDATE T001**. The database interface modifies table T001 on the database and the buffer entry for instance A at the same time. Thus, the buffer of the local SAP instance A is *updated synchronously*. At this time, the buffers of all SAP instances except for A are not up-to-date.
2. After table T001 has been changed in the database, the database interface (DBIF) for SAP instance A, logs the change by writing an entry to the database table DDLOG.
3. Table DDLOG is periodically read by all SAP instances. On the basis of the DDLOG entry, the buffer entry for table T001 is *invalidated*. The buffers of the SAP instances are still not updated, but the content of table T001 in the buffer is marked as being invalid.

4. If table T001 is read again on an SAP instance other than A, the database interface can recognize that the data in the buffer is no longer valid. The data is reloaded from the database into the buffer. In this way, the buffers of all SAP instances other than instance A are *asynchronously* updated.

Pending period

After an invalidation, the contents of a table are not immediately loaded into the buffer at the next read access. Rather, a certain waiting or *pending period* is observed. The next "n" accesses are redirected to the database. The buffer is only reloaded after the pending period. This protects the buffer from frequent successive invalidations and reloading operations.

The synchronization mechanism described here applies not only to table buffers but also to other SAP buffers (such as the program buffer).

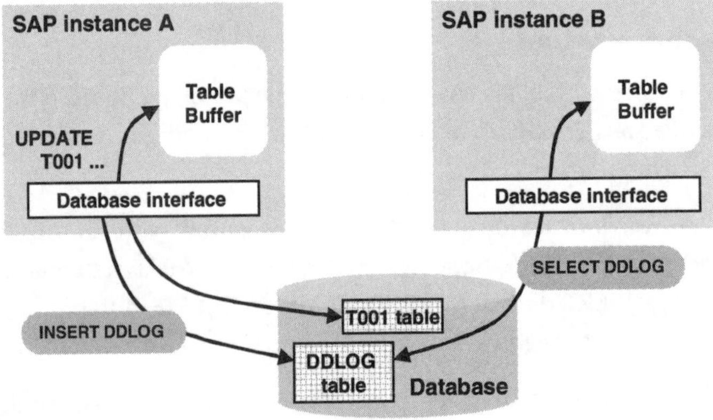

Figure 9.3 Buffer synchronization

rdisp/bufrefmode, rdisp/bufreftime

Buffer synchronization is controlled by the SAP profile parameters **rdisp/bufrefmode** and **rdisp/bufreftime**. For an SAP system with only one SAP instance the parameter **rdisp/bufrefmode** should be set to "sendoff, exeauto". The "sendoff" entry means that no DDLOG entries can be written (as there is no other SAP instance to be synchronized). "exeauto" means that table DDLOG is read periodically. This is necessary for buffer synchronization after an import using the transport programs `tp` or `R3trans`. (The SAP Change and Transport system (CTS) writes entries to the DDLOG table to enable buffer synchronization after the import of buffered objects (for example table contents and programs). In an SAP system with multiple SAP instances **rdisp/bufrefmode** must contain the value "sendon, exeauto". **rdisp/bufreftime** specifies the frequency of buffer synchronization. You should not change the default value of 60 (seconds). This means that table DDLOG is read every 60 seconds.

Granularity of table invalidation

Table entries are *invalidated* as follows:

- If a record is changed in a table with single record buffering, then just this record is invalidated. All other buffered table entries remain valid.
- If a record in a fully buffered table is changed, then the entire contents of the table are invalidated.
- If a record in a generically buffered table is changed, then the generic area in which this record is located is invalidated.

Thus, table contents are invalidated in the same units that they are filled.

A somewhat different buffer synchronization procedure is used when a buffered table is changed through an ABAP statement that uses a WHERE clause, for example with **UPDATE <dbtab> WHERE..., DELETE FROM <dbtab> WHERE...** This type of ABAP statement can be used to change several records in a table. In this case, as a result, the entire `<dbtab>` table in question is invalidated in the buffer of the local SAP instance (instance A in our example) and on all other servers. For this reason, changes with **WHERE** clauses can increase buffer management workload much more than change operations that do not use a **WHERE** clause.

When program or customizing settings are transported, invalidations also occur. Therefore, imports should not be carried out in a production system at times of high workload. It is recommended that imports should be scheduled once or twice per week at times of low workload.

Invalidations and displacements

Invalidations should not be confused with *displacements*, which are displayed in the SAP Memory Configuration Monitor (ST02) in the **Swaps** column. When there is not enough space in the buffer to store new data, the data that has not been accessed for the longest time is displaced. Displacement occurs asynchronously, determined by accesses to the buffer. It occurs when the space available in the buffer falls below a certain level or when access quality falls below a certain point.

Activating Buffering

1. To activate or deactivate buffering for a table, call the ABAP dictionary function by selecting:

   Tools • ABAP Workbench • Dictionary

2. Enter the table name, select the **Display** button and then **Technical settings**.

3. To activate buffering, select **Buffering switched on**. Finally, enter the buffering type (full, generic or single record) and, in the case of generic buffering, the number of key fields.
4. Save the new settings.
5. Once they have been saved, you can activate the changes. The settings should then show the status "active", "saved".

Since the technical settings of a table are linked to the SAP Change and Transport System (CTS), to change the buffering for a table you need a change request. Buffering can be activated or deactivated while the SAP system is running.

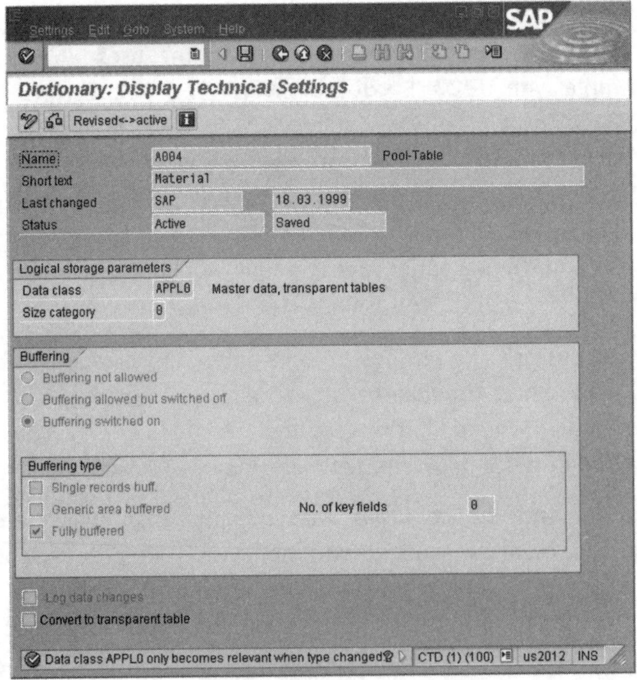

Figure 9.4 Technical settings of a table

There are three options for setting buffering:

- **Buffering not allowed**
  This setting deactivates buffering for a table. It is used if a table should not be buffered under any circumstances (for example, if it contains transaction data that is frequently changed).

- **Buffering allowed but switched off**
  This setting also deactivates buffering for a table. It means that it is possible to buffer this table, but in this particular system, for reasons of performance, buffering has been deactivated (for example, because the table is too large). Whether a given table with this characteristic should in fact be buffered can be ascertained from the analyses described later in this chapter.
- **Buffering switched on**
  This setting activates the buffering for the respective table.

If you try to activate buffering for a table that SAP has delivered with the setting **Buffering not allowed**, this is considered a modification of the SAP system and must be registered in the SAP Service Marketplace. You should activate the buffering for such tables only if you have been explicitly advised to do so by SAP.

If you set the buffering type for a client-dependent table to "full", the table will automatically be buffered as generic 1.

What Tables Should be Buffered?

Technical prerequisites

If tables are to be buffered, they must satisfy the following *technical prerequisites*.

- Buffered data will be stored redundantly on all SAP instances. As a result, buffering is only suitable for small tables that are read frequently.
- Buffer synchronization causes a rather considerable loss in performance when accessing buffered tables. Therefore, only tables that are not changed often should be buffered.
- Buffered tables are sorted and stored according to key fields. Table buffering is therefore optimal for statements that access the table through the key fields. Table buffers do not support searching using secondary indexes.
- Buffer synchronization occurs after a certain delay. Therefore, you should only buffer tables for which short-term inconsistencies are acceptable.

In the SAP system we differentiate between three types of data: transaction data, master data and customizing data.

Never buffer transaction data!

Transaction data includes, for example: sales orders, deliveries, material movements and material reservations which might be stored in the tables VBAK, LIKP, MKPF and RESB. These tables grow over time and can attain several MB or even GB in size. In principle, transaction data should not be buffered.

As a rule, do not buffer master data!

Typical *master data* includes, for example, materials, customers and suppliers, stored in the tables MARA, KNA1 and LFA1. Tables with master data grow slowly over time and can reach sizes of several hundred MB. For this reason, master data is generally not buffered. Another argument against buffering master data tables is that master data is normally accessed with many different selections and not necessarily via the primary key. Rather than buffering, accesses to these tables can be optimized by the use of secondary indices.

Customizing data is normally buffered!

Customizing data portrays, among other things, the business processes of your enterprise in the SAP system. Examples of customizing data include the definition of clients, the company codes, plant and sales organizations, for example in tables T000, T001, T001W and TVKO. Customizing tables are generally small and are seldom changed once the system has gone live. Therefore, customizing data is eminently suited to table buffering.

Table TCURR, for example, contains exchange rates for foreign currencies. The key fields in this table are MANDT (client), KURST (type of exchange rate), FCURR (source currency), TCURR (target currency) and GDATU (start of validity period). In most customer systems this table is small, it is rarely changed and thus meets all the conditions for buffering. As a result, it is delivered by SAP with the status "full buffering" set.

In some SAP systems, however, this table may grow quickly because many exchange rates are required and the rates are frequently changed. Because the table is fully buffered, older entries (entries with validity periods that have long since expired) are also loaded into the buffer, although they are no longer necessary for normal operation. As a result, once the table reaches a certain size, table buffering is no longer effective. If the table is changed during daily operation, invalidations and displacements reduce performance.

In this case, you should remove the table from buffering. You should also try to achieve a long-term application-specific solution: are all table entries really necessary? Could old entries be removed—for example by archiving? We will look at this example again in greater detail in the section "Detailed Table Analysis" on page 304.

Condition tables contain the customizing data for the central logical functions that determine such information as pricing, output determination, partner determination, account determination and so on. These functions are used in the logistics chain, for incoming sales orders, goods issue, billing and so on. Given that these transactions are extremely critical for performance in many SAP systems, the optimization of buffering for condition tables should receive special priority. **Condition tables**

Condition tables are: A<nnn>, B<nnn>, C<nnn>, D<nnn>, KOTE<nnn>, KOTF<nnn>, KOTG<nnn> and KOTH<nnn>, with <nnn> = 000–999. Tables with nnn = 000–499 are part of SAP standard and, with a few exceptions, are delivered with the attribute **Buffering switched on**. Tables with nnn = 500–999 are generated in customizing as required and are not initially buffered.

Table A005 contains customer and material-specific price conditions. In other words: In this table a price condition can be maintained for every combination of customer and material. In addition, a validity period can be set for the price condition. If the possibility of customer-specific prices is used intensively in an SAP system, and these prices are frequently changed, this table would grow very quickly. A problem similar to what we have described above in the example of table TCURR occurs: In this case the table would have to be removed from buffering. Other condition tables that would also grow quickly include A017 and A018 (prices for suppliers and material numbers).

Monitoring SAP Table Buffering

Problem areas

Three problems can occur in the area of SAP table buffering and they should be monitored:

- Tables are designed too small and, as a result, *displacements (swaps)* occur. Monitoring of displacements is described in Chapter 2 in the section "Analyzing SAP Memory Management" on page 98. Before continuing with a detailed analysis, make sure that the table buffer has at least 10% free space and at least 20% free directory entries.
- Tables may be buffered which, for reasons of performance, should not have been buffered, either because they are changed *(invalidated)* too often or because they are too large.
- Tables that should be buffered for reasons of performance are not buffered. This applies mainly to tables which are created in the customer system, whether explicitly in the ABAP dictionary or implicitly in customizing (for example, condition tables).

Monitoring table buffering is not a task that needs to be carried out periodically. Some examples of when table buffers should be examined:

- Users complain about occasional long response times in a transaction that normally runs quickly.
- On analyzing the shared SQL area or an SQL trace you find expensive SQL statements related to buffered tables, which would indicate reload processes caused by incorrect buffering.
- On analyzing the single record statistics (transaction code STAT), you frequently find the entry "Note: Tables were saved in the table buffer" (see also Chapter 4, "Single Record Statistics" on page 149).

The monitors and strategies described below help you to identify problems with incorrectly buffered tables.

Table Access Statistics

SAP Table Access Statistics (also called Table Call Statistics) is the most important monitor for analyzing SAP table buffering.

1. The Monitor can be started as follows:

   Tools · Administration · Monitor · Performance · Setup/Buffers · Calls

2. A selection screen appears. Here, you can select the time period, the SAP instance and the type of table to be analyzed. For this analysis, select "All tables", "Since startup", and "This server".
3. A screen is displayed that lists details on ABAP and database accesses and buffer status for all tables in the SAP system. You can navigate between different lists using the arrow buttons (from SAP Basis 4.0 on). By double-clicking on a row you can view all the information available for that table.

The most important fields are described in Table 9.1.

Field	Explanation
Table	Name of the table; if it is a pooled table, the name of the table pool is given first; for example, KAPOL A004.
Buffer State	The status of the table in the buffer—if this table can be buffered. See Table 9.2 for more information.

Table 9.1 The fields in the Table Calls Statistics Monitor

Field	Explanation
Buf key opt	Buffering type: "ful" indicates full buffering; "gen" indicates generic buffering; and "sng" indicates single record buffering.
Buffer size [bytes]	Space occupied by the table in the SAP table buffer
Size maximum [bytes]	Maximum size of the table in the SAP table buffer since system startup
Invalida-tions	Number of invalidations
ABAP/IV Processor requests	Number of ABAP table access requests received by the database interface, subdivided into *Direct Reads, Sequential Reads, Updates, Inserts, Deletes*
DB activity	Number of database operations (Prepare, Open, Reopen, Fetch or Exec) that the database interface has forwarded to the database, subdivided according to *Direct Reads, Sequential Reads, Updates, Inserts, Deletes*
DB activity—Rows affected	Number of rows that are transferred between the database and the SAP instance

Table 9.1 The fields in the Table Calls Statistics Monitor (contd.)

Request, Open, Fetch

A table access in an ABAP program is called a *request*. We differentiate between five different types of requests: **Direct Reads, Sequential Reads, Inserts, Updates** and **Deletes**. Direct Reads are **SELECT SINGLE** statements that have specified all the primary key fields in the **WHERE** clause with an **EQUALS** condition. All other select statements are known as sequential reads. Inserts, Updates and Deletes are referred to as *Changes*.

In a request, the ABAP program calls up the database interface of the SAP work process. The database interface checks to see if the data needed for the query can be provided by the table buffer in the SAP instance. If this is not the case, the database interface passes the SQL statement on to the database. An SQL statement performing a read is made up of an **OPEN** operation, which transfers the SQL statement to the database, and one or more **FETCHES**, which transfer the resulting data from the database to the SAP work process. An SQL statement that is performing a change is similarly made up of an **OPEN** operation and an **EXEC** Operation. For more detailed explanations of the **Prepare, Open, Reopen, Fetch** and **Exec** operations, see the section "Evaluating an SQL Trace" on page 155 in Chapter 4.

For tables that cannot be buffered, the database interface automatically passes each request on to the database. For direct reads, inserts, updates and deletes, each request corresponds to exactly one **OPEN** and one **FETCH**. For sequential reads the situation is more complex because for each request there can be more than one **OPEN** and more than one **FETCH**.

For tables that can be buffered, requests encounter one of three possible situations:

- The contents of the table are located in the buffer with the "valid" status: The required data can be read from the buffer. As a result, this request requires no database activity.
- The contents of the table are located in the "valid" buffer, but the SQL statement does not specify the correct fields, or it contains the clause **BYPASSING BUFFER** to prevent reading from the SAP buffer. A complete list of SQL statements that do not read from the SAP buffer can be found in the section "Buffer Accessing" on page 285. In this situation, database activity is required to satisfy the request.
- The table contents are not yet located in the buffer or are not valid: In this situation the data needed for the request cannot be read from the buffer. The database interface loads the buffer (if the table is not in the pending period).

During the initial buffer load process, the field **Database activity: Rows affected** is not increased. If a table has been loaded only once into the buffer and all subsequent requests are read from the buffer, the value in the **Database activity: Rows affected** field remains at zero in the table access statistics. If the table is invalidated or displaced and then reloaded into the buffer from the database or if the buffer is bypassed, the **Database activity: Rows affected** field is increased by the number of table rows that are read.

Buffer status

The **Buffer State** field shows the *buffer status* of a table. The various status possibilities are listed in Table 9.2.

Status	Explanation
valid	The table (or parts of it) is valid in the buffer, which means that the next access can be read from the buffer.
invalid	The table has been invalidated. It cannot yet be reloaded into the buffer because the operation that changed the table has not yet been completed with a "commit".

Table 9.2 Buffering status

Status	Explanation
pending	The table has been invalidated. It cannot be loaded at the next access because the pending period is still running.
loadable	The table has been invalidated. The pending period has expired and the table will be reloaded at the next access.
loading	The table is currently being loaded.
absent, displaced	The table is not in the buffer (because, for example, it was never loaded or it has been displaced).
multiple	Can occur for tables with generic buffering: Some generic areas are valid, others have been invalidated because of changes.
error	An error occurred while the table was being loaded. This table cannot be buffered.

Table 9.2 Buffering status (contd.)

Figure 9.5 shows the screen shot of a table access statistic in an SAP system (SAP Basis 3.1). The list is sorted according to the **DB activity—Rows affected** column which indicates the number of records read from the database. At the top of the list we find buffered tables, such as the condition tables A004, A005 and A952. The entry KAPOL preceding the name indicates that these tables are located in the KAPOL table pool. We shall return to the evaluation of this example in the next section.

Analyzing Buffered Tables

Identify buffered tables for which buffering reduces rather than increases performance. To do so, proceed as follows:

1. Start the SAP Table Call Statistics as follows:

   Tools · Administration · Monitor · Performance · Setup/Buffers · Calls

2. In the following screen select **All tables**, **Since startup** and **This server**.
3. The screen that then appears should resemble the one shown in Figure 9.5.

First step: Determine number of database accesses

In this *first step* sort the Table Call Statistics according to the "DB activity—Rows affected" column. The number of "rows affected" is an indication of the database load caused by accesses to the table in question. The tables with high database activity will appear at the top of

All tables (appserv5_DEN_00)

Tune Edit Goto Monitor System Hilfe

Choose Generic buffer Single record buffer Not buffered Overview <-> Detail Sort

System : appserv5_DEN_00 All tables

Date & time of snapshot: 05.05.1998 09:41:11 System Startup: 02.05.1998 03:33:06

TABLE	Buffer State	Buf key opt	Buffer size [bytes]	ABAP/IV Processor requests Total	Direct reads	Seq. reads	Changes	DB activity Open	Fetch	Rows affected
Total			27202.865	22681.402	17911.056	4.646.871	123.475	531.683	696.527	9.703.622
KAPOL A004	valid	gen	10273.552	6.475	0	6.475	0	0	7.074	6.076.943
KAPOL A005	valid	gen	3.111.279	1.545	0	1.545	0	0	1.464	811.580
A952	valid	gen	3.466.740	7.876	0	7.876	0	0	1.116	611.139
VBRK			0	408.014	763	407.251	0	763	6.583	407.974
S508			0	196.020	0	196.020	0	0	797	196.006
MDVM			0	135.437	0	132.395	3.042	0	222	140.740
MAKT			0	77.476	74.900	2.576	0	74.900	74.900	74.900
MARA			0	77.493	23.204	54.289	0	23.204	24.430	74.226
EBAN			0	77.744	3.507	74.028	209	3.507	6.796	74.138
unknown			0	65.143	34	65.109	0	52	331	65.125
MVKE			0	63.029	61.799	1.230	0	61.799	61.799	61.799
KONP			0	85.809	33.950	51.859	0	33.950	56.559	60.567
MBEW			0	56.491	54.545	989	957	54.545	54.545	55.502
MARD			0	66.340	3.119	63.221	0	3.119	12.321	55.241
MDBS			0	54.879	0	54.879	0	0	3.094	46.789
VBAK			0	59.394	43.084	16.310	0	43.084	44.717	44.717
CE1DEN2			0	224	0	224	0	0	723	39.042
KNA1			0	52.031	13.641	38.390	0	13.641	27.080	38.954
DOKIL			0	33.901	33.901	0	0	33.901	33.901	33.901
MDKP			0	32.388	11.420	6	20.962	11.420	11.420	32.382
VBAP			0	36.060	6.007	30.053	0	6.007	13.664	29.508
LIPS			0	30.801	316	30.436	49	316	8.425	27.231
VBDATA			0	25.084	0	0	25.084	0	0	25.084
VBMOD			0	25.084	0	0	25.084	0	0	25.084
TADIR	valid	sng	4.096	28.947	3.895	25.052	0	7	53	25.057
VBUP			0	27.697	4.739	22.839	119	4.739	8.334	22.758
MARC			0	24.291	21.807	2.484	0	21.807	21.819	21.819
MONI			0	20.386	0	14.222	6.164	0	3.022	19.535

DEN (1) (066) appserv5 OVR 09:45AM

Figure 9.5 Table Call Statistics (first example)

the list. These should be transaction data tables or large master data tables; for example, the tables VBAK, S508 and MDVM in Figure 9.5. For many of these tables the number of requests is approximately the same as the number of "rows affected".

For buffered tables the number of "rows affected" should be low, because for accesses to these tables, data should be read from the buffer and not from the database. Therefore, such tables should not appear towards the top of the list. If, as in Figure 9.5, you find buffered tables with a high number of "rows affected", there are two possible causes:

- The table is relatively large and has been changed or displaced. Reloading processes and database read accesses during the pending period are reflected in a high number of "rows affected". You should check to see if buffering should be deactivated for these tables.
- The type of buffering does not match the WHERE clause in the read accesses so the database interface cannot use the buffer.

If buffered tables appear among the top entries in Table Calls Statistics sorted according to "rows affected", this is a sure sign that buffering these tables is counter-productive. These tables should be analyzed in greater detail.

Second step: Analyzing the rate of changes and invalidations

In a *second step*, determine the rate of change of the buffered tables ("changes" / "requests" in the Table Calls Statistics) and the number of invalidations. To do this, sort according to the columns **Invalidations** or **Changes**. Using the guideline values given above, check to see if buffering should be deactivated for the tables with the highest rates of change and the most invalidations.

Third step: Determining table size

In a *third step* sort the Table Calls Statistics according to table size (the **Buffer size** column). First of all, you should check the buffering status of the largest table. It should be "valid". By comparing the values for "buffer size" and "size maximum" you can see if generic areas of the table have been displaced or invalidated. You should also check, using the guideline values given below, if buffering should be deactivated for the largest table.

The following counters may be of use in deciding whether a table should **4.0B**
be buffered or not: Tables that are smaller than 1 MB and with an invalidation rate of less than 1% do not generally present any technical problems and can be buffered. Tables between 1 MB and 5 MB should have an invalidation rate of less than 0,1%. For tables that are bigger than 5 MB, the developer must decide individually for each table whether buffering is worthwhile. Please note that these guideline values reflect experience at the time of this book's appearing in print.

Fourth step: logical analysis

Before deactivating buffering for a table, as a *fourth step* you should consider the following recommendations:

- **For customer-developed tables**
  Changes to table buffering status should only be made after joint consideration involving the developer and the system administrator.
- **For tables created by SAP**
  Occasionally you may need to deactivate buffering for a table which had buffering activated in the standard delivery. An example could be the TCURR table mentioned above or the SAP condition tables (such as Annn). However you should never deactivate buffering unless you have analyzed the table functions closely. This applies in particular for SAP basis tables, such as the tables DDFTX and USR*. If you find an SAP table for which you wish to deactivate buffering, you should first look for related notes in the SAP Service Marketplace.

Verifying the effects of changes

Once you have changed the buffering mode of a table, you should verify the success of your actions.

Ideally, you should know the programs and transactions that access the tables in question and be able to directly observe how the changes affect runtime.

In the Table Calls Statistics you can verify the success of your changes by comparing the number of "requests" to "rows affected". The purpose of a table buffer is to reduce the number of database accesses. This should be reflected in the ratio of "requests" to "rows affected". If by changing the buffering for a table you have not managed to increase this ratio, reanalyze the buffer and, if in doubt, undo the changes you made to buffering.

Example

Figures 9.5 and 9.6 show two screen shots of Table Calls Statistics from two real SAP systems. Both lists are sorted according to the **DB activity—Rows affected** column.

We shall first of all look at Figure 9.5. As mentioned above, we would expect that tables with transaction data or a large volume of master data would be at the top of the table, such as the tables VBRK, S508, MDVM. However, at the top of the list we see the buffered condition tables A004, A005 and A952. The buffering status of these tables is "valid", which means that these tables are located in the buffer. On comparing the columns **ABAP/IV Processor requests—Total** and **DB activity—Rows affected**, you will see that per request (that is to say, per ABAP access) an average of 1,000 rows are read from the table. For these three tables a total of around 7.5 million rows were read. This represents around 75% of the records read for all of the tables together (9.7 million). It is likely that the very high number of reads for these three tables is caused by frequent buffer load-processes.

To verify this suspicion, examine the number of invalidations and the size of the table in the buffer. To do this, double-click the row containing the table that you want to analyze. This takes you to a screen summarizing all the available information on this table. In our example you will see that tables A004, A005 and A952 are frequently invalidated, which means that they have an invalidation rate or more than 1% of the total requests. The size of the tables in the buffer (**Buffer size [bytes]** field in Figure 9.5) is between 3 and 10 MB. According to the guidelines for table buffering given above, these tables should not be buffered. By analyzing Table Calls Statistics in this case, we have come to the conclusion that buffering should be deactivated for tables A004, A005 and A952.

On looking at the **Changes** column in Figure 9.5, at first you may be surprised to see that tables A004, A005 and A952 are invalidated although there are no changes indicated in the column **Changes**. This is because the column **Changes** only displays the changes that are performed on the local SAP instance (here, "appserv5_DEN_00"). Modifications are not shown in the **Changes** field if they are executed on other SAP instances or if the changes to the customizing tables are carried out in another SAP system, such as the development system, and then transferred to the SAP system being examined. Nevertheless these changes from other SAP systems do cause an invalidation of the buffer entries and as a result start a local buffer reloading process.

An analysis similar to the one just carried out on the Table Calls Statistics shown in Figure 9.5 can also be carried out for Figure 9.6. In this example the list is also sorted according to **DB activity—Rows affected** and we also have a number of buffered tables at the top of the list. The entry "displcd" in the **Buffer State** column shows that table A005 was not invalidated because of a change, rather, it was displaced because of a lack of space in the buffer. Therefore, in this example two factors come together: On the one hand, tables were buffered that were possibly too large and changed too often for buffering; on the other hand, the table buffer is too small and this causes displacements. You can see if displacements occur in the table buffer by checking the **Swaps** column in the SAP Memory Configuration Monitor (transaction code ST02).

Since the example in Figure 9.6 reveals two problems, the corresponding solution strategy is more complex. First of all, the size of the table buffers should be increased. The size and number of invalidations in tables A005, A004, A006 and A017 should be examined in more detail, and using the guideline values listed above, you should decide whether buffering should be deactivated for these tables. For example, if you find that table A005 is larger than 1 MB and the number of invalidations is greater than 0.1%, you should deactivate buffering for this table. After this first optimization step, you should carry out a second analysis on the Table Calls Statistics to see if the number of database accesses to the buffered tables is noticeably reduced. If not, analyze the table statistics further to determine whether you need to enlarge the table buffer size or deactivate buffering for other tables.

All tables (bbafddi1_P11_00)

Tune Edit Goto Monitor System Hilfe

Choose Generic buffer Single record buffer Not buffered Overview <-> Detail Sort

System : bbafddi1_P11_00 All tables
Date & time of snapshot: 11.02.1998 13:55:00 System Startup: 11.02.1998 03:52:18

TABLE	Buffer State	Buf key opt	Buffer size [bytes]	ABAP/IV Processor requests Total	Direct reads	Seq. reads	Changes	DB activity Open	Fetch	Rows affected
Total			6.095.721	3.914.298	2.899.491	992.701	22.106	123.252	159.805	3.735.563
KAPOL A005	displcd	gen	0	2.338	0	2.338	0	0	2.499	1.406.353
KAPOL A004	valid	gen	979.282	488	0	488	0	0	847	539.694
KAPOL A006	valid	gen	940.632	612	0	612	0	0	853	455.149
KAPOL A017	pending	gen	0	392	0	392	0	0	364	128.818
T179	valid	gen	65.054	111.380	238	111.142	0	20	64	76.773
ATAB TMC73	pending	ful	0	580	0	580	0	0	58	62.818
ATAB TFAWX	pending	gen	0	14.039	0	14.039	0	0	106	62.492
T179T	valid	gen	124.992	551	491	60	0	178	215	57.754
VAPMA			0	48.757	0	48.757	0	0	207	46.894
VBUK			0	45.020	44.610	400	10	44.610	44.800	44.812
ATAB T130F	valid	gen	39.240	115.168	22	115.146	0	1	107	41.857
ATAB T156S	pending	gen	0	297	297	0	0	48	90	33.512
TFAWL	valid	gen	530.334	5.544	0	5.544	0	0	293	33.100
ICONT	valid	ful	115.895	513	502	11	0	46	75	30.148
T023T	valid	gen	44.847	510	498	12	0	39	49	20.519
ATAB TFAW	valid	gen	60.772	884	0	884	0	0	66	20.002

P11 (3) (066) bbafddi1 INS 01:55PM

Figure 9.6 Table Call Statistics (second example)

For computers with a large main memory it is not unusual for the generic buffer table to be configured with as much as 100 MB and single record buffers to be configured to 40 MB.

Analyzing Tables That are Currently not Buffered

In this section we will describe an analysis to help you decide if you should activate buffering for any tables that are currently not buffered. To perform the analysis, call up the Table Calls Statistics and proceed as follows:

First step: Access statistics

Requests To identify tables that are currently not buffered and may potentially benefit from being buffered, in a *first step* sort the Table Calls Statistics Monitor according to the **ABAP/IV Processor requests—Total** column. At the top of the list you will normally find the tables DDNTF and DDNTT. These are ABAP dictionary tables that are stored in the NTAB buffers—the "Field description buffer" and the "Table definition buffer". The next tables in the list will be as follows:

- Tables with transaction data or large master data tables, such as the tables MARA, MARC, VBAK, MKPF from SAP logistics modules and SAP update tables VBHDR, VBMOD and VBDATA. These tables cannot be buffered.
- Buffered tables with customizing data. Make sure that buffered tables with a high number of requests show the "valid" status.

If there are non-buffered customizing tables at the top of the list sorted by requests, you should consider activating buffering for these tables.

You should pay particular attention to customer-developed tables. These include tables explicitly created in the ABAP dictionary (for example, tables with names beginning with Y or Z) and condition tables generated during customizing (for example with Annn, nnn = 500).

The result from the first step is a list of tables that could potentially be buffered because they receive a high number of requests.

Second step: technical analysis

In the *second step* you can determine the invalidation rate and the size of the table with a technical analysis.

Changes

One criterion for deciding if a table should be buffered is the change rate, which can be calculated from the ratio of *Changes* to *Requests*. Note that the **Changes** column only displays the changes on the selected SAP instance but not changes performed on other SAP instances nor those that are imported as table content.

Table size

You should also determine the size of the table (see also the section "Detailed Table Analysis" on page 304).

Third step: logical analysis

In the *third step* check to see if the logical prerequisites for buffering are met (see also the section "What Tables Should be Buffered?" on page 291).

- **For customer-developed tables**
  To determine if the technical prerequisites for buffering are met, contact the developer responsible to find out the purpose of the tables and determine whether or not the tables should be buffered, from a logical point of view. For example, condition tables are usually suited to buffering, as mentioned above. The developer sets the type of table buffering. Note that single record buffering and generic buffering are only useful if the key fields are specified in the WHERE clause of the access requests.

  Changes to table buffering status should only be made after joint deliberation between the developer and the system administrator.
- **For tables created by SAP**
  The buffering status of SAP tables are already pre-set when the SAP system is delivered. Usually, most of the tables that can be buffered,

are buffered. If you find an SAP table that you feel should be buffered, check for relevant notes in the SAP Service Marketplace. You should never activate buffering for tables with the characteristic "Buffering not allowed", unless you have explicit instructions to do so from SAP.

Activating buffering can lead to logical inconsistencies because of asynchronous buffer synchronization. You should therefore never activate buffering if you are not sure how the table functions and what type of accesses are made to the table. Activating buffering can also cause performance problems if the table is too big and/or is changed too frequently.

Detailed Table Analysis

With detailed table analysis you can determine the size of a table, the number of table entries and the distribution of the generic regions in a table.

1. To start the detailed table analysis, mark a table in the Table Calls Statistics Monitor and select the **Analyze** button, or enter the transaction code DB05. For older SAP versions, start the report RSTUNE59.
2. Enter a table name and mark **Analysis for primary key**. Start the analysis. (*Please note:* This may take some time for large tables.) The results of the analysis are then shown.
3. Use this list to check the size of the table. In the upper part of the list you will find, among other things, the number of table entries and the size that the table would be if fully buffered. This size can be smaller or larger than the space needed for the table on the database. For example, database fragmentation can cause the table to consume unnecessary space on the database. In addition, unlike some databases, the table buffer does not compress empty fields to minimize the need for storage space.
4. Check the distribution of the generic areas of the table. You will find the necessary information in the lower part of the analysis screen.

Rows per generic key	Distinct values	1–10	11–100	101–1,000	1,001–10,000	10,000–100,000	> 100,000
MANDT	The following distribution applies to client 100						
1. KURST	41	10	14	11	0	6	
2. FCURR	1,311	877	209	175	50		
3. TCURR	5,188	1,921	2,920	347			
4. GDATU	169,795	169,795					

Table 9.3 Example of detailed analysis of generic regions for table TCURR

Table 9.3 shows an example of the possible distribution of generic regions in table TCURR. (Compare also the section "What Tables Should be Buffered?" on page 291.) The distribution displayed concerns production client 100. This distribution analysis is interpreted as follows:

▶ **KURST row**
The **Distinct values** column shows the number of generic regions, which in this example is the number of different types of currency exchange (KURST field). Table TCURR contains 41 different types of currency exchange. Of these, 10 types have between 1 and 10 entries in the table (1-10 column), 14 types have between 11 and 100 entries, and so on. Finally there are 6 exchange rates with between 10,000 and 100,000 entries. No exchange rate type has more than 100,000 entries.

▶ **FCURR row**
There are 1,311 different combinations of exchange rate types (KURST field) and source currencies (FCURR). There is no combination with more than 10,000 entries (The row 10,000–100,000 is empty).

▶ **Last row; GDATU**
There are 169,795 different entries with the combination MANDT, KURST, FCURR, TCURR and GDATU. This is also the total number of entries in client 100, because MANDT, KURST, FCURR, TCURR and GDATU make up the complete primary key for table TCURR.

Ultimately, one row of this distribution analysis shows the average number of rows read when one, two or n fields of the primary key are specified.

How does this distribution analysis actually help you to decide how table TCURR should be buffered?

- First of all you can see that table TCURR has 169,795 different entries in the live client. If TCURR has full or generic-1 buffering, a change operation always invalidates the client entirely. Therefore, after a change operation, 169,795 records must be reloaded into the buffer. In other words: the buffer loading process is justified only if users need to make over 100,000 read accesses. The invalidation rate for this table must have been very low to ensure that buffering the table does not cause too great a reduction in performance.
- Should you decide to set generic-3 buffering for table TCURR, a maximum of 1,311 generic regions would be buffered, as can be seen in the "FCURR" row of the "Distinct values" column. The largest regions (50 in total) contain between 1,001 and 10,000 records. If a record in the table TCURR is changed, then a maximum of 10,000 records would be invalidated and reloaded.
- It would also be possible to set generic-4 buffering. Up to 5,188 generic regions would then have to be buffered.

From this analysis it is clear that full buffering for table TCURR is out of the question. Depending on the invalidation rate, this table should be set to generic-3 buffering, or not be buffered at all.

The larger the table, the more you should favor generic buffering.

In the initial screen of the detailed table analysis you have the possibility of selecting the **Analysis for fields** function. This enables you to start analyses for any combination of table fields, to be specified in the fields **Field1**, **Field2**, and so on. With this analysis you can determine the selectivity of a secondary index. See also Chapter 11, "Optimizing SQL Statements Through Secondary Indexes" on page 339.

Monitoring Buffer Synchronization (DDLOG Entries)

The buffer synchronization monitor displays the remaining, undeleted entries in the DDLOG table.

1. The Monitor can be started as follows:

   Tools · Administration · Monitor · Performance · Setup/Buffers · Buffers · Detail analysis menu · Buffer Synchron

2. In the selection screen you can specify the buffer for which you wish to view the synchronization activities. With the **Select all** button you can select all buffers.
3. Then select **Read DDLOG**. A list appears, displaying the synchronization operations in accordance with the selection criteria entered.

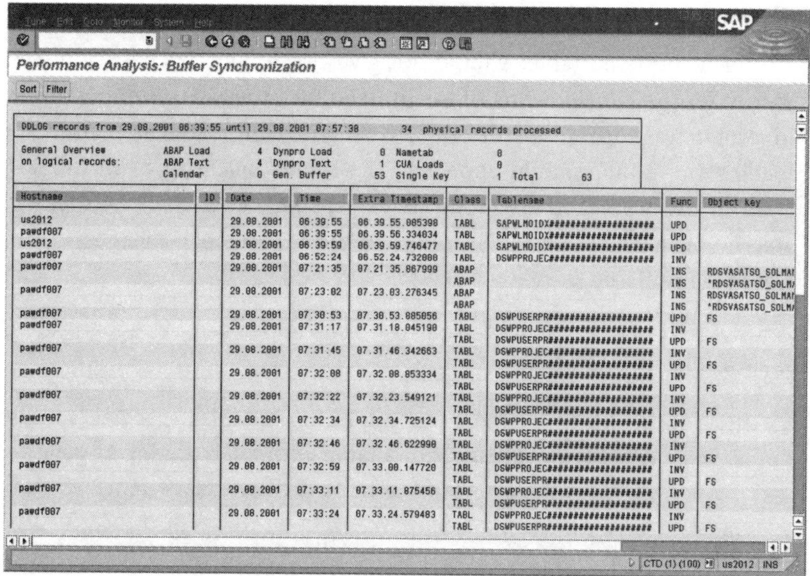

Figure 9.7 Buffer synchronization monitor

Figure 9.7 shows an example of the output of this monitor. Table 9.4 explains the various different fields.

Field	Explanation
Hostname	Name of the application server that has written the synchronization entry. If the referral originates from an import, this column shows the entry "tp" or "R3trans".
ID and SEQ.No.	Unique identification (for internal use)
Date and Time	Time stamp
Class	Name of the buffer: NTAB, ABAP, TABLP, TABL etc.
Tablename	Name of the table to be synchronized
Func	Database operation: INS, DEL, UPD
Object key	Relevant key, if the invalidated area is a generic region.

Table 9.4 Fields in the buffer synchronization monitor

Shared SQL Area and SQL Trace

Normally, buffered tables should not give rise to any database accesses, except for the initial loading of the buffer. Once the SAP system has been in production operation for some time, no SQL statements used for loading the buffer should appear in the *shared SQL area* or in the *SQL trace*. However, if these statements appear among the expensive statements in the shared SQL area or in the SQL trace, it means they are not being buffered properly.

An SQL statement that was used to load a buffer can be recognized as follows:

- The WHERE clause for the generic-n buffered tables specifies the first "n" fields with an equals sign. For a table with full buffering or generic-1 buffering, this is the client (if the table is client-dependent).
- The SQL statement contains an Order-by condition, which contains all the fields of the table key.

The following SQL statement loads the buffer for table TMODU, a generic-1 buffered table:

```
SELECT * FROM "TMODU" WHERE "FAUNA" = :A0 ORDER BY "FAUNA", "MODIF",
"TABNM", "FELDN", "KOART", "UMSKS"
```

If the table to be buffered is a pooled table, during buffer loading there is a database access to the table pool in which the table is located.

Pooled table A002 is fully buffered and is located in the KAPOL table pool. The SQL statement for loading the buffer is:

```
SELECT "TABNAME", "VARKEY", "DATALN", "VARDATA" FROM "KAPOL" WHERE
"TABNAME" = :A0 ORDER BY "TABNAME", "VARKEY"
```

ATAB and KAPOL are important table pools. ATAB contains many SAP Basis buffered tables (such as T<nnn>); KAPOL contains many condition tables (such as A<nnn>).

Summary

Buffering tables in the main memory of the SAP application server is an important instrument for optimizing performance. Table buffering is only effective if the following conditions are met:

- The table must be relatively small.
- The table must be accessed relatively often.

- The invalidation rate for the table must be low.
- The short-term inconsistency between the application servers, brought about by asynchronous buffer synchronization, can be tolerated.
- Access to the table must be using the first "n" fields of the primary key, where "n" is less than the total number of key fields.

The synchronization and loading processes of incorrectly buffered tables can cause a reduction in performance that far outweighs any gains in performance provided by buffering. In this case, users will sporadically notice long response times in a transaction that normally runs quickly.

The Table Calls Statistics Monitor is the central tool for monitoring SAP table buffering. Using these statistics you can decide whether the buffering of a particular table is effective or not. The main statistics to look at are the number of ABAP requests (ABAP/IV processor requests), the size of tables (buffer size [bytes]), the number of invalidations and the database activity (DB activity: Rows affected). Figure 9.8 shows the corresponding procedure roadmap for analyzing table buffering.

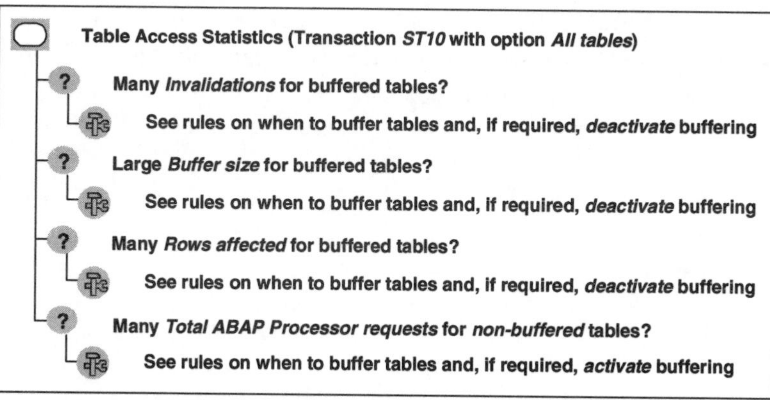

Figure 9.8 Procedure roadmap for analyzing the efficiency of table buffering

Important terms in this chapter

After studying this chapter you should be familiar with the following terms:

- Generic regions of a table
- Single record buffering, generic buffering
- Buffer synchronization
- Invalidation and displacement

Questions

1. Which of the following factors are reasons for not activating full buffering on a table?

    a) The table is very large.

    b) In the SQL statement most frequently used to access the table, the first two of five key fields are contained in an equals condition.

    c) The table is changed frequently.

2. Which statements apply with regard to buffer synchronization?

    a) During buffer synchronization, the application server executing the change instructs the message server to communicate to the other application servers the change made to the buffered table.

    b) After a transaction changes a buffered table, the change transaction must first be completed with a database commit before the table can be reloaded into the buffer.

    c) In a central system the SAP profile parameter **rdisp/bufrefmode** must be set to "sendoff, exeoff".

    d) In a central system, the entries in the table buffer are never invalidated, because the table buffer is changed synchronously after a database change operation.

10 Locks

In an SAP system many users can simultaneously read the contents of database tables. However, for changes to the dataset you must ensure that only one user can change a particular table content at a time. For this purpose, table content is locked during a change operation. The first section of this chapter introduces you to the concepts of locking for SAP systems and database systems.

If locks remain in place for a long time, wait situations can occur which limit the throughput of the SAP system. The second part of the chapter deals with the general performance aspects of using locks.

The SAP system uses special buffering techniques for availability checking with ATP logic and for number assignment for documents. These techniques reduce lock time and can maximize throughput. They are discussed in sections three and four.

When should you read this chapter?

You should read this chapter to help you:

- Find out more about database locks and SAP enqueues
- Analyze system problems that are caused by database locks or enqueues

This chapter does not offer instructions for the programming of SAP transactions; for this, use ABAP text books or SAP online help.

Database Locks and SAP Enqueues

To make a travel booking you must check that all the desired components are available, for example, flights, hotels, bus or boat transfers, and so on. The "all or nothing" principle applies; if no flights are available, you will not be needing a hotel room, and so on. Since the availability of the different components is usually checked one after the other, you want to be certain that no other user makes a change to any of the items in the sequence before the entire booking is completed.

To do this you can use locks, which will preserve data consistency. The locking concepts of the SAP system and the database system have the same ultimate purpose of preserving data consistency, but they are based on different technologies and used in different situations. Locks that are administered by the database system are known as *Database Locks*, locks administered by the SAP system are known as *SAP Enqueues*.

Database Lock Concept

Database locks are administered by the lock handler of a database instance. The locked entity is typically a row in a database table (special exceptions are detailed below). Database locks are set by all modifying SQL statements (**UPDATE, INSERT, DELETE**) and by the statement **SELECT FOR UPDATE**. Locks are held until the SQL statement **COMMIT** (database commit) finalizes all changes and then removes the corresponding database locks. The time interval between two commits is called a database transaction. A program can undo the effects of all modifying SQL statements by executing a database rollback with the SQL statement **ROLLBACK**. In this case all database locks are also removed.

A program using database locks to make a travel booking, for example, would use the SQL statement **SELECT FOR UPDATE**. With this statement a particular item of travel data is read and locked. When each relevant data item has been read and the booking is ready to be made, the data is changed in the respective table rows with the command **UPDATE** and then the **COMMIT** command is used to finalize changes and release all locks. Once a lock has been set, other users can still read the affected data (a simple **SELECT** is still possible), but they cannot lock it. Therefore, they cannot effect an **UPDATE** or a **SELECT FOR UPDATE**. This means that the original lock is *exclusive*.

After a transaction step the SAP work process automatically triggers a database commit (or a database rollback). This removes all locks. This means that a database lock does not last through multiple transaction steps (through multiple input screens in the SAP system).

SAP Enqueues

To lock through several SAP transaction steps use SAP's enqueue administration. SAP enqueues are administered by enqueue work processes in the enqueue table, which is located in the main memory. To retain these enqueues even when an SAP instance is shut down, they are also saved in a local file on the enqueue server.

An SAP enqueue locks a logical object. Therefore, an enqueue can lock rows from several different database tables if these rows form the basis of a single business document. An SAP enqueue can also lock one or more complete tables. SAP enqueue objects are defined and modified in the ABAP dictionary (see below "Locked objects"). They are closely related to the concepts *SAP transaction* and *SAP Logical Unit of Work (SAP LUW)*. Both of these are described extensively in the ABAP literature for dialog programming. The present chapter will therefore not discuss the functions and uses of these techniques as part of ABAP programs. Rather, we shall focus on the aspects related to performance analysis. If performance problems caused by the incorrect use of SAP enqueues are discovered, the responsible APAB developer must be consulted.

An SAP enqueue is a logical lock that acts within the SAP system. If a row in a database table is locked by an SAP enqueue, it can still be changed by an SQL statement executed from the database, or by a customer-developed ABAP program that does not conform to SAP enqueue conventions. Thus, SAP enqueues are only valid within the SAP system. Database locks, by contrast, resist all change attempts. They lock a table row "tight" for all database users and also prevent changes by users outside the SAP system.

For each object that can be held by an enqueue there are two function modules: an enqueue module and a dequeue module. To set an enqueue, an ABAP program must explicitly call the enqueue module, while to remove it, the program must call the corresponding dequeue module. As a result, SAP enqueues can be held in place through multiple transaction steps. At the completion of an SAP transaction, all SAP enqueues are automatically removed.

Let us explain how SAP enqueue administration works, using the example of the round trip: The trip includes several components such as flight, hotel reservations and bus transfers. The individual components of the trip are processes on different input screens—with several transaction steps—and are locked using SAP enqueues. After determining the availability of each component, the booking for the entire trip can be confirmed. This concludes the dialog part of the transaction. Under the protection of the enqueues, an update work process then transfers the changes to the database tables. Once the update has been completed, the SAP LUW is finished and the enqueues are unlocked.

An SAP LUW may also contain program modules that require an update2-type update. An SAP enqueue is not used for this. Modules that use this type of update should not be used to process data that requires the protection of enqueues.

Table 10.1 contrasts the main features of database locks and enqueues.

	DB locks	SAP locks (enqueues)
Locked object	Individual rows of a database table	Logical object, such as a document defined in the ABAP dictionary
How object is locked	Implicitly using modifying SQL statements (such as **UPDATE** and **SELECT FOR UPDATE**)	Explicitly by the ABAP program calling an enqueue module
How lock is removed	Implicitly with the SQL statement **COMMIT** or **ROLLBACK** Usually at the end of a transaction step	Explicitly by calling a dequeue module Usually at the end of an SAP transaction
Maximum duration	One transaction step	Over multiple transaction steps
Result of lock conflicts	Wait situation, referred to as exclusive lockwait	Program specific—for example the error message "Material X is locked"
How to monitor	Transaction code DB01, "Exclusive Lockwaits"	Transaction code SM12, "Enqueue Monitor"

Table 10.1 Features of database locks and SAP enqueues

Monitoring Database Locks

In this section you will find notes on how to monitor database locks and SAP enqueues.

Database Locks

Exclusive lockwaits

What happens in the event of a lock conflict, when a work process wants to lock an object that is already locked? With database locks, the second process waits until the lock has been removed. This wait situation is known as an *Exclusive lockwait*. Most databases do not place a time limit on these locks. If a program fails to remove a lock, the wait situation can continue indefinitely.

This could become a major problem if the program fails to release a lock on critical SAP System data, such as the number range table NRIV. There is a danger that one work process after another will be waiting for this lock. If all work processes are waiting, there is no work process available to allow you to intervene from within the SAP system. If the program holding the problem lock can be identified, as a last alternative it can be terminated through the operating system.

To monitor current lock wait situations, call the Database Lock Monitor (transaction code DB01), which you can start from the Database Monitor (transaction code ST04) by selecting

Detail analysis menu · Exclusive lockwaits

or from the system-wide Work Process Overview (transaction code SM66) by selecting

Goto · DB Locks

For a description of this monitor and notes on how to troubleshoot lock wait situations, see the section "Other Checks on the Database" on page 92 in Chapter 2. Lock wait situations increase database time and result in high database times in the statistics in the Workload Monitor. Some database systems explicitly monitor lock wait times, and these lock wait times can be viewed in the Database Performance Monitor (Transaction ST04).

Typical problems

Basically you should set programs to request locks as late as possible. It is preferable for a program to read and process data from the database before setting locks or making changes in the database. This is illustrated in Figure 10.1. The top part of the diagram shows how several changes are made during a database transaction and how as a result database locks are held for too long. The lower part of the diagram shows a more appropriate method of programming: The transaction is programmed so that it collects the changes in an internal table and then transfers these changes to the database as a group at the end of the transaction. This reduces the lock time in a database.

Performance problems due to delays in releasing locks frequently occur when customers modify the programming of update modules. The separation of update modules from dialog modules aims to reduce the number of locks needed in the dialog part of a transaction, since changes to the database and the associated locks are the task mainly of the update modules. However, sometimes the update module is modified, for example, to supply a customer-developed interface with data. This modification may cause problems if the update module has already set locks and, for example, the modification generates expensive SQL statements. The locks cannot be released until the SQL statements are fully processed, and lengthy lock waits may result.

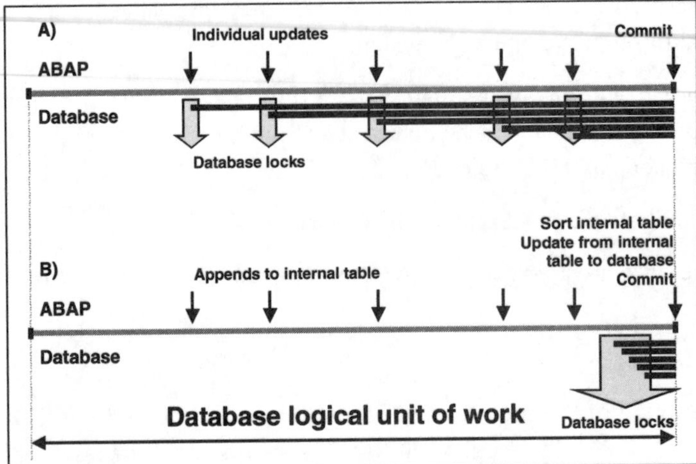

Figure 10.1 Locks should be set as late as possible

Another source of problems with locks are background programs that set locks and then run for several hours without initiating a database commit. If dialog transactions need to process the locked objects, they will be forced to wait until the background program finishes or initiates a database commit. To solve this problem you should either ensure that the background program initiates a database commit at regular intervals (without sacrificing data consistency) or that it runs only when it will not interfere with dialog processing. Similar problems may occur when background jobs are run in parallel—that is, when a program is started several times simultaneously. Parallel processing is recommended only when the selection conditions of the respective programs do not lock the same data.

While you are working in the ABAP debugger, databank commits are generally not initiated, and all locks stay in place until you are finished. You should therefore avoid using the debugger in a production SAP system.

Deadlocks

We shall now present an example for a situation known as a *deadlock*. Let us assume that work process 1 and work process 2 both want to lock a list of materials. Work process 1 locks material A and work process 2 locks material B. Then work process 1 tries to lock material B and work process 2 tries to lock material A. Neither work process is successful because the materials already have locks on them. The work processes block each other. This is known as a deadlock. It is identified by the database instance and solved by sending an error message to one of the work processes. The corresponding ABAP program is terminated and the error is logged in the SAP Syslog.

Deadlocks can be avoided by correct programming. In the present example, the program should be changed so that its internal material list is sorted before any locks are set. Then, the lock on material A will always be set before the lock on material B, and thus programs requiring the same materials are serialized and not deadlocked.

Deadlocks should occur very rarely. Frequent deadlocks indicate incorrect programming or incorrect configuration of the database instance.

Table locks

In some database systems, such as DB2 and SAP DB, if a work process places single-row locks on more than, for example, 10% of the single rows in a table, the locks are automatically replaced by *table locks*. Thus the database decides that it is more efficient to lock the entire table for a work process than to maintain several locks on individual rows. Table locking has consequences for parallel processing in background jobs, where each program is intended to update a different part of the same table at the same time. It is not possible to schedule background jobs so that, for example, one updates the first half of the table and the other updates the second half, because the database may decide to lock the table exclusively for one of the jobs. One program that is particularly affected by this is the period closing program in materials management.

There are database parameters you can use to specify when the database should convert single-row locks to a table lock.

Sometimes the database locks entire tables for administrative reasons. This happens when indexes are created or when particular tables and indexes are analyzed (for example, during the Oracle analysis **VALIDATE STRUCTURE**). If these actions are performed during production operation, substantial performance problems may result.

SAP Enqueues

SAP enqueues are administered in the enqueue table, located in the global main memory of the enqueue server (enqueue table). The work processes in the enqueue server directly access the enqueue table; the enqueue server also carries out lock operations for work processes from other application servers, which are communicated via the message service. The following abbreviations are used in Figure 10.2: DIA: dialog work process; ENQ: enqueue work process; MS: message service; DP: dispatcher; ENQ tab: enqueue table.

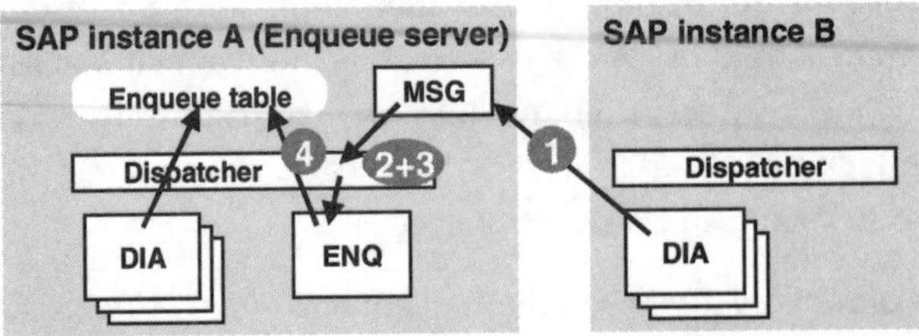

Figure 10.2 Communication for setting and removing SAP enqueues

For work processes in the enqueue server, setting and releasing locks takes less than 1 millisecond, for work processes in other application servers it takes less than 100 milliseconds.

Performance problems with SAP enqueues

If an *SAP enqueue* is requested but is already held by another user, the attempt to set a lock is rejected and a corresponding error message is sent back to the ABAP program. The application developer has to decide how to deal with this error message with suitable programming. For programs in dialog mode the error message is normally forwarded to the user, for example, with the message "Material X is locked by user Y". For background programs one will normally attempt to set the lock again at a later point in time. After a certain number of unsuccessful attempts, a corresponding error message is written to the program log.

If SAP enqueues are held for (too) long, performance problems can arise from the fact that after a failed attempt, the user will repeat the entry. Let us take the example that a user needs to process a material list and to do so, needs to set 100 SAP enqueues. If the attempt to set lock number 99 fails, the program is interrupted with the message "material number 99 is locked", and all of the work that the system has already performed has been in vain and must be repeated. Therefore rejected enqueue requests lead to higher system workload and restrict the throughput of transactions.

- You can get an overview of all SAP enqueues currently active using Transaction SM12:

  Tools · Administration · Monitor · Lock entries

- Start the test programs to diagnose errors:

  Extras · Diagnose

  or

  Extras · Diagnose in VB

  If errors are identified, check the SAP Service Marketplace for notes or contact SAP directly.

- With the menu option

  Extras • Statistics

  you can view statistics on the activity of the enqueue server. The first three values show the number of enqueue requests, the number of rejected requests (unsuccessful because the lock requested was already held by another) and the number of errors that occurred during the processing of enqueue requests. The number of unsuccessful requests should not be more than 1% of the total number of enqueue requests. There should be no errors.

Number Range Buffering

With many database structures it is necessary to be able to directly access individual database records. This is done with a unique key. *Number ranges* assign a serial number which forms the main part of this key. Examples of these numbers include order numbers or material master numbers. SAP number range management monitors the number status so that previously assigned numbers are not issued again.

The Fundamentals

A business object for which a key must be created using the number range is defined in the SAP system as a *number range object*. A number range contains a *number range interval* with a set of permitted characters. The number range interval is made up of numerical or alphanumeric characters and is limited by the fields from-number and to-number. One or more intervals can be assigned to a number range.

Technical implementation

The current number level of a number range, which is the number that is to be assigned next, is stored in the database table NRIV. If a program needs a number (for example from the number range MATBELEG), it goes through the following steps:

1. The program reads the current number level from the NRIV table and, at the same time, locks the MATBELEG number range. To set the lock, the SQL statement **SELECT FOR UPDATE** is applied to the line of table NRIV that corresponds to the number range MATBELEG.
2. The program increases the number range level by one by updating the table NRIV.
3. The number range in the database remains locked until the program completes its DB LUW by performing a database commit or database rollback. If an error occurs before the lock is released, the document

cannot be created, and the change in table NRIV is rolled back—that is, the previous number level is returned. This ensures that numbers are assigned *chronologically* and *without gaps*.

Bottlenecks can occur when many numbers are requested from a particular number range in a short period of time. Since the number range is locked in the database from the time of the initial reading of the current number level to the time of the database commit, all business processes competing for number assignment must wait their turn, and this limits transaction throughput.

A solution to this lock problem is provided by buffering the corresponding number range. SAP offers two ways of doing this: *Main memory buffering* and buffering for each SAP instance in an additional database table (NRIV_LOKAL).

Main memory buffering

By buffering number ranges in main memory the database table NRIV does not have to be accessed for each number assignment, rather the number is read from the buffer. The number range interval buffer is located in the main memory of the SAP instances. A certain amount of new numbers are stored in each buffer. When these numbers have been used up, a new set of numbers is obtained from the database. The number range level in the database table NRIV is increased by the range of numbers transferred to the buffer. When a number is taken from the buffer and assigned to a document, the number range level in the database remains unchanged.

Technically, entering a set of new numbers in a buffer involves several steps. They are as follows:

1. For example, a program needs a number from the MATBELEG number range, which is buffered in the main memory. It discovers that the number range buffer in its SAP instance is empty.
2. The program starts an asynchronous RFC call to fill the number range buffer. This RFC is processed in a second dialog work process. Table NRIV is read and locked, the number range buffer is filled, table NRIV is updated and the action is concluded with a database commit. The first work process, in which the original program is running, remains stopped while this takes place. In the Work Process Overview, the **Action** field shows "stopped" and **Reason** displays "NUM".
3. Once the number range buffer has been filled, the original program can resume its work.

During this process, the program that checked the buffer for a number and the program that refills the number range buffer must run in separate database LUWs. This is the only way to ensure that the commit of the second program can finalize the changes in table NRIV and release the lock without performing a commit for the database LUW of the first program. To accomplish this, the two programs are run in separate work processes.

To guarantee that work processes are available for refilling the buffer with new numbers, the work process dispatcher program gives preferential treatment to requests for new number sets.

Main memory buffering of number ranges has the following consequences:

- When an SAP instance is shut down, the remaining numbers in the buffer—that is, the numbers that have yet to be assigned—are lost. This causes a gap in number assignment.
- As a result of the separate buffering of numbers in the various SAP instances, the chronological sequence in which numbers are assigned is not reflected in the sequence of the numbers themselves. This means that a document with a higher number may have been created before a document with a lower number.

If you prefer to prevent gaps in the assignment of numbers to a particular document type or number range object, or if you are required to do so by law, you should not buffer this object in the main memory.

Buffering in NRIV_LOKAL

In this case, another buffering technique can be used: Instead of managing the number range for a particular type of document centrally in a single row of table NRIV, number intervals are selected for each SAP instance and managed in a separate database table (NRIV_LOKAL). In this table, the name of the SAP instance forms part of the primary key. Database locks associated with number assignments for new documents will then appear only in those areas of table NRIV_LOKAL that correspond to a particular SAP instance.

Extended local number range buffering (SAP Note 179224) means that you can buffer number range intervals for each SAP instance *and* buffer work processes locally. (The name of the SAP instance and the logical number of the work process form part of the primary key of the local number range.) With this buffering technique one lock problem is conclusively ruled out.

The following points should be borne in mind:

- Buffering in NIRV_LOKAL is useful only when the user is working simultaneously on several SAP instances. For a very high throughput, for example, processing POS entries in mySAP Retail, local buffering on instance level and work process level (or if possible, main memory buffering) is recommended.
- Numbers are not assigned to documents in numerical order, so that a document with a higher number may have been created before a document with a lower number.
- Some of the numbers in a particular interval may not be assigned—for example, at the end of a financial year or during the renaming of an instance. The RSSNR0A1 report shows details on the numbers that have not been assigned.

To enter a new set of document numbers in table NRIV_LOKAL, a new interval is *synchronously* read from table NRIV, and the affected row of table NRIV remains locked until the commit occurs. If the interval of numbers read from NRIV is too small, frequent accesses to NRIV to obtain new numbers during mass processing may cause lock waits. Therefore, when large quantities of similar documents are being created across a number of instances, ensure that the interval selected is sufficiently large.

Buffering type	Method	Advantages	Limitations	Example of use
No buffering	–	No gaps in number allocation, chronological order	Lock waits with parallel processing	Only if it is essential to have no gaps in number allocation, if numbers must be in sequence and only a low throughput is needed.
Main memory	In the main memory	No lock wait problems, fast access (main memory instead of database)	There may be gaps in number allocation, sequence not chronological	Standard for most number ranges

Table 10.2 Types of buffering for number ranges

Buffering type	Method	Advantages	Limitations	Example of use
Local, on instance level	Temporarily stored on the database table NRIV_LOKAL with number range and SAP instance forming part of key	Problems of lock waits reduced; number allocation almost gap-free	Sequence not chronological; locks occur within an instance; many instances necessary if throughput is high	Largely replaced by the following method
Local, on instance and work process level	Temporarily stored on the database table NRIV_LOKAL with number range, SAP instance and WP number forming part of key	No lock wait problems; number allocation practically gap-free	Sequence not chronological	POS-Inbound

Table 10.2 Types of buffering for number ranges (abbreviations: POS-Inbound: processing Point-of-Sale entries in mySAP Retail) (contd.)

Activating Number Range Buffering

To activate or deactivate number range buffering, proceed as follows:

1. Call the Number Range Maintenance transaction:

   Tools · ABAP/4 Workbench · Development · Other tools · Number ranges

   or enter the transaction code SNRO.
2. Enter an object name and select **Change**.
3. To activate the main memory buffering, from the menu, select:

   Edit · Set up buffering · Main memory

   Enter the quantity of numbers to be held on the buffer in the field **No. of numbers in buffer** and save the change. The desired amount of numbers from table NRIV will thus be buffered.

To activate buffering in table NRIV_LOKAL, in the menu of the number range maintenance transaction, select:

Edit · Set up buffering · Local file

To deactivate the buffering, from the menu, select:

Edit · Set up buffering · No buffering

Please note that these changes will be overwritten if the respective number range object is replaced, for example, with a new release. After every update, check whether number range buffering has been affected.

Finding out the current number level

To view the current *number level*, use Transaction SNRO. For buffered number range objects, the level indicated here is the next available number that has not yet been transferred to a buffer in an application server. The level indicated is higher than the last number assigned.

The current number level of the buffer for each SAP instance can be checked with Transaction SM56.

1. Call Transaction SM56, and in the menu select:

   Goto · Items

2. In the dialog box, enter the client, the relevant number range object and, if required, the relevant sub-object.

Monitoring Number Range Buffering

To identify performance problems related to number assignment, call the Exclusive Database Lock Monitor (Transaction DB01). At peak processing times, lock waits of several minutes for table NRIV are too long. If this occurs, from the initial screen of the Database Lock Monitor, proceed as follows:

1. Identify the number range involved:
   - If you are using an Oracle database, double-click the row showing the lock on table NRIV. This brings you to a screen with detailed information on the locked row. The name of the number range is indicated in the "Object" column (for example "RF_BELEG").
   - For other databases start an SQL trace for a user who is waiting for the database lock to be removed. With this SQL trace, you can identify the number affected by the lock in the SQL statement.
2. Find out the buffering status of the number range.
   - If buffering is not currently activated, check to see if the corresponding object can be buffered.
   - If the number range is already buffered, check whether the quantity of numbers in the buffer can be increased. Table NRIV will then be accessed less frequently.

Only experienced SAP developers or consultants should change the buffering mode for number ranges.

- Activating buffering may cause gaps in number assignment, which could be a problem if gap-free number assignment is mandatory or if it is assumed that it will be gap-free.
- Having too few numbers in the buffer can cause performance problems by requiring the buffer to be refilled too often. The disadvantage of having a range that is too large is that too many numbers are lost if the SAP instance is shut down.

There are notes on many number ranges in the SAP Service Marketplace. They contain details on buffering status and recommendations for how many numbers should be loaded into a number range buffer. You should never change buffering mode for a SAP default number range without first looking for relevant notes on the object. Some notes are listed in the appendix of this book.

ATP Server

The availability check establishes the availability of materials in the SAP logistics modules, for example, for sales orders or production orders. The availability check discussed in this book is based on ATP (available to promise) logic.

Performance during an availability check can be reduced by either of two factors:

- **Locks**
  The material being checked for availability must be locked with an SAP enqueue. When the lock is in place, it may block other users who need to work with the material, especially if the lock remains for a long time or the material is frequently worked on. As a result, we can see that locks limit the throughput of the availability check.
- **Read accesses for tables RESB and VBBE**
  An availability check is used to ensure that a material will be available at a specific time in the future. As part of the check, incoming movements planned before that time are added to the current stock, whereas planned outward movements are subtracted. In this context, totaling material reservations and secondary requirements for production orders is critical to performance, as is the totaling of customer requirements for sales orders, which are stored in tables RESB and VBBE respectively. Reading and calculating these

reservations and requirements can lead to a high runtime for the availability check.

Table RESB may be as large as 1 GB or even larger. Depending on the customizing, for each availability check all RESB records for a material, from the current date until the date on which the material should be available, must be read.

From SAP release 4.0 on, the availability check is carried out on a dedicated SAP instance—the *ATP server*. The ATP server has a buffer in the shared memory in which ATP-relevant information is stored. This significantly reduces the accesses to the database tables RESB and VBBE. The ATP server is not a separate installation. It is a logical service running on an SAP instance, and as such it forms part of the SAP system.

The Fundamentals

Figure 10.3 shows how an ATP server performs its work in the system landscape: If an SAP work process on SAP instance B has to check the availability of a material, it uses a Remote Function Call (RFC) to communicate the request through the network to the server where the ATP server resides. In Figure 10.3 the ATP server is configured on SAP instance A (step 1). This call is sent between the gateway services of the two SAP instances (2). The program that executes the availability check is processed by a dialog work process on the ATP server (3). The following abbreviations are used in Figure 10.3: DIA: dialog work process; GW: gateway service; DP: dispatcher; ENQ tab: enqueue table; E/I buffer: export/import buffer.

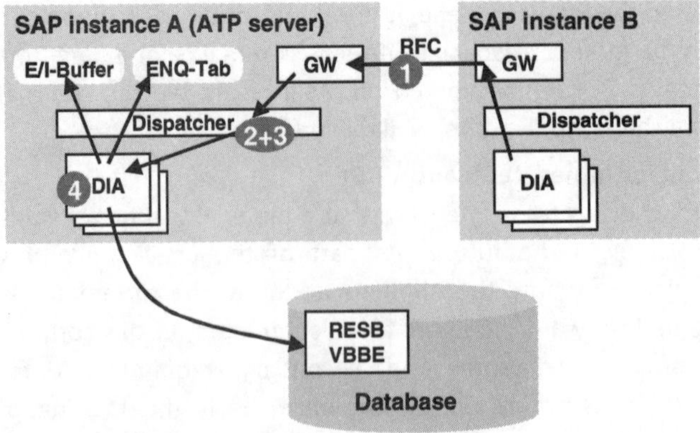

Figure 10.3 Communication during an availability check using the ATP server

For calculating the availability of a material the SAP work process on the ATP server uses subtotals, which have already been calculated for other availability checks and are stored in the main memory of the ATP server in the *export/import buffer*. These subtotals consist of a calculation for each day's material reservations (from table RESB) or sales requirements (from table VBBE) for every possible combination of material, plant, storage location, and batch. Daily totals per combination of material, plant, storage location and batch are compressed and stored in the export/ import buffer. The export/import buffer thus contains two groups of entries: one for RESB data and one for VBBE data. The size of the entries depends on the number of days for which subtotals exist.

On checking the availability of material, the work process does not read RESB and VBBE data from the database, rather it reads it from the export/ import buffer (Figure 10.3). This method means that performance is considerably improved. Special delta processing guarantees consistency between the buffer and the database.

While checking availability the SAP work process sets and removes SAP enqueues which are necessary to guarantee data consistency. To set and remove enqueues with only a minimum of performance loss, the ATP server and the enqueue server should be run on the same SAP instance.

Locking with quantity

In the availability check with the ATP server, a special SAP technique, called *locking with quantities*, is used. Instead of relying on exclusive SAP enqueues, which allow only one user to lock a material, this technique uses *shared enqueues*. Shared locks can be used by several users on the same object at the same time—which means that several users can check the availability of a material at the same time.

Locking with quantities during availability checks has been available since SAP release 3.0. In this case the availability check is also carried out centrally on the enqueue server, but without buffering the daily subtotals in the export/import buffer. Further information on this transaction is available in SAP online help notes on availability checks.

Configuring the ATP Server

Correctly configuring the ATP server is a technical measure that resolves two particular problems with the availability check, namely frequent accesses to the RESB and the VBBE tables. *However the ATP server does not solve all the problems associated with the availability check.* It is very important to optimize application-related aspects of the availability check during customizing. For example:

- Set sensible reorder times and planning horizons for materials
- Deactivate individual checking of materials used in bulk, such as screws or nails
- Regularly archive reservations

Application-related optimization measures are provided in the SAP Empowering Workshop "Technical Optimization of the Availability Check".

Tables RESB and VBBE are accessed by database views during the availability check. If you try the availability check with an SQL trace, in SAP release 4.0 you will access the views ATP_RESB or ATP_VBBE. In SAP Release 3.1 the SQL trace will show that table RESB is accessed through the view MDRS view.

Activate

To activate the ATP server, set the SAP profile parameter **rdisp/atp_server** to the name of the SAP instance that provides the ATP server (for example, enqhost_PRD_00). The value of this parameter must be identical for all SAP instances and should therefore be set in the default profile. The ATP server and the enqueue server should be run on the same SAP instance.

Sizing

The SAP profile parameters **rsdb/obj/buffersize** and **rsdb/obj/max_objects** configure the size and the maximum number of entries in the export/import buffer. The size of an entry in the export/import buffer depends on the number of days for which subtotals exist. For each added day, the size of the entry increases by around 50 bytes. If reservations are calculated for a combination of material, plant, storage location and batch for 20 days, the size of the entry would be around 1 KB. If in your company you expect a maximum of 10,000 combinations and for each combination there are an average of 20 days of daily reservation or sales requirement subtotals, you would set the size of the export/import buffer to 20,000 KB (parameter **rsdb/obj/buffersize**) and the maximum number of entries at 20,000 (parameter **rsdb/obj/max_objects**).

Activating locking with quantities

You should activate *locking with quantities* for all materials to be checked for availability using the ATP server. This is done using the checking group of each material. To activate locking with quantities for a checking group, proceed as follows:

1. Call up customizing:

   Tools · Business Engineer · Customizing · Continue

2. Then select:

   Implement projects · Display SAP reference IMG

3. Then select:

   Sales and distribution · Basic functions · Availability check and transfer of requirements · Availability check · Availability check with ATP logic and against planning · Define checking groups

   A screen appears in which you can set the characteristics of the checking groups for the availability check.

4. To set locking with quantities for a particular checking group, mark the check box in the **Block QtRq** column.

Other resources

On large installations many availability checks are carried out simultaneously, and as a result, on the enqueue server or the ATP server some parameters which may limit the number of RFC connections must be set to values that are sufficiently large. These parameters are listed in Table 10.3.

Parameter name	Description	Minimum size for "locking with quantities"
rdisp/tm_max_no	Number of maximum possible terminal connections (or size of table tm_adm)	= 500
rdisp/max_comm_entries	Number of maximum possible CPIC/RFC connections (or size of table COMM_ADM)	= 500
gw/max_conn	Number of maximum possible gateway connections (or size of table conn_tbl)	= 500
rdisp/wp_no_dia	Number of dialog work processes	= 5
em/initial_size_MB	Size of extended memory	= 250
rdisp/ROLL_SHM	Size of roll buffer in 8 KB blocks	= 4,000 (= 32 MB)

Table 10.3 Parameter settings for the ATP server or enqueue server when using *locking with quantities*

To ensure that there are sufficient dialog work processes available for the availability check, you require at least five dialog work processes on the enqueue/ATP server—even if there are no users working on this server.

The enqueue/ATP server also requires sufficient SAP extended memory. Monitor the use of extended memory at regular intervals.

For the most recent information on sizing for the export/import buffer, see SAP Notes 24762 and 99999.

Locking with quantities is available as of SAP Release 3.0, irrespective of the ATP server. You should also take note of the recommendations given in this last section ("Other resources") if you set "locking with quantities" without the ATP server.

Monitoring the ATP Server

Transaction ACBD offers monitoring and administration functions for the export/import buffer in the ATP server, such as:

- Complete or partial deletion of the export/import buffer (with regard to ATP data)
- Adjusting the export/import buffer to the database

This transaction allows data from the database to be preloaded into the export/import buffer. Otherwise, data loading does not occur until the first availability check is made for each respective combination of material, plant and table.

You can monitor the contents of the export/import buffer, from a technical point of view, in the SAP Memory Configuration Monitor (transaction code ST02). To do this, choose:

Detail analysis menu · Import/export buffer · Buffered Objects

The most important fields in this monitor are **Table name** ("ATPSB" for ATP server objects), **Object name** (this field contains the clients, the information, whether it is an RESB entry (RE) or a VBBE entry (VB), the plant and material number) together with the fields **Size** (size of an entry) and **Used** (number of accesses to this entry).

The shared enqueues, used when locking with quantities, can be monitored in the SAP Enqueue Monitor (transaction code SM12). They are indicated by the entry "ATPENQ" (in SAP Release 3.1: "EV03V") in the **Table** field and are marked with a cross in the column **Shared**.

Monitoring SAP enqueues is one of the regular tasks of system administration. SAP enqueues that are held over several hours are an indication that there is an error in a program or a program is being used incorrectly.

Summary

The database and the SAP system both offer their own lock concepts (database locks and SAP enqueues). Locks held for a long time can lead to performance problems and can even bring the system to a standstill. You can monitor exclusive database lock wait situations with the help of Transaction DB01 and wait situations caused by SAP enqueues with the help of Transaction SM12.

Special attention should be given to the locks associated with both number ranges (used to generate, for example, order numbers or document numbers) and availability checks. Sections three and four of this chapter show ways to identify bottlenecks in these areas and how they can be avoided. Key words in this respect are ATP server (for the availability check) and number range buffering (for number assignment).

Important terms in this chapter

After studying this chapter you should be familiar with the following terms:

- Database locks and SAP enqueues
- Locking with quantity
- ATP server
- Number range buffers

Questions

1. Which of the following statements are correct?
   a) When you set an SAP enqueue you lock one or more tables in the database.
   b) After an SAP enqueue has been placed, the corresponding database table can still be changed by an update request coming from programs, such as customer-developed reports.
   c) A database lock is usually released at the end of a transaction step, while an SAP enqueue is usually released at the end of an SAP transaction.
   d) A database lock that is held for too long can cause an SAP system to come to a *standstill*.

2. Which of the following statements are correct with regard to the ATP server?

   a) The ATP server should always be configured on the database server.

   b) The ATP server is an independent SAP installation with its own database on a separate computer.

   c) The ATP server reduces the number of accesses to tables RESB and VBBE.

3. When buffering number range objects in main memory, which of the following considerations should you bear in mind?

   a) Since buffering occurs in all SAP instances, buffer synchronization may cause some numbers to be assigned twice.

   b) Gaps occur in the number assignment when using buffered number ranges. You must check whether these gaps are permitted by law and are acceptable from a business point of view.

   c) If the quantity of numbers in the buffer is too small, performance problems will result (particularly during mass data entry using batch input or fast input).

   d) Sufficient physical memory must be available because number range buffering consumes a great deal of memory.

11 Optimizing SQL Statements

During application programming, SQL statements are often written without sufficient regard to their subsequent performance. Expensive (long-running) SQL statements slow performance during production operation, resulting in large response times for individual programs and placing an excessive load on the database server. Frequently you will find that 50% of the database load can be traced to a few individual SQL statements.

As the database and the number of users grow, so do the number of requests to the database and the search effort required for each database request. This is why expensive or inefficient SQL statements constitute one of the most significant causes of performance problems in large installations. The more a system grows, the more important it becomes to optimize the SQL statements.

The second edition contains new sections on "Optimizing the SQL Statement (**WHERE** clause)" and "Presetting Field Values in Report Transactions".

When Should You Read This Chapter?

You should read this chapter if you have identified expensive SQL statements in your SAP system and wish to analyze and optimize them. The first and second sections of this chapter can be read without previous knowledge of ABAP programming; the third section assumes a basic familiarity with ABAP programming.

This chapter is not an introduction to developing SQL applications. For this, refer to ABAP textbooks, SQL textbooks, or SAP Online Help.

Identifying and Analyzing Expensive SQL Statements

The following sections describe how to identify and analyze expensive SQL statements.

Preliminary Analysis

The preliminary step in identifying and analyzing expensive SQL statements is to identify those SQL statements for which optimization would be genuinely worthwhile. The preliminary analysis prevents you from wasting time with SQL statement optimizations that cannot produce more than trivial gains in performance.

For the preliminary analysis, there are two main techniques: using an *SQL trace* or using the *shared SQL area*. An SQL trace is useful if the program containing the expensive SQL statement has already been identified—for example, through the Workload Monitor (Transaction ST03), Work Process Overview (Transaction SM50 or SM66), or users' observations. By contrast, using the shared SQL area enables you to order statements according to the systemwide load they are generating. For both analysis techniques, the following sections describe the individual analysis steps.

The flowchart in Figure 11.1 shows the techniques for identifying expensive SQL statements that are worth optimizing. The following shapes are used in the diagram:

- *A round-cornered rectangle* indicates where you start a specific SAP performance monitor.
- A *diamond shape* indicates a decision point.

The parallelogram indicates the point at which you have successfully identified expensive SQL statements that are worth optimizing.

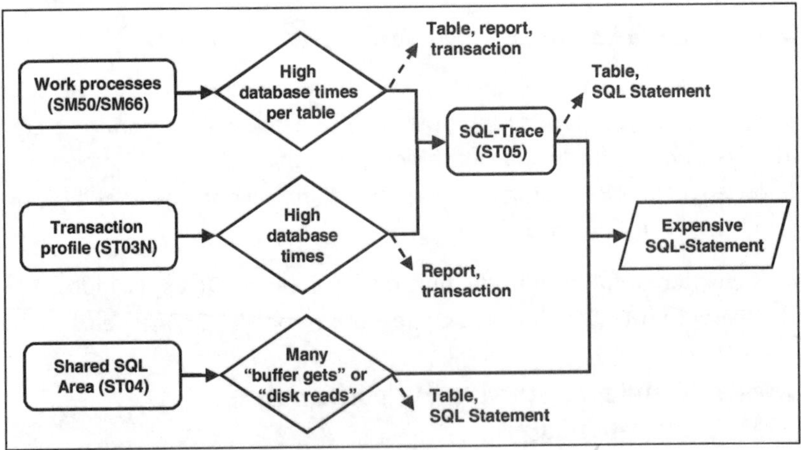

Figure 11.1 Techniques for identifying expensive SQL statements that are worth optimizing

Preliminary Analysis Using the SQL Trace

Create an SQL trace using Transaction ST05 as described in Chapter 4. Display the SQL trace results in one user session by choosing List trace. The Basic SQL Trace List screen appears. Call Transaction ST05 in another user session and display the compressed summary of the results by choosing

List trace · Goto · Summary · Compress

If you sort the data in the compressed summary according to the elapsed database time, you can find out the tables that were accessed for the longest time. Use these tables in the Basic SQL Trace List screen to look up the corresponding SQL statements. Only these statements should be considered for optimization.

In a third user session, from the Basic SQL Trace List screen, access a list of all identical accesses by choosing

Goto · Identical selects

Compare these identical selects with the user session showing the SQL trace results. Note which SQL statements receive identical selects; then, in the Basic SQL Trace List screen, examine the processing time for these SQL statements in the column Duration. By adding up these durations, you can estimate roughly how much database time could be saved by avoiding multiple database accesses. Unless this time saving is sufficiently large, there is no need for you to perform optimization.

As a result of this preliminary analysis, you will have made a note of any statements you wish to optimize.

Preliminary Analysis Using the Shared SQL Area Monitor

To monitor the shared SQL area in R/3, from the main screen in the Database Performance Monitor (Transaction ST04), choose **Detail analysis menu** and look under the header **Resource consumption by**. Then, for Oracle, choose **SQL request**, and for Informix, choose **SQL Statement**. In the dialog box that appears, choose **Enter**. The screen **Database performance: Shared SQL** appears. For an explanation of the screen, see Chapter 2. Expensive SQL statements are characterized by a large number of logical or physical database accesses. To create a prioritized list of statements, where the top-listed statements are potentially worth optimizing, sort the shared SQL area according to logical accesses (indicated, for example, as buffer gets) or physical accesses (indicated, for example, as disk reads).

Further Preliminary Analysis

Regardless of whether you begin your analysis from an SQL trace or the shared SQL area, before you proceed to a detailed analysis, perform the following checks:

- Create several SQL traces for different times and computers to verify the database times noted in the initial SQL trace. Determine whether there is a network problem or a temporary database overload.
- If the expensive SQL statement is accessing a buffered table, use the criteria presented in Chapter 9 to determine whether table buffering should be deactivated—that is, whether the respective buffer is too small or contains tables that should not be buffered because they are too large or too frequently changed.
- Check whether there are any applicable SAP Notes in the SAP Service Marketplace by using combinations of search terms, such as performance and the name of the respective table.

Detailed Analysis

Whether to Optimize the Code or the Index

After listing the SQL statements that are worth optimizing, perform a detailed analysis to decide the optimization strategy. Optimization can take one of two forms: optimizing the ABAP program code related to an SQL statement, or optimizing the database—for example, by creating indexes.

SQL statements that seek to operate on a great number of data records in the database can be optimized only by changes to the ABAP programming. The left-hand part of Figure 11.2 shows the activities of a statement requiring this kind of optimization. Data is depicted by the stacked, horizontal black bars. If you look at the amount of data records depicted both in the database process and in the application server, this shows that the statement has transferred much data to the application server. Therefore, a large number of data blocks (the pale rectangles containing the data bars) were read from the database buffer or the hard disk. For a statement like this, the relevant developer should check whether all this data is actually needed by the program, or whether a significant amount of the data is unnecessary. The amount of data that constitutes a significant amount varies. For a dialog transaction, where you expect a response time of around 1 second, 500 records that are transferred by an SQL statement are a significant number. For a reporting transaction, 10,000 records would normally be considered a significant number. For programs running background jobs (for example, in the SAP application module CO), the number of records that must be considered a significant number may be considerably larger yet again.

By contrast, an expensive SQL statement of the type requiring database optimization is shown in the right-hand part of Figure 11.2. Although you can see that only a few data records (represented by the horizontal black bars) were transferred to the application server by the SQL statement, the selection criteria has forced the database process to read many data blocks (the pale rectangles, some of which contain the data bars). As you can see, many of these data blocks do not contain any sought-after data; therefore, the search strategy is clearly inefficient. To simplify the search and optimize the runtime, it may be helpful to create a new secondary index. Alternatively, a suitable index may already exist, but is not being used.

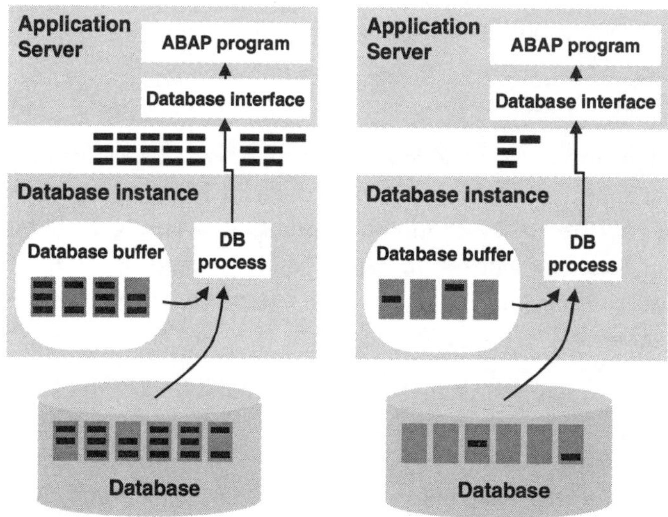

Figure 11.2 Expensive SQL statements (Left: The statement tries to transfer too much data. Right: The statement unnecessarily reads too many data blocks.)

Detailed Analysis Using an SQL Trace

For each line in the results of an SQL trace (Transaction ST05), looking at the corresponding database times enables you to determine whether a statement can be optimized through database techniques such as creating new indexes. Divide the figure in the column Duration by that in the column Rec (records). If the result is an average response time of less than 5,000 microseconds for each record, this can be considered optimal. Each **FETCH** should require less than around 100,000 microseconds. For an expensive SQL statement where a **FETCH** requires more than 250,000 microseconds, but targets only a few records, a new index may improve the runtime.

If the average response time is optimal, but the runtime for the SQL statement is still high due to the large volume of data being transferred, only the ABAP program itself can be optimized. To do this, from the screen Basic SQL Trace List, choose **ABAP display** to go to the ABAP code of the traced transaction and continue your analysis as described below.

Detailed Analysis Using the Shared SQL Area Monitor

Returning to the Shared SQL Area Monitor in Transaction ST04, you should now analyze the statistics more closely. The decisive data for evaluating an SQL statement's optimization potential is as follows: the number of logical read accesses for each execution (indicated as Gets/ Execution for Oracle and Buf.Read/Execution for Informix); and the number of logical read accesses for each transferred record (indicated as Bufgets/record for Oracle).

Statements that read on average less than 10 blocks or pages for each execution and appear at the top of the sorted shared SQL area list due to a high execution frequency cannot be optimized by using database techniques such as new indexes. Instead, consider improving the ABAP program code or using the program in a different way to reduce the execution frequency.

Good examples of SQL statements that can be optimized by database techniques, such as creating or modifying new indexes, include SQL statements that require many logical read accesses to transfer a few records. These are SQL statements for which the Shared SQL Area Monitor shows a statistic of 10 or higher for Bufgets/record.

For SQL statements where you need to change the ABAP code, you need to identify the various programs that use the SQL statement and improve the coding in each program. You can do this in ABAP Dictionary Maintenance. To access this transaction, use transaction code SE11, or, from the R/3 initial screen,

1. Select
   Tools · ABAP Workbench · Dictionary
2. Enter the name of the table accessed by the SQL statement you wish to optimize and choose **Where-used list**.
3. In the dialog box that appears, select **Programs**.
4. A list appears showing all programs in which the table is used. Check these programs to see if they use the expensive SQL statement that you want to modify.

The disadvantage of this search is that you may need to check a large number of programs. In addition, there may be a difference between the ABAP version of the SQL statement and the version created by the database interface. These factors mean that you may require considerable experience in using the ABAP programming language to identify the code causing the performance problem. For SAP Basis 4.5 or later, you can go directly from the shared SQL area to ABAP coding (**ABAP coding** button).

Further Detailed Analysis

After determining whether the SQL statement can be optimized through a new index or through changes to the program code, you require more detailed information about the relevant ABAP program. This information will be required when optimizing the SQL statements:

- The purpose of the program
- The tables that are involved and their contents—for example, transaction data, master data, or Customizing data; the size of the tables and whether the current size matches the size originally expected for the table
- The users of the program; the developer responsible for a customer-developed program

After finding out this information, you can begin with the tuning as described in the following sections.

Optimizing SQL Statements Through Secondary Indexes

To optimize SQL statements using database techniques such as creating new indexes, you require a basic understanding of how data is organized in a relational database.

Fundamentals of Database Organization

The fundamentals of relational database organization can be explained using a simplified analogy based on a database table corresponding to a Yellow Pages telephone book.

When you are looking up businesses in a Yellow Pages telephone book, you would probably never consider reading the entire telephone book from cover to cover. You are more likely to open the book somewhere in the middle and zone in on the required business by flipping back and forth a few times, using the fact that the names are sorted alphabetically.

If a relational database, however, were to try reading the same kind of Yellow Pages data in a database table, it would find that the data is generally not sorted, but is instead stored in a type of linked list. New data is either added—unsorted—to the end of the table or entered in empty spaces where records were deleted from the table. This unsorted Yellow Pages telephone book in the form of a database table is depicted in Table 11.1.

Page	Column	Position	Business Type	Business Name	City	Street	Telephone No.
			...				
15	2	54	Video rentals	Video Depot	Boston	Commonwealth Ave.	(617) 367-0788
			...				
46	1	23	Florist	Boston Blossoms		Boston	(617) 445-0044
46	1	24	Video rentals	Beacon Hill Video		Cambridge Street	(617) 350-6232
			...				

Table 11.1 Example of an Unsorted Database Table

One way for the database to deal with an unsorted table is by using a time-consuming sequential read, record for record. To save the database from having to perform a sequential read for every SQL statement query, each database table has a corresponding *primary index*. In this example, the primary index might be a list that is sorted alphabetically by business type, business name, and the location of each entry in the telephone book (see Table 11.2).

Business Type	Business Name	Page	Column	Position
...				
Florist	Boston Blossoms	46	1	23
...				
Video rentals	Beacon Hill Video	46	1	24

Table 11.2 Primary Index Corresponding to the Sample Table (Excerpt)

Business Type	Business Name	Page	Column	Position
Video rentals	Video Depot	15	2	54
...				

Table 11.2 Primary Index Corresponding to the Sample Table (Excerpt) (contd.)

Because this list is sorted, you (or the database) do not need to read the entire list sequentially. Instead, you can expedite your search by first searching this index for the business type and name (for example, video rentals and Video Depot), and then using the corresponding page, column, and position to locate the entry in the Yellow Pages telephone book (or corresponding database table). In a database, the position data consists of the file number, block number, position in the block, and so on. This type of data about the position in a database is called the *Row ID*. The Business Type and Business Name columns in the phone book correspond to the primary index fields.

A primary index is always *unique*—that is, for each combination of index fields, there is only one table entry. If the present example were an actual database index, there could be no two businesses of the same type with the same name. This cannot necessarily be said of a phone book, which may, for example, list two outlets of a florist in the same area with the same name.

Secondary Indexes

In the present example, the primary index helps you only if you already know the type and name of the business you are looking for. However, if you had only a telephone number and wanted to look up the business that corresponds to it, the primary index is not useful to you because it does not contain the field **Telephone No.** Consequently, you would have to sequentially read the entire telephone book. To simplify search queries of this kind, you could define a *secondary index* containing the field **Telephone No.** and the corresponding Row IDs or the primary key. Similarly, to look up all the businesses on a street of a particular city, you could create a sorted secondary index with the fields **City** and **Street** and the corresponding Row IDs or the primary key. In contrast to the primary index, secondary indexes are as a rule not unique—that is, there can be multiple similar entries in the secondary index. For example, "Boston, Cambridge Street" will occur several times in the index if there are several businesses on that street. The secondary index based on telephone numbers, however, would be unique, because telephone numbers happen to be unique.

Execution plan

Optimizer and Execution Plan

If you are looking up all video rental stores in Boston, the corresponding SQL statement would be as follows:

```
SELECT * FROM telephone book WHERE business type = 'Video rentals'
AND
city = 'Boston'.
```

In this case, the database has three possible search strategies: (1) to search the entire table, (2) to use the primary index for the search, and (3) to use a secondary index based on the field **City**. The decision as to which strategy to use is made by the *database optimizer* program, which considers each access path and formulates an *execution plan* for the SQL statement. The optimizer is a part of the database program. To create the execution plan, the optimizer *parses* the SQL statement. If you want to look at the execution plan (also called the explain plan) in the SAP system, you can use one of the following: SQL trace (Transaction ST05), Database Process Monitor (accessed from the Detail analysis menu of Transaction ST04), or **Explain** function in the shared SQL area (also accessed from the Detail analysis menu of Transaction ST04).

The examples presented here are limited to SQL statements that access a table and do not require joins through multiple tables. In addition, the examples are presented using the Oracle access types, which include *index unique scan*, *index range scan*, and *full table scan*. The corresponding access types of the other database systems are explained in Appendix B.

Index Unique Scan

An *index unique scan* is performed when the SQL statement's **WHERE** clause specifies all primary index fields through an **EQUALS** condition. For example:

```
SELECT * FROM telephone book WHERE business type = 'Video rentals'
AND
business name = 'Beacon Hill Video'.
```

The database responds to an index unique scan by locating a maximum of one record, hence the name unique. The execution plan is as follows:

```
TABLE ACCESS BY ROWID telephone book
   INDEX UNIQUE SCAN telephone book___0
```

The database begins by reading the row in the execution plan that is indented the furthest to the right (here, `INDEX UNIQUE SCAN telephone book___0`). This row indicates that the search will use the primary index telephone book__0. After finding an appropriate entry in the primary index, the database then uses the Row ID indicated in the primary index to access the table telephone book. The index unique scan is the most efficient type of table access—that is, the access type that reads the fewest data blocks in the database.

Full Table Scan

For the following SQL statement, a *full table scan* is performed if there is no index based on street names:

```
SELECT * FROM telephone book WHERE street = 'Cambridge Street'
```

In this case, the execution plan contains the row: `TABLE ACCESS FULL telephone`. Especially for tables greater than around 1MB, the full table scan is a very expensive search strategy, causing a high database load.

Index Range Scan

An *index range scan* is performed if there is an index for the search, but the results of searching the index are not unique—that is, multiple rows of the index satisfy the search criteria. An index range scan using the primary index is performed when the **WHERE** clause does not specify all the fields of the primary index. For example:

```
SELECT * FROM telephone book WHERE business type= 'Florist'
```

This SQL statement automatically results in a search using the primary index. Since the **WHERE** clause does not specify a single record, but rather an area of the primary index, the table area for business type "Florist" is read record by record. Therefore, this search strategy is called an index range scan. The results of the search are not unique, and zero to <n> records may be found. An index range scan is also performed through a secondary index that is not unique, even if all the fields in the secondary index are specified. Such a search would result from the following SQL statement, which mentions both index fields of the secondary index considered above:

```
SELECT * FROM telephone book WHERE city = 'Boston' AND street=
'Cambridge Street'
```

The execution plan is as follows:

```
TABLE ACCESS BY ROWID telephone book
   INDEX RANGE SCAN telephone book__B
```

The database first accesses the secondary index telephone book__B. Using the records found in the index, the database then directly accesses each relevant record in the table.

Without further information, it is difficult to determine whether an index range scan is effective. The following SQL statement also requires an index range scan: `SELECT * FROM telephone book WHERE business name LIKE 'B%'`. This access is very expensive since only the first byte of data in the index key field is used for the search.

Consider the following SQL statement:

```
SQL Statement
   SELECT * FROM mara WHERE mandt = :A0 AND bismt = :A1
```

and the corresponding execution plan:

```
Execution plan:
TABLE ACCESS BY ROWID mara
   INDEX RANGE SCAN mara___0
```

The primary index MARA___0 contains the fields MANDT and MATNR. Because MATNR is not mentioned in the **WHERE** clause, MANDT is the only field available to help the database limit its search in the index. MANDT is the field for the client. If there is only one production client in this particular SAP system, the **WHERE** clause with mandt = :A0 will cause the entire table to be searched. In this case, a full table scan would be more effective than a search using the index; a full table scan reads only the whole table, but an index search reads both the index and the table. You can therefore determine which of the strategies is more cost-effective only if you have additional information, such as selectivity (see below). In this example, you need the information that there is only one client in the SAP system. (For more discussion of this example, see the end of the next section.)

Methodology for database optimization

Exactly how an optimizer program functions is a well-guarded secret amongst database manufacturers. However, broadly speaking, there are two types of optimizers: the *rule-based optimizer (RBO)* and the *cost-based optimizer (CBO)*.

All database systems used in conjunction with the SAP system use a cost-based optimizer—except for the Oracle database, which has both a CBO and an RBO. For Oracle, the database profile parameter **OPTIMIZER_MODE** lets you change the default optimizer to a cost-based optimizer. If you are unsure which optimizer is being used, in the Database Performance Monitor (Transaction ST04), choose **Detail analysis menu ·**

Parameter changes · Active parameters. This screen alphabetically lists current parameter settings. If the parameter **OPTIMIZER_MODE** is set to CHOOSE, the cost-based optimizer is activated. If the parameter is set to RULE, the rule-based optimizer is activated. For SAP R/3 Release 3.x, this database parameter is set by default to the rule-based optimizer. For SAP R/3 Release 4.x, this parameter is set by default to the cost-based optimizer. Do not change the default setting of the parameter OPTIMIZER_MODE without explicit instruction from SAP.

Rule-Based Optimizer (RBO)

An *RBO* bases its execution plan for a given SQL statement on the **WHERE** clause and the available indexes. The most important criteria in the **WHERE** clause are the fields that are specified with an **EQUALS** condition and that appear in an index:

```
SELECT * FROM telephone book WHERE business type= 'Pizzeria' AND
business name = 'Blue Hill House of Pizza' AND city = 'Roxbury'
```

In this example, the optimizer decides on the primary index rather than the secondary index because two primary index fields are specified (business type and business name), while only one secondary index field is specified (city). One limitation on index use is that a field can be used for an index search only if all the fields to the left of that field in the index are also specified in the **WHERE** clause with an equals condition. Consider two sample SQL statements:

```
SELECT * FROM telephone book
  WHERE business type like 'P%' AND business name = 'Blue Hill House
of Pizza' and
SELECT * FROM telephone book WHERE business name = 'Blue Hill House
of Pizza''
```

For either of these statements, the condition business name = 'Blue Hill House of Pizza' is of no use to an index search. For the first of the two examples, all business types beginning with "P" in the index will be read. For the second example, all entries in the index are read since the business type field is missing from the WHERE clause. While an index search is thus greatly influenced by the position of a field in the index (in relation to the left-most field), the order in which fields are mentioned in the WHERE clause is arbitrary.

Cost-Based Optimizer (CBO)

To create the execution plan for an SQL statement, the *CBO* considers the same criteria as described for the RBO above, plus the following criteria:

- **Table size**
  For small tables, the CBO decides to avoid indexes in favor of a more efficient full table scan. Large tables are more likely to be accessed through the index.
- **Selectivity of the index fields**
  The selectivity of a given index field is the average size of the portion of a table that is read when an SQL statement searches for a particular distinct value in that field.

  For example, if there are 200 business types and 10,000 actual businesses listed in the telephone book, then the selectivity of the field business type is 10,000 divided by 200, which is 50 (or 2% of 10,000). The larger the number of distinct values in a field, the higher the selectivity and the more likely the optimizer will use the index based on that field. Tests with various database systems have shown that an index is used only if the CBO estimates that on average less than 5 to 10% of the entire table has to be read. Otherwise, the optimizer will decide on the full table scan.
- **Physical storage**
  The optimizer considers how many index data blocks or pages must be read physically on the hard disk. The more physical memory that needs to be read, the less likely that an index is used. The amount of physical memory that needs to be read may be increased by database fragmentation (that is, a low fill level in the individual index blocks).
- **Distribution of field values**
  Most database systems also consider the distribution of field values within a table column—that is, whether each distinct value is represented in an equivalent number of data records, or whether some values dominate. The optimizer's decision is based on the evaluation of statistics on the data—for example, it uses a histogram or spot checks to determine the distribution of values across a column.
- **Spot checks at time of execution**
  Some database systems—for example, SAP DB and SQL Server—decide which access strategy is used at the time of execution and not during parsing. At the time of parsing, the values that will satisfy the WHERE clause are still unknown to the database. At the time of execution, however, an uneven distribution of values in a particular field can be taken into account by a spot check.

To determine the number of distinct values per field in a database table, use the following SQL statement:

```
SELECT COUNT (DISTINCT <dbfield>) FROM <dbtable>.
```

To find out the number of distinct values for each field of a database table, use Transaction DB02 and (for Oracle)

1. Select **Detailed analysis**.
2. In the resulting dialog box, in the field Object, enter the name of the table and select **OK**.
3. Then select **Table columns**. The resulting screen lists each field of the selected table (under Database column). The corresponding number of distinct values is indicated under **Distinct values**. The corresponding menu path for other database systems is explained in SAP Online Help.

Table Access Statistics for the CBO

To make the right decision on the optimal access, the CBO requires statistics on the sizes of tables and indexes. These statistics must be periodically generated to bring them up to date. To ensure that this occurs, schedule the relevant generating program using the DBA Planning Calendar (Transaction DB13). If the *table access statistics* are missing or obsolete, the optimizer may suggest inefficient access paths, which can cause significant performance problems.

RBO or CBO? (Advantages and Disadvantages)

An advantage of using the RBO is that you do not need to generate table access statistics. Generating these statistics requires administrative work and places a load on the system. The program that generates the statistics must run several times a week at periods of low system load.

The advantage of the CBO is its greater flexibility because it considers the selectivity of specified fields. Recall the analysis example with table MARA that was considered above. The SQL statement was as follows: `SELECT * FROM mara WHERE mandt = :A0 AND bismt = :A1`. Here, the CBO, which knows that MANDT contains only one distinct value, would decide on a full table scan, whereas the RBO, automatically preferring an index, would choose the less effective index range scan.

Sometimes you can help the RBO to choose the correct index by appropriately rewriting the indexes. Rewriting indexes for the RBO is not covered in the present book. For Oracle, see the article "Improving SQL Statements by Secondary Indexes" posted on SAP's TechNet site on the Internet.

Including Hints in SQL Statements

Some database systems allow you to influence the execution plan for various purposes by including what are called *hints* in an SQL statement. For example, in conjunction with an Oracle database, you can force the use of a full table scan with the following SQL statement:

```
SELECT /*+ FULL likp */ * FROM likp WHERE …
```

The ABAP Open SQL interface supports hints for SAP Basis Release 4.5 or later. If a hint must be used with SAP Basis 4.0, you can implement it using ABAP Native SQL.

After an R/3 upgrade or a database upgrade, or even after a database patch, hints may become superfluous or, even worse, may cause ineffective accesses. Therefore, following an upgrade, all hints must be tested. To make system administration easier, use hints very rarely.

To see how indexes can improve performance for the execution of SQL statements, reconsider the above example of an SQL statement affecting table MARA:

```
SELECT * FROM mara WHERE mandt = :A0 AND bismt = :A1
```

In the SAP system, the table MARA contains material master records. The primary index MARA___0 contains the following fields: MANDT (which identifies the client system) and MATNR (the material number). Another field in the table MARA is BISMT, which indicates the old material number. This field is used when new material numbers are introduced because of internal company reorganization, but the old, familiar material numbers are required to remain available to make searches easier for users. The above SQL statement searches for a material using an old material number.

If there is no secondary index with the field BISMT, the database optimizer has two possible access paths: the full table scan or the index range scan through the primary index MARA___0. If there are no table access statistics, the optimizer cannot recognize that the field MANDT is very unselective. After locating the field MANDT in both the WHERE clause and the index, the optimizer therefore decides on an index range scan through the primary index MARA___0.

If statistics on the table MARA are available, the optimizer decides on a full table scan. Table 11.3 compares the runtimes of accessing table MARA in various situations, using a MARA with 50,000 entries. The full table scan has a runtime of 500,000 microseconds. This is clearly more effective than the index range scan through the unfavorable primary index MARA___0 (using fields MANDT and MATNR), which requires 3,500,000 microseconds. The runtime decreases dramatically to 3,000 microseconds after the creation of a secondary index based on the field BISMT. Using this secondary index thus represents a thousand-fold improvement over using the primary index.

	Access Path	With Index Based on Fields...	Runtime in Microseconds
Without table access statistics Without secondary index based on the field BISMT	Index range scan	MANDT, MATNR	3,500,000
With table access statistics Without secondary index based on the field BISMT	Full table scan	–	500,000
With table access statistics With secondary index based on the field BISMT	Index range scan	BISMT	3,000

Table 11.3 Comparison of Runtimes for an SQL Statement Affecting Table MARA Using Different Search Strategies

Result

This example shows that it is important to create the right secondary indexes for frequently used SQL statements. In addition, up-to-date table statistics are required for the database optimizer to determine the best access path.

Administration for Indexes and Table Access Statistics

Creating and Maintaining Indexes

Indexes are created and maintained in ABAP Dictionary Maintenance, which you can access by using Transaction SE11, or, from the R/3 initial screen, by choosing **Tools · ABAP Workbench · Dictionary**. To see the table fields of an existing index, after entering a table name, select Display. The screen **Dictionary: Table/Structure: Display fields** appears. The primary index fields of a table are marked in the column **Key**. To see the associated secondary indexes, select **Indexes**. The primary index is not included in the resulting list of indexes, since it is shown on the preceding screen.

1. To create a new secondary index for a table, select

   Tools · ABAP Workbench · Dictionary

2. and enter an index name. Select

   Goto · Indexes · Create

3. In the resulting screen, enter a short description, name the index fields, and select Save. The index now exists in the ABAP Dictionary, but has not yet been activated in the database.
4. To activate the index in the database, select

   Index · Activate

   After the index has been activated in the database, the screen displays the message Index MARA~T exists in database system Oracle.

The process of activating an index for a large table in the database is especially time-consuming. During this process, **INSERT**, **UPDATE**, and **DELETE** operations affecting the corresponding table are blocked. Therefore, avoid creating new indexes for large tables during company business hours. To activate indexes by an appropriate background job, use **Utilities** for ABAP Dictionary Tables (Transaction SE14).

After activating a new index, you may need to generate new table access statistics so the optimizer can consider the new index when calculating the execution plan.

As of SAP R/3 Release 4.0, the SAP system includes database-dependent indexes that are activated as required. In ABAP Dictionary Maintenance (Transaction SE11), an index of this type is indicated by the field for selected database systems being marked.

Although an index may be defined as a database index in SAP, it may be (or become) missing in the database—for example, due to not being activated or due to being deleted and not re-created during database reorganization. This type of index is called a *missing index*. To determine whether a database index is missing, use Transaction DB02 and choose Missing indexes. Alternatively, from the SAP initial screen, select

Tools · Administration · Monitor · Performance · Database · Tables/ Indexes · Missing indexes

In the resulting display, missing primary and secondary indexes are listed separately.

Missing primary indexes require the urgent attention of the database administrator. If a primary index is missing, duplicate keys may be written, and therefore the consistency of the data is no longer guaranteed. Additionally, the lack of a primary index leads to inefficient database accesses, causing performance problems for large tables.

Re-creating a Missing Primary Index in the Database

To solve the problem of a missing primary index, which is known to the ABAP Dictionary, but does not yet exist (or no longer exists) on the database, re-create that index in ABAP Dictionary Maintenance:

1. Use Transaction SE11, or, from the SAP initial screen, select

   Tools · ABAP Workbench · Dictionary

2. Enter the table name and select

   Display · Utilities · Database Utility · Indexes · Primary index · Create database index

If no errors occur, the index has now been created on the database. If errors occur—for example, due to duplicate keys—contact SAP.

Missing Secondary Indexes

Missing *secondary indexes* can cause performance problems if the index belongs to a table that is larger than around 1 MB. To create the index that was missing:

1. Use Transaction SE11, or, from the SAP initial screen, select

   Tools · ABAP Workbench · Dictionary

2. Enter the table name and select

   Display · Indexes

3. Select the missing index and then select

   Activate

Generating Table Access Statistics

You can schedule the program that generates table access statistics to run as a periodic background job using the DBA Planning calendar. To do this, use transaction code DB13, or, from the SAP initial screen, select

Tools · CCMS · DB administration · DB scheduling

The statistics generation programs are indicated in the calendar—for example, as AnalyzeTab for Oracle, Update sta0 for Informix, and Update Statistics for SQL Server.

To find out which programs need to be scheduled to run periodically and how to schedule them for a specific brand of database, see the SAP Notes in Appendix H and the SAP Online Help.

Updating or creating new table access statistics is a resource-intensive process with runtimes of several hours for an entire database. Most database systems use a two-step process: Requirement analysis: This first step finds out the tables for which statistics should be created. Statistics generation: This second step generates the statistics.

Statistics generation is controlled by the table DBSTATC. To view the contents of this table, use transaction code DB21, or, from the SAP initial screen, select

Tools · CCMS · DB administration · Cost based optimizer · Control statistics

The resulting screen lists the SAP tables whose cost-based optimizer statistics are to be checked and updated, and provides several columns of relevant information, such as

- column **Active**: Specifies how the table statistics are edited during an update. For example, an A indicates statistics should be generated. An N or R excludes the table from the analysis.
- column **Todo**: In this column, the control table DBSTATC sets an X if statistics for a given table are to be generated when the generation program runs next.

For each run of the statistics generation program, you can monitor the logs created.

1. To monitor these logs after a run of the statistics generation program `SAPDBA` for an Oracle database, select

   Tools · CCMS · DB administration · DB Logs

2. Then select

   DB Optimizer

   The resulting screen might show, for example, the following information:

```
Beginning of Action      End of Action        Fct  Object    RC
24.04.1998 17:10:12  24.04.1998 17:35:01  opt  PSAP%     0000
24.04.1998 17:36:30  24.04.1998 18:26:25  aly  DBSTATCO  0000
```

   In the first row, the value opt in the column **Fct** indicates that a requirement analysis was performed. The value PSAP% in the column **Object** indicates that the requirement analysis was performed for all tables in the database. Comparing the beginning and ending times in the first row, you can see that the requirement analysis took 25 minutes.

   In the second row, the value aly in the column **Fct** indicates that a table analysis run was performed. The value DBSTATCO in the column **Object** indicates that the table analysis was performed for all relevant tables. (These are all tables listed in the control table DBSTATC—usually only a small percentage of all database tables.) Comparing the beginning and ending times in the second row, you can see that the table analysis took almost an hour. The operations in both rows ended successfully, as indicated by the value 0000 in the column **RC**.

The SAP tools for generating table access statistics are specifically adapted to the requirements of the SAP system. Certain tables are excluded from the creation of statistics because generating statistics for those tables would be superfluous or would reduce performance. Ensure that the table access statistics are generated only by the generation program released specifically for SAP.

When SAP is used in conjunction with Oracle databases, *no* statistics are created for pooled and clustered tables such as the update tables VBMOD, VBHDR, and VBDATA. For these tables, the field **Active** in Transaction DB21 displays the entry R.

Therefore you must make sure to generate the table access statistics only using SAP tools. For further information, please refer to the SAP database administration online help.

To check whether statistics were generated for a particular table, use Transaction DB02, or, from the SAP initial screen, select

Tools · Administration · Monitor · Performance · Database · Tables/Indexes

Next, proceed as follows:

- For Oracle, select
  Transaction DB02 · Detailed analysis · <Choose a table> · Table columns or **Detailed analysis**
- for INFORMIX:
  Transaction DB02 · Checks · Update statistics · <Choose a table>
- for MS SQL-Server:
  Transaction DB02 · Detailed analysis · <Choose a table> · show statistics

Depending on the database system, the resulting screen indicates, for example, the following information: the date of the last analysis; the accuracy of the analysis; the number of occupied database blocks or pages; the number of table rows; and the number of different entries per column (distinct values).

Rules for Creating or Changing Secondary Indexes

Preliminary Checks

Creating or changing a secondary index changes the R/3 System and can improve or worsen the performance of SQL statements. Therefore changes to indexes should be performed only by experienced developers or consultants.

- Before creating or changing an index, check whether the SQL statement for which you want to create a new index originates from a standard SAP program or a customer-developed program.
  - If the SQL statement originates from a standard SAP program, check the relevant SAP Notes in the SAP Service Marketplace that describe ways of optimizing performance for the SQL statement. If there are no relevant SAP Notes, enter your proposal concerning the creation of an appropriate index in a problem message in the SAP Service Marketplace.
  - When optimizing customer-developed SQL statements, try to avoid creating secondary indexes on SAP transaction data tables. As a rule, transaction data tables grow linearly over time and cause a corresponding growth in the size of the related secondary indexes. Therefore, over time, searching in a secondary index will result in an SQL statement that runs more and more slowly. For transaction data therefore, SAP uses special search techniques such as matchcode tables and SAP business index tables such as the delivery due index.
- If the SQL statement originates from a customer-developed program, rather than create a new index, you may be able to either
  - rewrite the ABAP program in such a way that an available index can be used, or
  - adapt an available index in such a way that it can be used.
- Never create a secondary index on SAP Basis tables without explicit recommendation from SAP. Examples of these tables include table NAST and tables beginning with D010, D020, and DD.

Rules for Creating Secondary Indexes

The following rules are the basic rules of secondary index design. For primary indexes, in addition to these rules there are other considerations related to the principles of table construction.

- An index is useful only if each corresponding SQL statement selects only a small part of a table. If the SQL statement that searches by means of a particular index field would cause more than 5% to 10% of the entire index to be read, the cost-based optimizer does not consider the index useful, and instead chooses the full table scan as the most effective access method.

  Rule 1: Include Only Selective Fields in the Index

  Examples of selective fields normally include document numbers, material numbers, and customer numbers. Examples of nonselective fields usually include SAP client IDs, company codes or plant IDs, and account status.

- As a rule, an index should contain no more than four fields. If too many fields are used in the index, this has the following effects:

  Rule 2: Include Few Fields in the Index

  - Change operations to tables take longer because the index must also be changed accordingly.
  - More storage space is used in the database. The large volume of data in the index reduces the chance that the optimizer will regard it as economical to use the index.
  - The parsing time for an SQL statement increases significantly, especially if the statement accesses multiple tables with numerous indexes and the tables must be linked with a join operation.

- To speed up accesses through an index based on several fields, the most selective fields should be positioned furthest toward the left in the index.

  Rule 3: Position Selective Fields to the Left in an Index

- To avoid the optimizer not using an index, it is sometimes necessary to use nonselective fields in the index in a way that contradicts rules 1 to 3. Examples of such fields typically include the fields for client ID (field MANDT) and company code (field BUKRS).

  Rule 4: Exceptions to Rules 1 to 3

- Avoid creating nondisjunct indexes—that is, two or more indexes with largely the same fields.

  Rule 5: Indexes Should Be Disjunct

- Despite the fact that the ABAP Dictionary defines a maximum limit of 16 indexes for each table, as a rule you should not create more than 5 indexes. One exception is for a table that is used mainly for reading, such as a table containing master data. Having too many indexes causes similar problems to those that occur if an index has too many fields. There is also an increased risk that the optimizer will choose the wrong index.

  Rule 6: Create Few Indexes per Table

Keep in mind that every rule has exceptions. Sometimes the optimal index combination can be found only by trial and error. Generally, experimenting with indexes is considered safe, as long as you keep the following points in mind:

- Never change indexes for tables larger than 10 MB during company business hours. Creating or changing an index can take from several minutes to several hours and blocks the entire table. This causes serious performance problems during production operation.
- After creating or changing an index, always check whether the optimizer program uses this index in the manner you intended. Ensure that the new index does not result in poor optimizer choices for other SQL statements. This problem is discussed further below.

Optimizing SQL Statements (WHERE Clause)

Before creating a new index, you should check carefully whether it would be possible to rewrite the SQL statement in such a way that an available index can be efficiently used. This example will demonstrate the point.

Example: Missing unselective field in the WHERE clause

While analyzing expensive SQL statements in client-specific code, you notice the following statement:

```
SELECT * FROM bkpf WHERE mandt = :A0 AND belnr = :A1
```

Table BKPF contains FI invoice headers, and so can be quite large. The field BELNR is the invoice number. Access therefore appears to be very selective. Detailed analysis reveals that there is exactly one index, the primary index of the table, with the fields MANDT (client), BUKRS (booking account), and BELNR (document number). Since the field BUKRS is not in the SQL statement, the database cannot use all the fields that follow in the index for the search. In our example, the highly selective field BELNR is lost for the index search, and the entire table must be searched sequentially.

Such programming errors are frequent when the respective unselective field (the booking account in this case) in a system is not used (because there is only one booking account in the client system). The remedy is simple; an "equal" or "in" condition can be added to the unselective field of the **WHERE** clause. The efficient SQL statement would be

```
SELECT * FROM bkpf WHERE mandt = :A0 AND bukrs = :A1 AND
belnr = :A2.
```

Or, when the booking account is not known to the program at the time of execution but the developer is sure that only a certain number of booking accounts exists in the system, then the statement would be

```
SELECT * FROM bkpf WHERE mandt = :A0 AND belnr = :A2 AND bukrs IN
(:A3, :A4, :A5, ...).
```

The sequence of AND-linked partial clauses within the **WHERE** clause does not matter. The programming example "with index support" can be found in Transaction SE30 under "Tips and Tricks".

Example: Missing client in the WHERE clause

A performance problem from a similar cause occurs when you add **CLIENT SPECIFIED** to the ABAP SQL statement and forget to specify the client in the **WHERE** clause. Most SAP indexes begin with the client; therefore, for this SQL statement, the client field is not available for an efficient index search.

Although these may appear to be trivial errors, they are regrettably frequent in client-specific code. Table 11.4 lists the most important SAP tables where this problem can occur.

SAP Functionality	Table	Unselective Fields (must be specified in the SQL statement)	Selective Fields
FI	BKPF (document headers)	BUKRS (booking account)	BELNR (document number)
FI	BSEG (document headers, part of the cluster table RFBLG)	BUKRS (booking account)	BELNR (document number)
Comprehensive	NAST (message status)	KAPPL (application key)	OBJKY (object number)
WM	LTAK/LTAP (transfer order headers and items)	LGNUM (warehouse number)	TANUM (transfer order number)
MM	MAKT (material description)	SPRAS (language key)	MAKTG (material description in capital letters)

Table 11.4 Examples of tables with leading unselective fields in the primary index. When choosing the selective fields (fourth column), the unselective fields (third column) must, in every case, also be given.

Example: Alternative access

Occasionally, one can optimize an unselective access for which there is no index by first taking data from a different table. With the dummy data, one can then search for the desired data efficiently via an index search. Consider the following SQL statement:

```
SELECT * FROM vbak WHERE mandt = :A0 AND kunnr = :A1
```

This SQL statement from a client-specific program selects sales documentation (Table VBAK) for a particular client (field KUNNR). Since there is no suitable index in the standard program version, this statement requires the entire VBAK table, perhaps many GB in size, to be read sequentially. This access is not efficient.

This problem can be solved by creating a suitable secondary index containing the disadvantages already discussed, although a developer with some understanding of the SD data model would find a different way. Instead of directly reading from table VBAK, table VAKPA would first be accessed. The optimal access would be

```
SELECT * FROM vakpa WHERE mandt = :A1 AND kunde = :A2,
```

and then

```
SELECT * FROM vbak WHERE mandt = :A1 AND vbeln = vakpa-vbeln.
```

In this access sequence, table VAKPA (partner role sales orders) would be accessed first. Since there is an index with the fields MANDT and KUNDE, and the field KUNNR is selective, this access is efficient. (Over time, if a large number of orders build up for a client, access will begin to take longer.) Table VAKPA contains the field VBELN (sales order number), which can be used to efficiently access table VBAK via the primary index. You can optimize the access by replacing one inefficient access with two efficient ones, although you have to know the data model for the application to be able to do this. SAP Notes 185530, 187906, and 191492 catalog the most frequent client code performance errors in the SAP R/3 logistics modules.

Summary This section has described cases where it is possible to improve the performance of SQL statements radically without creating a new secondary index. This kind of optimization is naturally preferable. Every new index requires space in the database; increases the time required for backup, recovery, and other maintenance tasks; and affects performance when updating.

Monitoring Indexes in the Shared SQL Area

Before and after creating or changing an index, monitor the effect of the index in the shared SQL area:

1. To monitor the shared SQL area in R/3, from the main screen in the Database Performance Monitor (Transaction ST04), choose **Detail analysis menu** and under the header **Resource consumption by**: For ORACLE, choose **SQL request**; for Informix, choose **SQL Statement**. In the dialog box that appears, change the automatically suggested selection values to zero and choose **OK**.
2. Choose

   Select table.

   Specify the table for which you want to create or change the index and choose **Enter**. The resulting screen displays the SQL statements that correspond to this table.
3. Save this screen together with the execution plan for all SQL statements in a file.
4. Two days after creating or changing the index, repeat steps 1 to 3, and compare the results with those obtained earlier to ensure that no SQL statement has a loss in performance due to poor optimizer decisions. In particular, compare the number of logical or physical accesses per execution (these are indicated, for example, in the column Reads/ execution); and check the execution plans to ensure that the new index is used only where appropriate.

To check the index design using the Shared SQL Area Monitor in a development system or test system, ensure that the business data in the system is representative, since the data determines the table sizes and field selectivity considered by the cost-based optimizer. Before testing, update the table access statistics so they reflect the current data.

What to Do if the Optimizer Ignores the Index

If you find that the cost-based optimizer program refuses to include a particular secondary index in its execution plan despite the fact that this index would simplify data access,

- the most likely reason is that the table access statistics are missing or not up to date. Check the analysis strategy and determine why the table has not yet been analyzed (see SAP Online Help on database administration). You can use Transaction DB20 to manually create up-to-date statistics, and then check whether the optimizer then makes the correct decision.

- More rarely, the optimizer ignores an appropriate index despite up-to-date table access statistics. Possible solutions include:
  - If the **WHERE** clause is too complex and the optimizer cannot interpret it correctly, you may have to consider changing the programming. Examples are provided in the next section.
  - Sometimes *deleting* the table access statistics or even appropriately modifying the statistics will cause the optimizer to use a particular index. (For this reason, the generation program released specifically for R/3 chooses not to generate statistics for some tables. Therefore ensure that you create the table access statistics with the tools provided by SAP.)
  - In either of these cases, the solution requires extensive knowledge of SQL optimization. If the problem originates from the standard R/3 software, consult SAP or your database partner.

Optimizing SQL Statements in the ABAP Program

Database indexes can be used to optimize a program only if the selection criteria for the database access are chosen so that only a small amount of data is returned to the ABAP program. If this is not the case, then the program can only be optimized by rewriting it or by changing the user's work habits.

Rules for Efficient SQL Programming

This section explains the *five basic rules* for efficient SQL programming. It does not replace an ABAP tuning manual and is limited to a few important cases. Related programming techniques are explained with examples at the end of this section and in the following sections.

For a quick guide to efficient SQL programming, call ABAP Runtime Analysis (Transaction SE30) and choose Tips and Tricks. To do this, select

System · Utilities · ABAP Runtine Analysis · Tips and Tricks

The resulting screen lets you display numerous examples of good and bad programming.

Rule 1

Transfer Few Records

SQL statements must have a **WHERE** clause that transfers only a minimal amount of data from the database to the application server or vice versa. This is especially important for SQL statements affecting tables of more than 1 MB. For all programs that transfer data to or from the database:

- If the program contains **CHECK** statements for table fields in **SELECT... ENDSELECT** loops, then replace the **CHECK** statement with a suitable WHERE clause.
- SQL statements without **WHERE** clauses must not access tables that are constantly growing—for example, transaction data tables such as BSEG, MKPF, and VBAK. If you find such SQL statements, rewrite the program.
- Avoid identical accesses—that is, the same data being read repeatedly. To identify SQL statements that cause identical accesses, trace the program with an SQL trace (Transaction ST05), view the results, and select **Goto • Identical selects**. Note the identical selects and return to the trace results screen to see how much time these selects required. This tells you how much time you would save if the identical selects could be avoided.

Rule 2

Keep the Volume of Transferred Data Small

To ensure that *the volume of transferred data is as small as possible*, examine your programs as described in the following points:

- SQL statements with the clause **SELECT *** transfer all the columns of a table. If all this data is not really needed, you may be able to convert the **SELECT *** clause to a **SELECT LIST** (`SELECT <column 1> <column 2>`) or use a projection view.
- There is an economical and an expensive way of calculating sums, maximums, or mean values in relation to an individual table column:

  First, you can perform these calculations on the database using the SQL aggregate functions (**SUM, MAX, AVG**, etc.) and then transfer only the results, which is a small data volume. Second, you can initially transfer all the data in the column from the database into the ABAP program and perform the calculations on the application server. This transfers a lot more data than the first method and creates more database load.
- A **WHERE** clause searching for a single record often looks as follows:

```
CLEAR found.
```

```
SELECT * FROM dbtable WHERE field1 = x1.
   found = 'X'. EXIT.
ENDSELECT.
```

The disadvantage in this code is that it triggers a **FETCH** on the database. For example, after 100 records are read into the input/output buffer of the work processes, the ABAP program reads the first record in the buffer, and the loop processing is interrupted. Therefore, 99 records were transferred for no benefit. The following code is more efficient:

```
CLEAR found.
SELECT * FROM dbtable UP TO 1 ROWS WHERE field1 = x1.
ENDSELECT.
IF sy-subrc = 0. found = 'X'. ENDIF.
```

This code informs the database that only one record should be returned.

Use Array Select Instead of Single Select

Rule 3

The *number of fetches* must remain small. Using array select instead of single select creates *fewer, more lengthy* database accesses instead of *many short* accesses. Many short accesses cause administrative overhead and network traffic in comparison to fewer, more lengthy database accesses. Therefore, avoid the following types of code:

```
LOOP AT itab.
   SELECT FROM dbtable WHERE field1 = itab-field1.
   <further processing>
ENDLOOP.
```

or:

```
SELECT * FROM dbtable1 WHERE field1 = x1.
   SELECT * FROM dbtable2 WHERE field2 =
      dbtable1-field2.
      <further processing>
ENDSELECT.
ENDSELECT.
```

Both examples make many short accesses that read only a few records. For SAP R/3 Release 3.0 and later, you can group many short accesses to make a few longer accesses by using either the **FOR ALL ENTRIES** clause or a database view.

Rule 4

Keep the WHERE Clauses Simple

The WHERE clauses must be simple; otherwise, the optimizer may decide on the wrong index or not use an index at all. A **WHERE** clause is simple if it specifies each field of the index using **AND** and an equals condition.

Virtually all optimizers have problems when confronted with a large number of **OR** conditions. Therefore, you should use the disjunct normal form (DNF) whenever possible, as described in the example below on avoiding **OR** clauses.

Instead of the following code:

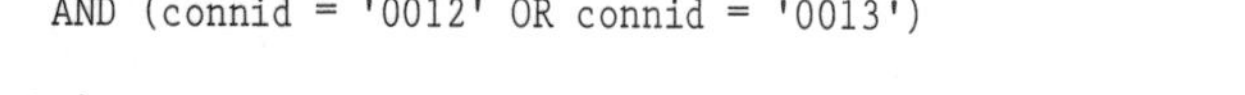

```
SELECT * FROM sflight WHERE (carrid = 'LH' or carrid = 'UA')
   AND (connid = '0012' OR connid = '0013')
```

it is better to use:

```
SELECT * FROM SFLIGHT
   WHERE ( CARRID = 'LH' AND CONNID = '0012')
      OR ( CARRID = 'LH' AND CONNID = '0013')
      OR ( CARRID = 'UH' AND CONNID = '0012')
      OR ( CARRID = 'UH' AND CONNID = '0013').
```

The other way of avoiding problems with **OR** clauses is to divide complex SQL statements into simple SQL statements and cause the selected data to be stored in an internal table. To divide complex SQL statements, you can use the **FOR ALL ENTRIES** clause (see below, under "More about FOR ALL ENTRIES Clauses").

Sometimes you can use an **IN** instead of an **OR**. For example, instead of `field1 = x1 AND (field2 = y1 OR field2 = y2 OR field2 = y3)`, use `field1 = x1 and field2 IN (y1, y2, y3)`. Try to avoid using **NOT** conditions in the **WHERE** clause. These cannot be processed through an index. You can often replace a **NOT** condition by a positive **IN** or **OR** condition, which can be processed using an index.

Rule 5

Avoid Unnecessary Database Load

Some operations such as sorting tables can be performed by the database instance as well as the R/3 instance. In general, you should try to transfer any tasks that create system load to the application servers, which can be configured with more SAP instances if the system load increases. The capacity of the database instance cannot be increased so easily. The following measures help to avoid database load:

- SAP buffering: This is the most efficient tool for reducing load on the database instance caused by accesses to database data. (See Chapter 9.)
- Sorting on the application server rather than in the database: If a program requires sorted data, either the database or the SAP instance must sort the data. The database should perform the sort only if the same index can be used for sorting as for satisfying the **WHERE** clause, since this type of sort is inexpensive. (See below, under "Sorting Techniques".)

Consider the table <DBTABLE> with the fields <FIELD1>, <FIELD2>, <FIELD3>, and <FIELD4>. The key fields are <FIELD1>, <FIELD2>, and <FIELD3>, and these comprise the primary index <TABLE__0>. To cause the data to be sorted by the database, you can use the following statement:

```
SELECT * FROM <dbtable> INTO TABLE itab
         WHERE <field1> = x1 and <field2> =  x2
         ORDER BY <field1> <field2> <field3>. Here, a database sort
is appropriate, since the primary index TABLE__0 can be used both to
satisfy the WHERE clause and to sort the data.
```

A sort by the fields <FIELD2> and <FIELD4> cannot be performed using the primary index TABLE__0 since the ORDER_BY clause does not contain the first primary index field. Therefore, to reduce the database load, this sort should be performed not by the database but by the ABAP program. You can use ABAP statements such as:

```
SELECT * FROM <dbtable> INTO itab
         WHERE <field1> = x1 and <field2> = x2.
SORT itab BY <field2> <field4>.
```

Similar considerations to those used in the case of sorting apply when using the **GROUP BY** clause or aggregate functions. If the database instance performs the **GROUP BY**, this increases the consumption of database instance resources. However, this must be weighed against the gain in performance due to the fact that the **GROUP BY** calculation transfers fewer results to the application server. (For more information on aggregate functions, see Rule 2 above.)

Example of Optimizing an SQL Statement in an ABAP Program

This section uses an example to demonstrate each step in optimizing an SQL statement.

Preliminary Analysis

In this example, a customer-developed ABAP program is having performance problems. As an initial response, run an SQL trace (Transaction ST05) on a second run of the program, when the database buffer has been loaded. The results of the trace show the information in Table 11.5.

```
Duration in Microseconds   Object    Oper      Rec    RC  Statement
    1,692  MSEG       PREPARE           0  SELECT WHERE MANDT ..
      182  MSEG       OPEN              0
   86,502  MSEG       FETCH       32    0
      326  MKPF       PREPARE           0  SELECT WHERE MANDT ..
       60  MKPF       OPEN              0
   12,540  MKPF       FETCH        1 1403
       59  MKPF       REOPEN            0  SELECT WHERE MANDT ..
    2,208  MKPF       FETCH        1 1403
       60  MKPF       REOPEN            0  SELECT WHERE MANDT ..
    2,234  MKPF       FETCH        1 1403
       61  MKPF       REOPEN            0  SELECT WHERE MANDT ..
    2,340  MKPF       FETCH        1 1403
     ... 28 more indiv. FETCHES
   43,790  MSEG       FETCH       32    0
       61  MKPF       REOPEN            0  SELECT WHERE MANDT ..
    2,346  MKPF       FETCH        1 1403
       60  MKPF       REOPEN            0  SELECT WHERE MANDT ..
    2,455  MKPF       FETCH        1 1403
     ...
```

The trace begins with a **FETCH** operation on table MSEG, which reads 32 records, as indicated by the 32 in the column Rec. Next, 32 separate **FETCH** operations are performed on table MKPF, each returning one record as indicated by the 1 in the column Rec. This process is repeated with another **FETCH** operation that reads 32 records from table MSEG and 32 further single-record **FETCH** operations on the table MKPF, and so on, until all records are found.

Now view the compressed summary. To do this from the SQL trace results screen, select **Goto · Summary · Compress**. The results are indicated in Table 11.6.

TCode/ Program	Table	SQL-Op	Accesses	Records	Time in Micro-seconds	Percent
SE38	MKPF	SEL	112	112	319,040	61.7
SE38	MSEG	SEL	1	112	197,638	38.3
Total					516,678	100.0

Table 11.5 Compressed Summary of an SQL Trace

The compressed summary shows that almost two-thirds (61.7%) of the database time is used for the individual **FETCH** operations on the table MKPF, and more than one-third (38.3%) is used for the **FETCH** operations on the table MSEG.

Detailed Analysis

The detailed analysis is the step prior to tuning. In this step, you find out the tables, fields, and processes that are important for tuning the SQL statements you identified in the preliminary analysis.

To increase the performance of specific SQL statements, you can either improve the performance of the database instance or reduce the volume of data transferred from the database to the application server.

In Table 11.5, the SQL trace results show that the response times per record are approximately 3,000 microseconds for the accesses to table MKPF, and approximately 1,800 microseconds for accesses to table MSEG. Since these response times are good, you can conclude that the performance of the database instance is good. The only remaining way of increasing the performance of SQL statements in the ABAP program is to reduce the amount of data transferred.

View the identical selects: From the SQL trace (Transaction ST05) results screen, choose **Goto · Identical selects**. In the present example, the resulting list shows 72 identical SQL statements on the table MKPF. This is around 60% of the total of 112 accesses to the table MKPF, as indicated in the compressed summary. Therefore, eliminating the identical accesses would result in about 60% fewer accesses and correspondingly less access time.

To access the code from the SQL trace results screen, position the cursor on the appropriate program in the column Object and click **ABAP display**.

In this example, accessing the code reveals that the following ABAP statements caused the database accesses analyzed in the SQL trace:

```
SELECT * FROM mseg INTO CORRESPONDING FIELDS OF imatdocs
         WHERE matnr LIKE s_matnr.
   SELECT * FROM mkpf WHERE mblnr = imatdocs-mblnr
         AND mjahr = imatdocs-mjahr.
      imatdocs-budat = mkpf-budat.
      APPEND imatdocs.
ENDSELECT.
ENDSELECT.
```

You now need to know from which tables the data is being selected. This is indicated in ABAP Dictionary Maintenance (Transaction SE11). In this example, the two affected tables, MKPF and MSEG, store materials documents for goods issue and receipt. MKPF contains the document heads for the materials documents, and MSEG contains the respective line items. The program reads the materials documents for specific materials from the database and transfers them to the internal table IMATDOCS. The materials are listed in the internal table S_MATNR.

The fields of these tables that you need to know in this example are as follows:

- Table MKPF:
  - MANDT: client (primary key)
  - MBLNR: number of the material document (primary key)
  - MJAHR: material document year (primary key)
  - BUDAT: posting date in the document
- Table MSEG:
  - MANDT: client (primary key)
  - MBLNR: number of the material document (primary key)
  - MJAHR: material document year (primary key)
  - ZEILE: position in the material document (primary key)
  - MATNR: material number
  - WERKS: plant

The above program excerpt selects the materials documents corresponding to the materials in the internal table S_MATNR and transfers the document-related fields MANDT, MBLNR, MJAHR, ZEILE, MATNR, WERKS, and BUDAT to the ABAP program. In the above SQL statement, S_MATNR limits the data volume to be transferred to the ABAP program from table MSEG. Because the field MATNR is in the table MSEG, the data selection begins in table MSEG rather than in MKPF. For each of the records selected in MSEG, the data for the field BUDAT is read from table MKPF and transferred to internal table IMATDOCS.

The program in this example resolves these tasks with a nested **SELECT** loop. As you can see in the excerpt, the external loop executes a **FETCH** operation that returns 32 records. Then each record is processed individually in the ABAP program, and a relevant record from table MKPF is requested 32 times. After this, the program resumes the external loop, collecting another 32 records from the database, then returns to the internal loop, and so on, until all requested documents are processed.

Once you have identified the SQL statements that have to be optimized (in the preliminary analysis)—and the related tables, fields, and processes (in the detailed analysis)—you can start to tune these statements as follows.

Tuning the SQL Code

Comparing the excerpted programming with the rules for efficient SQL programming reveals three areas where these rules are contradicted in the present example:

- Contradiction to Rule 1: Identical information is read multiple times from the database.
- Contradiction to Rule 2: **SELECT *** statements are used, which read all the columns in the table. These statements are, however, few in number.
- Contradiction to Rule 3: Instead of a small number of **FETCH** operations that read many records from table MKPF, the program uses many **FETCH** operations that read only one record. This creates an unnecessary administrative burden in terms of **REOPEN** operations and network traffic.

Two tuning solutions for this example of poor data accessing are provided in the following subsections.

Solution 1

Avoiding Identical SQL Statements

The identical database accesses occur because of the nested *SQL statements*. In the example, the first SQL statement accesses the table MSEG to obtain the following data: MANDT=100, MBLNR=00005001, MJAHR=1998, and the field ZEILE specifies the 10 rows from 0000 to 0010. The second SQL statement searches the table MKPF based on the keys MANDT=100, MBLNR=00005001, and MJAHR=1998, and reads identical heading data 10 times. Using nested SQL statements always poses the risk of identical accesses because the program does not recognize which data has already been read. To avoid identical accesses, read all the data from the table MSEG, and then read the heading data from the table MKPF only once, as indicated in the rewritten version of the program below.

Avoiding Select * Statements

To reduce the amount of data transferred for each table record, convert the **SELECT *** clause to a **SELECT LIST**.

Bundling Fetch Operations

To convert the numerous single record accesses to the table MKPF into larger *FETCH operations*, you can use the **FOR ALL ENTRIES** clause.

The program optimized in the above ways now looks as follows:

```
SELECT mblnr mjahr zeile matnr werks FROM mseg
                   INTO TABLE imatdocs
                   WHERE matnr LIKE s_matnr.
If sy-subrc = 0.
   SORT imatdocs BY mblnr mjahr.
   imatdocs_help1[] = imatdocs[]
   DELETE ADJACENT DUPLICATES FROM imatdocs_help1
                COMPARING mblnr mjahr.
   SELECT mblnr mjahr budat FROM mkpf
              INTO TABLE imatdocs_help2
              FOR ALL ENTRIES IN imatdocs_help1
              WHERE mblnr = imatdocs_help1-mblnr
                AND mjahr = imatdocs_help1-mjahr.
   SORT imatdocs_help2 BY mblnr mjahr.
   LOOP AT imatdocs.
      READ TABLE imatdocs_help2 WITH KEY mblnr = imatdocs-mblnr
                  mjahr = imatdocs-mjahr BINARY SEARCH.
      imatdocs-budat = imatdocs_help2-budat.
      MODIFY imatdocs.
ENDLOOP.
ENDIF.
```

Here are some comments on the optimized program:

1. The required data is read from the table MSEG. The **SELECT *** clause has been replaced with a **SELECT LIST**, and the **SELECT ... ENDSELECT** construction has been replaced with a **SELECT ... INTO TABLE....**
2. The statement **IF sy subrc = 0** checks whether records have been read from the database. In the following steps, the internal table IMATDOCS_HELP1 is filled. To avoid double accesses to the table MKPF, the table IMATDOCS is sorted by the command **SORT imatdocs**, and the duplicate entries in MBLNR and MJAHR are deleted by the command **DELETE ADJACENT DUPLICATES**.
3. Finally, the data that was read from the table MSEG and is now stored in the table IMATDOCS, and the data that was read from table MKPF and is now stored in the table IMATDOCS_HELP2, are combined and transferred to the ABAP program. To optimize the search in the internal table IMATDOCS_HELP2, it is important to sort the table and to include a **BINARY SEARCH** in the **READ TABLE** statement.

After performing these changes, repeat the SQL trace to verify an improvement in performance. Now, the SQL trace results look as follows.

```
Duration Object   Oper      Rec    RC
   1,417 MSEG     PREPARE           0
      65 MSEG     OPEN              0
  57,628 MSEG     FETCH     112  1403
   6,871 MKPF     PREPARE           0
     693 MKPF     OPEN              0
 177,983 MKPF     FETCH      40  1403
```

You can observe the following access improvements as compared with the previous version of the program:

- Using **SELECT LIST** to access the table MSEG now allows all 112 records to be transferred in a single **FETCH** operation. Using **SELECT *** enabled only 32 records per **FETCH** operation. The time for the MSEG access is reduced from 197,638 microseconds to 57,628 microseconds.
- By avoiding identical accesses to table MKPF and using the **SELECT LIST** and the **FOR ALL ENTRIES** clauses, you have reduced the MKPF access from 319,040 microseconds to 177,983 microseconds.

In summary, the *database access time is reduced by half*.

More about FOR ALL ENTRIES Clauses

The **FOR ALL ENTRIES** clause is used to convert many short SQL statements into a few longer SQL statements, especially for **LOOP ... ENDLOOP** constructions or, as in the above example, for nested **SELECT** loops.

When the **FOR ALL ENTRIES** clause is used, the database interface creates, for example, a **WHERE** clause that translates the entries of the internal driver table (in this example, IMATDOCS_HELP1) into separate conditions, which are then combined with each other through a disjunct normal OR. In this example, the database interface creates the following SQL statement:

```
SELECT
   "MBLNR" , "MJAHR" , "BUDAT"
FROM
   "MKPF"
WHERE
      ( "MANDT" = :A0 AND  "MBLNR" = :A1 AND  "MJAHR" = :A2 )
   OR ( "MANDT" = :A3 AND  "MBLNR" = :A4 AND  "MJAHR" = :A5 )
   OR ( "MANDT" = :A6 AND  "MBLNR" = :A7 AND  "MJAHR" = :A8 )
        <n times>
   OR ( "MANDT" = :A117 AND "MBLNR" = :A118 AND "MJAHR" = :A119)
```

To calculate <n>, the SAP work process takes the smaller of the following numbers: the number of entries in the internal driver table (here, IMATDOCS_HELP1); and the SAP profile parameter **rsdb/max_blocking_factor**. If the number of entries in the internal driver table is larger than **rsdb/max_blocking_factor**, the work process executes several similar SQL statements on the database to limit the length of the **WHERE** clause. The SAP work process joins the partial results excluding duplications.

The execution plan for the above statement is as follows:

```
Execution Plan
SELECT STATEMENT
   CONCATENATION
      TABLE ACCESS BY INDEX ROWID MKPF
         INDEX UNIQUE SCAN MKPF______0
      TABLE ACCESS BY INDEX ROWID MKPF
         INDEX UNIQUE SCAN MKPF______0
            <n times>
      TABLE ACCESS BY INDEX ROWID MKPF
         INDEX UNIQUE SCAN MKPF______0
```

When using the **FOR ALL ENTRIES** clause, observe the following prerequisites:

- The driver table (here, IMATDOCS) must not be empty: If the driver table is empty of data, the **FOR ALL ENTRIES** clause reads the entire database table. In the present example, the driver table contains the header information for the materials documents. If it is empty, line item data is not required, and the second, expensive SQL statement need not be executed. To avoid executing the second statement, cause the program to check that the driver table is empty by using the ABAP statement **IF sy subrc = 0**. This ensures that the SQL statement with the **FOR ALL ENTRIES** clause is processed only if the table IMATDOCS was previously filled.
- The driver table (here, IMATDOCS) must contain no duplicate entries: If the driver table contains duplicate entries, the corresponding data is obtained twice from the database. Therefore, there should be no duplicate entries in the driver table. In the above code example, duplicate entries are avoided by sorting the driver table and then deleting the duplicates.

Depending on the database system, the database interface translates a **FOR ALL ENTRIES** clause into various SQL statements. In the present example, the database interface uses the **FOR ALL ENTRIES** clause to generate equivalent conditions based on OR. Alternatively, the database interface can also translate the clause into SQL statements using an IN or a **UNION** operator. This is controlled through R/3 profile parameters whose settings should not be changed without explicit instruction from SAP.

Solution 2

The second way of optimizing the program requires you to create a database view on the tables MSEG and MKPF. In this example, this would be the view Z_MSEG_MKPF with the following properties:

- Tables: MKPF and MSEG
- Join conditions:
  - MSEG-MANDT = MKPF-MANDT
  - MSEG-MBLNR = MKPF-MBLNR
  - MSEG-MJAHR = MKPF-MJAHR

- View fields:
  - MSEG-MANDT
  - MSEG-MBLNR
  - MSEG-MJAHR
  - MSEG-ZEILE
  - MSEG-WERKS
  - MKPF-BUDAT
  - MSEG-MATNR

To create a database view, use ABAP Dictionary Maintenance (Transaction SE11).

With this view, the ABAP program can be formulated as follows:

```
SELECT mblnr mjahr zeile matnr werks budat FROM z_mseg_mkpf
                INTO TABLE imatdocs
        WHERE matnr LIKE s_matnr.
```

The SQL trace then displays the information shown below.

```
  Duration in Microseconds   Object    Oper      Rec    RC
      1,176 Z_MSEG_MKP REOPEN            0
    149,707 Z_MSEG_MKP FETCH      112 1403
```

Compared with the optimized version in Solution 1 above, the database time has again been reduced by half!

The execution plan is as follows:

```
Execution Plan
SELECT STATEMENT
   NESTED LOOP
      TABLE ACCESS BY INDEX ROWID MSEG
         INDEX RANGE SCAN MSEG~M
      TABLE ACCESS BY INDEX ROWID MKPF
         INDEX UNIQUE SCAN MKPF~0
```

Checking for identical accesses and joining data in the ABAP program are no longer necessary. The comparison of the two solutions—the first with the **FOR ALL ENTRIES** clause and the second with the database view—present a clear argument in favor of converting nested **SELECT** loops into database views. However, using a database view means that, in addition to selecting the right indexes, the database optimizer must make correct choices on the following issues:

- **The sequence of accessing the tables:**
  In the present example, the optimizer should decide to read first the table MSEG and then table MKPF.
- **The type of table join:**
  In the present example, the optimizer should decide on a *nested loop join* to join the data from both tables. The available join methods vary according to the database system (see the manufacturer's documentation).

You should monitor the performance associated with using a view. During the corresponding join operation, partial sort operations occur on the database, during which time performance problems may occur. If the database has problems choosing the appropriate execution plan for the SQL statement that accesses the view, it may be wiser to explicitly program the table accessing sequence and the joining of the data in the ABAP program.

Presetting Field Values in Report Transactions

Many times when display transactions are called, a screen appears with up to 10 or more selection fields. By entering appropriate selection criteria, the end user may limit the number of hits. If precise, focused selection criteria can be specified, then the database can more quickly find the information using an index. If no criteria whatsoever are entered, a full table scan may be performed on the corresponding database table.

This means that poor end-user habits create performance problems, which can be prevented in the following ways:

- End-user education: You can broadcast user messages to sensitize users to the problem of unproductive selections and their consequences (How do I make the right selection?). Selection screens should be filled with criteria that are as specific as possible. If at all possible, a value should always be entered into the first field (document number, requirement tracking number, material number, etc.), together with other entries (purchasing group, purchasing organization, plant, etc.). When selecting from supplier orders, the supplier should be specified, along with a time interval for the order date that is as short as possible. Users should be made aware that a selection result containing several hundred entries is not optimal.
- Changing field attributes on selection screens: You can change field attributes and, for example, designate certain very selective fields as required fields. Although this restrictive method effectively limits

selection possibilities, it must be adjusted to the special requirements of the end users. Alternatively, default values for fields can be pre-specified. The user can then overwrite any necessary default entries (for example, if the user is taking over for a co-worker who is away sick and needs to assume responsibility for a group).

To change field attributes and to specify user default values, changes must be made to the ABAP code for all previously listed transactions.

As an example, if you call Transaction ME57 to select purchase requisitions, then a window with more than 20 input fields is displayed. If no other values are entered into fields in this window, then a full table scan of table EBAN (purchase requisitions) will be performed. A discussion with the users responsible for the transaction and the business process would probably result in the following types of suggestions for improvement:

- Users could be required to enter a purchasing group (required field).
- End users are usually only interested in orders with the status "N" (not closed). If the processing status "N" is also given, then the statement is more efficient, because far fewer records will be read. Unfortunately, users often forget to enter the "N". Organizational methods cannot be expected to control this problem, since the transaction is executed by some 2,000 users. Instead, a simple solution would be to preset this field with the default value "N".
- To further limit the selection, the date range should be as narrow as possible, that is, the default date should be the current calendar date.

The following section describes the method for implementing these suggestions for improvement.

Defining Required Fields

First, determine the report name and the name of the field that will be made a *required field*:

1. To call the transaction to be optimized (in our example, Transaction ME57), from the SAP initial screen, select
2. **System · Status**. In the **Report** field, you will find the associated report (in our example, "RM06BZ00").
3. Leave the Status window (click **Continue**).
4. Using the cursor, select the field to be made a required field (in this example, **Purchasing Group**). Then, press the **F1** function key, which brings up context-sensitive Help for the **Purchasing Group** field.

5. Click **Technical Info** and, in the **Field Name** field, find "EKGRP", the name of the field to be changed.

Next, determine the place to be changed in the report code to make the field a required field. The field definition is either in the report or in a logical database. To find out whether the field definition is in the report itself:

1. Exit Help and transaction and call the ABAP editor (Transaction SE38).
2. In the **Program** field, enter the report name, which you have already found (RM06BZ00), and select **Source Code**, **Display**, then
3. select **Search** (glasses icon).
4. In the **Search** field of the dialog box that appears, enter the name of the field, which you have already found (EKGRP). In the **Search Range** section, select the field **Global in Program**.
5. If the field is found by the search, then you have found the place where the coding must be modified later.

If the field is not found, then search in the logical database to which this report is associated:

1. Call the ABAP editor (Transaction SE38).
2. In the **Program** field, enter the report name, which you have already found (RM06BZ00), and select **Attribute**, **Display**.
3. In the **Logical Database** field, you will find the logical database to which this report is associated (for example, "BAM").
4. Double-click the database name (here "BAM") to open a window with the definition of the logical database.
5. Use the arrow keys to go to the **Logical Databases: Editor Display Program DB<db>SEL** screen<db> is the name of the logical database. This screen contains the definition of the **EKGRP** field.

After you have identified the place to change in the code, you can make **EKGRP** a required field by adding the ABAP keyword **OBLIGATORY** to the corresponding line in the code.

To do this, change the line `ba_ekgrp FOR eban-ekgrp MEMORY ID ekg` to `ba_ekgrp FOR eban-ekgrp MEMORY ID ekg OBLIGATORY`. The next time you call Transaction ME57, the field **Purchasing Group** will be a required field—a question mark will appear on the screen.

This field will also be a required field in all reports that use the same logical database. The affected programs can be found using the where-used list.

Presetting Default Values

The second improvement mentioned involved entering default values in fields. To do this, first find the place in the code where the field is defined, as previously described. For example, find the definition of Processing Status (in our example, in Include FM06BCS1 of the report RM06BZ00). Then, change the line `s_statu FOR eban-statu` to `s_statu FOR eban-statu DEFAULT 'N'`. The next time you call Transaction ME57, the field **Processing Status** will already contain the value "N". The default value for the date can be set in the same way.

Other possible variable definitions besides **DEFAULT** and **OBLIGATORY** can include

- **NO-DISPLAY**
  The selection does not appear on the screen, but can be preset with default values.
- **NO-EXTENSION**
  The selection allows only one input line. That is, you cannot access the "Multiple Selection" screen, because its button does not appear on the selection screen.
- **NO INTERVALS**
  The **Select** option appears without an **until** field on the selection screen. The button for selecting the "Multiple Selection" screen appears immediately after the **from** field. This produces a simplified selection screen, which is especially helpful for a select option where normally no interval is used. For further information, see the context-sensitive Help (**F1**) for the **SELECT OPTIONS** ABAP statement.

Transaction Variants

With SAP Basis 4.0, you can assign a default variant to a transaction.

To do this, a system variant must be assigned to the report (RM06BZ00):

1. Call the ABAP editor (Transaction SE38).
2. In the **Program** field, enter the report name, which you have already found (RM06BZ00), and select **Variants, Display**.
3. In the **Variants** field, enter the name CUS&DEFAULT and select **Create**.
4. You can now create a variant, preset default values, hide fields, and make other specifications. For additional help in creating variants, please refer to the ABAP book series "ABAP Development Workbench". The volume "ABAP User's Guide: Reports and

Transactions" contains a chapter on "Pre-Setting Selections Using Variants".

The variant created must be a system variant, which means that it must begin with CUS&. To create a system variant, a correction order and a modification key are required from the SAP Service Marketplace. In addition, SAP Basis 4.0B contains an error in the code for creating a system variant. To resolve this issue, implement SAP Note 107619, after which you must ensure that the system variant you have created is automatically used at the transaction start:

1. Call the ABAP Repository Browser (Transaction SEU) and select **Other Objects**, **Edit**, which will bring you to the **Other Development Objects** screen.
2. Select **Transaction**, enter the transaction code (ME57) and select **Display**.
3. Select **Display—Change**.
4. In the **Start with Variant** field, enter the name of the system variant just defined (CUS&DEFAULT). Save the change—entering the system variant is considered a modification.

Now when you start Transaction ME57, the fields will reflect your changes.

The user interface will now have been modified to look like this:

- The Purchasing Group is now a required field (as a result of the ABAP code modification).
- The default value "N" has been set for the **Processing Status** field, so it is no longer available for entries (as a result of system variant customization).
- The **Delivery Date** field is automatically preset to the current calendar date, and to a date far in the future.

Besides the default variant, you can also create other variants, like those with different preset processing status indications. These variants can be viewed by selecting **Goto · Variants · Get**. You may want to authorize some users to create new variants, whereas other users can be restricted to using only those variants already created.

Summary and Related Tuning Measures

The options available for optimizing execution performance for SQL statements include creating or changing indexes, creating table access statistics, and optimizing ABAP code. Figure 11.3 shows a procedure roadmap covering these optimization techniques.

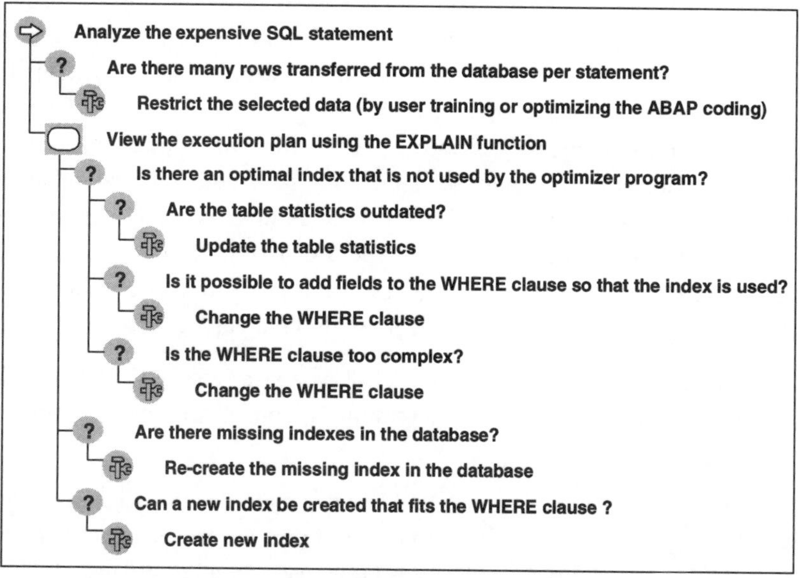

Figure 11.3 Procedure roadmap for optimizing expensive SQL statements

In addition to these techniques, it can be helpful to investigate the users' ways of using programs associated with expensive SQL statements. Users may not be aware that they are contributing to the long runtime of an SQL statement by not using appropriate limiting conditions when searching the database. For example, users should

- limit the kind of selection data they enter in SAP screens so that few records must be read
- use matchcodes when searching for business data
- Use SAP's information systems (EIS, VIS, LIS, and so on) instead of writing one-off programs to obtain ad hoc reports

The following sections explain additional tuning measures that you can use when you cannot further reduce the volume of data records transferred by an SQL statement and are sure that the optimal index is being used.

Reorganizing Indexes If an SQL statement is expensive even when there is an appropriate index and the ABAP code is optimal, check whether the cause of the database time is *index fragmentation*. To understand fragmentation, consider the example of an index containing a million records. If 99% of these records are deleted in the corresponding table and therefore in the index, in some databases, the blocks or pages that were occupied by the deleted records are not released, nor are the remaining valid entries automatically grouped together. Not only is the major part of the index now not serving any purpose, but the valid data is distributed across a large number of blocks. Therefore, an index range scan must read a large number of index blocks to return comparatively few data records. This condition is called fragmentation. To defragment the index, reorganize the index by deleting and re-creating it. An example of an index that typically may need reorganizing is the index RESB__M (see SAP Note 70513). The related table, RESB, contains the material reservations in production planning, and therefore undergoes extremely frequent changes.

Index fragmentation does not occur in all database systems. To find out if fragmentation affects your database system, consult the manufacturer's documentation.

Bitmap Indexes The indexes normally set up by the SAP system are B* tree indexes. Some database systems also offer other types of indexes—for example, *bitmap indexes*. These other types of indexes previously were seldom used in the SAP environment, but also provide a database-specific way of optimizing SQL statements. They are particularly significant in data warehouse applications like SAP's Business Information Warehouse.

Incorrect Buffer Settings Expensive SQL statements may also be due to incorrect settings for SAP buffering. The settings are incorrect if, for example, they make the buffer too small or perform buffering for tables that should not be buffered because they are too large or too often changed. Examine the tables accessed by the expensive SQL statements in the Shared SQL Area Monitor (within Transaction ST04) or in the SQL trace (Transaction ST05). If the tables accessed are the kinds of tables in Table 11.6, an incorrect buffer setting may be indicated. SQL statements that access these tables do not originate directly from an ABAP program, but are triggered on behalf of an ABAP program by the SAP Basis to obtain background information—for example, load ABAP programs, ABAP Dictionary objects, or buffered tables. For more information on buffering settings, see Chapter 2 and Chapter 7.

SAP Buffer	Related SAP Basis Table
Table definitions (TTAB)	DDNTT
Field definitions (FTAB)	DDNTF
Program (PXA)	D010*
Screen	D020*
Table buffer	ATAB, KAPOL

Table 11.6 SAP Buffers and Related SAP Basis Tables

The following SQL statement is an example of an SQL statement from the SAP Basis that reads the table D010S to load an ABAP program into the program buffer:

```
SELECT
  "BLOCKLG" , "BLOCK"
FROM
  "D010S"
WHERE
  "PROG" = :A0 AND "R3STATE" = :A1 AND "R3MODE" = :A2 AND "R3VERSION"
  = :A3 AND "BLOCKNR" = 1
```

DB Administration Tools

The Shared SQL Area Monitor (within Transaction ST04) may indicate expensive SQL statements (with many buffer gets) that do not originate from an R/3 application transaction, but from database monitoring programs such as the analysis program `RSORATDB`, the auxiliary program `SAPDBA` (for example, with the SAPDBA options -next, -check, -analyze), and non-SAP database monitoring tools. To avoid disrupting production operation, these programs should be run only during times of low workload. For example, the default setting for running `RSORATDB` causes it to run at 7 A.M. and 7 P.M. as a part of the background job SAP_COLLECTOR_FOR_PERFORMANCE.

You can identify SQL statements that are used for monitoring the database through table names such as DBA_SEGMENTS, DBA_INDEXES, and USER_INDEXES (for Oracle); or SYSTABLES and SYSFRAGMENTS (for Informix). To find out if an SQL statement belongs to the SAP system or to one of these database administration and monitoring tools, check whether the corresponding table exists in the ABAP Dictionary using Transaction SE11. If the table is not listed, the SQL statement is from a database administration and monitoring tool.

The following is an example of an SQL statement that is executed by SAP's administration and monitoring tool SAPDBA for Oracle:

```
SELECT
   OWNER,SEGMENT_NAME,SEGMENT_TYPE,NEXT_EXTENT/:b1,PCT_INCREASE
FROM SYS.DBA_SEGMENTS
WHERE TABLESPACE_NAME=:b2 AND(SEGMENT_TYPE='TABLE'
   OR SEGMENT_TYPE='INDEX' OR SEGMENT_TYPE='CLUSTER')
   AND NEXT_EXTENT/:b1*DECODE(PCT_INCREASE,0,:b4,
   ((POWER(1+PCT_INCREASE/100,:b4)-1)/(PCT_INCREASE/100)))>:b6
```

If administration programs like this cause expensive statements in a production system as indicated in the Shared SQL Area Monitor (within Transaction ST04) and are executed during times of high workload, they should be run infrequently.

Important Concepts in This Chapter

After reading this chapter, you should be familiar with the following concepts:

- Logical and physical read accesses (buffer gets, disk reads)
- Primary and secondary indexes
- Selectivity
- Database optimizer and execution plan
- Table access statistics

Questions

1. Which of the following statements is correct with regard to expensive SQL statements?
   A. They can lead to hardware bottlenecks (a CPU or I/O bottleneck) and negatively affect the runtime of other SQL statements.
   B. They can occupy a lot of space in the data buffer of the database, displace objects that are needed by other SQL statements, and negatively affect the runtime of other SQL statements.
   C. They can occupy a lot of space in the SAP table buffer and displace objects, which causes unnecessary reload operations.
   D. If they are performed after database locks were set by the same program, this can cause exclusive lock wait situations in the database, which in turn can cause a brief system standstill.

E. Expensive SQL statements in programs for reporting or in background programs are not normally a problem for the database.

2. In the results of an SQL trace, you find an SQL statement that has a runtime of 1 second and selects only 10 records. Which of the following could be the reason for the long runtime?

   A. There is a hardware bottleneck (a CPU or I/O bottleneck) on the database server.

   B. There is a network problem between the application server and the database server.

   C. The database optimizer has created an inefficient execution plan—for example, by choosing an inefficient index.

   D. There is no appropriate index for the SQL statement.

   E. There are exclusive lock waits in the database.

3. In the Shared SQL Area Monitor, you find an SQL statement with 10,000 logical read accesses per execution (indicated as Gets/Execution). Which of the following could be the reason for this high number of read accesses?

   A. There is a hardware bottleneck (a CPU or I/O bottleneck) on the database server.

   B. There is a network problem between the application server and the database server.

   C. The database optimizer has created an inefficient execution plan—for example, by choosing an inefficient index.

   D. There is no appropriate index for the SQL statement.

   E. There are exclusive lock waits in the database.

   F. A large number of records are being transferred from the database to the ABAP program.

A Performance Analysis Roadmaps and Checklists

Appendix A contains the most important procedure roadmaps and checklists for performance analysis of SAP-based software components.

The prerequisites for performing an analysis are as follows:

- That the component starts without error.
- There are still sufficient work processes available to run the performance analysis.
- If there are no available work processes, then you can call the SAP auxiliary program *dpmon*. This program is called on the operating-system level and enables you to access basically the same information as that found in the Work Process Overview.

The checklists for performance analysis contain references to other sections in this book that explain the available optimization options. Please ensure that you carefully consider the explanatory and cautionary notes in these sections before making any changes to your system.

Roadmaps

The roadmaps in this section explain how to proceed through the most important performance monitors. The following key explains the icons that appear in the procedure roadmaps (see Figures A.1 through A.9):

- **Rectangular monitor icon:**
  This tells you to start a particular performance monitor.
- **Question mark icon:**
  This indicates that you are at a decision point. If you can answer the question beside this icon with Yes, then you may proceed as described in the following line of the roadmap.
- **Exclamation mark icon:**
  This indicates the intermediate status of the analysis. Proceed to the next point on the roadmap.
- **Horizontal arrow icon:**
  This indicates another procedure roadmap. Continue the analysis in the roadmap indicated.
- **Tools icon:**
  This indicates possible solutions for performance problems. (See also the checklists for performance analysis in the next section.)

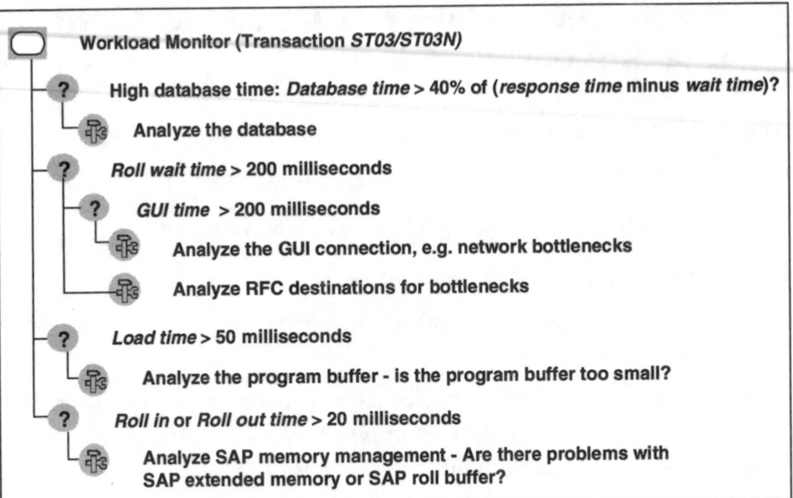

Figure A.1 Workload analysis I: General performance problems

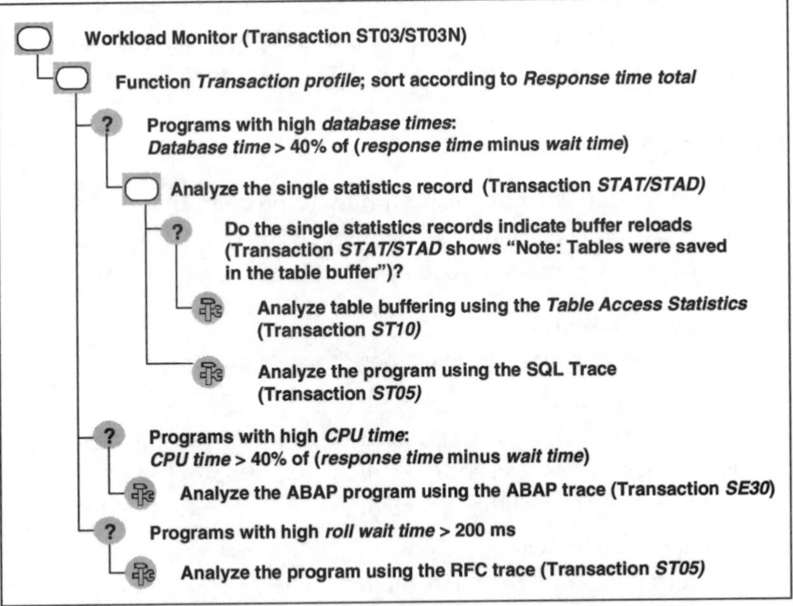

Figure A.2 Workload analysis II: Specific performance problems

You can access the monitors mentioned in the roadmaps as follows:

- To access the Systemwide Work Process Overview, use Transaction SM66; or from the SAP initial screen, select

  Tools · Administration · Monitor · Performance · Exceptions/Users · Active users · All processes.

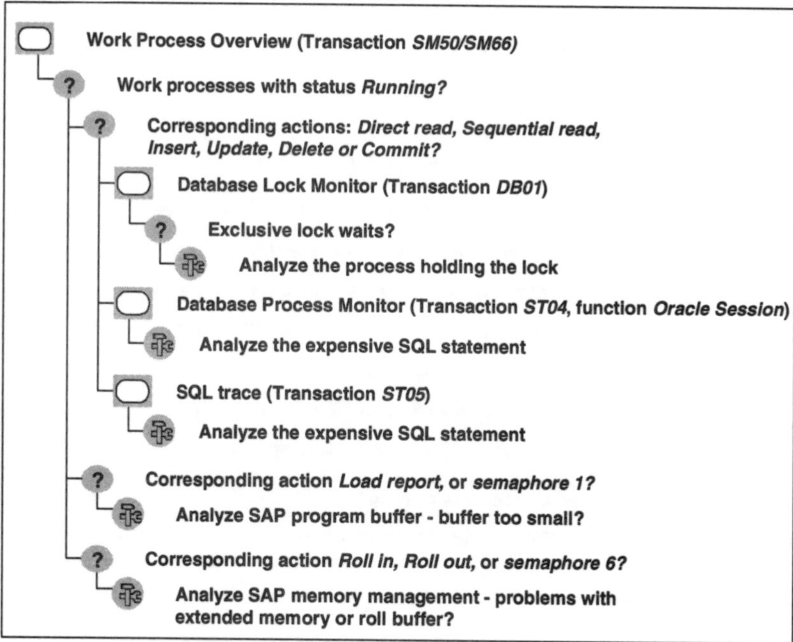

Figure A.3 Detailed analysis of SAP work processes

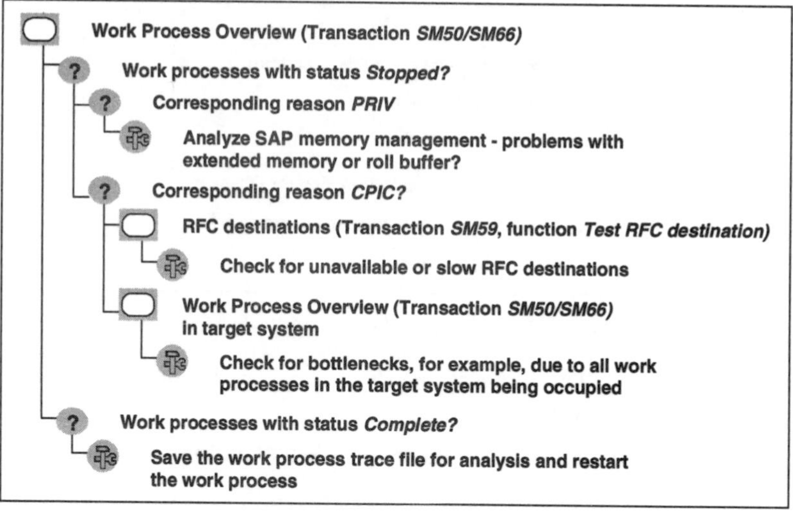

Figure A.4 Detailed analysis of SAP work processes

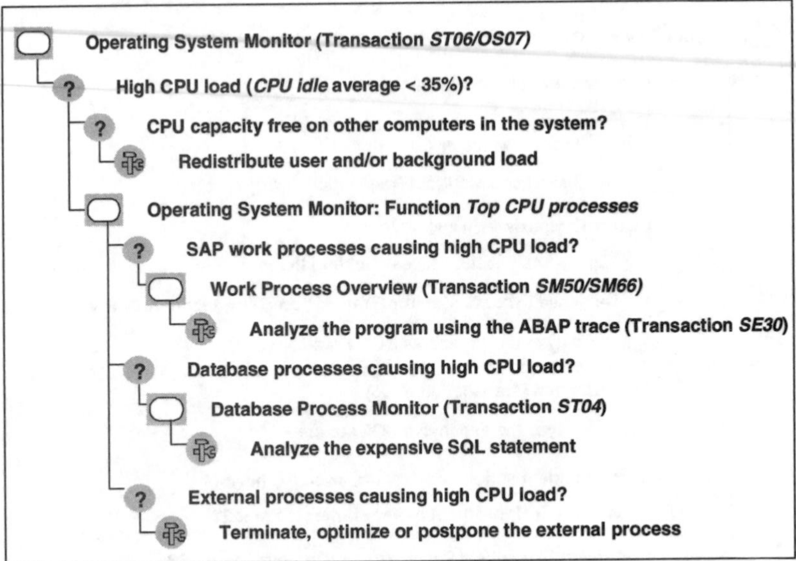

Figure A.5 Detailed analysis of a hardware bottleneck: CPU

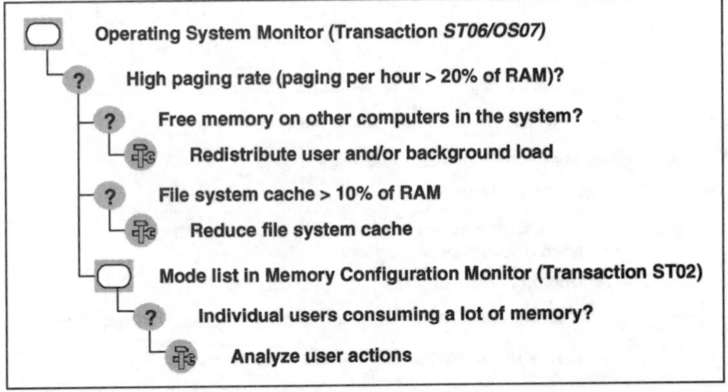

Figure A.6 Detailed analysis of a hardware bottleneck: Main memory

- To access the Alert Monitor, use Transaction RZ20; or from the SAP initial screen, select

  Tools • CCMS • Control/Monitoring • Alert Monitor.

- To access the Workload Monitor, use Transactions ST03 or ST03N; or from the SAP initial screen, select

  Tools • Administration • Monitor • Performance • Workload • Analysis

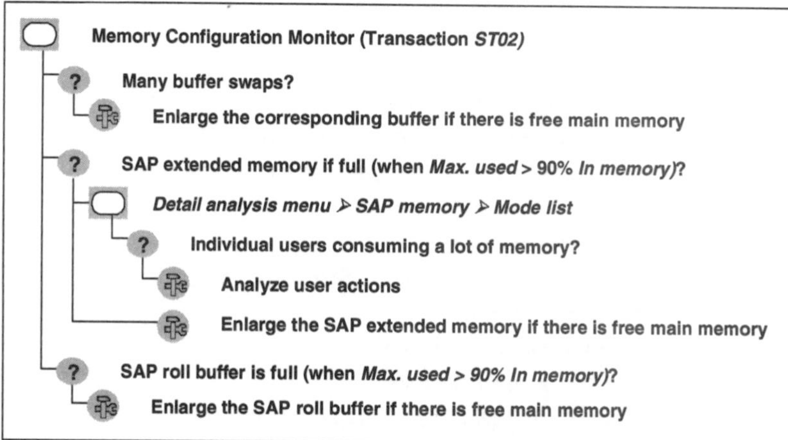

Figure A.7 Detailed analysis of SAP memory configuration

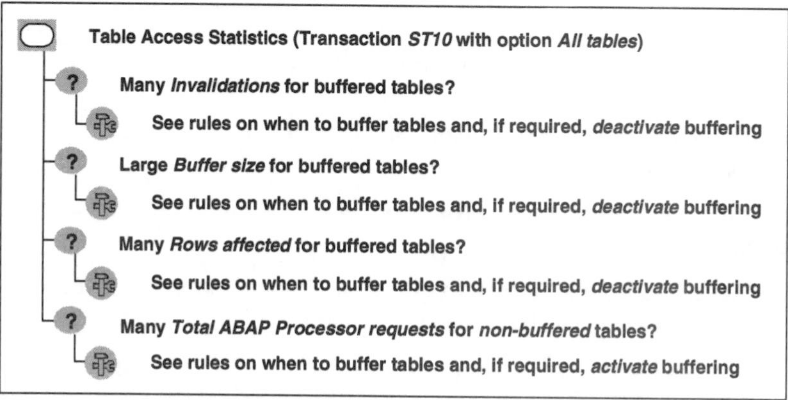

Figure A.8 Optimization of table buffering

- To access the Single Record Statistics, use Transactions STAD or STAD.
- To access the Remote Hardware Activity Monitor, use Transaction OS07; or from the SAP initial screen, select

  Tools · Administration · Monitor · Performance · Operating system · Remote · Activity
- Appendix B, "Database Monitors, Buffers, and SQL Execution Plans", contains a list of the menu paths for the performance monitors in the different database systems.

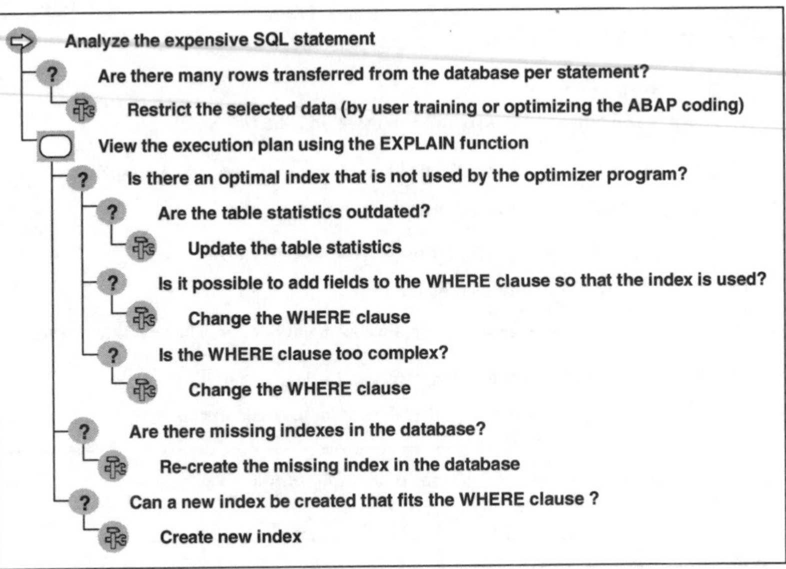

Figure A.9 Optimization of expensive SQL statements

- To access the Memory Configuration Monitor, use Transaction ST02; or from the SAP initial screen, select

  Tools · Administration · Monitor · Performance · Setup/Buffers · Buffers

- To access the Table Access Statistics, use Transaction ST10; or from the SAP initial screen, select

  Tools · Administration · Monitor · Performance · Setup/Buffers · Calls

  Make the appropriate selections and press **Enter**.

- To start, stop, or display a Performance Trace, use Transaction ST05; or from the SAP initial screen, select

  System · Utilities · Performance Trace

- To access the SAP Internet Transaction Server:

  Start the ITS administration instance in a browser, using the following URL address: `http://<sapwebserver>.<company.com>:<portnumber>/scripts/wgate/admin!`, where `<company.com>` is your company Internet address, `<sapwebserver>` is the ITS Web server, and `<portnumber>` is the TCP port over which the administration instance "listens".

Checklists

This section contains problem checklists—that is, short summaries for individual problems that are frequently identified in performance analysis. Each checklist classifies the degree of priority of the problem to be solved; provides indications and procedures for finding and analyzing the problem; gives applicable solutions as well as references to portions of this book relevant to the problem; and points out essential reading before attempting to solve the problem; and furnishes within a text box the reminder, "When using the checklists, do not perform any changes in your system without referring to the detailed information and warnings in the indicated sections of this book."

The following priorities are suggested in the checklists:

- *Very high* priority is reserved for when there is a danger that performance will soon cause system standstill and there are no longer sufficient free work processes available to analyze or solve the problem.
- *High* priority is for problems that are likely to drastically reduce systemwide performance.
- *Medium* priority is for problems that are likely to drastically reduce the performance of individual programs or application servers. Do not underestimate the impact of these problems on critical business processes or the possibility of the problem escalating.
- *Low* priority performance problems are not listed in the checklists.

Detailed Analysis of Hardware Resources

Problem:	CPU Bottleneck due to High Resource Consumption From Individual Processes
Priority	Medium to high.
Indications and procedures	A computer has less than 20% CPU capacity available. Check this using the Top CPU processes function in the Operating System Monitor. To access this function, use Transaction ST06 and select **Detail analysis menu • Top CPU processes**. The screen that appears shows individual processes that occupy considerable CPU over long periods of time.
Solution	Use the Work Process Overview (Transaction SM50 or SM66) to identify the SAP work process, the program and the user; then analyse the program or reschedule it. Identify the database processes in the Database Process Monitor (ST04 Detailed analysis menu Oracle Session [for example]), and optimize the corresponding SQL statement. For external processes with high CPU utilization: Optimize or terminate them.
See	Chapter 2, section "Monitoring Hardware" on page 70.

Problem:	CPU Bottleneck due to Non-Optimal Load Distribution
Priority	Medium: This problem can lead to high response times on specific computers.
Indications and procedures	In distributed system with multiple computers, you detect a hardware bottleneck on at least one computer, while other computers still have available, unused resources.
Solution	Redistribute the SAP work processes, after which you may need to reset the associated virtual memory areas, buffers and user distribution.
See	Chapter 2, section "Monitoring Hardware" on page 70, Chapter 5.

Problem:	Main Memory Bottleneck
Priority	Medium to high: This problem can lead to high response times on specific computers.
Indications and procedures	A computer displays high paging rates. High paging rates are especially critical for increased CPU usage. Calculate the main memory allocated by SAP instances and the database, and compare it with the physically available main memory on the individual computers. If the allocated memory exceeds the physically available main memory by more than 50%, and there are high paging rates, you have a main memory bottleneck.
Solution	If the load cannot be redistributed (same as the previous problem above), then the main memory will have to be expanded.
See	Chapter 2, section "Monitoring Hardware" on page 70.

Detailed Analysis of SAP Work Processes

Problem:	Terminated Work Processes
Priority	High to very high.
Indications and procedures	In the Local Work Process Overview (Transaction SM50), if you detect numerous terminated work processes (indicated as **complete** in the column **Status**) and find that you cannot restart them, it is likely that there is a problem with the R/3 kernel or with logging on to the database.
Solution	Check whether the SAP kernel version is up to date by calling Transaction SM51 and selecting **Release Info**. Refer to the SAP Service Marketplace for relevant SAP Notes or contact SAP Support.
See	Chapter 2, section "Analyzing SAP Work Processes" on page 107.

Problem:	Work Processes Stuck in Private Mode or in Roll In or Roll Out
Priority	Medium to high: This problem can lead to high response times on specific computers.
Indications and procedures	More than 20% of the work processes are indicated in the Work Process Overview (Transaction SM50 or SM66) as being in mode PRIV or in roll in or roll out. The problem is in SAP memory management.
Solution	Correctly set the parameters of SAP memory management—for example, **em/initial_size_MB and rdisp/ROLL_SHM, ztta/roll_extension**. See also the checklist for SAP Extended Memory Too Small.
See	Chapter 2, sections "Analyzing SAP Work Processes" on page 107, and "Analyzing SAP Memory Management" on page 98.

Problem:	Deactivated Update Service
Priority	Very high: This problem can cause a standstill in the SAP system.
Indications and procedures	All update work processes (indicated as UPD in the Work Process Overview) are occupied. Transaction SM13 indicates that the update has been deactivated.
Solution	Call the SAP system log (Transaction SM21) and check whether the update service has been deactivated. The system log contains an entry for the time, the user, and the reason for the deactivation. Resolve the reported problem—for example, a database error. Then reactivate the update service with Transaction SM13.
See	Chapter 2, sections "Analyzing SAP Work Processes" on page 107, and "Monitoring the Database" on page 79.

Problem:	High Database Response Times
Priority	Medium to very high.
Indications and procedures	The column Action in the Work Process Overview (Transaction SM50 or SM66) indicates Sequential read, Direct read, Waiting for DB lock, or other database activities for numerous work processes.
Solution	The problem is related to the database. Therefore, rather than increasing the number of SAP work processes, examine the database more closely. (See below, under "Detailed Analysis of the Database".)
See	Chapter 2, sections "Analyzing SAP Work Processes" on page 107, and "Monitoring the Database" on page 79.

Problem:	Long Runtimes for Individual Programs
Priority	Medium: This problem can lead to high response times for specific programs.
Indications and procedures	Work processes are blocked by programs with long runtimes. This is indicated in the Work Process Overview.
Solution	Determine whether the related ABAP program is still running properly. Analyze the affected programs and optimize or terminate them as appropriate.
See	Chapter 2, section "Analyzing SAP Work Processes" on page 107, and Chapter 4, "Performance Analysis for ABAP-Programs".

Problem:	Non-Optimal Load Distribution
Priority	Medium: This problem can lead to high response times on specific computers.
Indications and procedures	In a distributed system with multiple computers, you detect a work process bottleneck on at least one computer while other computers still have free work processes.
Solution	Call Transaction SMLG and check whether all the servers are available for load distribution with logon groups, or whether logon errors have been reported. Use Transaction SMLG to optimize the logon groups.
See	Chapter 2, section "Analyzing SAP Work Processes" on page 107, and Chapter 5, "Workload Distribution".

Problem:	Insufficient Work Processes
Priority	Medium: This problem can lead to high response times on specific computers.
Indications and procedures	None of the previously listed problems apply, but there is still a problem with work processes.
Solution	If the computer has sufficient reserves of CPU and main memory, increase the number of SAP work processes.
See	Chapter 2, section "Analyzing SAP Work Processes" on page 107, and Chapter 5, "Workload Distribution".

Detailed Analysis of the Database

Problem:	**Long Database Locks**
Priority	Medium to very high: This problem can cause a standstill in the SAP system.
Indications and procedures	Call the Database Lock Monitor with Transaction DB01. Refresh this monitor several times within a short time frame and check whether long-lasting wait situations occur because of database locks. In the Work Process Overview (Transaction SM50 or SM66), use the fields **Client host** and **Client PID** to determine the programs and the users holding the locks. Determine whether the related ABAP program is still running properly.
Solution	Terminate a program or a process manually if required, after consulting the affected users.
See	Chapter 2, section "Monitoring the Database" on page 79.

Problem:	**CPU Bottleneck on the Database Server**
Priority	High: This problem can lead to high database response times.
Indications and procedures	Call the Operating System Monitor (Transaction ST06) on the database server and see whether it shows a CPU bottleneck.
Solution	Check whether the CPU bottleneck originates from expensive SQL statements, incorrectly set database buffers, or an I/O bottleneck. You may need to reduce the load on the database server or increase its CPU capacity.
See	Chapter 2, sections "Monitoring the Database" on page 79, and "Monitoring Hardware" on page 70, and Chapter 5, "Workload Distribution".

Problem:	**Number of Logical Processors for the Database Instance**
Priority	High: This problem can lead to high database response times.
Indications and procedures	There is usually a profile parameter that specifies the maximum number of processors that are physically available to the database instance. Such parameters include MAXCPU (for ADABAS D) and NUMCPUVPS (for Informix). Check whether this parameter is optimally configured.
Solution	If necessary, adjust this parameter.
See	Chapter 2, section "Monitoring the Database" on page 79, and Chapter 5, "Workload Distribution".

Problem:	Database Buffer Too Small
Priority	Medium to high: This problem can lead to high database response times.
Indications and procedures	Call the Database Performance Monitor (Transaction ST04) and check whether the buffer quality and other key figures match the recommended values.
Solution	Increase the size of the respective buffer once by 25% and check whether the quality improves.
See	Chapter 2, section "Monitoring the Database" on page 79.

Problem:	Expensive SQL Statements
Priority	Medium to high: This problem can lead to high database response times.
Indications and procedures	In the Database Process Monitor, check whether there are any expensive SQL statements—that is, statements with either Disk reads that amount to more than 10% of the total physical reads, or Buffer gets that amount to more than 10% of the total reads. To access the Database Process Monitor, call the Database Performance Monitor (Transaction ST04). Then, for Oracle, select **Detail analysis menu • SQL request**, and for Informix, select **Detail analysis menu • SQL statement**. For other database examples, see Appendix B.
See	Chapter 2, section "Monitoring the Database" on page 79, and Chapter 11, "Optimizing SQL Statements".

Problem:	Database I/O Bottleneck
Priority	Medium to high: This problem can lead to high database response times.
Indications and procedures	Call the Database Performance Monitor (Transaction ST04). Then, for Oracle, select **Detail analysis menu • File system requests**, and for Informix, select **Detail analysis menu • Chunk I/O Activity**. Call the Operating System Monitor for the database server (Transaction ST06). Select **Detail analysis menu • Disk** (under the header Snapshot analysis). If the value in the column Util is greater than 50%, this indicates an I/O bottleneck. Check whether data files that are heavily written to reside on these disks.
Solution	Resolve the read/write (I/O) bottleneck by improving table distribution in the file system. Ensure that heavily accessed files do not reside on the same disk. These include the files for the swap space, the redo log, and the transaction log.
See	Chapter 2, sections "Monitoring the Database" on page 79, and "Monitoring Hardware" on page 70.

Problem:	Statistics for the Database Optimizer Are Obsolete or Not Available
Priority	Medium to high: This problem can lead to high database response times.
Indications and procedures	To check whether optimizer statistics are created regularly, call the DBA Planning Calendar. To do this, from the SAP initial screen, select (**Tools • CCMS • DB administration • DB scheduling**).
Solution	Schedule the program for updating statistics.
See	Chapter 2, section "Monitoring the Database" on page 79, and Chapter 11, "Optimizing SQL Statements", and SAP Online Help for topics in database administration.

Problem:	Missing Database Indexes
Priority	Very high, if a primary index is missing: This can cause data inconsistencies. Medium, if a secondary index is missing: This can cause high response times for individual programs.
Indications and procedures	Check whether there are any missing database indexes by calling the monitor for analyzing tables and indexes (Transaction DB02) and by selecting **Detail analysis menu • State on disk**: *Missing indices*.
Solution	Re-create the missing indexes.
See	Chapter 2, section "Monitoring the Database" on page 79, and Chapter 11, "Optimizing SQL Statements".

Problem:	Large Differences in Database Times Caused by Buffer Load Process
Priority	Medium to high: This problem can lead to high response times for specific programs.
Indications and procedures	To view occasional, long database accesses to buffered tables, use one of the following: the Local Work Process Overview (Transaction SM50), an SQL trace (Transaction ST05), or the single statistics records (Transaction STAT).
Solution	Call table access statistics and verify the efficiency of table buffering.
See	Chapter 9.

Problem:	Network Problems
Priority	Medium to high: This problem can lead to high response times on specific computers.
Indications and procedures	Determine whether there is a network problem between the database server and the application server by comparing SQL trace results on these two servers.

Problem:	Network Problems
Solution	Resolve the network problem between the two servers. A detailed analysis of network problems is not possible from within the SAP system, so use network-specific tools.
See	Chapter 2, section "Monitoring the Database" on page 79, and Chapter 4, section "Evaluating an SQL Trace" on page 155.

Detailed Analysis of Memory Management and the Buffers

Problem:	Extended Memory Is Too Small
Priority	High.
Indications and procedures	To determine whether either the extended memory or the roll buffer is too small, use the SAP Memory Configuration Monitor (Transaction ST02). See also the checklist entitled Work Processes Stuck in Private Mode or in Roll In or Roll Out.
Solution	Correct SAP memory configuration parameters such as **em/initial_size_MB, rdisp/ROLL_SHM, and ztta/roll_extension**. If you have sufficient main memory on the server, you can increase the memory size by 20 to 50%. Check whether this improves the situation.
See	Chapter 2, section "Analyzing SAP Memory Management" on page 98, and Chapter 8, "Memory Management".

Problem:	Displacements in SAP Buffers
Priority	Medium.
Indications and procedures	Look for displacements in the SAP buffers in the column Swaps in the SAP Memory Configuration Monitor (Transaction ST02). Displacements mean that the buffers are configured too small.
Solution	Increase the maximum number of buffer entries or increase the size of the respective buffer, provided that the computer still has sufficient main memory reserves.
See	Chapter 2, section "Analyzing SAP Memory Management" on page 98.

SAP Notes on Internet Transaction Server

Problem:	All ITS work processes (work threads) or all sessions are occupied.
Priority	High.
Indications and procedures	The ITS administration and monitoring tool indicates that all ITS work processes or all sessions are occupied.

Problem:	All ITS work processes (work threads) or all sessions are occupied.
Solution	Short term: Restart the ITS. Medium term: Increase the number of processes or optimize the load distribution.
See	Chapter 7, section "Performing a Bottleneck Analysis for the ITS" on page 239.

Problem:	Insufficient addressable (virtual) memory.
Priority	High.
Indications and procedures	Enter the problem in the AGate log (AGate.trc).
Solution	Start more AGate processes per ITS instance.
See	Chapter 7, section "Performing a Bottleneck Analysis for the ITS" on page 239.

Problem:	Standstill due to a lack of disk space.
Priority	Very high.
Indications and procedures	Enter the problem in the AGate log and in the operating system monitor.
Solution	Determine the cause of the rapid growth in data, for example, reorganized log files. Alternatively, the trace level may have been reduced after the generation of a detailed runtime analysis.
See	Chapter 7, section "Performing a Bottleneck Analysis for the ITS" on page 239.

B Database Monitors, Buffers, and SQL Execution Plans

The SAP Basis currently supports seven different relational database management systems, each with its own architecture:

- SAP DB
- DB2 UDB for UNIX and Windows; DB2 UDB for iSeries; DB2 UDB for zSeries
- INFORMIX Online for SAP
- ORACLE
- Microsoft SQL Server

However, the SAP Basis has database monitors that cover basic database functioning irrespective of the database system.

Database Process Monitor

The *Database Process Monitor* (see Table B.1) displays the currently active database processes, which are called agents, shadow processes, or threads, depending on the database system. The monitor displays the SQL statements that are being processed, and can indicate the SAP work process to which a database process is allocated.

Use the Database Process Monitor to identify currently running, expensive SQL statements. With the process ID (in the column **Clnt proc.**), you can find the corresponding SAP work process, SAP user, and ABAP program indicated in the Work Process Overview (Transaction SM50).

Database System	From the SAP Initial Screen, Select...
SAP DB	Tools • Administration • Monitor • Performance • Database • Activity • Detail analysis menu • DB processes
DB2 UDB for Unix and Windows	Tools • Administration • Monitor • Performance • Database • Activity • Performance • Applications
DB2 UDB for zSeries	Tools • Administration • Monitor • Performance • Database • Activity • Detail analysis menu • Thread Activity
Informix	Tools • Administration • Monitor • Performance • Database • Activity • Detail analysis menu • Informix session

Table B.1 Menu Paths for Accessing the Database Process Monitor According to Database System

Database System	From the SAP Initial Screen, Select...
ORACLE	Tools • Administration • Monitor • Performance • Database • Activity • Detail analysis menu • Oracle session
MS SQL Server	Tools • Administration • Monitor • Performance • Database • Activity • Detail analysis menu • SQL processes

Table B.1 Menu Paths for Accessing the Database Process Monitor According to Database System (contd.)

Shared SQL Area Monitor

For almost all database systems, you can monitor *statistics for the previously executed SQL statements* (see Table B.2). Monitoring these statistics is also known as monitoring the *shared SQL area* (which in some database systems is called the *Shared Cursor Cache* or *Shared SQL Cache*). These statistics on the shared SQL area help you to analyze expensive SQL statements. They cover, for example, the number of executions of an SQL statement; the number of logical and physical read accesses per statement; the number of rows that were read; and the response times. In some database systems, the system starts collecting these statistics when the database is started. For other database systems, statistics collection has to be activated explicitly.

Monitor the shared SQL area to identify and analyze expensive SQL statements that were executed previously.

Database System	From the SAP Initial Screen, Select...
SAP DB	Tools • Administration • Monitor • Performance • Database • Activity • Detail analysis menu • Diagnoses monitor
DB2 UDB for Unix and Windows	Tools • Administration • Monitor • Performance • Database • Activity • Performance • SQL Cache
DB2 UDB for iSeries	Tools • Administration • Monitor • Performance • Database • Activity • Detail analysis menu • SQL request Tools • Administration • Monitor • Performance • Database • Activity • Detail analysis menu • 50 slowest queries
DB2 UDB for zSeries	Tools • Administration • Monitor • Performance • Database • Activity • Detail analysis menu • Stmt Cache Statistics
Informix	Tools • Administration • Monitor • Performance • Database • Activity • Detail analysis menu • SQL statement

Table B.2 Menu Paths for Accessing the SAP Monitor for the Shared SQL Area According to Database System

Database System	From the SAP Initial Screen, Select...
ORACLE	Tools • Administration • Monitor • Performance • Database • Activity • Detail analysis menu • SQL request
MS SQL Server	Tools • Administration • Monitor • Performance • Database • Activity • Detail analysis menu • SAP Stats on SPs (SAP database interface statistics) or Tools • Administration • Monitor • Performance • Database • Activity • Detail analysis menu • SQL request (information form the SQL Server system tables, for SAP Basis 6.10 and later)

Table B.2 Menu Paths for Accessing the SAP Monitor for the Shared SQL Area According to Database System (contd.)

Hard Disk Monitor

To ensure optimal database performance, the load on the hard disks should be spread as evenly or symmetrically as possible—that is, all disks should show roughly equal numbers of read and write accesses.

When analyzing the distribution of I/O on the hard disk, use the Hard Disk Monitor (see Table B.3). This lets you identify files that are accessed especially frequently. These areas are sometimes called *hot spots*.

Database System	From the SAP Initial Screen, Select...
SAP DB	Tools • Administration • Monitor • Performance • Database • Activity • Detail analysis menu • Runtime environment
DB2 UDB for Unix and Windows	Tools • Administration • Monitor • Performance • Database • Activity • Performance • Tables Tools • Administration • Monitor • Performance • Database • Activity • Performance • Tablespaces
DB2 UDB for iSeries	Tools • Administration • Monitor • Performance • Database • Activity • Detail analysis menu • File activity
Informix	Tools • Administration • Monitor • Performance • Database • Activity • Detail analysis menu • Chunk I/O Activity
ORACLE	Tools • Administration • Monitor • Performance • Database • Activity • Detail analysis menu • Filesystem request
MS SQL Server	Tools • Administration • Monitor • Performance • Database • State on Disk • DB Analysis • I/O per File (SAP Basis 6.10 and later)

Table B.3 Menu Paths for Accessing the Hard Disk Monitor According to Database System

Database Lock Monitor

The SAP Basis provides the *Database Lock Monitor to help you identify exclusive lock wait situations on the database*. Use Transaction DB01 to call this monitor for almost all database systems, or, from the SAP initial screen, select

> **Tools · Administration · Monitor · Performance · Database · Activity · Detail analysis menu · Exclusive lockwaits**

or

> **Tools · Administration · Monitor · Performance · Database · Exclusive lockwaits**

With MS SQL Server, you can display a history of all lock wait situations that last more than one minute, by enabling the **Turn collector job on** option in the **Blocking lockstats** Monitor.

For DB2 UDB for Windows and UNIX, select

> **Tools · Administration · Monitor · Performance · Database · Activity · Performance · Lockwaits**

For DB2 UDB for iSeries, select

> **Tools · Administration · Monitor · Performance · Database · Wait situations**

Use the Database Lock Monitor to identify exclusive lock waits on the database.

Monitoring Database Buffers

Every database has different *buffers* in main memory to reduce the number of accesses to the hard disks. The buffers contain user data in tables and administrative information for the database. Accessing objects in main memory through these buffers is 10 to 100 times faster than accessing the hard disks. The main monitor for database buffers is the Database Performance Monitor. To call this monitor for any database system, use Transaction ST04, or, from the SAP initial screen, select

> **Tools · Administration · Monitor · Performance · Database · Activity**

The screen **Database Performance Analysis: Database Overview** is displayed.

SAP DB

SAP DB allocates the following areas in the virtual memory of the database server to accelerate database accesses:

- *Data cache*, which buffers table pages and index pages.
- *Converter cache*, which stores the logical numbering assigned to physical page numbers for database administration.
- *Catalog cache*, which stores the SQL statement context, including its table-accessing strategy or execution plan.
- *Rollback buffer (rollback cache)*, which is used to speed up rollbacks that may be required for incomplete transactions. In a normal SAP environment, this cache is not often used.

The buffer quality of the converter cache and the data cache is particularly important for the performance of an SAP DB database. The converter cache and data cache reside in the shared memory of the database server.

SAP DB converter cache

To speed up accesses to database data, pages from the converter area on the hard disk are held in the *converter cache* as a part of main memory. The converter area on the hard disk of an SAP DB database is used to assign physical page numbers to logical numbers for database administration. The size of a data page in an SAP DB database is 4 KB. The ideal size for the converter cache depends on the data volume in the SAP DB database. As a guideline value, the size of the converter cache should be equivalent to approximately 0.6% of the occupied pages in the database. The hit ratio for this cache should be around 98%. Extreme deviations from these guideline values can cause delays, especially when performing database backups. The size and hit ratio of the catalog cache are displayed in the **Catalog** row in the Database Performance Monitor.

An SAP DB database requires 50 GB of space on the hard disk. You can assume that converter pages require roughly 300 MB (0.6% of 50 GB). The optimal size of the converter cache is therefore 300 MB.

SAP DB Data Cache

To find out the size of the *SAP DB data cache* in the Database Performance Monitor (Transaction ST04), look in the screen area **Cache Activity** in the column **Size Kb** for the row **Data**. A hit ratio (indicated as the **Hitrate**) of at least 99% is optimal. The size of the data cache should be at least 160 MB, but may vary depending on the size of the database and the SAP application modules being used.

SAP DB Catalog Cache

For each active SAP DB database user, a *catalog cache* is created in the virtual memory of the database server. Note that a database user is not the same as a mySAP.com component user. Each SAP work process opens a connection to the database, so the number of database users is related to the number of configured SAP work processes. The catalog cache is used to buffer the context of the SQL statement, including the table-accessing strategy or execution plan of the statement. The catalog cache enables multiple executions of the same SQL statement to refer back to an execution plan that is already recorded in the catalog cache. Hit ratios of approximately 90% are desirable. The size and the hit ratio of the catalog cache are indicated in the Database Performance Monitor (Transaction ST04) in the row **Catalog**.

Sizing for the virtual memory areas of SAP DB database instances to be allocated at instance startup is performed using the SAP DB administration tool, **XControl**. Poor hit ratios are not always due to insufficient sizing, so investigate the causes of poor buffer quality before changing the size of the buffers. See Table B.4 for a summary of guideline values for evaluating SAP DB database buffers.

Database System	Name of Buffer	Hit Ratio Guideline Value	Parameter
SAP DB	Converter cache	≥ 98%	CONVERTER_CACHE
	Data cache	≥ 99%	DATA_CACHE
	Catalog cache	≥ 90%	CAT_CACHE_SUPPLY
	Rollback cache	≥ 90%	ROLLBACK_CACHE

Table B.4 Guideline Values for Evaluating the Performance of SAP DB Database Buffers

DB2 Universal Database (for Unix and Windows)

See the section "Analyzing the Database Buffer" on page 80 in Chapter 2.

DB2 Universal Database for iSeries

Since the database and the operating system are so closely linked in iSeries, the analysis of performance problems should always start with the Operating System Monitor (Transaction ST06). Memory pool paging, disk utilization, and the OS/400 system values are critical for system performance, as is CPU utilization.

The main memory is partitioned into memory pools, which applications can utilize as needed. An overview of the main memory configuration can be displayed by selecting **Detailed Analysis Menu · Pool** in the Operating System Monitor (ST06), or by means of the command *WRKSYSSTS* on the operating system level.

The paging parameter "DB Fault + Non-DB Fault" for the *MACHINE pool should remain significantly below the value of 10 missing pages/sec. For the *BASE pool, the number of dialog steps must be considered when determining the maximum permissible paging value. The empirical formula for this is

*Y [msec] = mean((DB Faults + Non-DB Faults) / (number of dialog steps)) * 10 msec*

where Y is the time per dialog step that is spent reading from and writing to the hard disk. The value of 10 msec is an overall estimate of the hard disk service time; for a sufficiently allocated system, the time is usually much lower. A higher paging rate could be an indication of a main memory bottleneck.

The main memory configuration output contains a right-hand column with the heading "Paging Option". In this column, the value *CALC should be set for the memory pool to which the SAP system is associated. *CALC activates the expert cache, which contains data for frequently processed SQL queries in the main memory, thereby reducing the need for hard disk access.

With iSeries, the hard disks play an important part in determining the system performance. The % busy rate (operating system command *WRKDSKSTS*) should be less than 30% per disk. Values in excess of this have a major impact on total system performance. High % busy rate values are often caused by poor data distribution on the hard disk. This problem can be resolved on the operating system level by using the tools TRCASPBAL and STRASPBAL.

Furthermore, the OS/400 system value settings should be checked; suggested values can be found in SAP Note 428855.

A memory-resident database monitor is available for analyzing time-consuming SQL statements. This monitor is contained in SAP Basis 4.6B and later. For earlier versions, the monitor can be installed separately (SAP Note 135369). The database monitor is activated by the SAP profile parameter **as4/dbmon/enable = 1**. Data for SQL queries executed on the system are first stored in main memory, and are then copied in regular intervals by SAP jobs to corresponding tables. Transaction ST04 takes you to a screen that shows statistical information, the current status of data, and the number of physical and logical read accesses. **Detailed Analysis Menu · 50 slowest statements** produces a list of the 50 most time-consuming SQL statements. You can sort on the database time that the respective SQL statement used since the program was last loaded.

The display contains the name of the SQL packet and various execution times. The SQL packet is usually used to determine the table name or ABAP report, in which the statement in question was executed. Furthermore, you can click the SQL packet name to show the SQL explain which provides information about the implementation of the SQL query.

In addition, the submenus **Detailed Analysis Menu · Index Advised** and **Detailed Analysis Menu · Index Created** in Transaction ST04 are important for a first-order analysis. This submenu shows SQL statements for which the database optimizer either suggests a suitable index (from the viewpoint of the optimizer) or temporarily creates an index. Temporary index creation for frequently used statements can put an especially large load on the database. Therefore, you should check if system performance would be improved by creating a permanent index, although you should remember that the addition of indexes in tables that are frequently changed can also be disadvantageous, because these indexes always need to be updated.

DB2 Universal Database for OS/390 and z/OS

DB2 allocates various buffers in the main memory on the database server:

- The data buffer contains several (virtual) buffer pools and hiperpools (optional), and buffers table and index pages.
- The record identifier (RID) pool buffers index pages that are accessed with the list **Prefetch**.
- The sort pool buffers data used to control the sorting of data.
- The dynamic statement cache buffers execution plans of SQL statements. It consists of the system-wide Environment Descriptor Manager (EDM) pool and local database thread caches.

Data Buffer

With DB2 V5, buffer pools can be created for 4-KB and 32-KB pages; for DB2 V6 and V7, 8-KB and 16-KB pages can also be created. The number of possible buffer pools depends on the DB2 version. The size of a buffer pool can be changed with the command **ALTER BUFFERPOOL**. The *Read*

Random Hit Ratio measures the quality of a buffer pool; that is, for random read accesses, the number of successful pool accesses is compared with the number of disk accesses. A hiperpool, which resides in expanded storage, can optionally be associated with each buffer pool, as long as the hardware has expanded storage. A hiperpool is considered to be efficiently utilized if it can be used mostly for read operations, with only a few write operations to the hiperpool. This ratio is assessed by means of the indicator *Hiperpool Efficiency*. If all table spaces are buffered by only one buffer pool, then the tables will compete for table spaces on this buffer. In order to achieve the best possible data buffering, table spaces that are frequently accessed should be associated with their own buffer pools (buffer pool tuning). The attributes of these buffer pools can be set to optimize the access mode (random or sequential) and properties (size, number of changes).

Dynamic Statement Cache

The SAP Basis database interface uses dynamic SQL statements, which are executed in two phases (stages): The first phase is the "Prepare Phase", in which the database optimizer determines the optimal access path. The second phase is the "Execution Phase", in which this optimal access path is used to access data. During the prepare phase, a *Skeleton* is created for every different SQL statement. A skeleton consists of the executable (prepared) statement and the statement string (the statement written in a character set). Skeletons are first buffered locally in the local cache of the respective thread. The DB2 parameter **CACHEDYN = YES** ensures that a skeleton for each different dynamic SQL statement is also stored in the EDM pool. The EDM pool also contains skeleton cursor tables, skeleton package tables, cursor tables, and package tables, as well as database descriptors. With DB2 V6 and later, the EDM pool can optionally use a data space.

Because SAP programs run with the bind option **KEEPDYNAMIC(YES)**, statement skeletons (in addition to COMMIT time points) remain in the local thread caches. When a statement is executed, the local cache and the EDM pool are searched for a prepared statement. If one is found, then the prepare and execution phases are avoided or shortened.

The *Global Cache Hit Ratio* measures how well the EDM pool acts as a system-wide buffer for SQL statement skeletons. The *Local Cache Hit Ratio* measures the quality of all local thread caches; that is, the number of immediately used statements is compared to the number statements that are displaced from the local cache. The *Reprepare Ratio* measures the number of statements that were displaced from the local cache, because the maximum number (MAXKEEPD) of statements that can be held in the local cache was exceeded. The size of all local caches is indirectly set by the DB2 parameter MAXKEEPD (the number of prepared dynamic SQL statements, in addition to the COMMIT time point). The local caches occupy a significant portion of the main memory.

Database System	Name of Buffer	Hit Ratio Guideline Value	Parameter
DB2 for OS/390 and z/OS	Data buffer (buffer pools und hiperpools)	Read random hit ratio ≥ 95% hiperpool efficiency ≥ 10%	
	RID pool		MAXRBLK
	Sort pool		SPRMSP
	EDM pool and EDM pool data space (global part of the dynamic statement cache)	Global cache hit ratio ≥ 95%	EDMPOOL EDMDSPAC CACHEDYN
	Thread-local cache (local part of the dynamic statement cache)	Local cache hit ratio ≥ 50%, reprepare ratio < 50%	EDMPOOL EDMDSPAC MAXKEEPD CACHEDYN

Table B.5 Guideline Values for Evaluating the Performance of DB2 for OS/390 and z/OS Database Buffers

Informix

Informix Data Buffer

In the initial screen of the SAP Database Performance Monitor (Transaction ST04), under the header **Data Buffers**, you will find the most important information about the size and performance of the Informix data buffer. The size of the data buffer is defined with the parameter **BUFFERS** in the file *ONCONFIG*.

To evaluate the Read Quality of the database buffer, you can apply the general rule that the Read Quality should be higher than 95% and the Write Quality should be higher than 82%.

Database Memory Areas

In an Informix database system, *memory is divided* into three areas, whose respective sizes are shown under the header **Shared Memory** in the Database Performance Monitor (Transaction ST04):

- The *Resident Portion* of the shared memory contains, among other things, the data buffer and the buffer for the database log. When the database is started, the Resident Portion is allocated and is mainly taken up by the data buffer.
- The *Virtual Portion* of the shared memory covers, among other things, the memory for database processes called session pools. Their sizes are defined by the parameter **SHMVIRTSIZE** at database startup.
- The *Message Portion* is small and of no importance for tuning.

The Virtual Portion of the shared memory has the special feature that it can enlarge itself while the database is running. However, the enlargement process is resource intensive. If you set the initial size of the Virtual Portion parameter (**SHMVIRTSIZE**) too small, you get continual enlargements during production operation, which negatively impacts database performance. Therefore, ensure that the database instance allocates sufficient memory to the Virtual Portion at startup. To verify the initial size of the Virtual Portion, before you stop the database, compare the current size of the Virtual Portion displayed in the Database Performance Monitor with the parameter **SHMVIRTSIZE**. If the current size of the Virtual Portion exceeds the size in **SHMVIRTSIZE**, you must increase the parameter accordingly.

If the operating system cannot provide sufficient memory, errors can occur when the Virtual Portion automatically enlarges. SAP Notes containing explanations and solutions for the errors are listed in Appendix H.

Database System	Name of Buffer	Key Figures (and Guideline Value)	Parameter
Informix	Data buffer	Read quality > 95%	BUFFERS
		Write quality > 82%	BUFFERS
	Virtual portion	Virtual Portion = SHMVIRTSIZE	SHMVIRTSIZE

Table B.6 Guideline Values for Evaluating the Performance of Informix Database Buffers

ORACLE

An Oracle database instance allocates memory in three areas:

- *Data buffer*, allocated as shared memory and indicated in Transaction ST04 as **Data buffer**.

- *Shared pool*, allocated as shared memory and indicated in Transaction ST04 as **Shared pool**. The data buffer and the shared pool form the *system global area (SGA)*.
- *Program global area (PGA)*, allocated as variable local memory by Oracle database processes. As a guideline, for each database process, you can allocate from 2.5 MB to 5 MB. To find out the number of Oracle database processes, use Transaction ST04 and choose **Detail analysis menu · ORACLE session**.

The total size of the allocated memory in an Oracle database equals the sum of the sizes of these three areas.

Oracle Data Buffer

The size of the Oracle data buffer is defined by the parameter **DB_BLOCK_BUFFERS** (in 8KB blocks) in the file *init_<SID>.ora*. Under the header Data buffer in the initial screen of the Database Performance Monitor (Transaction ST04), the number of logical read accesses to the data buffer is indicated as **Reads**. The number of physical read accesses is indicated as **Physical reads**.

If the database is using a rule-based optimizer, the quality of the data buffer (indicated as **Quality %**) is optimal if it is at least 97%. If a cost-based optimizer is being used, the quality of the data buffer is optimal if it is at least 95%.

Oracle Shared Pool

Oracle uses the *shared pool* to store administrative information. The shared pool consists of the *row cache* and the *shared SQL area*:

- The row cache contains, for example, the names and the characteristics of tables, indexes, extents, fields, and users.
- The shared SQL area stores the execution plans for SQL statements so that these do not have to be continuously recalculated.

Under the header *Shared Pool* in the initial screen of the Database Performance Monitor (Transaction ST04), the field **Size** indicates the allocated size of the shared pool in KB. The size of the shared pool is defined in bytes by the parameter **SHARED_POOL_SIZE** in the file *init_<SID>.ora*.

There are two indicators for the buffer quality of the shared pool. One is the buffer quality of the shared SQL area, indicated in ST04 under the header Shared pool as **pinratio**. This value should be at least 98%. The other indicator is the quality of the row cache, indicated as the ratio of user calls to recursive calls (in ST04 under the header Calls). *User calls* is the number of queries sent by the SAP system to the database. To respond to each query, the database requires administrative information from the row cache. If the database cannot obtain this information from the row cache, it performs a *recursive call* to import the information from the hard disk. Therefore, the ratio of user calls to recursive calls should be as large as possible and should not be less than 2:1. A typical size for the shared pool in a production SAP system is between 100 MB and 300 MB.

Database System	Name of Buffer	Guideline Value	Parameter
ORACLE	Data buffer	Data buffer quality should be at least: ≥ 97% for the rule-based optimizer ≥ 95% for the cost-based optimizer	DB_BLOCK_BUFFERS
	Shared pool	The ratio of user calls to recursive calls should be at least 2:1.	SHARED_POOL_SIZE
		The pinratio should be at least 98%.	SHARED_POOL_SIZE

Table B.7 Guideline Values for Evaluating the Performance of Oracle Database Buffers

SQL Server Database

SQL Server allocates memory in three areas:

- *Data cache*, for buffering table pages and index pages.
- *Procedure cache*, for buffering recently used stored procedures and the associated execution plans at runtime. *Stored procedures* are what the SAP database interface transforms SQL statements into in order to optimize performance for an SQL Server database instance. The procedure cache is thus equivalent to the Oracle shared SQL area. The procedure cache is about 20–50 MB in size.
- A fixed portion of memory totaling from 20 MB to 100 MB, depending on the size of the system, is allocated—for example, for connections between the R/3 work processes and the database (around 400 KB of memory for each work process), database locks (around 60 bytes of memory for each lock), and open objects (around 240 bytes of memory for each open object).

With regard to the total memory allocation, the SQL Server database offers you a choice between two different strategies: Either you assign the database a fixed memory size, or you leave it up to SQL Server to allocate memory within certain limits.

In the Database Performance Monitor (Transaction ST04), the current total memory allocated by SQL Server to the database is indicated as **Dynamic memory KB**. The limits within which SQL Server can decide how much memory to allocate are indicated as **Maximum memory KB** and **Minimum memory KB**. If the Database Performance Monitor shows that *auto growth* is activated, the database memory can vary dynamically. The parameters for defining memory limits are **MIN SERVER MEMORY** and **MAX SERVER MEMORY**.

Maximum allocations are as follows:

- 2 GB with Windows NT.
- 3 GB with Windows NT and Enterprise Edition.
- 64 GB with SQL Server 2000 and Windows 2000 Data Center.

If an SAP instance is located on the database server, it is currently recommended that you assign a fixed memory size for the SQL Server database, rather than allow the size of the allocated memory to vary dynamically.

SQL Server Data Cache

The Database Performance Monitor (Transaction ST04) indicates the size of the SQL Server data cache as **Data cache KB**. The performance of the data cache is reflected in the buffer quality, indicated as **cache hit ratio**. In production operation, cache hit ratio should be higher than 97%.

SQL Server Procedure Cache

In the Database Performance Monitor (Transaction ST04), the size and utilization of the *procedure cache* are indicated as **Procedure cache KB** and **Hit ratio%**.

Database System	Name of Buffer	Hit Ratio Guideline Value	Sizing Parameters
SQL Server	Data buffer	> 97%	MIN SERVER MEMORY, MAX SERVER MEMORY

Table B.8 Guideline Values for Evaluating the Performance of SQL Server Database Buffers

At runtime, SQL Server dynamically defines the sizes of the procedure cache and the fixed portion of database memory (see above). The remaining portion is used for the data cache. Therefore, the size of the data cache is determined by the total memory allocated to the SQL Server database and does not require separate adjustment by the database administrator. Note that this memory total is the memory available to the database server, not to one database instance alone, as in other database systems. If there is more than one database on a database server, SQL Server distributes the configured buffers to the various databases. You cannot influence this distribution. Therefore it is best not to run additional databases, such as test systems or training systems, on the same computer as the database of the production SAP system.

Summary

The guideline values provided for each database system are simply rules of thumb for good performance. A database instance may still be able to run well even if the buffer quality is poor. Thus, to avoid unnecessarily investing time and energy in optimizing the buffer quality, check the database response times using the workload analysis. See the section "Analyzing the Database Buffer" on page 80 in Chapter 2, on how to proceed in the case of a poor buffer quality.

Execution Plans for SQL Statements

When an SQL statement is executed, there are often several possible access paths for locating the relevant data. The access path adopted is called the *execution plan* and is determined by the database optimizer program.

This appendix provides examples of execution plans for various database systems. The examples illustrate accesses to a single database table, without taking into consideration database views and joins. Furthermore, we will focus on the following three questions:

- How do you recognize whether an index is being used for a search?
- How do you recognize which index is being used?
- How do you identify the index fields being used for the search?

The execution plans have been abbreviated in some places.

All the examples involve searches on the table MONI. The table MONI has the key fields RELID, SRTFD, and SRTF2. These form the primary index MONI0. In the SAP systems on which the sample execution plans were created, the table MONI consists of approximately 2,000 to 2,500 rows.

For each database, the following four different types of accesses to the table MONI are illustrated:

Sequential Read (Full Table Scan)

1. Sequential read using a full table scan: In this type of access, no WHERE clause is specified:

   ```
   SELECT * FROM "MONI"
   ```

   Because the SQL statement contains no information on how to limit the search, the database table is read sequentially with a full table scan. A full table scan is also executed if the limiting information provided does not match the available indexes.

Direct read

2. In this type of access, all three of the key fields in MONI's primary index are specified with an EQUALS condition. This is known as a fully qualified access or a *direct read*:

   ```
   SELECT * FROM "MONI" WHERE "RELID" = :A0 AND "SRTFD" = :A1 AND
   "SRTF2" = :A2
   ```

   The SQL statement contains all the information required to directly access data through the primary index.

Sequential read using the first primary key field:

3. In this type of access, the first key field of the primary index is specified with an EQUALS condition:

   ```
   SELECT * FROM "MONI" WHERE "RELID" = :A0
   ```

   The database instance reads the database rows that fulfill the specified WHERE clause through the primary index MONI~0.

Sequential read using the second primary key field:

4. In this type of access, the second key field of the primary index is specified with an EQUALS condition:

   ```
   SELECT * FROM "MONI" WHERE "SRTFD" = :A0
   ```

   This type of access does not result in a binary search.

To show what is meant by a binary search and a sequential search, consider a telephone book, which is sorted by surname (first primary key field) and then by first name (second primary key field). If you are searching for the surname, you begin by entering the list at a more or less random point and try to get closer to the correct name in jumps, doing as little name-by-name scanning as possible. For a computer, this is known as a binary search, because a computer's jumps decrease by a factor of two each time. However, if you are searching by first name only, you must sequentially search the entire telephone book. A sequential search is equivalent to a full table scan.

Instead of using a binary search, a sequential read using the second primary key field uses one of two database access strategies:

- Indexes are not used at all, or the first field in an index may be missing. In this case, an access must use a full table scan.
- Indexes are read sequentially to subsequently access the appropriate table row through a direct read: This strategy is advantageous if the index in the database occupies far fewer blocks or pages than the table and only a small number of table fields are being sought.

Oracle

Chapter 11 explains the Oracle execution plans, but they are included here to enable you to compare them more easily with the execution plans of the other database systems.

Sequential Read Using a Full Table Scan

1. Execution plan

```
Execution Plan
   SELECT STATEMENT ( Estimated Costs = 108 )
      TABLE ACCESS FULL MONI
```

   In this case, the optimizer estimates the access cost to be 108, as indicated by the entry "Estimated Costs = 108". For an ORACLE database, access costs are specified in blocks.

Direct Read

2. Execution Plan (Index Unique Scan)

```
Execution Plan
   SELECT STATEMENT ( Estimated Costs = 2 )
    TABLE ACCESS BY INDEX ROWID MONI
         INDEX UNIQUE SCAN MONI~0
```

   The row *INDEX UNIQUE SCAN MONI~0* indicates that the index MONI~0 is used. The use of the search strategy *Index Unique Scan* means that all the key fields are specified. Therefore, the search uses the primary index.

Sequential Read Using the First Key Field

3. The row *INDEX RANGE SCAN MONI~0* indicates that the index MONI~0 is used.

```
Execution Plan
   SELECT STATEMENT ( Estimated Costs = 103 )
    TABLE ACCESS BY INDEX ROWID MONI
         INDEX RANGE SCAN MONI~0
```

Sequential Read Using the Second Key Field

4. Here the optimizer program has decided that the specified field is of no help when limiting the blocks to read, since no index exists for a second primary key field. The optimizer thus decides to perform a full table scan.

SAP DB

Sequential Read Using a Full Table Scan

1. Execution plan

```
OWNER   TABLENAME   COLUMN OR INDEX   STRATEGY
SAPR3   MONI                          TABLE SCAN
```

As this is a full table scan, no index is used.

Direct Read

2. Execution plan

```
OWNER   TABLENAME   COLUMN OR INDEX   STRATEGY
SAPR3   MONI                          EQUAL CONDITION FOR KEY
COLUMN
                    RELID             (USED KEY COLUMN)
                    SRTFD             (USED KEY COLUMN)
                    SRTF2             (USED KEY COLUMN)
```

The search strategy identifies the fields RELID, SRTFD, and SRTF2 as relevant for the search. The strategy *EQUAL CONDITION FOR KEY COLUMN* shows that all the fields of the primary index are specified. This enables a direct read of the table.

Sequential Read Using the First Key Field

3. Execution plan

```
OWNER   TABLENAME   COLUMN OR INDEX   STRATEGY
SAPR3   MONI                          RANGE CONDITION FOR KEY COLUMN
                    RELID             (USED KEY COLUMN)
```

SAP DB stores tables sorted by key fields, so that a table and its primary index constitute one database object. Here, with the field RELID as the first key field, the table is accessed without an index using the strategy *RANGE CONDITION FOR KEY COLUMN*.

Sequential Read Using the Second Key Field

4. Since only the field SRTFD is specified, SAP DB also performs a full table scan. Therefore, this execution plan is identical to that in the first example.

In contrast to many other database systems, SAP DB differentiates between accesses through the primary index and the secondary index. For primary index accesses, it uses the access strategy *RANGE CONDITION FOR KEY COLUMN*. For accesses through a secondary index, it uses the access strategy *RANGE CONDITION FOR INDEX*.

DB2 UDB for Unix and Windows

1. Execution plan

Sequential Read Using a Full Table Scan

```
Execution Plan ( Opt Level = 5 )
  SELECT STATEMENT ( Estimated Costs = 12.623 [timerons] )
      TBSCAN MONI
```

2. Execution plan

```
Execution Plan ( Opt Level = 5 )
   SELECT STATEMENT ( Estimated Costs = 2.503 [timerons] )
       FETCH MONI
          IXSCAN MONI~0 #key columns:  3
```

The search strategy *Key row positioning using 3 key field(s)* identifies all three fields of the index MONI~0 as relevant for the search and therefore performs a direct read.

3. Execution plan

Sequential Read Using the First Key Field

```
Execution Plan ( Opt Level = 5 )
   SELECT STATEMENT ( Estimated Costs = 2.503 [timerons] )
       FETCH MONI
          RIDSCN
             SORT
          IXSCAN MONI~0 #key columns:  1
```

The row *IXSCAN MONI~0* shows that the index MONI~0 is used to access the table. The number of "key columns" indicates how many index fields are used for the search.

4. Execution plan

Sequential Read Using the Second Key Field

```
Execution Plan ( Opt Level = 5 )
    SELECT STATEMENT ( Estimated Costs = 1.308 [timerons] )
       FETCH MONI
          IXSCAN MONI~0 #key columns: 0
```

The access in the fourth example results in a sequential index scan using the index MONI~0. Similar to DB2 UDB for zSeries, DB2 UDB for Unix and Windows should decide to read the index MONI~0 next, in order to localize the appropriate pages of the table. Since the field SRTFD in the WHERE clause is the second field in the index and the first field is not specified, the index must be read sequentially. Therefore, in this example, the number of used "key columns" is "0".

Sequential Read Using a Full Table Scan

1. Execution plan

```
MAIN LEVEL 1
   SUBSELECT LEVEL 1
      File R3B46DATA/MONI            processed in join position 1
                                     using arrival sequence.
         Arrival sequence used to perform record selection
            Reason code:             T1 No indexes exist.
```

Direct Read

2. Execution plan

```
MAIN LEVEL 1
   SUBSELECT LEVEL 1
      File R3B46DATA/MONI            processed in join position 1
                                     using access path "MONI+0".
         Index R3B46DATA/"MONI+0"    was used to access records
                                     from file R3B46DATA/MONI
            Reason code: I1 record selection
            Key fields of the access path used:
               RELID
               SRTFD
               SRTF2
            Key row positioning using 3 key field(s).
```

The search strategy *Key row positioning using 3 key field(s)* indicates that all three fields of the index MONI~0 will be used for the search.

Sequential Read Using the First Key Field

3. Execution plan

```
MAIN LEVEL 1
   SUBSELECT LEVEL 1
      File R3B46DATA/MONI            processed in join position 1
                                     using access path "MONI+0".
         Index R3B46DATA/"MONI+0"    was used to access records
                                     from file R3B46DATA/MONI
            Reason code: I1 record selection
            Key fields of the access path used:
               RELID
               SRTFD
               SRTF2
            Key row positioning using 1 key field(s).
```

The database optimizer chooses the index MONI~0. The search strategy *Key row positioning using 1 key field(s)* indicates that the first field RELID will be used for the search.

4. Execution plan

Sequential Read Using the Second Key Field

```
MAIN LEVEL 1
   SUBSELECT LEVEL 1
      File R3B46DATA/MONI         processed in join position 1
                                  using arrival sequence.
         Arrival sequence used to perform record selection
            Reason code:          T3 Query optimizer chose table
                                  scan over available indexes.
```

The database optimizer will decide on the full table scan because this will be more efficient than access through an index. The reason code, "The optimizer preferred a full table scan to an index scan", explains this.

Related Tuning Measures

Since the database optimizer generates an SQL packet that persistently stores access information when an SQL statement is first run, the first execution (PREPARE phase) takes a relatively long time (shown in the SQL trace). If there is already an SQL packet, the database optimizer can use its contents when the statement is executed again, without having to re-determine the optimal access path (see CHECK PREPARED statement). The command sequence *ODP CLEANUP* in the SQL trace represents a further special requirement. When an SQL query is executed, a portion of the information is stored in ODPs (open data paths). For performance reasons, only the most recent 800 ODPs per SAP work process are used. If more ODPs are needed, the least used ones are deleted by means of an algorithm. This process usually occurs via a **Commit** statement, and is shown in the SQL trace; the amount of time needed depends on the system

You can obtain patches for the operating system and iSeries database software from IBM in the form of CUM packages, DB fix packs and individual PTFs. Once the corrections have been implemented, the SQL packet may have to be deleted to get rid of the problem, or the database optimizer may have to be invoked in order re-determine the execution plan. A note in the PTF "readme" file will indicate if this is necessary. For CUM packages and DB fix packs, the SQL packets should be deleted as a preventative measure. System performance may suffer until the SQL packets are re-built. For iSeries, the background updating of optimizer statistics is not necessary, because the statistics are managed by the system and are always up to date.

DB2 UDB for zSeries

Sequential Read Using a Full Table Scan

1. Execution plan

```
Explanation of query block number: 1   step: 1
Performance is bad. No Index is used. Sequential Tablespace Scan
Method:   access new table.
           new Table:  SAPR3.MONI
          Accesstype: sequential tablespace scan.
```

Direct Read

2. Execution plan

```
Explanation of query block number: 1   step: 1
Performance is optimal. Index is used. Index Scan by matching Index.
Method:   access new table.
           new Table:  SAPR3.MONI
       Accesstype: by index.
               Index: SAPR3.MONI~0 (matching Index)
                         Index columns (ordered): RELID SRTFD SRTF2
                         with 3 matching columns of 3 Index-Columns.
```

The search strategy *with 3 matching columns of 3 Index-Columns* indicates that all three fields of the index MONI~0 will be used for the search.

Sequential Read Using the First Key Field

3. Execution plan

```
Explanation of query block number: 1   step: 1
Performance is good. Index is used. Index Scan by matching Index.
Method:   access new table.
           new Table:  SAPR3.MONI
       Accesstype: by index.
               Index: SAPR3.MONI~0 (matching Index)
                         Index columns (ordered): RELID SRTFD SRTF2
                         with 1 matching columns of 3 Index-Columns.
```

The database optimizer chooses the index MONI~0. The search strategy *with 1 matching column of 3 Index-Columns* indicates that the first field of the index MONI~0 will be used for the search.

4. Execution plan

Sequential Read Using the Second Key Field

```
Explanation of query block number: 1 step: 1
Performance is good. Index is used. Index Scan by nonmatching Index.
Method: access new table.
        new Table: SAPR3.MONI
    Accesstype: by index.
       Index: SAPR3.MONI~0 (nonmatching Index)
                     Index columns (ordered): RELID SRTFD SRTF2
      DB2 can at least use the index to pick out those
      pages from the table space, that contain data of
                the table: MONI
```

The database optimizer chooses to use the index MONI0 for the search. Since the field SRTFD specified in the SQL statement is the second field, and the first field RELID is missing from the WHERE clause, the index must be read sequentially. This is indicated by the access strategy *Index Scan by nonmatching Index.*

The comments on performance visible in the DB2 UDB for zSeries execution plans are automatically displayed depending on the access type. However, they should not be understood as a valid description of the current performance situation. For a sequential tablespace scan (a full table scan), the automatic text is `performance is bad`; for an index range scan, the text is `performance is good`; and for an index unique scan, the text is `performance is optimal`. However, a full table scan on a small table does not cause a performance problem, whereas an index range scan on a large table with selection conditions that do not strictly limit the data volume can considerably reduce performance.

Informix

1. Execution plan

Sequential Read Using a Full Table Scan

```
Execution plan of a select statement (Online optimizer)
Estimated # of Rows Returned: 10
1) sapr3.moni: SEQUENTIAL SCAN
```

Informix gives the access cost in rows.

2. Execution plan

Direct Read

```
Execution plan of a select statement (Online optimizer)
Estimated # of Rows Returned: 1
1) sapr3.moni: INDEX PATH
   (1) Index Keys: relid srtfd srtf2
```

```
Lower Index Filter: (relid = ... AND (srtfd = ... AND
                                        srtf2 = ...))
```

The third line *sapr3.moni: INDEX PATH* indicates that Informix accesses the table through an index. The next line lists the fields in the index: RELID, SRTFD, and SRTF2. To determine the name of the index used from the listed fields, check the fields as listed in the ABAP Dictionary (Transaction SE11). The fifth line *Lower Index Filter* indicates which fields of the index will be used for the search. Here they are RELID, SRTFD, and SRTF2.

Sequential Read Using the First Key Field

3. Execution plan

```
Execution plan of a select statement (Online optimizer)
Estimated # of Rows Returned: 3
1) sapr3.moni: INDEX PATH
   (1) Index Keys: relid srtfd srtf2
       Lower Index Filter: sapr3.moni.relid = 'DB'
```

The line *sapr3.moni: INDEX PATH* signifies that Informix accesses the tables through the index. The line *Index Keys: relid srtfd srtf2* indicates which index keys are in the index. The line *Lower Index Filter: sapr3.moni.relid = 'DB'* indicates which index field will be used for the search. In this execution plan, it is the field RELID.

Sequential Read Using the Second Key Field

4. Here Informix decides to perform a sequential scan—in other words, a full table scan.

SQL Server

Sequential Read Using a Full Table Scan

1. Execution plan

```
Clustered Index Scan(EW4..MONI.MONI~0)
```

The SQL Server database stores tables sorted by their key field. The primary index is a clustered index. Therefore, even when reading the entire table, SQL Server accesses the table through the clustered index MONI0.

Direct Read

2. Execution plan:

```
Clustered Index Seek(EW4..MONI.MONI~0, SEEK:(MONI.RELID=@1 AND
MONI.SRTFD=@2 AND MONI.SRTF2=@3) ORDERED)
```

The search strategy is indicated in the parentheses after *SEEK*, and shows that the fields RELID, SRTFD, and SRTF2 will be used for the search.

3. Execution plan

   Sequential Read Using the First Key Field

   ```
   Clustered Index Seek(EW4..MONI.MONI~0, SEEK:(MONI.RELID=@1) ORDERED)
   ```

   The search strategy *Clustered Index Seek* indicates that the index MONI~0 and the field RELID will be used for the search.

4. Execution plan

   Sequential Read Using the Second Key Field

   ```
   Clustered Index Seek(EW4..MONI.MONI~0, WHERE:(MONI.SRTFD=@1))
   ```

   Here SQL Server also chooses the clustered index. This is indicated by the use of the search function WHERE. (In the previous SQL Server examples, the search function was SEEK.) However, since the WHERE condition specifies the field SRTFD, which is the second field in the index, and the first field, RELID, is not specified, the index is of little use for the search.

In contrast to many other database systems, SQL Server differentiates between accesses through the primary index and the secondary index. The access strategy using the primary index is called *Clustered Index Seek*. The access strategy using the secondary index is called *Index Seek*.

C Configuration Performance Parameters

This appendix lists the configuration parameters that are relevant to performance. Please note:

- To display the list of current parameter settings for a given SAP instance, call the SAP Memory Configuration Monitor (Transaction ST02). Then select **Current parameters**.
- As exact configuration suggestions do only make sense for concrete SAP systems and rather quickly become obsolete, there are no such direct suggestions in this book.
- Parameters can be changed either directly in the profile files or by using Transaction RZ10.
- There may be operating-system limits affecting memory management for your SAP release. Ensure that the operating system can administer the memory size you wish to configure. For information on operating-system limits, see Chapter 5.
- When changing memory management parameters, always keep a backup of the old instance profiles. This backup will enable you to revert to the former parameter values if required. Before restarting the instance, test the new instance profiles using the auxiliary program **sappfpar** on the operating-system level. After instance restart, verify that the instance is running without error. To obtain a description of the program **sappfpar**, execute the operating-system command *sappfpar ?*.
- You can change the SAP ITS using the ITS administration and monitoring tool.

When you are seeking to change particular parameters, warnings may appear indicating that changes should not be made without express instructions from SAP. You must heed these warnings. Instructions from SAP on changing the parameters can be provided by SAP employees, by hardware or database partners who have analyzed your system, or through an SAP Note. SAP Notes can be found in the SAP Service Marketplace or on SAP's Internet site, SAPNet. Ensure that the SAP Note applies to your SAP system, database, operating system, and the respective versions of these systems.

For help on SAP Basis profile parameters, use Transaction RZ11.

1. Enter Transaction RZ11.
2. Enter the SAP profile parameter for which you require more information, and
3. Select **Documentation**.

SAP Buffer Parameters

Table Group C.1 contains a table for each SAP buffer describing the buffer and the related SAP profile parameters.

Buffer Name: Table Definition (TTAB)	
Parameter	**Description**
rsdb/ntab/entrycount	This parameter specifies the maximum number of entries in the TTAB buffer.
The size of the TTAB buffer is approximately equivalent to the maximum number of entries multiplied by 100 bytes.	

Buffer Name: Field Description (FTAB)	
Parameter	**Description**
rsdb/ntab/ftabsize	Buffer size allocated at instance startup in KB.
rsdb/ntab/entrycount	Maximum number of buffer entries / 2.

Buffer Name: Initial Record (IRDB)	
Parameter	**Description**
rsdb/ntab/irbdsize	Buffer size allocated at instance startup in KB.
rsdb/ntab/entrycount	Maximum number of buffer entries / 2.

Buffer Name: Short Nametab (SNTAB)	
Parameter	**Description**
rsdb/ntab/sntabsize	Buffer size allocated at instance startup in KB.
rsdb/ntab/entrycount	The maximum number of buffer entries in the IRBD buffer equals double the value of this parameter.

Buffer Name: Program (PXA)	
Parameter	**Description**
abap/buffersize	Buffer size allocated at instance startup in KB.

Table C.1 Parameters for SAP Buffers (see SAP Note 103747)

Buffer Name: CUA	
Parameter	**Description**
rsdb/cua/buffersize	Buffer size allocated at instance startup in KB.
The maximum number of buffer entries in the CUA buffer equals half the value of the buffer size.	

Buffer Name: Screen	
Parameter	**Description**
zcsa/presentation_buffer_area	The buffer size allocated at instance startup (in bytes) equals half the value of this parameter.
sap/bufdir_entries	This parameter specifies the maximum number of buffer entries.

Buffer Name: Export/Import (v4.0 and later)	
Parameter	**Description**
rsdb/obj/buffersize	Buffer size allocated at instance startup in KB.
rsdb/obj/max_objects	This parameter specifies the maximum number of buffer entries.
rsdb/obj/large_object_size	Typical size of the largest objects in bytes.

Buffer Name: Calendar	
Parameter	**Description**
zcsa/calendar_area	Buffer size allocated at instance startup in bytes.
zcsa/calendar_ids	This parameter specifies the maximum number of buffer entries.

Buffer Name: Generic Key Table	
Parameter	**Description**
zcsa/ table_buffer_ area	Buffer size allocated at instance startup in bytes.
zcsa/db_max_buftab	This parameter specifies the maximum number of buffer entries.

Buffer Name: Single Record Table	
Parameter	**Description**
rtbb/buffer_length	Buffer size allocated at instance startup in KB.
rtbb/max_tables	This parameter specifies the maximum number of buffer entries.

Table C.1 Parameters for SAP Buffers (see SAP Note 103747) (contd.)

SAP Memory Management Parameters

SAP currently supports a number of operating systems for the implementation of the SAP application level:

- UNIX dialects AIX, HP-UX, Linux, ReliantUNIX (Sinix), Solaris
- Windows, Windows NT, Windows 2000
- IBM iSeries, IBM zSeries

Detailed information about available platforms can be found in the SAP Service Marketplace under www.service.sap/platforms.

Table C.2 lists the SAP profile parameters for SAP Memory Management.

With Zero Administration Memory Management, the parameters marked with)[1] in Table C.2 are automatically set at instance startup. These automatic settings are overwritten if there are differing values for these parameters in the instance profile. If Zero Administration Memory Management is used in your system, SAP recommends deleting the parameters listed in Table C.2 from the instance profile and configuring only the parameter `PHYS_MEMSIZE`. See also Chapter 8 and SAP Note 88416.

The following classifications are shown in the column **Type** in Table C.2: P denotes parameters that directly affect the performance of the SAP system. S denotes parameters that ensure the secure operation of the SAP system under high load.

Parameter	Description	Type
ztta/roll_area)[1]	Total local SAP roll area for all work processes.	S/P
ztta/roll_first)[1]	Portion of the local SAP roll area allocated to a dialog work process before SAP extended memory is allocated.	P
rdisp/ROLL_SHM)[1]	Size of the SAP roll buffer in shared memory.	P
rdisp/PG_SHM)[1]	Size of the ABAP paging buffer in shared memory (for SAP Release 4.0 and later, this has little effect on performance).	P
rdisp/ROLL_MAXFS)[1]	Size of the global SAP roll area, which comprises the SAP roll buffer plus the SAP roll file.	S

Table C.2 Parameters for SAP Memory Management (see SAP Notes 103747 and 88416)

Parameter	Description	Type
rdisp/PG_MAXFS)[1]	Size of the ABAP paging area, which comprises the ABAP paging buffer plus the ABAP paging file.	S
em/initial_size_MB)[1]	Initial size of the SAP extended memory.	S/P
em/max_size_MB)[1]	Maximum size of the R/3 extended memory. Some operating-system limits keep the size of SAP extended memory smaller than this value.	S/P
em/blocksize_KB)[1]	Size of a block in SAP extended memory. The default value of 1,024 KB should not be changed without explicit instructions from SAP.	P
em/address_space _MB)[1]	The address space reserved for the SAP extended memory (currently applies only under Windows NT).	S/P
ztta/roll_extension)[1]	Maximum amount of SAP extended memory that can be allocated for each user context.	S/P
abap/heap_area_dia)[1]	Maximum SAP heap memory for each dialog work process.	S
abap/heap_area _nondia)[1]	Maximum SAP heap memory for each nondialog work process.	S
abap/heap_area_total)[1]	Maximum SAP heap memory for all work processes.	S
abap/heaplimit)[1]	A limit in the SAP heap memory that flags work processes so they are restarted after the end of the current transaction and can thus release the heap memory.	S
em/global_area_MB	Size of the Global Extended Memory (SAP EG Memory), for SAP Basis 4.6D and later.	S

Table C.2 Parameters for SAP Memory Management (see SAP Notes 103747 and 88416) (contd.)

Additional Parameters

Parameter	Description
rdisp/mshost	Name of the computer where the message server is running.
rdisp/msserv	Name of the message service.

Table C.3 SAP Profile Parameters for Load Distribution

Parameter	Description
rdisp/enqname	Name of the SAP instance where the enqueue server is running.
rdisp/atp_server	Name of the SAP instance where the ATP server is running.
rdisp/wp_no_dia	Number of dialog work processes (per SAP instance).
rdisp/wp_no_btc	Number of background work processes.
rdisp/wp_no_enq	Number of enqueue work processes.
rdisp/wp_no_spo	Number of spool work processes.
rdisp/wp_no_vb	Number of update work processes.
rdisp/wp_no_vb2	Number of work processes for update2 updates.
rdisp/vb_dispatching	Activates or deactivates update dispatching. If the parameter is set to 1 (this is the default setting), update dispatching is activated. If the parameter is set to 0, update dispatching is not activated.
rdisp/vbstart	This parameter controls the behavior of the update service at SAP system startup. At startup, the update service checks its queue to see whether there are any update requests that have not yet been processed. Such requests are specially marked and then processed. If the parameter is set to 1 (this is the default setting), the update service processes update requests that have not yet been processed. If the parameter is set to 0, waiting update requests are not automatically processed.
rdisp/max_wprun_time	This parameter limits the maximum runtime of a transaction step in a dialog work process (in seconds). When this time has expired, the user request is terminated with the error message TIME_OUT. The default setting for this parameter is 300 seconds.
	Warning: If a COMMIT WORK command is executed in a program, this runtime starts again. While an SQL statement is being processed on the database, the program is *not* terminated even when this runtime expires.
rdisp/gui_auto_logout	If there is no GUI activity for *rdisp/gui_auto_logout* seconds, then the front end is automatically logged off. If the parameter has the value 0, then there is no automatic logoff.

Table C.3 SAP Profile Parameters for Load Distribution (contd.)

Parameter	Description
login/disable_multi_gui_login	If this parameter is set to 1, then multiple dialog logon connectionss (for the same client with the same user name) are blocked by the system. This parameter works for SAP GUI logon connections. This parameter has no effect on someone logging on using the Internet Transaction Server (ITS) or Remote Function Call (RFC).
login/multi_login_users	This list contains the names of users who are authorized for multiple logon connections. The user names (without client entry) are separated by commas.
rdisp/max_alt_modes	This parameter specifies the number of parallel modes per logon sessions that a user is authorized to open. This should only be done for specific reasons (acute memory bottleneck). The system itself may, depending on the situation, automatically create invisible parallel modes.

Table C.3 SAP Profile Parameters for Load Distribution (contd.)

Parameter	Description
rsdb/max_blocking_faktor	Split factor for dividing the results of ALL ENTRIES queries in SQL statements into smaller blocks. See the section "Analyzing Buffered Tables" on page 297 in Chapter 9. *Warning:* This parameter should not be changed without explicit instructions from SAP.
dbs/io_buf_size	Size of the data area in an SAP work process, through which data is transferred to or copied from the database by an SQL statement (in bytes). *Warning:* This parameter must not be modified without prior recommendation by SAP.

Table C.4 SAP Profile Parameters for the Database Instance

Parameter	Description
rdisp/bufrefmode	Defines the type of buffer synchronization. Possible settings: sendon or exeauto (for a distributed system) and sendoff or exeauto (for a central system).
rdisp/bufreftime	Time interval between two buffer synchronizations (in seconds).

Table C.5 SAP Profile Parameters for Buffer Synchronization

Parameter	Description
rdisp/tm_max_no	Maximum number of front-end connections in table tm_adm.
rdisp/max_comm_ entries	Maximum number of CPIC/RFC connections that can be administered in the communication table comm_adm.
gw/max_conn	Maximum number of CPIC/RFC connections that can be administered by the gateway service in table conn_tbl.
rdisp/rfc_max_login	Limit for number of RFC logon connections to SAP instance. If this limit is exceeded, then no resources are made available to the affected user.
rdisp/rfc_max_own_login	Limit for number of individual RFC logon connections to SAP instance. If this individual limit is exceeded, then no resources are made available to the affected user.
rdisp/rfc_max_comm_entries	Limit for the number of communication entries used for RFCs. If this limit is exceeded, then no resources are made available to the affected user. The number of communication entries is set via the profile parameter *rdisp/max_comm_entries*.
rdisp/rfc_max_own_used_wp	Limit for the number of dialog work processes used for RFCs by an individual user. If this limit is exceeded, then no resources are made available to the affected user.
rdisp/rfc_min_wait_dia_wp	Limit for the number of dialog work processes to be reserved for non-RFC users. If this limit is exceeded, then no resources are made available to the affected users.
rdisp/rfc_max_wait_time	Maximum number of seconds for which a work process can receive no resources before going to "sleep".

Table C.6 SAP Profile Parameters for Interface Configuration (see SAP Note 74141)

Parameter	Description
rstr/file	Name of the SQL trace file.
rstr/max_diskspace	Size of the SQL trace file in bytes.
abap/atrapath	Path name for the ABAP trace files.

Table C.7 SAP Profile Parameters for Configuring Monitoring Tools

Parameter	Description
abap/atrasizeQuote	Size of the ABAP trace files.
rdisp/wpdbug_max_no	Maximum number of work processes that can be run simultaneously in debugging mode.

Table C.7 SAP Profile Parameters for Configuring Monitoring Tools (contd.)

Internet Transaction Server

Parameter	Description
MaxSessions	Maximum number of possible user sessions.
MaxWorkThreads	Maximum number of ITS work processes (work threads).
MinWorkThreads	Minimum number of ITS work processes (normally equal to MaxWorkThreads).
MaxAGates	Maximum number of Agate processes (operating system level processes).
MinAgates	Minimum number of AGate work processes (normally equal to MaxAGates).
StaticTemplates	A value of "1" deactivates the runtime parsing of HTML templates. The default setting for production operation is "1". This means that, for performance reasons, changes to templates are not implemented.
CacheSize	Size of the HTML template cache.
ProductionMode	A value of "1" activates the caching of RFC function module/BAPI repository data. The default setting for production operation is "1". This means that changes to RFC function modules are not identified.
Caching	A value of "1" activates the caching of ITS log files. The default setting is "1".
TraceLevel	The trace level. The default setting is "1".
Debug	A value of "ON" activates debugging. The default setting is "OFF".
TimeoutPercentage	Percentage limit for the portion of timeouts for high load sessions.
~http_compress_level	Compression level (0 to 9). The default setting is 7.
~http_use_compression	A value of "1" activates data compression between ITS and Web browsers. The default setting is 1.

Table C.8 SAP Profile Parameters for Configuring the Internet Transaction Server

D Selected Transaction Codes

AL11	Display SAP directories
AL12	Display table buffer (buffer synchronization)
BALE	ALE administration and monitoring
DB02	Analyze tables and indexes (missing database objects and space requirements)
DB05	Table analysis
DB12	Overview of backup logs (DBA protocols)
DB13	DBA Planning Calendar
DB20	Generate table access statistics
OSS1	Log on to the SAP Service Marketplace
RZ01	Job Scheduling Monitor
RZ02	Network graphics for SAP instances
RZ03	Control Panel for operation modes and server status
RZ04	Maintain SAP instances
RZ10	Maintain profile parameters (by profile)
RZ11	Maintain profile parameters (by parameter)
RZ20	Central SAP monitor
SE11	Maintain ABAP Dictionary
SE12	Display ABAP Dictionary
SE14	Utilities for ABAP Dictionary tables
SE15	ABAP Repository information system
SE16	Data Browser for displaying table contents
SE38	ABAP Editor
SEU	SAP Repository Browser
SM01	Lock Transactions
SM02	System messages
SM04	User Overview
SM12	Display and delete SAP enqueues
SM13	Display update records
SM21	System log

SM37	Background Job Overview
SM39	Job analysis
SM49	Execute external operating-system commands
SM50	Local Work Process Overview
SM51	List of servers
SM56	Reset or check the number range buffer
SM58	Asynchronous RFC error log
SM59	Display or maintain RFC destinations
SM63	Display or maintain operating modes
SM65	Execute tests to analyze background processing
SM66	Systemwide Work Process Overview
SM69	Maintain external operating-system commands
SMLG	Maintain logon groups
ST01	SAP system trace
ST02	SAP Memory Configuration Monitor (also known as the function Setups/ Tune Buffers)
ST03	Workload Monitor
ST04	Database Performance Monitor
ST05	Start, stop, or view SQL trace, enqueue trace, or RFC trace
ST06	Operating System Monitor
ST07	Application Monitor
ST08	Network Monitor
ST09	Network Alert Monitor
ST10	Display statistics on table accesses (table call statistics)
ST11	Display developer traces
ST14	Application analysis—statistics relating to business document volume
ST22	ABAP runtime error analysis
STAT	Single statistics records on the application server
STMS	Transport Management System
STUN	SAP Performance Menu
TU02	Parameter changes—display active parameters and a history of changes

E Review Questions and Answers

Chapter 2

Questions

1. Which of the following can cause a CPU bottleneck on the database server?

   A. External processes that do not belong to the database or an SAP instance are running on the database server.

   B. The SAP extended memory is configured too small.

   C. Work processes that belong to an SAP instance running on the database (for example, background or update work processes) require CPU capacity.

   D. There are expensive SQL statements—for example, those that contribute 5% or more of the entire database load in the Shared SQL Area.

   E. The database buffers are set too small, so that data must be continuously reloaded from the hard disks.

2. Which of the following are necessary to achieve optimal database performance?

   A. Table analyses (through a program such as Update Statistics) must be regularly scheduled.

   B. The number of SAP work processes must be sufficiently large, so that there are enough database processes to process the database load.

   C. The database buffers must be sufficiently large.

   D. You should regularly check whether expensive SQL statements are unnecessarily occupying CPU and main memory resources.

   E. The database instance should be run only on a separate computer without SAP instances.

3. Which points should you take into consideration when monitoring SAP memory management?

   A. The total memory allocated by the SAP and database instances should not be larger than the physical main memory of the computer.

   B. The extended memory must be sufficiently large.

   C. If possible, no displacements should occur in the SAP buffers.

4. In the Local Work Process Overview, the information displayed for a particular work process over a considerable time period is as follows: Running, Sequential Read, and a specific table name. What does this tell you?
   A. There may be an expensive SQL statement which accesses the table and can be analyzed more closely in the Database Process Monitor.
   B. There may be a wait situation in the dispatcher, preventing a connection to the database. The dispatcher queue should be analyzed more closely.
   C. There may be an *exclusive lock wait* that you can detect in the monitor for exclusive lock waits.
   D. There may be a network problem between the application server and the database server.

Answers

1. A, C, D, E
2. A, C, D
3. B, C
4. A, C, D

Chapter 3

Questions

1. Which of the following statements are correct?
   A. The CPU time is measured by the operating system of the application server.
   B. The database time is measured by the database system.
   C. High network times for data transfers between the presentation server and the application server are reflected in an increased response time in the Workload Monitor.
   D. High network times for data transfers between the application server and the database server are reflected in an increased response time in the Workload Monitor.

E. The roll out time is not part of the response time because the roll out of a user occurs only after the answer has been sent to the presentation server. Nevertheless, it is important for the performance of the SAP system to keep the roll out time to a minimum, as during the roll outs, the SAP work process remains occupied.

2. How is the term load defined in the SAP environment?

   A. The load generated by a particular process is defined as the percentage of time which that process occupies the CPU of a computer, and can be monitored in the Operating System Monitor as CPU utilization.

   B. Load is the sum of response times. Thus, total load refers to the total response time, CPU load refers to the total CPU time, and database load refers to the total database time.

   C. Load means the number of transaction steps for each unit of time.

3. The Workload Monitor displays increased wait times for the dispatcher, such that Av. wait time is much greater than 50ms. What does this tell you?

   A. There is a communication problem between the presentation servers and the dispatcher of the application server—for example, a network problem.

   B. There is a general performance problem—for example, a database problem, a hardware bottleneck, or insufficient SAP extended memory; or there are too few SAP work processes. This statement does not provide enough information to pinpoint the exact problem.

   C. An increased dispatcher wait time is normal for an SAP system. It protects the operating system from being overloaded, and can be ignored.

Answers

1. A, D, E
2. B
3. B

Chapter 4

Questions

1. What do you have to consider when you perform an SQL trace?
   A. There is only one trace file in each SAP system. Therefore, only one SQL trace can be performed at a time.
   B. The user whose actions are being traced should not run multiple programs concurrently.
   C. You should perform the SQL trace on a second execution of a program because the relevant buffers are then already loaded.
   D. SQL traces are useful on the database server, but not on application servers, which yield inexact results due to network times.
2. When should you perform an ABAP trace?
   A. If a problem occurs with the table buffer.
   B. For programs with high CPU requirements.
   C. For I/O problems with hard disks.

Answers

1. B, C
2. B

Chapter 5

Questions

1. Where should background work processes be configured?
   A. Background work processes should always be located on the database server. Otherwise, the runtime of background programs will be negatively affected by network problems between the database server and the application server.
   B. If background work processes are not located on the database server, they must all be set up on a dedicated application server known as the background server.
   C. Background work processes can be distributed evenly over all the application servers.

2. How should you configure and monitor the dynamic user distribution?
   A. By setting the appropriate SAP profile parameter—for example, **rdisp/wp_no_dia**.
   B. By using Transaction SM04, User Overview.
   C. By using Transaction SMLG, Maintain Logon Groups.

Answers

1. C
2. C

Chapters 6 and 7

1. What is a high roll wait time?
   A. A unique index for a GUI communication problem, for example, in the network between the presentation server and the application server.
   B. A unique index for an RFC communication problem with SAP or non-SAP systems.
   C. A unique index for a GUI or RFC communication problem.
   D. A problem caused by an ineffective network between the application and the database level.
2. In a transaction step, a transaction is processed and controls are used, but no external RFC is called. Which of the following statements are correct?
   A. The GUI time is greater than the roll wait time.
   B. The RFC time is greater than the roll wait time.
   C. The roll wait time is always greater than zero.
   D. The roll wait time is normally greater than zero, although it can also be zero.
   E. The roll wait time is always zero.
3. In a transaction step, a program that uses no controls and no synchronous RFCs is processed, although asynchronous RFCs are called. Which of the following statements are correct?
   A. The GUI time is greater than the roll wait time.
   B. The RFC time is greater than the roll wait time.
   C. The roll wait time is always greater than zero.

D. The roll wait time is normally greater than zero, although it can also be zero.

E. The roll wait time is always zero.

4. A Web application that uses ITS and an SAP system is running "too slowly". What analyses do you perform?

   A. Use the ITS administration and monitoring tool or the central CCMS Monitor to check if all work processes or sessions are running on the ITS or if the CPU is constantly running.

   B. In the Work Process Overview for the connected SAP system, check if all work processes are running.

   C. Using a performance trace and the single record statistics, analyze the response time of the connected SAP system and compare it with the user-measured response time for the presentation server.

   D. Using an analysis tool on the presentation server (for example, PERFMON), check the data transfer volume to the browser and the compilation time for an HTML page on the browser, and compare the required time with the total response time.

Answers

1. C
2. A, D
3. B, E
4. A, B, C, D

Chapter 8

Questions

1. Which SAP profile parameters define the amounts of extended memory and heap memory that should be kept in the physical main memory or in the paging file?

   A. SAP extended memory is always kept completely in the physical memory, and SAP heap memory is created in the operating-system paging file.

   B. None. The memory areas in the physical main memory and the paging file (that is, the page-out or page-in process) are automatically distributed by the operating system. An application program (such as SAP or a database program) cannot influence the distribution.

C. The SAP profile parameter **ztta/roll_extension** defines the amount of SAP extended memory in the physical memory. The parameters **abap/heap_area_ dia** and **abap/heap_area_nondia** define the amount of SAP heap memory.

2. Which of the following can cause an SAP instance to not start, or to start with an error message, after you change SAP parameters for memory management?

   A. The program buffer size specified in the parameter **abap/buffer_size** exceeds the limit that exists due to address space restrictions.

   B. There is not enough physical memory to allow the new settings.

   C. The paging file is not large enough to allow the new settings.

   D. The amount of SAP extended memory specified in the parameter **em/initial_size_MB** exceeds the limit that exists due to address space restrictions.

Answers

1. B
2. A, C, D

Chapter 9

Questions

1. Which of the following factors are reasons for not activating full buffering on a table?

   A. The table is very large.

   B. The SQL statement that is used most frequently to access the table contains the first two of five key fields in an EQUALS condition.

   C. The table is changed often.

2. Which of the following statements are correct with regard to buffer synchronization?

   A. During buffer synchronization, the application server where the change occurred sends a message through the message server to implement the change in the respective buffered table on the other application servers.

   B. After a transaction changes a buffered table, the transaction must first be completed with a database commit before the table can be reloaded into the buffer.

C. In a central SAP system, the SAP profile parameter **rdisp/bufrefmode** must be set to sendoff, exeoff.

D. In a central SAP system, the entries in the table buffer are never invalidated, because the table buffer is changed synchronously after a database change operation.

Answers

1. A, C
2. B

Chapter 10

Questions

1. Which of the following statements are correct with regard to locks and SAP enqueues?

   A. An SAP enqueue locks one or more tables in the database.

   B. After an SAP enqueue has been placed, the corresponding database table can still be changed by an update request coming from programs such as customer-developed ABAP reports.

   C. A database lock is usually released at the end of a transaction step, while an SAP enqueue is usually released at the end of an SAP transaction.

   D. A database lock that lasts too long can cause an SAP system *standstill*.

2. Which of the following statements are correct with regard to the ATP server?

   A. The ATP server should always be configured on the database server.

   B. The ATP server is an independent SAP installation with its own database on a separate computer.

   C. The ATP server reduces the number of accesses to tables RESB and VBBE.

3. When buffering number range objects in main memory, which of the following considerations should you keep in mind?

   A. Since buffering occurs in all SAP instances, buffer synchronization may cause some numbers to be assigned twice.

B. Gaps occur in the number assignment when using buffered number ranges. You must check whether these gaps are permitted by business law and are acceptable from a business viewpoint.

C. If the quantity of numbers in the buffer is too small, performance problems will result, particularly during mass data entry using Batch Input or Fast Input.

D. Sufficient physical memory must be available, because number range buffering consumes a good deal of memory.

Answers

1. B, C, D
2. C
3. B, C

Chapter 11

Questions

1. Which of the following statements is correct with regard to expensive SQL statements?

   A. They can lead to hardware bottlenecks (a CPU or I/O bottleneck) and negatively affect the runtime of other SQL statements.

   B. They can occupy a lot of space in the data buffer of the database, displace objects that are needed by other SQL statements, and negatively affect the runtime of other SQL statements.

   C. They can occupy a lot of space in the SAP table buffer and displace objects, which causes unnecessary reload operations.

   D. If they are performed after database locks were set by the same program, this can cause exclusive lock wait situations in the database, which can cause a brief system standstill.

   E. Expensive SQL statements in programs for reporting or in background programs are not normally a problem for the database.

2. In the results of an SQL trace, you find an SQL statement that has a runtime of 1 second and selects only 10 records. Which of the following could be the reason for the long runtime?

   A. There is a hardware bottleneck (a CPU or I/O bottleneck) on the database server.

B. There is a network problem between the application server and the database server.

C. The database optimizer has created an inefficient execution plan—for example, by choosing an inefficient index.

D. There is no appropriate index for the SQL statement.

E. There are exclusive lock waits in the database.

3. In the Shared SQL Area Monitor, you find an SQL statement with 10,000 logical read accesses per execution (indicated as Gets/Execution). Which of the following could be the reason for this high number of read accesses?

   A. There is a hardware bottleneck (a CPU or I/O bottleneck) on the database server.

   B. There is a network problem between the application server and the database server.

   C. The database optimizer has created an inefficient execution plan—for example, by choosing an inefficient index.

   D. There is no appropriate index for the SQL statement.

   E. There are exclusive lock waits in the database.

   F. A large number of records are being transferred from the database to the ABAP program.

Answers

1. A, B, D
2. A, B, C, D, E
3. C, D, F

F Glossary

ABAP: Advanced Business Application Programming
Object oriented, SAP-specific programming language. ABAP is one of the three mySAP.com programming languages (along with Java and C/C++).

ABAP Dictionary: Central storage facility for SAP-based metadata (e.g., table structures).

ACID Principle: A business logic principle that a transaction (or logical unit of work, LUW) must obey: atomicity, consistency, isolation, durability.

address space of a process: → Virtual storage that can be addressed by a process. The size of the addressable storage (in 32-bit architecture) ranges from 1.8 to 3.8 GB (→ 2^{32} = 4 GB), depending on the operating system.

ALE: Application Link Enabling
ALE is a technology for building and operating distributed applications. The basic purpose of ALE is to ensure distributed, yet integrated mySAP.com components. It comprises a controlled business message exchange with consistent data storage in nonpermanently connected SAP applications.
Applications are integrated not through a central database, but through synchronous and asynchronous communication.
ALE consists of three layers:

- application services
- distribution services
- communication services

Alert Monitor: Graphical monitor for analyzing system states and events.

ANSI: American National Standards Institute

application server: A computer on which at least one SAP instance runs.

ArchiveLink: Integrated into the SAP Basis component, a communications interface between the mySAP.com components and external components. ArchiveLink has the following interfaces:

- user interface
- interface to the SAP applications
- interface to the following external components:
  - archive systems
  - viewer systems
  - scan systems

archiving object: A logical object comprising related business data in the database, which is read from the database using an archiving program. After it has been successfully archived, a logical object can be deleted by a specially generated deleting program.

ASAP: AcceleratedSAP
Standardized procedural model to implement SAP R/3 and additional mySAP.com solutions.

background processing: Processing that does not take place on the screen. Data is processed in the background, while other functions can be executed in parallel on the screen. Although the background processes are not visible for a user and run without user intervention (there is no dialog), they have the same priority as online processes.

BAPI: Business Application Programming Interface
Standardized programming interface that provides external access to business processes and data in the SAP system.

Batch Input: Method and tools for rapid import of data from sequential files into the SAP R/3 database.

Benchmark: → Standard Application Benchmark

browser: Web browser
A GUI program based on the HTML/HTTP protocols. Alternatively, a third-party browser can be used instead of the SAP GUI program.

Business Connector: SAP Business Connector (SAP BC)
Interface software: among other things, SAP BC is used to exchange XML documents between systems over the Internet.

button: Element of the graphical user interface. Click a button to execute the button's function. You can select buttons using the keyboard as well as the mouse. To do this, place the button cursor on the button and select Enter or click the Enter button. Buttons can contain text or graphical symbols.

CATT: Computer Aided Test Tool
You can use this tool to generate test data and to automate and test business processes.

CCMS : Computing Center Management System
Tools for monitoring, controlling, and configuring mySAP.com components. The CCMS supports 24-hour system administration functions from within the SAP system. You can use it to analyze the system load and monitor the distributed resource requirements of the system components.

CO: Customizing Organizer
Tool to administer change and transport requests of all types in an SAP system.

client: From a commercial, legal, organizational, and technical viewpoint, a closed unit within a mySAP.com solution, with separate master records within a table.

context switch on the operating-system level: On the operating-system level, there are generally more processes (SAP work processes, database processes, etc) than available processors. To distribute the CPU capacity among all processes, the processors serve them in time frames. A context switch occurs when a processor switches from one process to another.

context switch on the SAP level: In the SAP System, there are generally more users logged on than available SAP work processes. The → user contexts are therefore attached only to the SAP work process when the SAP work process processes a user request. A context switch on the SAP level occurs when an SAP work process switches from one user to another. Switching between user contexts consists of a roll out and a roll in of user context data.

Control Panel: Central tool for monitoring the SAP System and its instances.

CPI-C: Common Programming Interface-Communication
Programming interface—the basis for synchronous, system-to-system, program-to-program communication.

CTO: Change and Transport Organizer
Set of tools used to manage changes and development in the SAP system, as well as to transport these changes to other SAP systems.

Customizing: Adjusting a mySAP.com component to specific customer requirements by selecting variants, parameter settings, etc.

data archiving: Removing data that is no longer needed from the relational database and storing it in archives (→ see also archiving object).

database: Set of data (organized, for example, in files) for permanent storage on the hard disk.

database instance: An administrative unit that allows access to a database. A database instance consists of database processes with a common set of database buffers in → shared memory. There is normally only one database instance for each database. DB2/390 and Oracle Parallel Server are database systems for which a database can be made up of multiple database instances. In an SAP R/3 system, a database instance can either be alone on a single computer or together with one or possibly more SAP instances.

database locks: Like → enqueues on the SAP level, database locks help to ensure data consistency. Database locks are set by all data-changing SQL statements (`UPDATE`, `INSERT`, `DELETE`) and by the statement `SELECT FOR UPDATE`. Database locks are released by the SQL statements `COMMIT` (used for database commit) and `ROLLBACK` (used for database rollback).

database optimizer: Part of the database program that decides how tables are accessed for an SQL statement (for example, whether an index is used).

database server: A computer with at least one database instance.

DBA: Database administrator

DCL: Data Control Language
SQL statements to control user transactions.

DDL: Data Definition Language
SQL statements to define relationships.

deadlock: Mutual blocking of multiple transactions that are waiting for each other to release locked objects.

DIAG protocol: Communication protocol between SAPGUI and dialog work processes on the SAP application level.

dialog work process: SAP work process used to process requests from users working online.

dispatcher: The process that coordinates the SAP work processes of an SAP instance.

DML: Data Manipulation Language
Language commands to query and change data.

dynpro: The DYNamic PROgram that consists of a screen and the underlying process logic.

EDI: Electronic Data Interchange
Electronic interchange of structured data (for example, business documents) between business partners in the home country and abroad who may be using different hardware, software, and communication services.

enqueues on the SAP level: Like → database locks, SAP enqueues help to ensure data consistency. An SAP enqueue is set explicitly within an ABAP program by an enqueue function module and is explicitly released by a dequeue function module. SAP enqueues can continue to be in effect over several steps within an SAP transaction. Remaining SAP enqueues are released at the end of the SAP transaction.

Enterprise IMG: Company-specific Implementation Guide.

entity: Uniquely identifiable object—may be real or imaginary. The connections between entities are described by relationships.

EWT: Easy Web Transaction
Web-ready dialog-based transaction within a mySAP.com solution, enabled by means of → ITS.

execution plan: A strategy created for an SQL statement by the database optimizer tool to define the optimal way of accessing database tables.

extended memory: Storage area for storing → user contexts in the → shared memory of the application server.

FDDI: Fiber Distributed Data Interchange

firewall: Software to protect a local network from unauthorized access from outside.

GUI : Graphical User Interface
The medium through which a user can exchange information with the computer. You use the GUI to select commands, start programs, display files, and perform other operations by selecting function keys or buttons, menu options, and icons with the mouse.

heap memory on the operating-system level: The local memory of an operating-system process. The operating-system heap of an SAP work process includes the permanently allocated and the variable local memory of the SAP work process.

heap memory on the SAP level: Variable local memory of an SAP work process for storing → user contexts. SAP heap memory is temporarily allocated by the SAP work process and released when no longer required.

high availability: Property of a service or a system that remains in production operation for most of the time.
High availability for a mySAP.com component means that unplanned and planned downtimes are reduced to a minimum. Good system administration is decisive here.
You can reduce unplanned downtime by using preventive hardware and software solutions that are designed to reduce single points of failure in the services that support the SAP system. You can reduce the planned downtime by optimizing the scheduling of necessary maintenance activities.

Hot Package: → Support Package.

HTML: Hypertext Markup Language
Language for presenting text and graphics on the Internet.

HTTP: Hypertext Transport Protocol
Protocol for the transmission of files from a Web server to a Web browser over the Internet.

IAC: Internet Application Component
Web-ready SAP R/3 transaction, replaced by Easy Web Transaction (EWT).

IDES: International Demo and Education System
IDES contains multiple model companies, which map the relevant business processes of the SAP R/3 system. Using simple user guidelines and different master and transaction data, scenarios with large data volumes can be tested. IDES is therefore well suited as a training tool to assist in instructing project teams. There is an IDES not only for an SAP R/3 system, but also for other mySAP.com components.

IDoc: Internal Document
An IDoc type filled with real data.

IDoc type: Internal Document type.
SAP format, into which the data of a business process is transferred. An IDoc is a real business process formatted in the IDoc type.
An IDoc type is described by the following components:

- A control record. Its format is identical for all IDoc types.
- One or more records. A record consists of a fixed administration segment and the data segment. The number and format of the segments differ for different IDoc types.
- Status records. These records describe stages of processing that an IDoc can go through. The status records have the same format for all IDoc types.

IMG: Implementation Guide
A tool for making customer-specific adjustments to a mySAP.com component. For each component, the Implementation Guide contains

- all steps to implement the mySAP.com component, and
- all default settings and all activities to configure the mySAP.com component.

The IMG hierarchical structure

- maps the structure of the mySAP.com component, and
- lists all the documentation relevant to the implementation of the mySAP.com component.

instance: SAP instance
Administrative unit that groups together processes of an SAP system that offer one or more services.
An SAP instance can provide the following services:

D: Dialog

V: Update

E: SAP enqueue management

B: Background processing (Background)

S: Printing (spool)

G: SAP gateway

An SAP instance consists of a dispatcher and one or more SAP work processes for each of the services, as well as a common set of SAP buffers in the shared memory.
The dispatcher manages the processing requests. Work processes execute the requests.
Each instance provides at least one dialog service and a gateway. An instance can provide further services. Only one instance can be available that provides the SAP enqueue management service.
In accordance with this definition, there can be two (or more) SAP instances on an application server. This means that with two or more instances on one server, there are two or more dispatchers and SAP buffers. See also → database instance.

Intranet : A company-internal network that is based on Internet technology.

IPC: Inter Process Communication

ITS: SAP Internet Transaction Server
The interface between the SAP system and a Web server for generating dynamic HTML pages. The Web applications SAP GUI for HTML, Easy Web Transaction (EWT) and Web-RFC are enabled by means of ITS.

Java: Platform-independent, object- and network-oriented programming language. Java is one of the three mySAP.com programming languages (along with ABAP and C/C++).
The home page of the "Java Community" is www.java.sun.com, where you can find further information about the following terms: Java Server Pages (JSP), Enterprise JavaBean (EJB), Java to Enterprise Edition (J2EE), and Java Application Server. Information about the SAP-specific In-Q-My Java application server can be found at www.inqmy.com. www.appserver-zone.com has a list of all Java application servers.

LAN: Local Area Network
Network within a specific location. Ethernets or token rings are typical LANs. The typical transfer speed of a LAN lies in the range from MBits/sec to GBits/sec.

local memory of a process: → Virtual memory that is allocated to only one operating-system process. Only this process can write to or read from this area of memory (see also → shared memory).

locks: See → database locks and → enqueues on the SAP level.

LUW: Logical Unit of Work
From the viewpoint of business logic, an indivisible sequence of database operations that conform to the ACID principle.
From the viewpoint of a database system, this sequence represents a unit that plays a decisive role in securing data integrity.
See also→ transaction.

mode: User session in a SAP GUI window.

NSAPI: Netscape Server API (Application Programming Interface).

OLAP: Online Analytical Processing

OLE: Object Linking and Embedding

OLTP: Online Transaction Processing

operation mode: Defined numbers and types of work processes for one or more instances in a particular time period. Operation modes can be automatically changed.

optimizer: See→ database optimizer.

OS: operating system

paging on the operating-system level: See→ swap space.

paging on the SAP level: Memory area used by particular ABAP statements, consisting of a local paging area for each SAP work process, an SAP paging buffer in → shared memory, and possibly an SAP paging file on the hard disk of the application server.

PAI: Process After Input.
Technical program processes, after data is entered in a screen (for ABAP applications).

PBO: Process Before Output.
Technical program processes, before a screen is output (for ABAP applications).

performance: Measure of the efficiency of an IT system.

pop-up window: A window that is called from a primary window and is displayed in front of that window.

Q-API: Queue Application Programming Interface
The interface to buffered, asynchronous data transfer between decentralized applications and SAP R/2 and R/3 systems, based on CPI-C.

R/3: Runtime System 3

RAID: Redundant Array of Independent Disks
Hardware-based technology that supports disk redundancy through disk mirroring and related methods.

RDBMS: Relational Database Management System

RFC: Remote Function Call
RFC is an SAP interface protocol that is based on CPI-C. It allows the programming of communication processes between systems to be simplified considerably. Using RFCs, predefined functions can be called and executed in a remote system or within the same system. RFCs are used for communication control, parameter passing, and error handling.

roll in: See → context switch on the SAP level.

roll memory: Memory area used to store the initial part of → user contexts. It consists of a local roll area for each SAP work process, a roll buffer in → shared memory, and possibly a roll file on the hard disk of the application server.

roll out: See → context switch on the SAP level.

SAP GUI: SAP Graphical User Interface
See → GUI.

SAProuter: A software module that functions as part of a firewall system.

SAPS: → Standard Application Benchmark

SAP system service: Logical function in the SAP Basis
The DBMS service and the application services are functions that are needed to support the SAP system. The application services are Dialog, Update, Enqueue, Batch, Message, Gateway, and Spool—not all are absolutely necessary.

server: The term server has multiple meanings in the SAP environment. It should therefore be used only if it is clear whether it means a logical unit, such as an SAP instance, or a physical unit, such as a computer.

Service Level Management: A structured, proactive method whose goal it is to guarantee the users of an IT application an adequate level of service—in accordance with the business goals of the client, and at optimal cost. SLM consists of a Service Level Agreement (SLA), an agreement between the client (the owner of a business process) and the contractor (service provider) covering service targets and service level reporting or monitoring, that is, regular reporting on the achievement of targets. Useful information about SLM can be found at www.nextslm.org.

Session Manager: The tool used for central control of SAP R/3 applications. The Session Manager is a graphical navigation interface used to manage sessions and start application transactions. It can generate both company-specific and user-specific menus. The Session Manager is available as of Release 3.0C under Windows 95 and Windows NT. Replaced by the mySAP workplace.

shared memory: → Virtual memory that can be accessed by multiple operating-system processes. Where there are several SAP instances or an SAP instance and a database instance on the same computer, a semaphore management system ensures that the processes of each instance access only the shared memory of that instance, and not the global objects of other instances. The maximum size of the shared memory is limited on some operating systems. You can set the size of the shared memory using operating-system parameters. See also → local memory.

SID: SAP System Identifier
Placeholder for the three-character name of an SAP system.

SQL: Structured Query Language
A database language for accessing relational databases.

Standard Application Benchmark.: Available from SAP since 1993, a suite of benchmarks from SAP applications, available for many business scenarios (sales and distribution, financials, retail, assembly-to-order, banking, SAP ITS, etc.). Benchmark results received from hardware partners are certified by SAP before being made widely available. Further information (e.g., all published benchmark results) can be found on the Internet at service.sap.com/sizing (SAP-specific information) and at www.ideasinternational.com (general information). The unit used in SAP benchmarks for measuring hardware efficiency is called SAPS (SAP Application Benchmark Performance Standard).

Support Package.: Software fixes or updates provided by SAP for a specific release version of a mySAP.com component (previously known as Hot Package).

swap space: Storage area on a hard disk or other device used for storing objects that cannot currently be stored in the physical memory (also called a paging file). The processes of storing objects outside the physical memory and retrieving them are known as page out and page in, respectively.

system landscape: A real system constellation installed at a customer site.
The system landscape describes the required systems and clients, their meanings, and the transport paths for implementation and maintenance. Of the methods used, client copy and the transport system are particularly important. For example, the system landscape could consist of a development system, a test system, a consolidation system, and a production system.

TCP/IP: Transmission Control Protocol/ Internet Protocol

TDC: Transport Domain Controller
Application server of an SAP system in the transport domain, from which transport activities between the SAP systems in the transport domain are controlled.

TemSe: Temporary sequential objects
Data storage for output management.

TMS: Transport Management System
Tool for managing transport requests between SAP systems.

TO: Transport Organizer
Tool for managing all the change and transport requests with more extensive functionality than the → CO and the → WBO.

transaction:

1. Database transaction: a database → LUW. A unit of database operation that conforms to the ACID principles of atomicity, consistency, isolation, and durability.
2. SAP transaction: an SAP LUW. SAP transactions conform to the ACID principles over multiple transaction steps. For example, creating a customer order is an SAP transaction in which the ACID principles are adhered to in several successive screens up to completion of the SAP transaction at order creation. An SAP transaction may consist of several database transactions.
3. Reference to an ABAP program: for example, Transaction VA01. (See also → Transaction code.)

Transaction code: Succession of alphanumeric characters used to name a transaction, that is, a particular ABAP program in the SAP system.

transport: Term from software logistics: data export and import between development, quality assurance, and productivity systems.

transport domain: Logical group of SAP systems between which data is transported in accordance with fixed rules. The Transport Domain Controller exercises control over the transport domain.

TRFC: Transactional RFC
Remote Function Control to which the ACID principles are applied.

URL: Uniform Resource Locator
Address in the Internet.

user context: User-specific data, such as variables, internal tables, and screen lists. The user context is stored in the memory of the application server until the user logs off. A user context is connected with a work process only while the work process is working on the user request (→ context switch on the SAP level). User contexts are stored in → roll memory, → extended memory or in → heap memory.

virtual memory: In all operating systems, you can allocate more virtual memory than is physically available. Virtual memory is organized by the operating system either in the physical main memory, or in → swap space.

WAN: Wide Area Network
Network that connects widely separated locations, such as a central office with branch offices. For example, a WAN can be an ISDN line with a transfer speed of 64 kbits/sec.

WBO: Workbench Organizer
Tool for managing change and transport requests that are generated from the use of the ABAP Workbench.

WP : Work process
The application services of the SAP system have special processes—for example, for

- dialog administration
- updating change documents
- background processing
- spool processing
- enqueue management
- Work processes are assigned to dedicated application servers.

WWW: World Wide Web
The part of the Internet that can be accessed using a Web browser.

XML: Extensible Markup Language
An extensible language used to create structured (business) documents. XML is one of the preferred formats for the electronic exchange of documents between systems on the Internet.

G Information Sources

Sources of information for topics covered in this book are the SAP online Help, SAP training courses and workshops, and the SAP Service Marketplace. You can also find additional information on the Internet and in bookstores.

SAP Online Help

To access the SAP online Help in the SAP system:

- for SAP R/3 Release 4.0 or later: **Help · Application help**
- for SAP R/3 Release 3.1 or earlier: **Help · Extended help**

Then, for help on SAP performance monitors, choose

Basis · Computer Center Management System · System monitoring

Training Courses

SAP currently offers the following training courses for performance optimization:

- BC315: Workload Analysis and Tuning (Performance Training for Administrators)
- BC490: ABAP Program Optimization (Performance Training for Developers)

SAP Service Marketplace

The SAP Service Marketplace can be found on the Internet at http://service.sap.com. SAP employees, customers, and partners can access the SAP Service Marketplace.

Information about SAP services in the performance environment can be found at the following addresses:

- SAP Solution Manager: `http://service.sap.com/solutionmanager`
- SAP EarlyWatch Service: `http://service.sap.com/earlywatch`
- SAP EarlyWatch Alert Service und Service Level Management: `http://service.sap.com/ewa`
- SAP Going Live Check: `http://service.sap.com/goinglivecheck`

For further performance-related information on the SAP Service Marketplace:

- Monitoring infrastructure in the SAP Computing Center Management System (CCMS): `http://service.sap.com/systemmanagement`

- General performance information: http://service.sap.com/performance
- SAP benchmarking: http://service.sap.com/benchmark
- Hardware sizing: http://service.sap.com/sizing
- Released platforms for SAP software components: http://service.sap.com/platforms
- Database consolidation: http://service.sap.com/onedb
- Network configuration: http://service.sap.com/network

External Internet addresses:

Other Internet addresses that are relevant to the topics covered in this book:

- Information and discussion forum on service level management: http://www.nextslm.org
- Information on benchmarking: http://www.ideasinternational.com
- Information on monitoring tools (in particular, tools for monitoring Web sites): http://dmoz.org/Computers/Software/Internet/Site_Management/Monitoring/

Books

Online bookstore catalogs contain numerous books that focus on performance topics. These catalogs also give you access to reader reviews. There are many ways to search for material; the following suggested search terms should provide good results:

- "performance*" and the name of a database or an operating system.
- "Service Level Management"

Please note that there is a book published by SAP PRESS that provides a very good description of the IT infrastructure for SAP solutions from a hardware standpoint:

- Mißbach, Michael / Hoffmann, Uwe M.: SAP Hardware Solutions: Servers, Storage, and Networks for mySAP.com. Prentice Hall, 2001

Please also note the following reference, which was mentioned in the introduction:

- Will, Liane: SAP R/3 System Administration. The Official SAP Guide. San Francisco: Sybex, 1999

H Selected SAP Service Marketplace Notes

This appendix contains selected SAP Notes that are of central importance for performance optimization. Use these SAP Notes and the further references they may contain to keep up to date with current developments and recommendations. All SAP Notes can be found at the SAP Service Marketplace, http://service.sap.com.

SAP Notes on System Configuration and Load Distribution

SAP Note number	Title
131 030	Performance 4.0/5.0—collective note
203 924	Performance 4.6—collective note
203 845	mySAP workplace performance—collective note
19 466	Downloading a patch from SAPSERVx
39 412	How many work processes to configure
21 960	Two instances/systems on one UNIX computer
26 317	Set up LOGON group
51 789	Bad user distribution in logon distribution
388 866	Multiple components on a database
67 739	Problem report priorities

SAP Notes on SAP Memory Management According to Operating System

SAP Note number	Title
103 747	Performance 4.0/4.5/4.6: parameter recommendations
97 497	Memory Management Parameter (3.0/3.1)
146 289	Recommendations for SAP 64-bit kernel
146 528	Configuration of SAP systems on hosts with substantial RAM
33 576	Memory Management for Release 3.0C and later, Unix and NT
38 052	System Panic, terminations due to low swap space

SAP Note number	Title
68544	Memory Management under Windows NT
88416	Zero administration memory management for 40A/NT and later

SAP Notes on Enqueues, Number Range Buffering, and ATP Server

SAP Note number	Title
5424	Questions and answers on enqueue/locking
97760	Enqueue: performance and resource consumption
62077	Info: internal number assignment is not continuous
37844	Performance document number assignment RF_BELEG
23835	Buffering RV_BELEG / number assignment in SD
75248	Performance during direct input w. ALE Distribution
40904	Performance during availability check
24762	Blocking with quantities and late exclus. block
99999	ATP server installation and sizing
179224	Document number assignment for unbuffered numbering systems

SAP Notes on System Requirements

SAP Note number	Title
85524	R/3 sizing (Quick Sizer)
89305	Resource requirements for SAP R/3 4.0
113795	Resource requirements for SAP R/3 4.5
151508, 178616, 323263	Resource requirements for SAP R/3 4.6
26417	SAPGUI resources: hardware and software
164102	Network resource requirements for SAP R/3 4.6

SAP Notes on Performance Monitors

SAP Note number	Title
12103	Contents of table TCOLL
16083	Standard jobs, reorganization jobs
23984	Workload analysis: duration of data storage
209834	CCMS monitoring: using agents technology

SAP Notes on Internet Transaction Server

SAP Note number	Title
321426	SAP Internet Transaction Server (ITS) 4.6D: new functionality
350646	condensing HTML
203845	mySAP workplace performance

Index

C

D

E

F

G

H

I

J

K

L

M

N

O

P

Q

R

S

X

Z

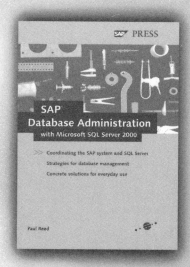

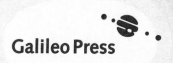